Somewhere

Praise for this book

'*Somewhere to Live* is an exhaustive and optimistic introduction to the urban land and housing challenge faced by countries in the global North and South alike. It addresses the complex and integrated issues of urban economic and social development and cultural respect and conservation in the contemporary context of climate change and pathogenic pandemic, in great analytical detail. It is fully supported by illustrative case studies that draw on Geoffrey Payne's extensive worldwide research and policy advice to governments, non-governmental organisations and international development aid agencies. The book is essential reading for students of urban development and policy makers and urban planning and management professionals, universally.'
    Patrick Wakely, *Professor Emeritus of Urban Development, University of London, (former Director, Development Planning Unit DPU, University College London UCL)*

'Geoffrey Payne has been a leading global expert on land and housing for many decades. This book pulls together an extraordinary amount of knowledge about local conditions, project initiatives, and policy dilemmas. The result is a major contribution to the global debate in this field. Payne shows that, despite the staggering number of people needing "somewhere to live", global accomplishments in providing shelter, in changing ideas, and finding a balance between efficiency and equity are considerable. Nonetheless, as a Swahili proverb reminds us, "Those who have arrived have a long way to go".'
    Michael Cohen, *Professor of International Affairs and Director of the Doctoral Program in Public and Urban Policy, The New School, USA*

'Geoff offers an impressive global coverage of historical and geographical precedents of themes associated related to access to housing: the origin of difficulties and the ingenuity of attempted solutions. The reader is exposed to a savvy collection of illustrations to how and where people find, or does not, a place to survive in world cities.

Among the many issues covered in the book, how land connects to housing stands out. Land is villainized often as one if not 'the' main impediment for a wider, more socially responsible provision of affordable housing. Land speculation being the usual suspect, though seldom convincingly explained how exactly the connection is made. The remedy is yet more abstract and unspecific! Geoff does a great and opportune job filling this gap. The reader will find in this book an authoritative rationalization of concrete experiences contributing to more sensible and effective policies.'
    Martim Oscar Smolka, *Senior Fellow and Director of the Latin America and the Caribbean Program, Lincoln Institute of Land Policy*

'For decades, Geoffrey Payne has been at the forefront of studies and policy advice on issues of housing the urban poor in developing countries. Through his studies of land issues, his work on intermediate forms of land tenure and his recommendation to adapt regulatory frameworks to the needs of the poor, Payne has made significant contributions to the understanding of urban poverty and housing and to the refinement of policies and programmes. In this new book, Payne goes one step further and places the urban low-income housing problems in the context of global economic inequality, the climate crisis and the Covid-19 pandemic, a situation which, he argues, is not accidental, but the intended outcome of a form of economic management designed to benefit a small elite at the expense of the vast majority of people.'

Yap Kioe Sheng, Thailand, Independent consultant

'The book is an outstanding contribution dealing with issues of land and housing that are so important in today's globalizing world. It is theoretically framed whilst providing many useful and excellent examples based on the author's impressive portfolio of work. The book adds great value to professionals, politicians, community groups, NGOs and everyone concerned about this important topic.'

Professor Georgia Butina Watson, Oxford Brookes University

'*Somewhere to Live* is a compelling argument for turning wider social, economic and environmental challenges facing humanity into opportunities for promoting pragmatic people-centric approaches for the provision of urban land and housing, enabling future cities that are congenial, socially diverse, and adaptable.'

Banashree Banerjee, Independent Architecture & Planning Consultant, India

'Building on over 50 years of experience, Geoff Payne provides us with a comprehensive examination of international land and housing policy that is both broad in scope and methodically executed in terms of rigour, detail of information and critical analysis. Utilising a range of case studies from around the globe – representative of different approaches to land and housing delivery from state management to market transition and delivery – it undertakes an intelligent critique of the neoliberal model while setting out practical alternatives for achieving a sustainable and just urban development. This latter point is what is often missing in many critiques of neo-liberal development model. I would wholly commend this book to both novice students who can easily follow the storytelling approach of the narrative and established researchers and academics who would appreciate its depth of analysis, range of information and engaging policy debates.'

Ramin Keivani, Head of School of the Built Environment, Oxford Brookes University

'Building on the foundations of the great names in land and housing studies and based on five decades of his own personal experience, Geoffrey Payne takes us with him on a beautifully illustrated walk through all of the complexity of the contemporary urban challenge. Ambitious in its scope and wise in its insights, this is essential reading for any serious urban scholar and practitioner, ultimately offering clear recommendations based on a realistic vision of a more equal and happy urban future for all.'
Mark Napier, Principal Researcher at CSIR and Visiting Professor at University of the Free State

'Somewhere to Live offers a synopsis of shelter challenges globally, including ongoing research on the sustainability transitions, and how to deal with affordable housing in the context of the SDGs. Geoffrey Payne provides an essential foundation for understanding the complexity of finding a place to live, the positive as well as negative features, and the options for achieving affordability. It is essential reading for all involved in addressing the housing and urban development issues in the world where the relationship between Somewhere to Live and the various forces that formulate the built environment is critical to social, economic, and political development.'
Professor Ahmed M. Soliman, Alexandria University, Egypt

'Not having a place to live is a reality for increasingly more people in this time of colonization of land and housing by finance. This book will not only help you to understand why but also to demonstrate that another destiny is possible, through its valuable and practical suggestions of planning and land management policies.'
Professor Raquel Rolnik, UN Special Rapporteur on the Right to Adequate Housing 2008–2014; architect, urban planner, and author

Somewhere to Live

Rising to the global urban land and housing challenge

Geoffrey Payne

Practical Action Publishing Ltd
27a, Albert Street, Rugby,
Warwickshire, CV21 2SG, UK
www.practicalactionpublishing.org

© Geoffrey Payne, 2022
The moral right of the author to be identified as author of the work has been asserted under sections 77 and 78 of the Copyright Design and Patents Act 1988.

All rights reserved. No part of this publication may be reprinted or reproduced or utilized in any form or by any electronic, mechanical, or other means, now known or hereafter invented, including photocopying and recording, or in any information storage or retrieval system, without the written permission of the publishers.

Product or corporate names may be trademarks or registered trademarks, and are used only for identification and explanation without intent to infringe.

A catalogue record for this book is available from the British Library.

A catalogue record for this book has been requested from the Library of Congress.

ISBN 978-1-78853-179-5 Paperback
ISBN 978-1-78853-096-5 Hardback
ISBN 978-1-78853-183-2 Electronic book

Citation: Payne, G., (2022) *Somewhere to Live*, Rugby, UK: Practical Action Publishing <http://dx.doi.org/10.3362/9781788531832>.

Since 1974, Practical Action Publishing has published and disseminated books and information in support of international development work throughout the world. Practical Action Publishing is a trading name of Practical Action Publishing Ltd (Company Reg. No. 1159018), the wholly owned publishing company of Practical Action. Practical Action Publishing trades only in support of its parent charity objectives and any profits are covenanted back to Practical Action (Charity Reg. No. 247257, Group VAT Registration No. 880 9924 76).

The views and opinions in this publication are those of the author and do not represent those of Practical Action Publishing Ltd or its parent charity Practical Action.

Reasonable efforts have been made to publish reliable data and information, but the authors and publisher cannot assume responsibility for the validity of all materials or for the consequences of their use.

Cover photo shows La Paz, in Bolivia. Credit: Geoffrey Payne
Cover design by: Vijay Sebastian
Typeset by vPrompt eServices, India

To Nico, Mika
and their generation

Contents

Photos, Figures, Boxes and Table	ix
Acknowledgements	xiii
Foreword	xvii

Part I: Key issues

1. Setting the scene	3
2. The cultural context	9
3. Cities, growth, and the climate crisis	21
4. The scourge of inequality	33
5. People on the move	43
6. Utopia or dystopia? Changing visions of urban development	53

Part II: How we value urban land and housing

7. To have and to hold	67
8. The global move to market	85
9. From feudal to market in the UK: A property-owning democracy?	99
10. State land and housing management in China, Cuba, Ethiopia, and Vietnam	113
11. From state to market in Mongolia, Albania, and Cambodia	133
12. From customary to market: Lesotho and Vanuatu, with lessons from part two	151

Part III: What needs to be done

13. Growth and sustainability	169
14. Managing urban land markets: From problems to progress in land management	187

15. Promoting tenure security and diversity	205
16. Spatial planning and land use for adequate housing	223
17. Homes not housing	247
18. Making it happen	259
References	269
Index	307

Photos, Figures, Boxes and Table

Photos

2.1	A traditional *ger* in Mongolia, equipped with a solar panel for cooking and a satellite dish providing internet access enabling its elderly pastoralist resident to watch Korean soap operas. The ultimate in nomadic self-sufficiency	10
2.2	Traditional hutong environment in northern China recreated for tourism	16
2.3	Main thoroughfare and courtyard in Rouse Avenue, New Delhi	18
3.1	Parts of Jakarta are sinking at a rate of 25 cm a year	27
3.2	Inner-city settlement in Phnom Penh, Cambodia	30
5.1	Self-planned and built *gecekondu* settlements in Ankara in the 1970s	51
6.1	Royal Vinh residential complex, Hanoi, Vietnam, complete with shopping malls, ice rink, and multiplex cinema	56
6.2	Typical housing in Kigali, Rwanda	57
6.3	Kigali, as proposed by OZ Architects from Denver, USA	57
6.4	Typical apartment blocks and villas in Ashgabat, Turkmenistan	61
9.1	Guinness Trust social housing projects were of a high standard and in prime locations	104
9.2	Lillington Gardens Estate in Pimlico, London. One of the architects was only 26 years old	105
10.1	Public rental housing project in Shanghai	115
10.2	Rooms for rent in the historic centre of Havana	118
10.3	Building in need of refurbishment in Havana	119
10.4	Typical inner-city settlement in Addis Ababa	122
10.5	IHDP housing in Addis Ababa	123
10.6	Typical 'Tube' housing development in urban Vietnam	127
10.7	Urban housing in the low-lying Mekong Delta Province, Vietnam	129

11.1 Typical *ger* settlement in Ulaanbaatar ... 134
11.2 Terraced inner-city housing and communal gardens in Ulaanbaatar ... 138
11.3 Repainted official apartment buildings in Tirana, Albania ... 144
11.4 Residents of unapproved settlements in central Phnom Penh, Cambodia ... 145
12.1 Housing on land allocated by a local chief in Maseru, Lesotho ... 153
12.2 Traditional *nakamal* in Nguna Island, Vanuatu ... 157
12.3 Typical low-income housing in Port Vila ... 159
15.1 Improved services and footpaths in a Surabaya *kampung*, Indonesia ... 214
15.2 Cooperative housing project with communal land lease on Bang Kaen Canal, Bangkok ... 218
16.1 Improved infrastructure in Comuna 13 settlement, Medellin, Colombia ... 225
16.2 Entrance to an upgraded *kampung* settlement in Surabaya, Indonesia ... 227
16.3 *Gecekondus* being replaced by apartment blocks in Ankara ... 228
16.4 Initial stage of urban development in Ismailia, Egypt, by settlers ... 231
16.5 Stage two of incremental housing development and road layouts in Ismailia ... 231
16.6 A separate entrance for rental housing enables owners to finance home improvements with permanent materials ready for use in Ismailia ... 232
16.7 Investment by some residents also increases the value of other homes in the area ... 232
16.8 Public bike sharing system and autonomous bus in Kaohsiung ... 245
17.1 Communal space and individual houses, Marmalade Lane co-housing project, Cambridge, UK ... 252

Figures

7.1 Notional typology tenure categories, degrees of security and associated property rights ... 69
7.2 Perceived tenure security in Sarvodaya Nagar, Bhandup, Mumbai ... 71

11.1	Possible unintended outcomes from plot sharing	143
13.1	The doughnut of social and planetary boundaries	182
14.1	Closed or restricted housing supply system	191
14.2	Open housing supply system	191
15.1	Likely consequences of providing titles to 'owners' of squatter houses	206
15.2	Likely consequences of improving property rights in unauthorized settlements	209
15.3	Urban land tenure levels of risk	210
16.1	Social clustering and housing across the infrastructure grid hierarchy	239

Boxes

8.1	A tale of two housing subsidies – Chile and the Philippines	91
8.2	Airbnb as a case study in adaptive regulation	93

Table

16.1	Allocating land uses by category	238

Acknowledgements

Over the five decades of research, teaching, and consultancy that has enabled me to write this book, I am indebted to so many people that thanking them all would take me well over the permitted word limit. However, I am indebted to the late Professors Bijit Ghosh and D.V.R. Rao at Delhi University and to Professor Ruşen Keleş in Ankara for their advice and support when I started my international career, and to the breadth of vision on people and place of Paul Oliver and John F.C. Turner who also provided my early career opportunities in the UK. I also owe a great debt to the many capable and committed colleagues within academia, the World Bank, UN-Habitat, other international development agencies and civil society organizations that spend their waking hours addressing issues of urban development. Central to these are David Allen, Johnny Astrand, Richard Baldwin, Banashree Banerjee, Somsook Boonyabancha, Meskerem Brhane, Billy Cobbett, Cormac Davey, Forbes Davidson, Alain and Maylis Durand-Lasserve, Ore Fika, Dao Harrison, Robert Hutchison, Ramin Keivani, Christophe Lalande, Ruşen Keleş, Tony Lloyd-Jones, Vicente del Rio, Raquel Rolnik, Oumar Sylla, Graham Tipple, Han Verschure, and Willi Zimmermann.

I am greatly indebted to many great friends for specific contributions to the research and editing of this book. Hamish Stewart provided invaluable assistance throughout, while specific advice and information was provided by Uma Adusumilli, Doris Andoni, Chinzorig Batbileg, Jamie Clark, Billy Cobbett, Natalie Daniels, Forbes Davidson, Dania González-Couret, Christopher de Gruben, Dao Harrison, Corrado Minnervini, Matthias Nohn, Poonam Pillai, Jaime Royo-Olid, Ahmed Soliman, Li Sun, Michele Vianelo, Georgia Butina Watson, Elias Yitbarek, and Yan Zhang.

It has been my privilege to collaborate with many younger professionals who have contributed in various ways and over many years to helping me with research. Among these, I am particularly grateful to Taimaa Almashriki, Eugene Chigbu, Emma Johnson, Priya Kanchan, Aleksei Luguvoi, Martina Manara, Daniela Muñoz Levy, Venkat Narayan, Bereket Neguse, Itzel Obregon, Sonia Roitman, Brigid Sammon, Anshika Suri, Evelyn Tehrani, Francesca Vanelli, Wenes Widiyani, Peter Williams, Boris Zerjav, and Cemre Sahinkaya-Özer, who has been extremely helpful throughout. Of course, I bear sole responsibility for interpreting the information received.

I am greatly indebted to UN-Habitat for providing financial support to enable me to undertake research in preparation for this book, though I take full personal responsibility for the text. The production of the book was made possible and even enjoyable thanks to the help from Jenny Peebles, Rosanna Denning and Chloe Callan-Foster at Practical Action Publishing and the editing support from Shantanu Raut, Emma Johnson, and my daughter Tania. My great thanks to Vijay Sebastian for designing the book cover. Most importantly, it is thanks to Tania and my wonderful wife Rita that I was able to undertake all the travelling and spend the time preparing this book. To them, I owe my greatest debt and thanks.

Finally, I am very conscious that consultants and researchers such as myself have the privileged role of meeting a vast range of people, asking questions, visiting amazing places, and providing proposals, before leaving those responsible for putting ideas into action to fend for themselves. While one does one's best, it is they, and the millions of resourceful people and communities struggling to obtain somewhere decent to live, who face the real challenge of putting ideas into action on the ground. My hope is that this book provides a useful basis to enable them to succeed.

Foreword

How is it possible that, in 2022, a significant proportion of the world's population still lives in poor, unhealthy, unsafe and inadequate shelter? Providing access to land and affordable and acceptable housing should not represent a daunting challenge: we have the skills, experience and resources. What is obvious is that if both the challenges and the solutions were primarily technical then the problem would long ago been fully resolved.

Drawing on over four decades of international experience, Geoff Payne has deployed his formidable intellect and integrity to try and make sense of our collective failure, seeking to identify and understand the complex set of relationships that frame the relationship between urban land and decent housing. Written in an easy and approachable style his examination embraces culture, history, economy, the meaning of place, the primacy of politics, greed, patronage and corruption, and more. Much more: the impacts of climate change, and the resultant dislocation of millions of economic and climate refugees, are already being experienced but too slowly understood by policy makers.

Somewhere to Live not only shows the rich diversity of the actual construction of housing, but also explores the social meaning and values that different societies ascribe to the provision of this, one of the most basic of human needs. If providing access to urban land and housing is the question, then Payne demonstrates that there are many different answers. These range from the innovative to the appalling.

This rich cultural diversity is demonstrated by examples from different regions including Iraq, China, Turkey and Cambodia, introducing the uninitiated reader to such extraordinary places as the City of the Dead, where up to 500,000 residents share space with ancient human remains in the Cairo Necropolis. The flexibility and adaptability of housing solutions is as evident in a Mongolian Ger as it is missing in a south London high-rise.

Throughout this volume, Payne demonstrates how societies make conscious choices, more often driven by ideology than addressing need. Generally, it is the connected elites that ensure the setting of standards and regulations, and it is the poor that live with the consequences, too often through multi-generational poverty.

Indeed, controlling access to land and housing has been explicitly used to pursue larger social and political agendas, to exclude and to marginalise the poor, but never so far that they might not be able to provide constant low-cost labour and service. This was exemplified most strikingly in the design of colonial cities and taken to a systemic level in *apartheid* South Africa, where access to housing and the city was the fulcrum for excluding people officially determined as surplus.

However, regressive legislation is not always necessary – similar patterns of exclusion can be achieved through perfectly legal practices such as red-lining by banks, or dispossession as an entirely predicated outcome of the increased financialisation of housing.

Different examples are used to demonstrate the role that housing continues to play in the growing inequality visible in cities in different parts of the world: Payne's own home city, London, is often referred to as the money-laundering capital of the world, largely through speculation in the high-end property market. At the lower end of the scale, Nigerian politicians scorn court rulings to violently evict thousands of urban poor living on land suitable for extracting super-profits.

Payne keeps reminding the reader of the links between housing outcomes, and the economic models pursued by different societies. In an era where technical solutions are assumed to somehow provide the answers, **Somewhere to Live** shows their inadequacy in addressing fundamental social and political issues of choice. These include

- the increasingly visible shift, wherein access to land and housing changes from being a precondition for individual, communal and social progress, to that of a tradeable asset: the impact of the commodification of the sector significantly contributes to rampant local, national and global inequality;
- the central importance of open, transparent and effective urban land markets, which are extremely rare.
- the fact that, although access to urban land is one of the most pressing developmental needs of the urbanising poor, most urban land markets are inefficient, dysfunctional and opaque, effectively blocking any notion of a Right to the City;
- the extent to which land and housing is too often viewed through a European and American lens, obscuring the lessons, experience and interests of the majority of the world's population; and
- the tension between professionals and citizens, in which local and vernacular approaches are either discounted or ignored because they fail to fit into the playbook. This is despite the fact that, very often, local solutions are generally the most efficient and effective.

In demonstrating that universal access to land and housing is primarily a political choice, Payne points to the continued growth of slums – the poverty of the inhabitants is ensured through the fact that those extracting and extorting wealth through rent, service charges, bribery and corruption have the consent and protection of the social and political elite.

The connected reality, consistently ignored by policy makers and most development institutions, is that it is neither the state nor the formal private sector that produce housing solutions for those that need it most: globally it is the urban poor themselves that build the most houses, more often than not *despite* the actions of the public sector.

Access to land and housing remains one of the most visible physical indicators of the values of different societies: housing as a mechanism for underwriting a shared citizenship and suggesting a common future, or as a socially acceptable means of accumulation and exclusion. **Somewhere to Live** demonstrates that all governments have the means at their disposal to regulate urban land and housing markets in the public interest, although many choose not to. The book provides a wealth of examples for us to understand and demystify our choices and, more critically, to pressurise governments to fulfil their responsibilities.

William Cobbett, Director of Cities Alliance 2006–21 and previously UN-Habitat's Acting Chief of the Shelter Branch in Nairobi and Director General of the National Department of Housing in South Africa under President Mandela.

PART 1
Key issues

CHAPTER I
Setting the scene

Why is it that, despite economic growth that has lifted hundreds of millions out of poverty globally, access to urban land and housing is becoming more difficult? After all, the first thing all creatures, including humans, need to do on leaving the nest is to find somewhere to live. Somewhere within reach that is safe from the elements and from predators. For people, where that is, and what form it takes, depends not just on personal preferences, but on the political, economic, environmental, and cultural conditions at a given time and place. The options for finding a place that enables individuals, families, and communities to enjoy a productive, peaceful, and positive quality of life are proving increasingly constrained on a planet where unlimited wants are in conflict with finite resources, of which the most obvious is urban land.

The present situation is not accidental, but the intended outcome of a form of economic management designed to benefit a small elite at the expense of the vast majority of people, in countries at all levels of economic development. Even more seriously, it has coincided with a global pandemic that has exacerbated ongoing levels of social inequality, and the climate crisis, which could see many parts of the world becoming completely uninhabitable within the lifetime of people born in the 21st century. Inequality and the climate crisis will force ever higher levels of migration as people are forced to leave their homes, and even their countries, seeking somewhere to live.

The impact of these combined crises presents individuals, governments, and the international community with arguably the greatest challenge humanity has ever faced. Do we fully understand and accept the nature, extent, and urgency of the situation? Do we have the tools, resources, and force of will to address them? Do we already have examples we can learn from of successful efforts to overcome these kinds of challenges? Now that more than half of the world's population live in urban areas, and this is projected to increase to two-thirds by 2050, what implications are there for policies relating to urban management and the provision of services to enable this number of people to live sustainable and fulfilling lives? Do we need to redefine what we mean by development and how we measure its progress? If you work for government or an international development agency, what advice should you be giving? If you are a concerned citizen struggling to find somewhere decent and affordable to live, what pressure can you apply to make sure that appropriate policies are developed and implemented?

It is increasingly accepted that we cannot carry on as we have and that the virus and the climate crisis are here to stay. It is not clear what a new 'normal' will be like, or how to achieve it for all, not just a few. Market forces have become so dominant in recent decades that nation states have become subservient to investors and speculators, and economies are now managed in ways that serve the interests of a small elite at the expense of the vast majority. Land and housing prices in expanding urban areas have risen far faster than incomes, making home ownership increasingly unaffordable, and pushing up rents. Despite decades of economic growth, living in overcrowded, insecure, substandard, poorly located, and under-serviced housing has become the new 'normal' for millions of people.

It does not have to be this way.

The pandemic has demonstrated that, in a major crisis, it is the state, not markets, to which we turn for help. When states assert their authority, they can effect real change, and the same applies to the management of urban land and housing. As this book seeks to demonstrate, land and housing markets can be made to work well for the benefit of both investors and those in need, providing national, and particularly local, governments have the necessary will and skill. The book provides the means in the form of examples from all over the world that can be adapted and applied elsewhere.

Having worked on housing and urban development issues in the Global South for five decades, I have repeatedly felt the need to apologize for being a white British male providing policy advice in contexts that might appear far removed from the land and housing reality in my own country. However, the context of British experience is not as far removed as it seems: planning and building regulations, standards, laws, and procedures that the British once imposed around the world created the basis for policies and practices that continued even after colonized countries had achieved independence. Colonialism may have ended more than half a century ago but, even in India, an emerging global economic power, the Land Acquisition Act of 1894 imposed under colonial rule was only repealed in 2015. The experiences of India, other former colonies, and current overseas territories demonstrate that colonialism has cast a very long shadow over approaches to urban development, land ownership, and urban administration around the world. The fact that access to adequate and affordable housing is no longer available to large sections of the population in the UK, as well as most other economically advanced countries, means that the issues are no longer confined to the Global South and are now worldwide. It has become necessary to challenge the concepts and policies originating in the Global North that have contributed to the present global land and housing crisis. Systemic and structural change is required to address global inequality and the climate crisis, and to implement progressive and sustainable approaches.

The urgent need for change raises the question of how the urban land and housing sectors can be managed in ways that are more socially, economically, and environmentally sustainable. Most countries have endorsed the Paris Climate Agreement and the Sustainable Development Goals adopted in 2015, as well as the New Urban Agenda agreed at Habitat III in 2016. However, the scale of formal, planned development for affordable and adequate housing continues to lag far behind demand. It would therefore be a serious indictment of land and housing professionals, as well as governments and the international community if, in 2030, we were to look back with nostalgia at the current situation.

During my initial research on housing in India in 1970, I repeatedly asked residents of slums what they wanted. Invariably, the answer was 'basic security, basic services and to be left alone'. However, it became very clear that this was not the response that those in positions of influence wanted to hear and India was not alone in executing massive slum clearance programmes. This antipathetic approach to the needs of the urban poor is common in many countries today, even though settlements classified, or considered, to be slums contain many positive features. In fact, most put land to far more productive, efficient, and socially acceptable uses than developments planned by professionals, and make ingenious use of land that nobody else wanted, at least initially. As documented decades ago by Abrams (1966), Mangin (1967), and Turner (1967, 1968, 1976), these self-planned and developed urban settlements have much to teach us and are a central part of the solution to socially sustainable urban development. This requires professionals to approach such developments with an open mind to see what elements – standards, procedures, forms – may reflect norms that official requirements should incorporate. We are all in this together and need to learn from best practice everywhere we find it.

Organizing the evidence and examples

This book seeks to understand the challenges we face, drawing from a diverse range of perspectives to show how the single issue of finding somewhere to live can be part of a wider agenda for change that will enable people to live in harmony with nature and each other. For those wanting to explore specific issues and options in more depth, it provides a menu of policy options taken from examples throughout the world and offers links to a vast wealth of international experience gained by many academics, activists, and practitioners. Part One of the book provides a review of key issues and how they relate to urban land and housing. This raises the question of how land and housing are valued, which is explored through in-depth case studies in Part Two, while the chapters in Part Three provide a range of options and examples that offer ways forward.

Criteria for assessing best practice need to take into account the lessons provided by the global Covid-19 pandemic. This provided a timely reminder of the need to treat both the planet and each other as the greatest of priorities. The way that we manage land and housing has a vital role to play in realizing these objectives, and requires a holistic approach towards the social, economic, and environmental factors involved. A key consideration is the significance of the values we ascribe to our definition of development, and progress towards it is in how land and housing are managed, so that everyone can live fulfilling lives as part of a community. Since housing is ultimately a personal issue, Chapter 2 explores the cultural factors that exert powerful influences and values on our environment.

Of course, cultural values are not static and need to adapt to changing circumstances. Nowhere is this more critical than in the need to address the climate crisis and dramatically reduce carbon emissions, the theme explored in Chapter 3, which assesses the extent to which urban areas contribute to, and suffer from, more frequent and intense storms, floods, rises in sea level, and air pollution, and the impacts these have on the most vulnerable groups. As the Intergovernmental Panel on Climate Change (IPCC, 2021) notes, human activity is unequivocally responsible and unless there are immediate, rapid, and large-scale reductions in greenhouse gas emissions, it will be too late to limit the average temperature increase to 1.5°C, or even 2°C. That humanity has done more damage to the planet during the decades since we realized it was a problem shows that we have not yet been able to generate an adequate response to our existential crisis.

The second major theme explored in the book is that of increasing levels of global and local inequality and how this has made access to decent housing impossible for millions of people in countries at all levels of economic development. Although inequality has always existed, Chapter 4 records how it intensified as a direct result of neoliberal advocates who promoted market-based forms of economic governance which treated land and housing as commodities to be traded as any other asset. Record low interest rates have made property an extremely attractive investment, despite the setbacks of the 2008 financial crisis, forcing up prices and leading to social segregation that has not only undermined the social contract, but denied people the opportunity to meet their basic needs for safety, a sense of belonging, and self-actualization (Maslow, 1943).

Among the many manifestations of the current crisis are the increased levels of forced migration within and between countries. Chapter 5 reviews the ways in which the combination of social unrest, economic inequality, and the climate crisis are generating increased levels of migration, and the impact that this is having on urban areas. Responses by host governments and communities have varied widely but tend to focus on attempts to control numbers without addressing the causes.

While poverty and inadequate housing are increasing even in rich countries, the challenge remains greatest in scale and intensity in the rapidly urbanizing countries of the Global South as more and more people move to urban areas in the hope that they, or their children, will have a better life. While the proportion of the global urban population living in absolute poverty decreased from 11 per cent in 2013 to 10 per cent in 2015 (World Bank, 2018a), the rate of reduction has slowed and the numbers themselves have actually increased, putting in doubt the aim of eliminating poverty by 2030.

Globally, more than a billion people live in substandard, insecure housing without access to basic utilities, representing more than half the total urban population in many countries. A large proportion of these substandard settlements are in countries which have already urbanized to a large extent, such as Brazil, China, and Indonesia. However, the greatest challenge faces the towns and cities of sub-Saharan Africa, which need to improve the living conditions of the 60 per cent of urban dwellers already living in under-serviced, informal settlements, and provide land, housing, and services for nearly 800 million additional residents by 2050. This is equivalent to the combined existing urban population of Europe, Canada, the USA, and Mexico which took more than a century to achieve, so the challenge facing under-resourced African countries is without precedent. If the present proportion of slum-dwellers continues, this could mean that about 2 billion people could be living in degraded conditions by 2050, posing a major threat to social stability.

Intense competition for land and weak urban governance have provided ample opportunities for corruption in land management in countries at all levels of economic development. This presents professionals and policymakers with an immense challenge and Chapter 6 charts the evolving role of urban visionaries and practitioners under conditions of increasing social segregation. It reviews how development proposals reflect the aspirations of an affluent minority, or authoritarian leaders, rather than responding to the needs of the majority, posing serious challenges for the many built-environment professionals trying to promote more progressive approaches.

Having reviewed the key issues relating to urban land and housing in Part One, the chapters in Part Two move discussion to the evolving debate about land tenure and property rights, and the political economy of urban land and housing. This focuses on how land and housing are defined and valued, socially as well as economically, and includes a range of case studies from countries all over the world that provide examples of feudal, state-led, market-led, religious, and customary systems of land and housing management. Although most countries are in transition towards market-driven systems of governance, their previous ways of managing urban land and housing will significantly influence which approaches and policy instruments are most appropriate for improving access to decent housing.

Building on the evidence from Parts One and Two, the chapters in Part Three focus on what needs to be done to meet the needs of all social groups in both the Global South and North for access to adequate housing and a sustainable quality of life. Addressing inequality and the climate crisis raises the basic question of what we mean by development and how to measure progress. Chapter 13 explores the distinction between needs and wants and considers options that relate assessments of economic performance within a broader framework of social and environmental sustainability.

The remaining chapters report on a wide range of innovative and progressive policies and projects that demonstrate how the principles for achieving a decent quality of life and somewhere to live can be achieved for all. Of course, ingrained attitudes and assumptions can be even harder to change than policies and laws, so progress will be dependent upon generating public support for more sustainable approaches and progressive policies, which will threaten those with vested interests in the status quo. They may argue that the poor have always constituted a proportion of the population, and even the best intentions of governments and the international community have been unable to eliminate urban poverty. However, any acceptance of entrenched poverty as an inevitable part of human society undermines the demand for major policy changes that can achieve lasting change. An increasing proportion of young and even middle-income people in affluent, urbanized countries are also now facing major barriers to accessing land for housing, so they may present the greatest force for achieving fundamental change. The examples provided in Chapters 14–18 provide a wide-ranging menu of options that have already been tried and tested, and may be applicable in a variety of contexts. Summaries of their characteristics, strengths, and limitations will equip the professional reader to select locally appropriate options, or enable the well-informed citizen or community group to apply pressure for their adoption or adaptation. This is where the book can be a tool for everyone.

At present, urban land and housing have become physical manifestations of the wider social, economic, and environmental challenges facing humanity. The lesson of this book is that they can and should become part of the solution.

CHAPTER 2
The cultural context

Opening one's eyes

Where are you from? This is probably the second question that most of us ask after exchanging names with a stranger. This is for a good reason. Where we are born, and the environment in which we grow up, exerts a powerful influence on how we see the world and the values that we bring to key issues. While climate and topography also affect us, the cultural context provided by the lifestyles of parents, neighbours, and communities establish a set of values that permeate our world view. When the resident of a community housing project in Liverpool, UK, was asked where he was born, he pointed to a place on a new local road. It transpired that the project was replacing an area bombed during the Second World War and he had been born in a house that stood on the land now occupied by the road. So clear was he on his origins that he still thought of the physical location of the road as his place of birth. Similarly, the family names given to residents of Gaza City in the Palestinian territories are often those of the villages from which they were evicted by Israel, entwining their loss of home with the loss of their identity and aggravating the political tensions by making them intensely personal.

The concepts with which we perceive and use space are like a language; we use them without thinking of the structures involved. Yet there are hundreds of mutually unintelligible languages, all with their own distinct dialects, so why should there not be diverse ways of perceiving and using space? At a time when Western attitudes and practices are extending their reach through globalization, we should consider that non-Western ways of perceiving and using space provide people with an important sense of their own identity. They may offer lessons for application or adaptation in other contexts and should form an integral component of development programmes designed for upgrading existing settlements or planning new developments funded or supported by international donor agencies. To achieve this, a more holistic and multi-disciplinary approach to settlement planning is essential for success.

Historically, the vast range of cultural systems that have evolved in different parts of the world have generated an equally diverse range of building types and settlement forms. Underground villages in China and Turkey, floating villages in Cambodia and Vietnam, the City of the Dead in Egypt, where half a million people live above graves, and the Torre de David in Caracas, possibly the tallest informal development in the world, are just some of the creative innovations in design and development that demonstrate unique vernacular solutions to the need for somewhere to live. Most are materially, socially, and economically compatible with their environments, even under extreme topographical, economic, and climatic conditions. For example, technically and aesthetically attractive solutions for air conditioning that use prevailing wind conditions in Pakistan and Iran demonstrate that when people collaborate over time to meet their various needs, human ingenuity knows no limits.

Such a broad conception of housing and its social role includes the black tents of the Qashqai nomads of Iran, Inuit igloos, yurts and *gers* in central Asia (see Photo 2.1), and the reed houses of the Marsh Arabs in southern Iraq, which could be moved and re-erected when and where needed. This inclusive definition of housing acknowledges that even living on the street, an increasingly common practice today in affluent countries of the Global North as well as throughout the Global South, is a form of housing that not only meets the need for basic shelter but, in some cases, even benefits from legal protection (Ho, 2019).[1] This demonstrates that housing needs to be seen within a broad context of requirements that include a sense of security or community, essential services, and, above all, livelihoods. All these needs are defined according to cultural perceptions of the world based on the location and values of the community in which we grow up.

Just as there are hundreds of languages and dialects, there are also many ways of perceiving the environment and using land. For example, when native Americans offered European settlers the island of Manhattan for a string of

Photo 2.1 A traditional *ger* in Mongolia, equipped with a solar panel for cooking and a satellite dish providing internet access, enabling its elderly pastoralist resident to watch Korean soap operas. The ultimate in nomadic self-sufficiency
Credit: Geoffrey Payne

trade beads and other goods, they were not offering them the best commercial deal of all time, but simply the right to trade. The deal represented two completely distinct and different cultural perceptions of land. This was expressed eloquently by a Native American leader as:

> Our land is more valuable than your money. It will last forever. It will not even perish by the flames of fire. As long as the sun shines and the waters flow, this land will be here to give life to men and animals. We cannot sell the lives of men and animals; therefore we cannot sell this land. It was put here for us by the Great Spirit and we cannot sell it because it does not belong to us. You can count your money and burn it within the nod of a buffalo's head, but only the great Spirit can count the grains of sand and the blades of grass of these plains. As a present to you, we will give you anything we have that you can take with you, but the land, never (Crowfoot, circa 1853).

Similar concepts of humanity's relationship to land apply in much of the world where land is held under customary forms of tenure. As one African tribal leader is reputed to have said, 'how can we *own* land? It sustains us and we return to it when we die. Therefore, land owns *us*'.

Much of the literature on this subject has tended to adopt a highly ethnocentric approach by assuming or implying that European and American concepts of space are universally relevant. In reviewing the origins of urban form, Morris (1972, 1979) focused on European and American examples, adding a chapter for the third edition (1994) on the Islamic city, together with appendices on China, Japan, Indian mandalas, and Indonesia. Similarly, Lynch (1981) identifies characteristics of good urban form (vitality, sense, fit, access, control, efficiency, and justice), which are illustrated primarily through Western examples. This limited awareness of different traditions did not provide an analysis of why these other societies had evolved such distinct urban traditions. The launch of the journal *Urban Design International* in 1997 reflected an increasing interest among Western urban designers in the traditions by which non-Western societies organize the built environment. However, a rich vein of examples exist which have not perhaps received the recognition they deserve.

Space and place

One of the earliest examples of a non-Western way of perceiving and organizing space was illustrated by the 1964 publication of *Architecture Without Architects* by Rudofsky (1964, 1977), which provided numerous examples of culturally distinct responses to local topographic and climatic conditions around the world. One of the oldest is the Chinese concept of *feng shui*, meaning 'Wind and Water', which is a central factor in locating sites for homes and villages by identifying and locating the vital energy, or *ch'i*, and the way it flows.

Feng shui predates Confucianism and Taoism and has been practised for over 3,000 years. According to Kingston (1996: 18), the concept was first used 'to determine the most auspicious sites for the tomb of ancestors, in order to give them the best vantage to help their living descendants. Later, it started being used to site palaces, important government buildings and monuments, until finally whole cities were designed and built according to Feng Shui principles'. It remains a common factor in planning homes and settlements today, and Kingston claims that 90 per cent of all properties in Hong Kong are built according to *feng shui* principles. It can also be exploited, and she cites the case of the 70-storey Bank of China building in Hong Kong which had sharp angles pointing at neighbouring buildings, sending arrow-like 'killing-ch'i' energy at competitors. They responded by erecting *feng shui* mirrors to reflect the energy back to its source – commencing litigation.

Nitschke (1966)[2] cites Chinese concepts as the basis for the organization of the early Japanese capitals of Nara and Kyoto. Within this system, residential areas were organized on three scales into the *bo*, *ho*, and *cho* in which a block of about 120 m (*cho*) formed a quarter of a *ho* and that in turn was a 16th of a *bo*. However, the somewhat rigid Chinese geometry did not suit Japanese conditions, in which large areas of level ground were rarely available. As a result, the plans as built reflected a different ethos based on the Japanese concept of *ma*, or a sense of place, which Nitschke (1966: 117) defines as the 'simultaneous awareness of the intellectual concepts form+non-form, object+space, coupled with subjective experience'. Place-making within this framework developed several levels of order: 1) apparent disorder, in which human efforts to impose themselves on nature are unsophisticated; 2) geometric order, in which humans seek to impose an intellectual concept of order upon nature; and 3) sophisticated order, which only emerges when humans discover the order of an organic, constantly changing universe. He illustrates the latter (1966: 133) with the example of the *Katsura Rikyu* (Katsura Imperial Villa) which 'permits new elements, of the same or different quality and size, to be added or taken away as required; in other words it permits "change" in its three elements of growth, fulfilment and decay, to take place ... Each phase of growth is complete and beautiful in itself; nothing seems to be missing'.

In earlier papers, Nitschke (1964) demonstrates how this ability to embody both flux and transformation in the built environment was central to the ideas of the Metabolists, an emerging Japanese group of architects similar in some ways to the Archigram group in the UK (see Chapter 6), which also explored more dynamic and organic approaches to urban form that incorporate change. They shared a common desire to create forms which were both complete at any one point in time, yet were capable of evolving, as found in nature and embodied in the concept of *ma*. For example, key elements of many Japanese temples are rebuilt on adjacent sites every 20 years, but the new buildings are still regarded as ancient because they still house the gods. In the same vein, the famous Golden Temple in Kyoto was rebuilt in 1959 but is still considered to have been built in the 16th century. This is relevant to the restoration, or rebuilding, of historically and culturally important buildings such as Notre-Dame cathedral and the Mackintosh School of Art in Glasgow after they were gutted by fires started, ironically, during restoration work. While the new timber structures will not be original, they will perform the same structural purpose and be true to the original plans.

Japan is by no means the only country to have culturally specific approaches to perceiving, defining, and organizing the built environment. The Indian concept of *vastu*, or *vaastu*, has much in common with *feng shui* in that it organizes the flows of energy within and between spaces. It also determines the location of living, sleeping, cooking, and sanitary functions within housing. These functions are correlated to the four quadrants of the compass, and it recommends that kitchens, a source of negative energy, should be located in the south-east of the house and bedrooms face south-west.

A further example is found in the Middle East where there is a concept called *al-fina'* that refers to in-between spaces that demarcate public and private spaces along streets in Islamic cities (Nooraddin, 1998).

Two attributes that are generating widespread interest beyond their national boundaries are the Danish concept of *hygge* and the German concept of *gemütlich*, both of which embody a quality of cosiness and comfortable conviviality that engenders a feeling of contentment or wellbeing. While not directly related to the built environment, they embody qualities that can be applied to the local environment, and housing in particular. These more organic approaches to the built environment contrast strongly with classical European forms in which symmetrical design is pervasive. Such forms suggest imposed power, order, stability, and control, rather than harmony and adaptability with nature.

Place and identity

These examples of culturally based concepts of perceiving and organizing the built environment all relate to the notions of place-making and place-identity. This is associated with significant events and experiences that play out in a particular location. Thus, places where people gather to celebrate or protest acquire a quality that helps to build or reinforce a sense of collective endeavour and, therefore, identity.

In a comprehensive review of the literature on place-identity, and an impressive analysis of the ancient city of Erbil in Iraq, Almukhtar (2018)[3] cites Cresswell (2014: 19) who saw place as a fundamental component in "how we make the world meaningful and the way we experience the world'. Almukhtar (2018: 17) defined place as 'the physical location in which people construct their social relationships and develop a sense of connection and association with particular places to which they attach meanings. Therefore, place is fundamental for people to experience meaningful attachment at various scales from local to belonging to the wider world'.

As cultural values respond to exogenous influences, so the factors that influence place-identity change, albeit slowly. This was noted by Rapoport (1980) who recorded the variability of solutions and forms and their relation to lifestyles and cultures. He observed that people gave up some elements and organizations easily, while retaining others. He developed the concept of the 'cultural core' and the 'cultural periphery' to explain how societies were willing to accept changes such as technological innovations quickly and easily, providing they did not threaten their sense of cultural identity. However, where such innovations questioned their cultural core, change would take place slowly over generations, if at all. In response to the cultural impacts of mass mobility of populations and rapid cultural change, he considers that lifestyle is the most useful component of culture in relation to the built environment (Rapoport, 2002).

Imposed concepts and built forms

The built environment provides a powerful means of expressing identity and Castells (2010) reviews how both individuals and communities demonstrate multiple dimensions of affiliation according to power relations and perceived priorities. Colonialism and more recently globalization have disrupted indigenous symbols of place-identity, and encourage elites, who identify with built forms and technologies associated with the Global North, to replace them with imported concepts.

Just as Erbil experienced periods when it was expanded and redeveloped by invaders, so major new urban centres around the world were developed, or existing ones modified, by expanding empires. New capitals as diverse as Port Moresby in Papua New Guinea, Honiara in the Solomon Islands, Mexico City in Mexico, and Nairobi in Kenya are just a small sample of urban settlements imposed on local communities by invading forces throughout the world. Other cities, such as Hong Kong, Mumbai, Rio de Janeiro, and Cuzco, were planted by European colonialists as bases for controlling the local populations or extracting resources such as gold, silver, or cotton to finance their own development. In some cases, such as New Delhi and Johannesburg, the native population was only permitted to even access the new colonial areas in order to provide services required by the colonial residents. Lutyens' plan for New Delhi consisted of roundabouts linking up to six wide roads to enable a small number of policemen to supervise access to the areas occupied by the Indian princes and senior British officials whose large residential plots and bungalows occupied most prime locations. The colonialist arrogance of Lutyens and his disdain for the local population was illustrated by planning the houses 'according to the "line of climax", which rises from the houses of poor Indians to those of poor whites and up to the larger villas of the rich whites' (Nilsson, 1973: 72).

The impact of tourism, migration, and lifestyles

The erosion, or even complete loss, of local traditions in perceiving space and developing the built environment has continued beyond the end of colonialism through the process of economic globalization. However, one aspect of globalization has led to a re-awakening of interest in cultural traditions: the massive expansion of tourism. While conservative tourists may judge other places in relation to their homeland, the more adventurous seek something that reflects different ways of living. This has led to a resurgence of interest in maintaining and reviving traditional built forms, even if these no longer reflect local priorities. For example, an Egyptian student once submitted a diploma proposal for a tourist project on the Mediterranean coast that consisted of two distinctly different components. Part of the project included an air-conditioned skyscraper, while the other comprised a group of mud huts situated among palm trees. When challenged to justify proposing two incompatible architectural forms, he explained that the skyscraper was designed for Egyptian tourists who wanted to live like rich foreigners for their holiday and the mud huts were for rich foreigners who wanted to live like Egyptians for two weeks. He received a distinction for being so sensitive to the needs of both groups.

Of course, focusing on the built forms and spaces that command local respect and affection is not enough to ensure that the cultural values they once embodied can be recreated. The government of Uzbekistan has understandably sought to realize the massive tourist potential of the famous historic settlements along the Silk Road from China to Europe, and has spent large sums on restoring cities such as Khiva, Bukhara, and Samarkand. As a result, the cities have increasingly been regarded as cash cows, with large proportions of the population now serving the needs of foreign tourists. Factory workers, which include school-age girls, are employed to meet the increasing need for carpets and other handicrafts, while dancers and musicians exist in prominent locations to entertain visitors. However, places that symbolize some of the greatest achievements of human enterprise have become stage sets in which the local population live out their cultural traditions solely for the benefit of foreigners. This commercialization of the places and the cultural activities that took place in them undermines their authenticity and social value.

Similar processes are under way in China where parts of Inner Mongolia have been promoted as the location of the mythical Shangri-La. New developments comprising traditional architecture and cobbled streets are being built in open country as a lure for foreign tourists looking for the image of China's traditional urban environments, including courtyard houses, or *hutongs* (see Photo 2.2), which have been systematically destroyed within the main cities to be replaced by vast, standardized tower blocks. These tourist areas will become the only places where the Chinese themselves will be able to remember how they once lived.

16 SOMEWHERE TO LIVE

Photo 2.2 Traditional *hutong* environment in northern China recreated for tourism
Credit: Geoffrey Payne

What would help the residents of cities such as those along the Silk Road, and cities in other countries now exploiting their historic areas for tourism, are ways to retain those traditional elements of place-identity in developing new urban areas and projects in ways that avoid such tokenism. This would require the codification of a set of rules that are so deeply embedded in their cultures that they are probably applied instinctively and without conscious effort. Such organic processes can be most easily and clearly observed in vernacular settlements and building traditions where the underlying rules and procedures are widely understood and shared by those making key decisions about the areas in which they live. Alternatively, the opportunity to adapt the existing urban environment to reflect cultural traditions can enliven an area for both local residents and visitors. London has a justified reputation for creating areas that are dominated by different cultural and ethnic groups which recreate the forms, character and place-identity of their places of origin. Urban planning and land management that facilitates such processes can be socially, economically, and environmentally enriching and therefore deserve to be encouraged.

This principle was well illustrated in an analysis of the development and management of an inner-city settlement at Rouse Avenue, behind the commercial centre of New Delhi. The settlement consisted of single storey structures accommodating nearly 2,000 people on less than a hectare.

THE CULTURAL CONTEXT   17

The obvious question posed by these settlements was why would people leave often decent housing in rural areas to live in crowded, poorly or un-serviced urban settlements, with no security of tenure? When asked by a cultured Indian lady what I thought needed to be done about such settlements, I told her that the residents wanted basic services, basic security, and to be left alone, an answer she clearly did not want to hear. I soon discovered that many people like her from middle and upper income groups felt such settlements challenged a vision of progress, as represented by official standards and norms that had once been imposed on them but they had since adopted as their own. Some considered that India was 'over-urbanized' in that the level of urbanization was higher than had been justified by the level of industrialization originally experienced by European countries when first urbanizing (Payne, 1977).[4]

The conventional view was that poverty was concentrated in the rural areas and that government policy should therefore focus on rural development so that people would not feel it necessary to leave their villages and move to urban areas for a better life. While laudable and understandable, the vast number of villages needing investment imposed a burden on central and state government resources that they were simply unable to bear. As a result, people moved to the cities in larger numbers than the formal land and housing markets could provide for, leaving them no alternative but to occupy unoccupied or developed land and build what they could. The Rouse Avenue settlement was one of numerous examples in New Delhi, India and countries around the world undergoing similar processes.

The research demonstrated that the way people managed to survive under such conditions was due in large part to the symbiotic relationship between public and private space which enabled the latter to be used for different purposes at different times. The main thoroughfare effectively became a multi-functional outdoor living area (see Photo 2.3), while small *chowks*, or open spaces, under trees became communal meeting, working, and commercial spaces due to the shade they offered. The multi-functional use of communal space throughout the day meant that the effective space was far greater than the actual area, an attribute that was later found to exist in most inner-city settlements developed by the people living in them and particularly in cases where the residents had been at least partly in control of the development.

Despite the visual squalor that so offends the more affluent urban population, settlements and housing provided by the residents themselves invariably prove to be far more effective in putting land to socially and culturally efficient use, and in ways appropriate to their circumstances, than housing provided either by the state or the formal private sector. They also reflect many of the traditional urban forms of great Asian and Middle Eastern cities, such as Cairo and the Walled City of Lahore, where narrow paths combine with small *chowks* to provide opportunities for social interaction and economic activity.

Photo 2.3 Main thoroughfare and courtyard in Rouse Avenue, New Delhi
Credit: Geoffrey Payne

A more pragmatic approach to urbanization and serving the needs of the poor can be seen in the early days of the development of Ankara after its designation as the capital of Turkey in 1923. The government promoted modernization, industrialization, and urbanization as part of a secular development strategy, as a result of which in-migration accelerated and the population regularly doubled every decade. Under the Ottoman Land Act of 1858, villagers in the under-populated Anatolian plateau were permitted to occupy unused state land, providing they developed or cultivated it. Naturally, rural-urban migrants were quick to exploit this and occupied public land around the city. The outcome was a rapid expansion of informal *gecekondu*[5] settlements, mostly on public land. Initial settlements were planned to disorientate outsiders, especially the authorities, and prevent them from entering, though the settlers later learned to exploit legal loopholes which prevented completed dwellings from being demolished without a court order. This saw planning layouts gradually change to a more open, regular pattern as they felt more secure.

Connecting space, culture, and identity

Research on these issues builds on a body of pioneering work by Oliver (1969, 1971, 1997), Abrams (1966), Turner (1967), Mangin (1970), Rapoport (1969), and others engaged in the field of housing, spatial organization, and the role of communities in housing and settlement planning. Turner (1976) had already published seminal papers on informal settlements in Peru and created models explaining the logic behind their development, while King (1976, 1995, 2015) provides comprehensive analyses of colonial ways of perceiving and using space as a means of social control. He ranges from the impact of colonialism on the planning of cities to dwelling design, showing how the bungalow was based on traditional Bengali forms adapted to impose separation of the local servants from their colonial masters.

These leading thinkers on the impact of culture on housing and the built environment provide a conceptual framework for relating a range of interacting factors that later generations have sought to build on. The link between space as perceived and used, not just seen, was illustrated during an international study visit to Ben Guerir, a small town north of Marrakesh in Morocco. A multi-disciplinary group of master's degree students[6] were invited to prepare proposals based on interviews with local people and observe how they lived. While the planning and architecture students presented visually attractive proposals, an anthropology student presented the existing town map on which he had simply inserted red dots. He explained that when walking around the town, he had seen rich and poor men, dressed in Western or traditional clothes, in buses, cars, and on foot. He had also seen professional women in cars and on foot everywhere. However, the only places where he had seen poorer, traditionally dressed women was in locations where he had placed a mark. He explained that all these places had one thing in common – they were semi-private, communal extensions of the domestic environment in which these women felt comfortable to interact socially and economically. He recommended that, to ensure future plans for the town reflected the needs of this group, they should include many such spaces.

Gender considerations have not been as fully subject to studies on cultural aspects of the urban environment as they deserve to be. The issue is naturally more important in contexts where the gender divide is great. While the public spaces in the Salahaddin area of Erbil were popular with families, this was largely because women enjoyed greater autonomy than in the older parts of the city. Similarly in other parts of the Middle East, it has been found that small, communal spaces make it easier for women to socialize and interact economically.

In addition to meeting cultural needs, public open space also has class and societal roles to play, as illustrated by Suresh Gogte, a senior planner of Navi Mumbai, India. Sitting under a tree in a public space near his home, he became aware that, in the mornings, maids would meet to chat and complain about the women they were employed by. Later, middle-class women met to complain about their maids. During the lunch break, office workers met to complain about their managers, while in the afternoon, mothers came to complain about their teenage children. Finally, in the evening, the teenagers met to escape and complain about their parents. Gogte concluded that the provision of congenial places to meet and interact is a vital safety valve for healthy communities and families. The same social value of communal space can be seen in the favelas of Rio de Janeiro (de Paulo, 2021).

Learning from the experts

It is therefore abundantly clear that any professionals influencing the built environment need to acknowledge from the outset that the real experts are the people they are hoping to help. The danger of possessing a professional or academic qualification is that it can encourage the tendency to believe that one knows more than people who may lack the same intellectual qualifications and social status.

This raises major questions for contemporary urban planning and development since those making decisions may not come from within the community being affected, or even the same social class, culture, or country. However, local communities possess a wealth of lived experience so a degree of humility must be a pre-condition for being able to make a positive contribution. As Oliver (1987) observed from worldwide experience, providing standardized housing units that do not take into consideration cultural mores is seldom successful. Even emergency housing provided to those made homeless is unlikely to be accepted if it fails to reflect both cultural and practical needs. Oliver noted that, even 12 years after the major earthquake in Kerenköy, Kütaya, Turkey, when housing was in dire need, houses provided by the State remained unoccupied while only one in three post-earthquake houses of sprayed polyurethane supplied by the Bayer company and the German Red Cross near Managua, Nicaragua, were occupied. Even in less fraught contexts, experience similarly shows that people will reject proposals that do not reflect their needs and cultural values as they themselves define them. The lessons are clear. Local communities should be directly involved in decisions that will affect their neighbourhoods, and professionals planning new developments should be willing to learn from existing areas developed by residents themselves, especially where their social mores are different from those of the professionals. It is the professionals who are the students and the residents who are the experts.

Notes

1. In the United States, San Francisco and Oakland have proposed safe parking zones where individuals living in vehicles can securely leave their belongings without fear of removal for an allotted period of time.
2. See also Payne (2006).
3. See also Castells (2010), Hague and Jenkins (2005), Healey (2010), Relph (1976), and Watson and Bentley (2007).
4. See Payne (1977: 33–4) for a discussion of 'over-urbanization'.
5. *Gecekondu* literally means 'to land by night'.
6. The Building and Urban Design in Development (BUDD) course, established and directed by the author at the Development Planning Unit, University College London.

CHAPTER 3
Cities, growth, and the climate crisis

Measuring development

While researching this book, a pile of yellowed, musty-smelling documents confirmed not only that current forms of economic development are unsustainable and that humanity faces an existential threat, but that this has been known at least since 1962 when Rachel Carson (1962) exposed the environmental damage caused by pesticides. In 1972, Barbara Ward and René Dubos published *Only One Earth* (1972) for the Stockholm Conference (UN, 1972), which proposed a far-reaching agenda for environmental management, followed by another book by Ward (1976) that ends with a chapter on planetary housekeeping. Also in 1972, the influential *Limits to Growth* was commissioned by the Club of Rome (Meadows et al., 1972), and in 1980, the Brandt Commission published its report on international development issues. This was followed by the Brundtland Commission (WCED, 1987) report, *Our Common Future*, which defined sustainable development as 'meeting the needs of the present without compromising the ability of future generations to meet their own needs'. A year later, the World Meteorological Organization and United Nations Environment Programme (UNEP) established the Intergovernmental Panel on Climate Change (IPCC) and, in 1989, a major speech by the British Prime Minister, Margaret Thatcher, to the UN General Assembly (Thatcher, 1989) was a prelude to the Earth Summit in Rio de Janeiro in 1992 which established Agenda 21 as a non-binding action plan of the United Nations with regard to sustainable development. Another Earth Summit was held in Johannesburg in 2002, followed by the Rio+20 summit in 2012 and the UN Conference on Sustainable Development in New York in 2015 that established the Sustainable Development Goals. Al Gore's book and film *An Inconvenient Truth* of 2006 led to him being jointly awarded the Nobel Peace Prize with the IPCC in 2007, indicating a global recognition of the challenge.

Given all the words spoken and air miles consumed in discussing more sustainable ways of living, cynics could feel justified in considering that the hot air generated has only increased emissions. The evidence certainly gives no ground for complacency. In 1992, the authors of *Limits To Growth* published a sequel (Meadows et al., 1992) which argued that, in many areas, we had already overshot our ecological footprint limits. Meadows (2004: 237) published a 30-year update that provided even more sobering warnings, suggesting that 'society has limited capacity for responding to those limits with wise, farsighted, and altruistic measures that disadvantage important players in the short term'. The 10 warmest years on record globally have all occurred since 2005 and the five warmest years have all come in the 2010s (Climate Central, 2020). These trends changed the debate from global warming to the *climate crisis* and according to Wallace-Wells (2019: 4) 'we have done as much damage to the fate of the planet and its ability to sustain human life and civilization since Al Gore published his first book on climate than in all the centuries – all the millennia – that came before'. The IPCC (2021a) confirms that climate change is widespread, rapid, and intensifying and that this is a direct result of human action. It finds that 'unless there are immediate, rapid and large-scale reductions in greenhouse gas emissions, limiting warming to close to 1.5°C or even 2°C will be beyond reach' (IPCC, 2021b). Since massive storms, wildfires, and droughts have already caused widespread suffering, an increase to 1.5°C can only result in many areas of the globe becoming uninhabitable, and anything above that will be catastrophic. We have now received a final warning and future generations will judge us by our response.

The IPCC report throws into question assumptions regarding the ability of the planet to support continued human demands. The ecological footprint of a country has been measured by Rees (1999) who assessed the area of productive land required to produce/absorb the material/energy flows associated with particular patterns of consumption. This suggested that at least two additional Earths would be needed to bring the human population up to North American levels of resource consumption standards. Allowing for later population growth, at least three additional Earths would now be required. We have now reached the point at which the planet can no longer sustain continued economic growth of an increasing global population. This raises two key questions in seeking to reduce human demands on the planet. First, should priority be given to reducing population growth rates; and, second, are the indicators we use for measuring economic growth appropriate and reliable?

Food for thought

In addressing the impact of population growth on the demand for non-renewable resources, a number of factors need to be considered. First, the total world population is expected to reach 8.6 billion in 2030, 9.8 billion in 2050, and 11.2 billion in 2100. With roughly 83 million people being added every year, the upward trend in population size is expected to continue throughout this century, even assuming fertility levels continue to decline. It has been widely argued since Malthus (1798) that increases in food supply stimulate increases in population at a faster rate, negating the benefit and leading to starvation. This was known as the 'Malthusian trap'. However, later evidence in Europe showed that social and economic development reduced fertility rates and resulted in a lower rate of population growth. This led to the 'demographic transition' theory whereby high birth rates and high infant death rates in societies with minimal technology, education (especially of girls), and economic development, were replaced over several stages by low birth and death rates. While the theory is widely accepted, cultural, economic, and other factors influence local outcomes. Nonetheless, the majority of the countries with the highest rates of population growth are also among the poorest and most are in sub-Saharan Africa (Hajjar, 2020), while countries with the lowest population growth rates are among the most affluent and many have fertility rates below replacement levels.

A second consideration is the impact that areas with the highest population growth rates have on the consumption of food and other resources. Given the general tendency for poor countries to consume less, it is not surprising that obesity is most common in middle and high income countries (Ritchie and Roser, 2017). This suggests that progress in reducing consumption of food and other resources globally can best be achieved by 1) stimulating social and economic development in poorer countries, particularly in sub-Saharan Africa; and 2) reducing consumption and obesity levels in more affluent countries and those in the Global South, such as Mexico, Egypt, and the Pacific Islands where obesity levels are also high (World Population Review, 2021).

The evidence is overwhelmingly clear that, unless radical action is taken immediately, both globally and locally, humanity faces an imminent existential crisis. About 75 per cent of the world's population will be at risk of potentially deadly heat exposure for more than 20 days a year by 2100, and this will negatively impact living conditions and economic productivity (Mora et al., 2017). Meat, aquaculture, eggs, and dairy use around 83 per cent of the world's farmland and contribute 56–58 per cent of food-related emissions, despite providing only 37 per cent of our protein and 18 per cent of our calories (Poore and Nemecek, 2019), promoting obesity while imposing unsustainable demands on land and creating excessive carbon emissions.

Even without climate change, water to produce food and supply industrial and human consumption is scarce and difficult to access in vast areas of the globe. Some 97 per cent of all the Earth's water is saline and three-quarters of the 3 per cent that is fresh water is concentrated in inaccessible areas, such as polar regions and glaciers (de Rivero, 2010).

In assessing the ways in which human activity is consuming more than the planet can support, the indicators used for defining development and measuring progress towards it are clearly not fit for purpose. Currently, the universal indicators of progress are gross domestic product (GDP) and gross national income (GNI). While the former is most commonly used to measure the rate at which a national economy grows or shrinks, GNI is used by the World Bank to assess national incomes and to rank countries according to whether they are low, lower-middle, upper-middle, or high-income status. The indicators exclude aspects which cannot be quantified financially, such as wellbeing, and it has been claimed that both fail to account for 'external diseconomies' (Mishan, 1967; Hodson, 1972) such as pollution of the land, air, and water resulting from industrialization or the impacts on human health.

For example, if you decide to walk or cycle to work, you have generated no emissions, possibly apart from sweat, while travelling by car is expensive and polluting. Yet, a car journey is more likely to contribute to GDP, especially if an accident were to require the services of hospital and insurance companies, lawyers, and the police. While the first journey improves wellbeing, the second increases GDP *at the expense* of wellbeing.

Fioramonti (2013) records how the term GDP became a powerful propaganda tool for comparing the economic performance of the USA and the Soviet Union during the Cold War. By measuring progress through the growth of GDP, issues such as wellbeing and the impact on the planet could be conveniently ignored. He details how the search for alternative measures, such as the Gross National Happiness index developed in Bhutan, the short-lived Green GDP of China, and the Human Development Index, launched by the UN in 1990, all failed to gain global acceptance. When a potential president of the World Bank was seen to have criticized the use of the term GDP, he was branded 'anti-growth' and was only appointed after recanting. A further limitation of both GDP and GNI as measures of progress is that they fail to take into account the relative *distribution* of income and wealth.

Rising tides

The focus on economic growth as the major measure of development and progress towards it has increased carbon emissions from the exploitation of non-renewable resources such as oil and coal to levels that are generating multiple threats: sea levels are threatening coastal regions, wild fires are destroying settlements, and intense cyclones are causing widespread death and destruction.

Rising global temperatures are causing both land ice and sea ice to melt in the Arctic and Antarctic. Since 1958, Arctic ice has lost about two-thirds of its thickness, older ice has shrunk substantially in area, rendering both regions increasingly vulnerable to climate heating (Cassella, 2018; Kwok, 2018; NASA, 2020). Melting Himalayan and Andean glaciers mean the water supply in parts of Peru, Pakistan, China, India, and Nepal will soon decline (Ohio State University, 2018). If average global temperatures were to reach 4°C above pre-industrial levels by 2100, when many who are now children will still be alive, the world would be on the way to becoming ice-free and sea levels would be perhaps two metres higher than today. Many of the world's coastal regions, where a high proportion of the global urban population lives, would be uninhabitable. It is therefore vital to keep the global average temperature increase to 1.5°C above pre-industrial levels with correlating global greenhouse gas emission pathways (IPCC). Even this is 30 per cent higher than the current level.

Sea level rise poses a major threat to social and economic development in many countries, including China, where rapid industrialization and urbanization in the Pearl River Delta has generated enormous energy demand by manufacturing industries, transportation, and residential consumers, resulting in greater emissions of CO_2 and other greenhouse gases, and an average temperature increase of 1.19°C since the 1970s (He and Yang, 2011). In Vietnam, 11 per cent of the population would face inundation if sea levels rise by 1 metre, climbing to 26 per cent if sea levels rise by 3 m (Dasgupta, 2018). Large swathes of the country's Mekong Delta Province are being replaced by largely unoccupied industrial estates that do not absorb rainfall efficiently. A predicted sea level rise of 17 cm by 2030 and 30 cm by 2050 increases the risk of flooding and saltwater penetration into remaining agricultural areas, adversely affecting the entire province.

According to the World Bank, 2.1 billion people already live without access to enough drinking water, and 4.5 billion lack safely managed sanitation services (World Bank, 2021). Climate change is likely to exacerbate this shortage. Droughts following increased temperatures have triggered extensive wildfires in Australia, the USA, and Canada (Hausfather, 2018), causing deaths and extensive destruction of residential areas. The Asian Development Bank (2013) described Pakistan as one of the most 'water-stressed' countries in the world, with a fivefold per capita drop in supply since independence in 1947, and about the same level as drought-stricken Ethiopia.

Island nations are the most vulnerable globally as many have no high ground to which people can move. The Maldives, a nation composed of 26 ring-shaped atolls and coral islands in the Indian Ocean, is actively considering the purchase of land in Sri Lanka and Australia to relocate people, while the island of Kiribati in the South Pacific is purchasing land in Fiji in case sea levels continue to rise (RNZ, 2017). Vanuatu is arguably the most environmentally vulnerable country in the world as it has to cope with cyclones, sea level rise, earthquakes, and active volcanoes, and has already seen the evacuation of Ambae Island in response to flash flooding and volcanic ash (World Bank, 2018c). Modelling of sea level rise during future decades (see Climate Central 2021) indicates the extent to which countries and urban centres are likely to be affected.

Another major concern is that the world's largest desert, the Sahara, which covers an area similar to the USA, has expanded by about 10 per cent since 1920 and in some areas is growing by 50 km annually (University of Maryland, 2018), adversely affecting the viability of agricultural production and food security for vast swathes of sub-Saharan Africa. This is a significant factor in promoting out-migration, most of which leads to the growth of urban areas, increasing pressure on land, while some migrants move to other countries where they are being accommodated in emergency settlements. Those remaining in countries like Senegal hear from the minority who make it to Europe or other countries, but not from those who perish on the way, fuelling further migration.

The expansion of the Sahara also has a massive impact on the climate in other parts of the world. As the increasingly hot, dry air from the desert drifts westward with the trade winds, it mixes with the moist air over the

Atlantic Ocean, which is itself getting warmer. This generates intense areas of low pressure that drift towards the Caribbean and southern USA. Hurricane Katrina inundated New Orleans in 2005; Hurricane Matthew devastated much of Haiti in 2016; and Hurricane Maria flattened much of Puerto Rico in 2017. The intensity, if not the frequency, of hurricanes and storms has increased significantly in recent years and this is likely to become even more common as the Sahara expands and sea temperatures continue to rise. The proportion of tropical storms that rapidly strengthen into powerful hurricanes has tripled during the last 30 years and the 2017 hurricane season is estimated to have caused damage costing US$282 bn, increasing the costs of insurance which many people are unable to afford. As always, it is the most vulnerable groups that suffer the most.

Urban influences and impacts

Cities contribute significantly to, and suffer from, greenhouse gas emissions. The ways that we manage land in both urban and rural areas have a major influence on this trend and are therefore a key factor in formulating policies and programmes to address it. While rural communities are likely to suffer increased threats to the viability of agricultural activity that sustains their livelihoods and communities, those in cities will be exposed to higher temperatures and water shortages. Cities contribute no less than 40 per cent of global greenhouse emissions and, given current demographic trends, this is likely to increase over time (Rosenzweig et al., 2011). Urban areas constitute 'heat islands' as a result of building activity, transport systems, and energy consumption and it is projected that average temperatures in many cities will increase by between 1°C and 4°C by the 2050s, 50 years ahead of the global average (see above).

The 55 per cent of the world's population now living in cities is projected to increase to 68 per cent by 2050, representing an additional urban population of 2.5 billion in just over 30 years (UN DESA, 2018). Rosenzweig et al. (2011) conclude that climate change will have significant impacts on four sectors in most cities: the local energy system; water supply, demand, and wastewater treatment; transportation; and public health. Many power plants are less than 5 m above sea level, rendering them vulnerable to flooding. Increased temperatures may increase demand for power for air conditioning, while hydropower may not be effective if water sources reduce. Similarly, the quantity and quality of water supply will be significantly affected by projected increases in flooding and droughts. For example, in Lagos, 60 per cent of the population uses informal distribution systems which are far more vulnerable to drought-induced stoppages. The authors also note that vehicle emissions represented 23 per cent of greenhouse gas emissions related to energy in 2004 and are a major cause of bad health in cities around the world. Finally, higher population numbers and densities in urban areas exacerbate existing health risks and create new ones, including water-borne

Photo 3.1 Parts of Jakarta are sinking at a rate of 25 cm a year
Credit: Geoffrey Payne

diseases and respiratory illnesses, which have been made far worse by the 2020 Covid-19 pandemic.

With 10 per cent of the world's population and 13 per cent of the urban population living in areas less than 10 metres above sea level (McGranahan et al., 2007), the need for urban planning to protect key groups and activities is compelling. Flooding not only destroys what valuables the urban poor possess, including their homes, but spreads water-borne diseases, impeding their recovery. Parts of Jakarta are sinking at a rate of 25 cm a year (see Photo 3.1) due to water extraction from groundwater aquifers, and parts of north Jakarta are nearly 3 metres below sea level, requiring three barriers to stop the area from being completely uninhabitable. This has prompted the government to announce the relocation of the capital 1,200 km from the main island of Java to Kalimantan province on the island of Borneo. Subsidence in Mexico City is also increasing as water is abstracted at rates higher than aquifers can replenish. Large numbers of the urban poor in coastal cities are forced by high land costs into the most vulnerable locations. Disease resulting from this exposure reduces their ability to work and earn enough to replace what they have lost, let alone lift themselves out of poverty. This situation is recreated in insecure, badly serviced settlements globally. In Vietnam's economic powerhouse, Ho Chi Minh City, storms that delivered 100 mm of rainfall in three hours previously occurred once in four years, but now occur four times annually, and the drainage system is unable to cope, causing regular flooding in predominantly low-lying residential areas.

While urbanization exposes more people to floods, it exposes others to severe water shortage. In Cape Town, California, and northern China, water shortages are already common and leading to drastic policy responses

(*The Economist*, 2018; Muller, 2018), while Beijing, New Delhi, and São Paulo are among many other expanding cities suffering shortages.

Bastin et al. (2019: 1) estimate that '22% of the world's cities are likely to exist in a climatic regime that does not currently exist on the planet today. The situation is even more pronounced in the tropics, with 30% of cities experiencing novel climate conditions essentially because the climate will get drier'. They describe how:

> Cities in northern latitudes will experience the most dramatic shifts in extreme temperature conditions. For example, across Europe, both summers and winters will get warmer, with average increases of 3.5°C and 4.7°C, respectively. These changes would be equivalent to a city shifting ~1,000 km further south towards the subtropics, i.e. a velocity ~20 km.year-1, under current climate conditions … [while] Cities in the tropical regions will experience smaller changes in average temperature, relative to the higher latitudes. However, shifts in rainfall regimes will dominate the tropical cities. This is characterized by both increases in extreme precipitation events (+5% rainfall wettest month) and, the severity and intensity of droughts (−14% rainfall driest month). With more severe droughts, tropical cities will move towards the subtropics, i.e. towards drier climates. (Bastin et al., 2019: 6–8)

The failure to expand public utility networks, such as water supply and wastewater treatment, in line with increased urban populations and the climate crisis, imposes major health risks. For example, the public sewer system in Chennai, India, had not been expanded significantly since the original network was installed during the colonial period. Unsurprisingly, just weeks after the city was designated as one of India's 100 'smart' cities, the pipes burst, causing widespread flooding. Then the water supply failed in 2019 as the reservoir supplying it was drained, with urban management failing to develop or implement contingency plans. To escape such problems, some affluent groups are moving out of existing cities into new, privately developed towns and cities such as Lavasa in India and Daoyan in China, to live in splendid isolation, though still within reach of the benefits of the cities to which they now pay no taxes.

Breathing bad

According to the Health Effects Institute (2019: 2), 'Air pollution consistently ranks among the top risk factors for death and disability worldwide. Breathing polluted air has long been recognized as increasing a person's chances of developing heart disease, chronic respiratory diseases, lung infections, and cancer'. The World Health Organization (WHO, 2018) estimates that air pollution killed 7 million people in 2016, with more than 90 per cent of air pollution-related deaths occurring in low-and middle-income countries, mainly in Asia and Africa, followed by low-and middle-income countries of the eastern Mediterranean region, Europe, and the Americas. In China, 1.26 million people died during 2017 from air pollution (Yin et al., 2020), and although the Covid-19 shutdowns during 2020 can be expected to have saved more lives from improved air quality than were lost from the pandemic, pollution levels have increased to even higher than pre-pandemic levels since the shutdown was relaxed (Edmond, 2020). IQAir (2020: 4) reports that 'As in previous years, South and East Asian locations emerge as the most polluted globally. Bangladesh, China, India, and Pakistan share 49 of the 50 of the most polluted cities worldwide'. However, it is not only deaths from breathing bad air that need to be considered. The hearts of young city dwellers contain billions of toxic air pollution particles which contribute to heart disease (Calderón-Garcidueñas et al., 2019). Ninety per cent of the world's population lives with toxic air and the impact on the lives of children growing up in, or near, polluted areas will be irreversible, leading the WHO to declare a global public health emergency (Ghebreyesus, 2018).

Cities constitute heat islands due to the concentration of buildings, people, and traffic, and as ambient temperatures increase, urban temperatures will increase even faster. The buildings and construction sector accounted for 36 per cent of final energy use and 39 per cent of energy and process-related carbon dioxide (CO_2) emissions in 2018, 11 per cent of which resulted from manufacturing building materials and products such as steel, cement, and glass. This is made worse by the extensive and increasing use of glass in high-rise buildings, which depend upon air conditioning. In this way, such buildings are increasing global warming and extreme temperatures. In the case of London, this trend is estimated to lead to a fivefold increase in CO_2 emissions in the city centre by 2050 (Kolokotroni et al., 2012). While the affluent minority can afford the comfort of air conditioning, this will not be affordable to the majority who will suffer from the increased temperatures. In some countries, extreme temperatures will also require food to be grown in air-conditioned environments, creating a vicious cycle of ever-increasing heat and air pollution.

The poor pay the price

High consumption patterns and energy usage have combined to generate the climate crisis and reflect the macro-economic and environmental processes by which the global economy has been managed, or mismanaged, for many decades. While urban areas in the Global North have the financial, institutional, and technical resources to redirect economic activity towards a more, circular economy or 'steady state' form of economic management, cities in the Global South are more exposed, and the poor in those cities are the most vulnerable of all – and least able to cope.

Despite economic growth, 20.3 million urban residents will slip below the poverty line even with low climate impacts, while 77.3 million face a return to poverty with higher climate impacts (World Bank, 2016). UNEP (2021: 13) has declared a planetary emergency and states that:

> The well-being of today's youth and future generations depends on an urgent and clear break with current trends of environmental decline. The coming decade is crucial. Society needs to reduce carbon dioxide emissions by 45 per cent by 2030 compared to 2010 levels and reach net-zero emissions by 2050 to limit warning to 1.5°C as aspired to in the Paris Agreement, while at the same time conserving and restoring biodiversity and minimizing pollution and waste.

An inevitable outcome of recent and current forms of economic management is that the poorest groups are paying the price for the lifestyles of more fortunate groups. Responsibility for meeting this challenge therefore rests squarely on the primary consumers of resources and producers of pollution in the Global North. Exporting their environmental footprint to poorer countries through trade and the disposal of waste only compounds the crisis. While affluent groups are able to escape the most serious consequences of their lifestyle by insurance policies and other remedial actions, the poor cannot. They are forced into locations (see Photo 3.2) that are most exposed to environmental threats and less well connected to basic utilities such as clean water and effective drainage systems, without the resources to protect

Photo 3.2 Inner-city settlement in Phnom Penh, Cambodia
Credit: Geoffrey Payne

themselves. Many spend their lives living in settlements that are insecure, clearing up the waste produced by an affluent minority.

Fortunately, campaigners such as the nonagenarian David Attenborough and teenager Greta Thunberg have succeeded in raising public awareness of the climate crisis to a hitherto unprecedented level and this is a precondition for change by governments and the international community. Achieving a more sustainable environment that protects not only humans, but the diversity of species that sustains the entire ecosystem will require sustained pressure. Powerful vested interests in the fossil fuel industries spend vast sums to challenge the science and protect their interests, and 'climate deniers' have gained political support from populist leaders in many countries. Economic nationalism has also seriously constrained the speed and scale of the international collaboration required to achieve systemic change as governments demand that others take greater steps to meet internally agreed objectives. Confronting this challenge will require evidence that more sustainable forms of managing land and other environmental resources is not only vital for our future but can actually improve quality of life if well managed. Developing and implementing options for affordable land and adequate housing in areas exposed to environmental risks requires that social and environmental considerations be given equal weight to those of market efficiency in managing the growth of urban areas and land management. We will return to the options for realizing these objectives in Chapters 12 and 13.

CHAPTER 4
The scourge of inequality

The rise of the right

Despite substantial economic growth in the last century, this is arguably the first time in human history that the young cannot be confident that their lives will be better or more comfortable than those of their parents. Incomes have not risen in real terms for large sections of the global population, employment is less secure, and pension benefits have declined. The poor also have significantly shorter life expectancies than the affluent minority and those lives are less healthy and happy. Many working people in affluent countries are dependent upon food banks for their survival, threatening a return to a Hobbesian state in which life for many is nasty, brutish, and short, while a small elite basks in unlimited luxury.

This situation has not come about by accident. It is the result of a process predicated on achieving this very outcome and it was implemented on our watch. The economic philosophy that has resulted in the current crisis is that of unrestrained market capitalism, or neoliberalism. Building on the liberal ideas of Adam Smith (1776), neoliberalism started as an attempt to find a balance between classical liberalism and socialist planning by Ludwig von Mises (1944) and his pupil Friedrich Hayek. They argued in the 1940s that the most efficient form of economic management was one in which free markets were the most efficient means of meeting peoples' needs and realizing development through competition. They considered that any government involvement in the economy would lead society down 'the road to serfdom' (Hayek, 1944) and responded to what they saw as the visionary appeal of socialism, particularly to the young, by encouraging academics, journalists, teachers, and other 'secondhand' dealers in ideas (Hayek, 1949: 372) to provide evidence of the efficiency of markets in meeting social needs. To this end, they created the Foundation for Economic Education (1946) and the Mont Pèlerin Society (1947) with funding from wealthy individuals and corporations dedicated to illustrating the merits of a neoliberal approach (Mitchell, 2009). This network later expanded to include the American Enterprise Institute, the Heritage Foundation, the Institute of Economic Affairs, the Centre for Policy Studies, and the Adam Smith Institute.

Conditions following the Second World War were not amenable to their ideas, so another original member of the Mont Pèlerin Society, Milton Friedman (1962, cited in Klein, 2007: 7), developed the concept of 'shock therapy' and observed that 'only a crisis – actual or perceived – produces real change. When the crisis occurs, the actions that are taken depend on the ideas that are lying around. That, I believe, is our basic function: to develop alternatives to existing policies, to keep them alive and available until the politically impossible becomes politically inevitable'. Friedman had the opportunities to apply the shock doctrine in Chile with the installation of General Pinochet as president from 1973 to 1990, and following the 1973 oil crisis. Political support came from Reagan and Thatcher, who used the opportunity to promote the privatization of state assets, including social housing, education, and health services. Friedman's 1976 television programme *Freedom to Choose*, was adopted wholeheartedly by Reagan (Capitalism Common Sense, 2011) and served as the basis for 'Reaganomics'. The approach was also adopted by the World Bank in the 1980s by imposing 'structural adjustment programmes' to promote market-based approaches on low-income countries applying for loans, forcing them to liberalize their markets and open them up to foreign competition. This was most dramatically played out in the privatization of Russian and other Eastern European bloc countries' state assets through the 1990s following the dissolution of the Soviet Union in December 1991.

Another opportunity to apply the 'shock doctrine' arose with the 1997 Asian financial crisis when International Monetary Fund (IMF) policies made matters even worse for Indonesia and Thailand. According to Stiglitz (2003: 15), the policies not only failed to stabilize emerging economies and help them recover from a crisis, but actually made things worse and contributed to global instability. He also pointed out (2003: 31) the irony that the USA and European countries only agreed to such liberalization for themselves after 1970 when their economic situation was more secure and the requisite regulatory apparatus was far more developed. As Stiglitz noted, both the IMF and the World Bank, and later the World Trade Organization, founded in 1995, are driven by the collective will of the G7 group of the most important, and affluent, industrial countries.

Income inequality

Were they still alive, Hayek and Friedman could look back with satisfaction at the scale of their impact. Neoliberalism has reduced education, housing, and healthcare to commodities assessed as providing 'value for money', and many tax-paying citizens are now referred to by governments as 'customers'. Light touch regulation, reduced worker representation, and low corporate tax regimes, plus a proliferation of tax havens, have concentrated benefits at the top and allowed private corporations and a few individuals to acquire vast wealth.

According to Oxfam reports to the annual Davos World Economic Summits, the richest 85 individuals in the world had as much combined wealth as the poorest half of the world's population in 2015; by 2016, the number had shrunk to the richest 62 persons and by 2017 to eight persons. The 2018 report stated that the richest 1 per cent bagged 82 per cent of wealth created during the previous year, while the poorest half of humanity got nothing. The 2019 report stated that total incomes for billionaires increased by US$2.5 bn a day while the poorest half of the world's population became 11 per cent poorer (Oxfam, 2019). During 2020, while more than a billion people lived in overcrowded, substandard housing, Jeff Bezos is said to be 'worth' $189 bn, more than the oil rich state of Qatar and almost equivalent to the GDP of Greece (Carter, 2020).[1] Bezos' wealth increased in a single day by $13 bn in 2020 because of online shopping during the Covid-19 pandemic (Neate, 2020), while the share value of Apple Corporation doubled from $1 tn to $2 tn in just five months.

At the same time that the ultra-rich are keeping such wealth for themselves, global wage growth in real terms declined from 2.4 per cent in 2016 to just 1.8 per cent in 2017 and from 1.8 per cent to 1.1 per cent, excluding China (ILO, 2019). The United Nations Development Programme (2011: 29) reports that 'the gap between the rich and the poor widened over the last two decades in more than three-quarters of OECD countries and in many emerging market economies'. Income has also become more concentrated among top earners in China, India, and South Africa. In China, for example, the top 20 per cent of income earners had 41 per cent of total income in 2008, and the Gini coefficient (World Bank, 2013b)[2] for income inequality rose from 0.31 in 1981 to 0.42 in 2005. While this number may appear small, it is a significant proportional increase.

It could be expected that higher levels of inequality may be inevitable in countries at the early stages of economic development, when some groups better placed through education, financial resources or good connections to those in power can benefit more quickly than others. However, since an affluent minority can be assumed to be capable of looking after itself, institutions like the IMF and World Bank can only justify their existence if their policies can improve the living conditions of the remaining majority.

The two institutions have somewhat different priorities in that the IMF aims to promote economic growth, while the World Bank seeks to achieve 'A world free of poverty'. Some progress has been achieved in the latter's objective with more than a billion people being lifted out of extreme poverty since 1990 (Barne and Wadhwa, 2018). They also report that the proportion of people in extreme poverty in 2015 was down 10 per cent, the lowest level in recorded history. However, that still left over 700 million people living on less than $1.90 a day, of whom 41 per cent are in sub-Saharan Africa. If informal sector workers are included, global inequality is even higher. For example, about 30 per cent of China's urban population operate in the informal economy and are officially invisible (Sun and Liu, 2015), so ineligible for access to urban health services.

While economic growth per se has brought humanity's relationship with the planet and all other species and life support systems to a crisis, the *form* of such growth has brought us to a crisis in our relationship with each other. It is now clear that massive and increasing levels of inequality are the inevitable outcome of an economic system in which the role of the state has been reduced to meeting the interests of markets, not one where markets are required to meet the needs of people. By focusing on competition rather than collaboration, they also undermine the 'social contract' that ensures social cohesion and stability.

According to Alvaredo et al. (2018: 9), 'since 1980, income inequality has increased rapidly in North America, China, India, and Russia. Inequality has grown moderately in Europe. From a broad historical perspective, this increase in inequality marks the end of a post-war egalitarian regime'. The date is not coincidental. It was the year after the Thatcher government launched the UK 'Right to Buy' policy to sell off public assets at a substantial discount and establish neoliberalism as the basis for economic policies that were then vigorously exported. Jenkins et al. (2007: 49) note that:

> a new trans-national community is emerging, made up of people from different nations, but with similar ideas and values as well as patterns of behaviour. On the other hand, national societies are undergoing a process of disintegration, including the destruction of indigenous economies and concentrations of property and income. The resulting process of marginalisation leads to increasing repression and authoritarianism in both under-developed and developed countries.

Wealth inequality and land

Contemporary discussion on inequality focuses too much on income inequality when the real challenge is on inequality in wealth. The first survey to measure national wealth in the UK focused not on incomes but on land. As noted by Fioramonti (2018), William Petty conducted the first survey of national wealth in 1652 by systematically analysing the value of land conquered by Oliver Cromwell in Ireland. It was instrumental in equipping government with new information to raise taxes and limit the amount of wealth owned by private individuals and avoid concentrations of capital in the hands of potential opponents. The failure to replace GDP with other measures of economic performance must come as a great comfort to a global elite whose wealth is based on land and property since these are no longer the key factors in defining economic health or, more importantly, the basis of taxation. While income can be declared in locations with low – or no – tax rates, land and property cannot be moved, even if the declared ownership can be registered elsewhere. Consequently, if assets are included in measures of inequality, global inequality is even higher than that of incomes.

The extent to which the concentration of landholdings reinforces the interests of the established order is well illustrated in the case of the UK. According to Cahill (2006),[3] the British sovereign is by far the largest landowner in the world and has legal ownership of one-sixth of the planet's surface, including the whole of Canada, British dependencies that include some of the world's largest tax havens, and even all freehold property in the UK. While a few bask in the wealth that they have inherited, elites in other countries also have vast landholdings as part of their wealth. For example, the King of Saudi Arabia has the right to dispose of all land in the country (Cahill 2006: 62), while it is claimed (2006: 64) that 52 families own most of the land in Spain (Cahill 2006: 64). In other countries, such as Ethiopia, Lesotho, and Vietnam, the head of state or the government own all land and can use this as a means of protecting their interests. However, it is the new rich, consisting mainly of oligarchs and private equity firms, who are acquiring vast tracts of land and property in prime areas around the world. More than 80 per cent of all land and property sales in high end property in London have recently been attributed to foreign buyers, many of whom never live in them and only visit occasionally. During the protests and civil unrest in Hong Kong in late 2020, about £200 m was invested in London property, demonstrating the city's attractiveness to global investors. Even this is a small component of a far larger process which led to a UK government committee concluding in 2016 that the London property market was the primary avenue for the laundering of illicit money worth £100 bn a year, making London the global capital of money laundering (Benjamin 2016; Persaud, 2017; Transparency International 2017). As the Panama Papers scandal also revealed, vast sums have been invested in London by global tycoons to create property empires registered in tax havens (Pegg et al., 2016; UK Gov, 2019). Landholdings now represent a major component of wealth accumulation and inequality at both national and international levels and shows no sign of reducing. This has inflated property prices in central London, reinforcing the process first observed by Engels (1872–73)[4] by which centrally situated land prices force workers towards the outskirts.

The end of history and a new global financial architecture

The collapse of state-managed economic systems under the Soviet Union in 1989 allowed and even encouraged market fundamentalists to conclude that the approach to economic management they had adopted was fully justified and that humankind had reached 'the end of History' (Fukuyama, 1989, 1992). However, the opportunity for triumphalism was short-lived. The collapse of Lehman Brothers in September 2008 was the largest bankruptcy in US history, while J.P. Morgan bank agreed to forfeit $1.7 bn to settle criminal charges, revealing the scale of financial mismanagement under 'light-touch' regulation. As we will see in Chapters 7 and 8, this triggered the 2008 global recession from which the world has still not recovered. Despite this, no significant change has been introduced so far and criminal charges are notable by their absence.

The political elites in all major economies have bought into the neoliberal agenda so fully that they are now completely isolated from the mass of voters. Record low interest rates are punishing the thrifty, and encouraging short- rather than long-term investments. Governments are competing with each other to attract foreign investment by reducing corporate tax rates and proposing tax-free ports in a 'race to the bottom' that increases the wealth and political power of multinationals, hedge funds, and private equity consultancies. The Covid-19 pandemic has added another potentially deadly threat to the global economy, and the financial system has become so unrelated to the real global economy that even respected financial sources are speculating that a crisis even more serious than that of 2008 is inevitable (Wolf, 2020).[5]

While multinational corporations and ultra-rich individuals are able to minimize their exposure to taxes on incomes and wealth, the vast majority of people struggle to feed and house themselves, let alone prosper. Welcome, if belated, action is being proposed in some quarters to require some corporations to pay taxes in locations where revenues are generated, though nothing has been done at the scale required to reduce evasion and opacity. Unexplained Wealth Orders have recently been introduced in the UK to force those suspected of using property as a means of money laundering to declare the source of their wealth, though only one case has so far come to court. While the rich use tax havens to hide their wealth, not all local residents benefit. For example, although the British Virgin Islands provides a secure home for foreign investors, only a small proportion of local residents had hurricane insurance and were therefore denied assistance after Hurricane Irma struck in 2017. Residents of tax havens pay taxes, commonly indirect taxes on consumption rather than property, meaning low-income households pay a proportionately higher rate of tax than foreign investors.

Public sector collusion in the current form of economic mismanagement has resulted in public and private debt rising to more than $246 tn, three times global GDP of $80 tn, so even a modest increase in interest rates, which began in early 2022, is likely to promote a global crisis, especially after Russia's invasion of Ukraine. Free-market capitalism is being propped up at vast cost through creative financial mechanisms such as 'quantitative easing', by which governments print vast sums of money and give it to the banks to build up their reserves. The crisis had an even more corrosive impact on human welfare by effectively disempowering people as citizens and glorifying them as producers or consumers (Fioramonti 2013: 48).

Global disaffection with the status quo is manifest in many ways, none of which appears to be addressing the need to contain demands on natural resources or reduce inequality. In posing the question of how a political party can generate support from people who would suffer from its policies, Krugman (2009) argues that they have become effective at deploying weapons of mass distraction, techniques that are still being widely applied.

For anyone inclined to conclude that currently high levels of inequality are sustainable, it is worth remembering that they were particularly high just before the First World War and after the financial crash in 1929 with continued high inequality levels up until the Second World War.

Living with inequality

Long-term research among countries for which reliable data is available has demonstrated that high levels of inequality have widespread negative social and health consequences for both the impoverished majority *and* affluent minority. Wilkinson and Picket (2010, 2018) report that levels of trust, mental illness, life expectancy, infant mortality, obesity, children's educational performance, teenage births, homicides, imprisonment rates, and social mobility are all adversely affected in countries with high inequality levels. As levels of inequality change, so do the data on all these social and health aspects, irrespective of the level of economic development. They also report that where income differences are bigger, social distances are bigger and social stratification more important. The Covid-19 pandemic has thrown these inequalities into sharp relief as it is the poor and ethnic minorities living in deprived areas who have suffered the most. For the wealthy minority, who could be considered to be suffering from financial obesity, the desire to live in a pristine environment separated behind barriers from the poorer (and financially starving) majority, has resulted in a large increase in the development of gated communities. Such exclusive, homogeneous communities are increasingly common in countries as diverse as Argentina, Brazil, India, Indonesia, Pakistan, South Africa, the USA, and Vanuatu. Roitman and Recio (2020) and Caldiera (2000) review the extent to which rising global inequality has accelerated the development of gated communities since the 1990s. In another study, Roitman and Phelps (2011) report that gated communities in Argentina have become so widespread in the urban suburbs of Buenos Aires that they have taken on the form of 'private cities'.

In India, real estate developers have developed completely new towns for those willing and able to pay for a good quality environment within commuting distance of existing cities. In India, Gurgaon, 32 km from the capital New Delhi, has expanded to a population of more than 1.5 million, and residents' organizations and private companies provide most of the infrastructure. The area attracted many global companies to establish offices that, in turn, attracted young professionals and older affluent families wanting to take advantage of the shopping malls and golf courses. The original rural landowners, however, were only provided with basic accommodation and live in cramped areas with their livestock wandering the locality. In another example, a private developer planned and built the city of Lavasa, near Pune and a four hour drive from Mumbai, as a city of 300,000 people spreading over hills and modelled on the Italian hillside town of Portofino. However, widespread media coverage reports that only a third of the development is occupied, essential facilities like schools are lacking, refuse collection is sporadic, and maintenance is late or non-existent.

The extent to which socially and physically segregated developments adversely affect social and urban development has been increasingly acknowledged in China where Sun et al. (2017) report that social segregation and spatial fragmentation have become so extensive that the government is proposing to 'ungate' the country's urban super-blocks and prohibit the construction of new gated communities in order to improve connectivity, one of the key features of any healthy city.

For the majority of people in expanding urban areas, the segregation of an affluent minority into self-financed and managed settlements should enable local governments to focus on meeting the needs of the majority of citizens. However, if the minority are not contributing their fair share of property taxes or service charges, local governments struggle to generate sufficient revenues and technical resources to meet the basic needs of the majority. In an increasingly divided world, this does not augur well for the future, especially as the most vulnerable groups are forced into the most environmentally vulnerable locations and are exposed to the greatest risks to health and wellbeing. It could even be argued that the Global North has itself become a gated community as migration is being restricted and refugees are turned back.

A central tenet of free market neoliberal ideology is that personal freedom can enable anyone to succeed through hard work, enabling those who rise to the top to claim a moral justification for their success. However, as Sandel (2020) points out, this implies that others deserve to fail. He shows how the focus on equality of opportunity has been used to justify the gross inequality this has generated and how it has fuelled the current widespread resentment among those who feel neglected. He argues that by embracing market values, centre-left political parties throughout Europe and the USA became more congenial to the professional classes than to the blue-collar and middle-class voters who constituted their base, a process that opened the door to political populists. In this poisonous political environment, he concludes that inequality of income and wealth are now so pronounced that they lead us into separate ways of life and 'public spaces that gather people together across class, race, ethnicity and faith are few and far between' (Sandel, 2020: 226).

Market fundamentalists made the fundamental error when interpreting Adam Smith (1776) of assuming that when left to themselves, market forces would drive economies to efficient outcomes 'as if by an invisible hand'. However, as Stiglitz (2003: 73) notes, whenever information and markets are incomplete, which is to say always, the invisible hand works most imperfectly and government intervention is needed. Also, neoliberalists conveniently fail to acknowledge that Smith was a moral philosopher before he was an economist[6] and consistently stressed the need for *enlightened* self-interest in a similar way to Tocqueville's concept of 'self-interest properly understood' (Stiglitz 2012: 288). He observed that by adopting a long-term approach, businesses would not abuse their customers and, if that wasn't enough, he looked to the government to enforce laws. Today, such considerations have been replaced by rampant, short-term, self-interest by market traders intent on maximizing short-term gain, privatizing profits, and socializing losses.

In 2012, the wealth of the richest 1 per cent amounted to $110 tn, equivalent to 65 times the total wealth of the bottom half of the world's population (Oxfam, 2014).[7] And what do they want to spend such wealth on? Apparently, 16 per cent already own a ski chalet, 12 per cent are interested in one, and 40 per cent already own beachfront property, while a further 23 per cent are interested in one (Dorling, 2015: 100).[8] By 2021, global wealth had increased to $418 tn and the number of dollar millionaires rose to 56 million. However, more than half the world's population lived on incomes of less than $10,000 a year (Credit Suisse, 2021: 17). In the event of glaciers melting and sea levels rising, the wealthy elite may need to seek alternative investment options.

Notes

1. Given the extreme reservations concerning the usefulness of GDP as a measure of value, these comparators simply indicate the scale of inequality.
2. The Gini coefficient is the measure of the deviation of the distribution of income among individuals or households within a country from a perfectly equal distribution. A value of 0 represents absolute equality, a value of 100, absolute inequality. In some cases, data are presented as between 0.0 and 1.0.
3. Cahill notes that 'fee simple' is a medieval term for the sum paid to represent the fact that freehold was actually a tenancy and that the monarch was the ultimate landowner.
4. The original texts were published in a German newspaper during 1872–73, combined and published with amendments in 1887 and re-published in English in 1975 by Progress Printers, Moscow.
5. Wolf states that the current situation 'is much the biggest crisis the world has confronted since the second world war and the biggest economic disaster since the Depression of the 1930s. The world has come into this moment with divisions among its great powers and incompetence at the highest levels of government of terrifying proportions'.
6. Adam Smith self-published *The Theory of Moral Sentiments* in 1759.
7. Oxfam's report cites information from Credit Suisse that total wealth amounts to $240.8 tn. Share of wealth for the bottom half of the population is 0.71 per cent and for the richest 1 per cent is 46 per cent (amounting to $110 tn).
8. Dorling cites Frank Knight research in *The Wealth Report 2012*, London Citi-Private Bank <https://content.knightfrank.com/research/83/documents/en/2012-800.pdf> [accessed 22 September 2021]

CHAPTER 5
People on the move

Photos of the limp body of a young child washed up on a beach, or migrants found dead in a refrigerated container, provide all too graphic coverage of the desperate attempts people make to seek a safer or better life. Of course, migration has been a constant feature ever since *Homo sapiens* first emerged from Africa to colonize the planet. Initially, communities moved from one area to another in search of more fertile land or to conquer those already working it. The rise and fall of empires can be seen in the maps of the land and settlements they conquered and lost. The industrial revolution accelerated migration to urban areas, increasing pressure on land, though the numbers involved were relatively small, as the global population was only 1 billion in 1800 and the population of Manchester, arguably the world's first industrial city, was less than 100,000. Since then, the global population has increased sevenfold, triggering mass migration into urban areas, which themselves became larger than ever before.

The impacts of industrialization, colonialism, urbanization, globalization, and climate change on intra- and international migration are unprecedented. Historical examples include the forced migration of more than 12 million Africans to the New World as slaves between 1525 and 1866, while more than 40 million Europeans migrated to the New World between 1850 and 1913, leaving countries with abundant labour and low living standards and entering countries with scarce labour and high living standards (Hatton and Williamson, 1992). During the 20th century, countless millions migrated, often under duress, and the 21st century has already witnessed mass movements of people from areas of conflict or economic hardship in search of security and opportunities to build a better life, though, sadly, many die en route, end up in slavery, or linger in encampments.

Drivers of contemporary migration

According to the International Organization for Migration (2020), international migrants in 2019 accounted for almost 272 million people, or 3.5 per cent of the global population, of which nearly two-thirds were labour migrants. However, migration within national boundaries accounts for an equally vast number, with 290 million rural-urban migrants in China alone in 2019 (Government of China, 2020).

With nearly half the world's population living on less than US$5.50 a day (World Bank, 2018b), extreme poverty is a key driver of migration. Hundreds of thousands of mainly young people in sub-Saharan Africa leave home to seek a better future in Europe, though many end up in slavery in North Africa or perish crossing the Sahara or Mediterranean, while migrants in South America trek across Central America to the USA, a traditional beacon of hope for those seeking a better life.

Some migration is seasonal and Central and South America have well-established histories of intra-regional seasonal migration by agricultural sector workers seeking employment. On a yearly basis, there are migrations from northern Panama to southern Costa Rica and from northern Guatemala to southern Mexico, among other routes (Shifter and Huerta, 2020). Northward migration from Central America and the Caribbean has resulted in the systematic and regular transfer of funds from the United States and other countries to families and relatives that remain in the countries of origin, accounting for $75 bn in 2017 (Orozco et al., 2018). Over 3 million Venezuelans have fled in response to the deepening political and economic crisis in their country, seeking a better life in the USA, though with limited success.

Of all the reasons for population movement, the most dramatic and traumatic, is that of families forced by conflict to abandon their homes, livelihoods, and communities and flee with what they can carry to places of safety. Personal items that are part of their identity are invariably destroyed or abandoned. Being separated, or seeing family members killed en route to safety, leaves scars from which many will never fully recover, while arriving in areas where they may be unwelcome only serves to reinforce the suffering. The global scale of such displacement is vast. According to the United Nations High Commissioner for Refugees (UNHCR, 2019), 79.5 million people had been forcibly displaced at the end of 2019, including 5.6 million Palestinians under UNRWA's mandate (United Nations Relief and Works Agency for Palestine Refugees in the Near East)[1] and 4.2 million asylum seekers. Each of these represents a personal tragedy, especially as the figure includes an estimated 40 per cent of the total who were children below 18 years of age, whose lives will be permanently harmed. Approximately 73 per cent of refugees moved to neighbouring countries.

Refugees escaping from conflict tend to do so in waves, rather than incrementally. This requires the immediate large-scale provision of medical, educational, and other services, often at very short notice. For some, the United Nations provides safety in refugee settlements. In Uganda, such camps accommodated refugees escaping the Lord's Resistance Army and in the neighbouring Democratic Republic of the Congo, over 800,000 have been accommodated, stretching the resources of UNCHR in obtaining land with services and shelter. Some refugee camps have now grown so large and have been in existence for so long that they have become refugee cities, accommodating long-term residents. While camps may be able to provide basic services and essential medical support, they also serve as a permanent reminder of their residents' displaced status. At the same time, nearly a million Rohingyas (UN OCHA, 2017) have been forced to flee Myanmar following persecution there to seek shelter in Bangladesh. As a geographically small country with over 160 million citizens, Bangladesh is ill-equipped to care for such a large influx of displaced people. The international community has largely ignored its responsibility under international law to intervene and provide meaningful additional support to the Rohingyas (ICRC, 2018).

The global increase in forced migration has generated a major backlash in countries as diverse as Australia, Brazil, Colombia, Hungary, Italy, Peru, and Poland, enabling populist politicians to blame refugees for the failure of domestic policies. Sadly, the scale and frequency of conflicts in many parts of the world show few signs of decreasing. In addition to inequality and conflict, environmental hazards represent a third major driver of migration and are made more intense and frequent by the climate crisis. As global heating continues, this could prove to be the most challenging for urban policymakers and managers in the coming decades. Every year since 2008, an estimated 26.4 million people around the world have been forcibly displaced by floods, windstorms, earthquakes or droughts, the equivalent to one person every second (Apap, 2019) and even more are likely in future.

As discussed in Chapter 3, the melting of glaciers and the Arctic ice-cap, combined with the expansion of water through warming, is causing widespread flooding that is likely to be followed by permanent drought, making agriculture impossible on vast swathes of land, forcing millions in sub-Saharan Africa and other parts of the world to migrate to areas that are less affected. Other migrants opt to seek their future across the Sahara Desert to North Africa in the hope of building a new life in Europe, though thousands die in the attempt. Those who succeed put increased pressure on other regions and countries. Immigration has become a toxic issue globally and threatens to become even more sensitive as climate change accelerates and the number of people forced to migrate increases.

Since the International Conference on Population and Development in 1994 (UNFPA, 1994), international migration and its impact on economic development has risen steadily up the agenda of the international community. The 2030 Agenda for Sustainable Development includes several migration-related targets and calls for regular reviews of progress towards their achievement. In response to increasing movements of refugees and migrants around the world, the UN General Assembly adopted the New York Declaration for Refugees and Migrants (United Nations, 2016). However, urban land and housing policy has not been explicitly addressed in the process of acknowledging the socio-economic rights of migrants. For current waves of migrants entering Europe, safe, accessible housing is essential to their successful resettlement (European Commission, 2016). The challenge of integrating land and housing policy more fully into international and national frameworks on migration is still to be addressed. Many need easy access to health and education services which requires the provision of land in areas where these services are readily available. However, the costs of land make the acquisition of adequate areas problematic and migrants risk being accommodated in separate areas which can then be considered as ghettos. Where cultural traditions and values of migrants are significantly different from those of the host community, the increased pressure on local resources can provoke hostility from receiving communities, provoking incidents of racism and further alienation that triggered the initial need for migration. However, a large proportion of migration resulting from climate change remains within national borders and results in moves from particularly vulnerable locations, such as flooded valleys or coastal areas exposed to cyclones, or floods.

The greatest cause for concern is the potential for forced migration as either agriculture becomes unsustainable, or floods make heavily populated areas, such as Dhaka, Jakarta, Mumbai, Miami, Shanghai, and other conurbations uninhabitable. As Himalayan glaciers melt, major floods, followed by permanent drought as rivers run dry, could affect vast numbers of people in South and East Asia. The need to take action to restrict climate heating is unanswerable, though the need for contingency planning should the worse happen, cannot be delayed.

A key difference between migrants is that while those moving on their own initiative to seek a better life tend to be the most enterprising, and therefore able to adapt to their new environment and contribute to the host country, those seeking refuge from conflict are likely to be in need of medical, social, and psychological support to address the trauma they have suffered, and the scars are likely to take time to heal before they can rebuild their lives and contribute to their host society. Both groups require access to land and housing in order to be successfully resettled and remain vulnerable to exploitation throughout the transition.

Cities as magnets

What makes contemporary migration into urban areas challenging is both its speed and scale. The UK and other European countries had more than a century to evolve political and institutional frameworks for absorbing and housing urban migrants. This was at a time when the numbers were relatively small and the countries were masters of their destiny as emerging global powers. Today, most central and local governments responsible for managing the same processes struggle to provide land, housing, and services for a far larger number of urban migrants who have arrived over a far shorter period of time and with relatively fewer resources. Another key difference between 19th-century urbanization and that taking place today is that when European countries were urbanizing, they could export those considered to pose a threat to the established order to their colonies where land was readily expropriated from indigenous peoples and given, often for free, directly to new migrants. Countries experiencing large migrant influxes today do not have these opportunities. However, this has not stopped some countries, notably Australia (Chia, 2021), and potentially the UK (Bourke, 2021), from processing applications by migrants and refugees in remote offshore locations. This sends a signal to potential migrants that they are not welcome and makes it easier for those who do move to be conveniently abandoned and forgotten.

Migration into urban areas accelerated during and after the 1950s, when countries that had been part of European empires gradually became independent, allowing freedom of movement for the native populations, which had been prevented by the colonial powers. Urban population growth rates of 7–10 per cent a year were not uncommon in many countries, meaning that city populations doubled every seven to ten years, imposing new demands for the provision of affordable land and housing that neither central nor local governments were equipped to address. It is estimated that China and India will together account for over half of the global urban expansion up to 2030 (World Bank, 2013c). In 1978, less than a fifth of China's population resided in cities, yet by 2009 urban residents comprised half the population and by 2030 this share is expected to be nearly two-thirds, representing an addition of around 13 million urban residents each year over a decade (ibid.: 23), all of whom will require access to land, housing, and services.

Elsewhere in Asia, rural-urban migration is an even stronger driver of urbanization trends. By 2030, South-east Asia – spanning Cambodia, Indonesia, Malaysia, the Philippines, Singapore, Thailand, and Vietnam – will see urban populations grow by another 100 million. Issues of economic and gender inequality persist and may be amplified as rural-urban migration continues to reshape land use and growth patterns across the region (Tacoli, 2017) and areas where agriculture is no longer viable are reclaimed by nature.

While the numbers of people migrating to urban areas present Asian countries with daunting challenges, the numbers projected for Africa are even greater. At present, around 40 per cent of the continent's population live in cities, compared to just 14 per cent in 1950 (UNICEF, 2017). Rural to urban migration continues to accelerate and by the late 2030s the majority of the continent's population will live in urban areas. The number of children is projected to increase by 170 million between now and 2030, taking the number of the continent's under-18s to 750 million, out of a projected total of around 2 billion (UNICEF, 2017). Making adequate amounts of affordable land and housing available will be one of the largest challenges facing the continent's booming cities. The urban population of sub-Saharan Africa is projected to increase by approximately 790 million people between 2010 and 2050, equivalent to the existing *total* urban population of Europe, the USA, and Mexico (Durand-Lasserve et al., 2018). Even allowing for the uncertainties involved in such projections, the order of magnitude is clear and those responsible for economic and urban development in Africa face a challenge without precedent. Added to this is the need to improve living conditions for the existing urban population. If the current proportion of slum dwellers continues in the region, this could result in 2 billion people having to live in substandard city districts by 2050, carrying with it the potential for societal destabilization (German Advisory Council on Global Change, 2016). National and local governments will need all the support the international community can provide in meeting this challenge.

Many climate migrants also end up in urban centres, only to exchange living on exposed rural land for living on exposed urban land. This poses an increasing challenge for hard-pressed urban authorities seeking to meet the increasing need for land as they lack the resources to obtain expensive land for low-income migrants, especially when they have been unable to make land available on affordable terms for their existing populations.

International efforts to assist the victims of conflict have changed from accommodating refugees in camps to encouraging them to move into urban areas where economic opportunities to rebuild their lives are greater. According to the UNHCR (2021), a total of 82.4 million people in 2019 were forcibly displaced, of which 26.4 million were refugees and 48.0 million were internally displaced people. Most live with family and friends in urban centres as close as possible to their homes, usually in a neighbouring country. This is in stark contrast to the past, when most refugees were deliberately housed by hosting nations in rural settlements or 'camps' far from city centres (Muggah, 2018). Of the 3.5 million Syrian refugees who have settled in Turkey, only 6 per cent are in camps, with the rest living in Turkey's urban areas (Cajaptay and Yalkin, 2018); Turkey has hosted the largest number of refugees of any country for five consecutive years. This increased population has inevitably created pressure on the local infrastructure and around 500,000 Syrian children are enrolled in Turkey's school system (Cunningham and Zakaria, 2018). For most refugees, Turkey was a staging post in their efforts to reach northern Europe, and particularly Germany, which was initially open in accepting refugees. However, the rise of nationalist governments in eastern Europe resulted in large numbers travelling by boat via Greece, resulting in many deaths from drowning. To stem the flow, and ensure that Turkey accommodated the majority of refugees, the European Union negotiated a deal with Turkey to help share the cost, though the influx has inevitably generated local tensions and many find it difficult to obtain employment (del Carpio et al., 2018), while refugees in Greece were moved from the mainland to islands where they were forced to live in squalid conditions (Long, 2018).

Cities are on the frontline for receiving and accommodating refugees. However, international support for cities hosting them is inadequate (Couldrey and Peebles, 2020), though given the scale and sensitivity of the issues involved, as well as the limited resources, this is perhaps understandable. UNHCR has promoted the Cities of Light movement (Watson, 1988) to disseminate examples of good practice, while Zetter and Deikun (2012) report on a private sector initiative in the Philippines that developed low-cost medium-rise apartments for those able to pay modest rents.

Official responses to migration

Understandably, an early reaction by governments and professionals struggling to cope with ever-increasing demands, was to seek to reduce the challenge to more manageable levels by stemming the tide of rural–urban migration and investing in rural areas so migration would not be necessary. As urbanization increased, a literature developed on the subject of 'over-urbanization' (Sovani, 1964) on the basis of comparisons between the levels of industrialization, economic development, and urbanization in Europe when it was undergoing the urban transition and contemporary levels of urbanization in developing economies. However, there is no reason to take the European experience as an appropriate model for countries currently experiencing urbanization and it has been claimed that urban-rural wage differentials suggest that Europe may have been *under*-urbanized (Williamson, 1988).[2]

Attempts to discourage or restrict rural-urban migration were implemented in several countries. In the 1970s, entry permits were required for residence in Jakarta, though this proved ineffective at halting the city's rapid growth. On a larger scale, China has imposed a *hukou* or resident permit system on all citizens since 1958 which restricts legal access to land and essential services to a person's place of birth. Despite strong central government powers, this has also proved ineffective and some estimates show that over a third of all urban housing in China is on land developed and occupied by people without a local *hukou* (Sun and Ho, 2018). Migrants without a *hukou* account for about 9.5 million people, or nearly 40 per cent of Shanghai's 24.28 million population and are not legally entitled to access the city's education or even health facilities, so many migrants are forced to leave their children in their village to be looked after by grandparents (Sun, 2015). The number of these 'left-behind' children is estimated at nearly 70 million nationally, raising major problems for both ageing relatives and the mental health and career prospects for the 'left-behind' children (Sudworth, 2016). While unqualified migrants suffer, Shanghai and other Tier 1 Chinese cities are competing with each other to attract highly qualified 'talented professionals' and Shanghai offers them a local *hukou* and substantial subsidies to rent good quality, heavily subsidized, housing.

The increased speed and scale of rural-urban migration has had a major impact on urban land management and coincided with a period of economic globalization that has promoted the concept of land as a tradable commodity, enabling investors to raise prices in urban areas where demand is increasing. Migrants to cities therefore face a major barrier in being able to obtain affordable land with tenure security and reasonable access to essential services and livelihood opportunities as they must compete with global capital for access to land. The result has been the expansion of various forms of non-formal, or extra-legal land development in cities all over the world and, in many cities in the Global South, these now represent the majority of all urban land development and continue to increase faster than authorized development. In India alone, the urban population is expected to increase by more than 200 million by 2030, requiring up to 8 million hectares of land for residential use (World Bank, 2015c), more than twice the area of Belgium. Demands for infrastructure and industry could add a similar amount, adding up to a total land demand of 5 to 10 per cent of the land area currently used for agriculture nationally. If not handled well, such massive land use change will further increase vulnerability, food and water shortages, rent-seeking, environmental problems, social dislocation, inequality, and conflict (World Bank, 2015c).

National responses to the provision of land for migrant groups vary considerably. The Gulf States, which include some of the wealthiest countries in the world, employed 23 million migrant workers from South Asia and the Far East prior to the Covid-19 pandemic, accounting for more than half of the total workforce (Batta, 2020). Yet workers receive limited rights and protection from employers. Housing for migrant workers is completely segregated from the indigenous population and from migrants with professional backgrounds under conditions that often attract criticism for poor standards. This has exposed many workers to the Covid-19 pandemic and many countries have repatriated workers exposed to the risk. Singapore, another rich country, has over a million migrant workers, many living in high-density government licensed dormitories. Such cramped conditions exposed them to the Covid-19 pandemic, yet many still went to work to avoid losing their incomes. Prior to the pandemic, India provided de facto security of tenure for migrants into large cities such as Mumbai, where even those living on the streets are legally protected under national law. Following initial attempts to clear those living on the streets, an appeal was eventually brought to the Supreme Court which ruled that under India's constitution, all citizens had the right of free movement and that pavement dwellers could only be moved if the authorities provided alternative accommodation (Tellis, 2015). As this would only have attracted even more people to live on the streets in order to obtain housing, the programme was abandoned, though occasional evictions continue.

One of the most progressive and pragmatic responses to rural-urban migration was adopted in the capital of Turkey, Ankara, which experienced such high rates of rural-urban migration during the 1970s that the population was doubling every decade or less. This approach applied traditional self-help and communal support practices developed in the villages from which the migrants came and enabled most migrants to find a plot of land on the edge of the city and build a home with help from neighbours. They took advantage of legal plurality in the land tenure system to claim that they were bringing 'dead' public land to use as permitted under the 1858 Ottoman Land Act (see Photo 5.1) and although the approach broke with conventional planning policy, it was highly successful in enabling Ankara to assimilate masses of migrants in a socially and economically successful manner.

Conclusions

Migration within and between countries continues to challenge the ability of governments, professionals, and the international community to find ways and means of providing urban land, housing, and services in sufficient amounts and on terms that enable migrants to contribute to and benefit from social and

Photo 5.1 Self-planned and built *gecekondu* settlements in Ankara in the 1970s
Credit: Geoffrey Payne

economic development at a time of massive change. Experience shows that when people migrate from their existing homes, either for economic prospects of a better future, to escape conflict, or due to the climate crisis, they tend to move into cities. This places, and will continue to place, enormous challenges on urban policymakers and managers to absorb potentially vast increases in urban populations, most of whom will have limited financial resources.

Approaches to land use and land management in urban and peri-urban areas are urgently needed that are based on the needs and resources of migrants. While some countries have made a massive effort to absorb migrants as a positive factor in development policies, others have found it difficult to accept the need for more realistic and pragmatic approaches. Since there is evidence that migrants are net contributors to social and economic development, not just beneficiaries, and that many Western economies with ageing populations will be reliant on inward migration in coming decades (OECD, 2008), there is every good reason why government policies should be willing to acknowledge this and make land, housing, and services available to enable them to achieve their full potential.

Unfortunately, many affluent countries of the Global North have responded to the migration challenge by imposing borders and restricting the movement of people, even those who are eligible to claim asylum. Many migrants and refugees are even deported to other countries or to detention camps which are themselves evolving into large urban settlements, offering little hope for those fleeing from economic hardship, violence, or both. This is both inhuman and cynical, given that the same countries are happy to attract ultra-high-net worth international migrants while failing to provide an effective policy framework for the social and economic integration of large numbers of working age migrants of more modest means (Gurría, 2016). In so doing, the affluent Global North is turning into a vast gated community in which finance is free to move, but people from the Global South are excluded. As many regions, and even some countries, become unable to sustain human life, the numbers of people forced to move will only increase unless the Global North does more to address the fundamental causes of migration.

Notes

1. See: https://www.unrwa.org/palestine-refugees [accessed 13 October 2021].
2. Cited in McGranahan (1991).

CHAPTER 6
Utopia or dystopia? Changing visions of urban development

Making a mark

From the Egyptian and Mayan pyramids, the vast tombs of the Chinese emperors with their terracotta armies, the temples of Angkor Wat and Borobudur, to the planning of complete cities such as Mohenjo-Daro, Alexandria, Machu Picchu, Samarkand, and the short-lived Fatehpur Sikri, vast monuments have always been an effective way of leaving a mark. More recently, architects, planners, and other visionaries have presented ambitious proposals for urban living that range from nostalgic reinterpretations of a mythical past, such as the English town of Poundbury; carefully considered exercises in self-sufficiency, like the New Towns movement; grandiose concepts such as Brasilia and Neom; and blatant assertions of power, as in the master plan for New Delhi.

Romance and idealism

Three motives appear to dominate contemporary urban developments, elitism, nationalism, and profit, though not necessarily in that order, nor any one exclusively. When not making proposals themselves, many professionals seem more than happy to serve these interests. However, it was not always so. Building on the original concept of utopia by Thomas More (1516),[1] and seeking to address the poverty and squalor prevailing in the industrial cities, 19th- and early 20th-century British idealists such as Robert Owen, John Ruskin, Patrick Geddes, Ebenezer Howard, and William Morris envisaged ways of living in which people could work, live, and play in harmony with each other and nature. In *News from Nowhere*, Morris (1890) picked up the baton from Henry George, Owen, and others to advocate a form of 'utopian socialism' that included common ownership and democratic control over the means of production. He proposed a multi-nodal urban complex that provided access to services, facilities, and nature, and considered it so self-evidently sensible that class conflict could be avoided and people would adopt it willingly. While many individuals have adopted elements of this approach, especially through the Covid-19 pandemic, such thinking has yet to gain traction politically.

While Ruskin inspired the Romantic movement that put architecture and planning into a social context, Geddes developed the concept of 'conservative surgery', intended to meet primary human needs as part of a holistic approach to civic engagement (Haworth, 2000). He adopted this approach in preparing town plans for nearly 50 Indian cities, all founded on a careful survey of physical, cultural, and natural conditions (Geddes, 2021). As the founder of the garden cities movement, Howard (1898, 1902) had a far-reaching impact on urban planning globally and inspired the creation of Letchworth and Welwyn Garden cities in the UK, and later generations of new towns, including Milton Keynes, which applied the principles of land value capture, community governance, and long-term stewardship to create truly sustainable communities for public benefit (Yang, 2021).

The need to rebuild after two World Wars and provide housing for those who had suffered spurred the post-war recovery of Western European and Japanese cities and is a testament to the power of government and private sector collaboration to build world cities out of burning rubble. The Universal Declaration of Human Rights (1948) and later the International Covenant on Economic, Social and Cultural Rights (1966) were both the product of a fleeting post-war consensus on universal human rights, and included reference to housing. Article 25 of the Declaration states that 'everyone has the right to a standard of living adequate for the health and well-being of himself and of his family, including food, clothing, housing and medical care and necessary social services' (United Nations, 1948).

Technology to the fore

As economic recovery enabled people to rebuild their lives during the 1950s, the social focus that had inspired utopian visions of urban living were replaced by the possibilities of new technology, and a range of utopian fantasies emerged that sought to accelerate the creation of new forms of urban living. The Japanese Metabolists group built on the traditional organic approach to design discussed in Chapter 2 and generated a range of futuristic proposals during the 1960s in which buildings were in a constant state of flux and evolution to permit cellular changes and frictionless expansion. Proposals included a floating city in Tokyo Bay, helicoidal towers, and a range of buildings that could evolve over time.

At the same time in the UK, an avant-garde group of architects collaborated under the Archigram architectural banner to promote new ways of using technology to build dynamic and flexible urban environments. They drew heavily on the ideas and images of Antonio Sant'Elia, a founder of the Futurists movement, whose proposals for vast multi-storey buildings with high level walkways, terraces, and bridges inspired films such as Fritz Lang's *Metropolis* and Ridley Scott's *Bladerunner*. Buckminster Fuller's structural innovations in making maximum use of minimal resources produced the 'Dymaxiom' house and car, tensegrity structures, and the geodesic dome concept that inspired the futuristic Eden Project structure in Cornwall, UK.

All of these ideas and examples were a breath of fresh air at a time when architectural and planning education were focusing on the ideas of the great masters of modernism, such as Le Corbusier, Mies van der Rohe, and Frank

Lloyd Wright, even though none had been formally trained as an architect. According to Fishman (1977), they all hated the cities of their time with an overwhelming passion and saw the salvation of civilization in their own urban vision. While Mies van der Rohe's concept of 'more is less' became a watchword for engineering efficiency rather than the more deserving need to make more use of scarce finite resources for environmental sustainability, Wright's reinterpretation of vernacular traditions produced impressive designs, though his famous Fallingwater house was structurally flawed, requiring massive maintenance and repair costs. However, it was Le Corbusier who produced arguably the most physically original but socially authoritarian ideas and projects. His 'Plan Voisin' even sought to eliminate public life at street level (Scott, 1998: 103–46) while his view of housing as 'a machine for living in' demonstrated his priority for technocratic efficiency over congeniality. Projects for high-rise housing at Unité d'Habitation in Marseilles and Berlin were based on the concept of 'vertical garden cities' and provided maisonettes on 18 floors for up to 1,600 residents with a wide range of social facilities, including kindergartens, medical facilities, recreational spaces, and rooftop gardens, all surrounded by open space. The concept was widely adopted, though the falsity of the assumption that professionals know what is best for people in the design of housing was amply demonstrated in another award-winning design of individual prefabricated houses at Pessac, near Bordeaux, France. Because the designs did not reflect how people lived, it was difficult to find purchasers for the houses, and when people did move in, they radically changed the buildings to reflect their needs. To his credit, Le Corbusier later acknowledged that 'it is life that is right and the architect who is wrong' (Boudon, 1972: 2). This preoccupation with visual order and social discipline does not provide a basis for success when the social backgrounds of residents are so markedly different from those of the designers, as amply illustrated in the case of a massive Indian city beautification programme when Sanjay Gandhi, the son of the Prime Minister, forcibly relocated about 500,000 people from inner-city settlements to the urban periphery.

The limitations of such elitist approaches to housing can also be seen in the work of the Egyptian architect Hassan Fathy, the title of whose book *Architecture for the Poor* (Fathy, 1973) revealed his paternalistic assumptions about what people need. Despite his well-intentioned application of traditional, environmentally sustainable building forms that were later to win an international award (World Habitat Awards, 2016), his project to re-house residents from the village of Gourna, to New Gourna, were rejected by the local community. Fathy failed to appreciate that domes were popularly associated with mosques and mausolea, not homes, and that internal courtyards were not culturally applicable in the region. He even designed the houses without running water, arguing that this would preserve old rituals of social interaction by forcing people to visit the village well regularly. Unsurprisingly, many abandoned the newly constructed homes and even vandalized them, a response that was an 'incomprehensible mystery' to Fathy himself (Pyla, 2009).

Photo 6.1 Royal Vinh residential complex, Hanoi, Vietnam, complete with shopping malls, ice rink, and multiplex cinema
Credit: Geoffrey Payne

Elsewhere, the global influence of maximizing land values by constructing self-contained, high-rise developments that embody none of the elements of traditional place-identity risks creating individual and collective alienation and anomie (Photo 6.1).

Elitist aspirations

As the last region of the world to urbanize, it is understandable that national leaders in Africa want to demonstrate that their countries are catching up with other regions that have already developed high-tech cities. Given the massive projected urban population of sub-Saharan Africa by 2050 (Durand-Lasserve et al., 2018), it is clearly vital to think big. However, the ability of high cost, high-tech new developments to provide serviced land and affordable housing for this number of people, given predominantly low incomes, raises concern that their primary aspiration is to be accepted by the international business community as having 'arrived', rather than help the majority of their citizens. Numerous examples of such aspirational planning exist throughout Africa. The master plan for Kigali, an extension of Dar-es-Salaam, Tanzania, and the Eko Atlantic development in Lagos reflect a prioritization of form over function, and aspiration over reality.[2] In these cases, international architects, planners, and financiers were engaged to put physical form to grandiose visions that bear no resemblance to the existing practices or lifestyles. In Kigali, American architects (OZ-Architecture, Denver, CO) were appointed in 2004 to prepare the Kigali City Master Plan (KCMP). Excluding detailed analysis of land values, household incomes, tenure systems,

UTOPIA OR DYSTOPIA? CHANGING VISIONS OF URBAN DEVELOPMENT 57

or needs, the consultants put emphasis on physical planning, including a proposal to replace the existing congenial, affordable, high density, self-built housing (Photo 6.2), with a mass of glass fronted towers (Photo 6.3) that would impose heavy burdens on air conditioning, but convey the government's image as the 'Switzerland of Africa'.

Photo 6.2 Typical housing in Kigali, Rwanda
Credit: Geoffrey Payne

Photo 6.3 Kigali, as proposed by OZ Architects from Denver, USA
Source: Image reproduced with permission from V. Watson (2013) 'African urban fantasies: dreams or nightmares?' *Environment and Urbanization*, vol. 26, (1): 215–231

The proposed plan eliminates key social and economic variables and processes, as if the KCMP were intended to be implemented on empty land with no existing settlements. For this reason, the plan was prudently renamed 'Kigali Conceptual Master Plan' in 2008. This poses the question: can a 'concept' be enforced? If understood as a vision of what strategic options might be available in future, rather than an operational planning proposal, a conceptual master plan can be seen either as a useful tool for decision-making regarding long-term physical planning options, or as an elegant academic exercise. The plan also seeks to attract inward investment and therefore make the city profitable for investors – a combination of all three contemporary motives for urban development. The extent to which this approach reflects the needs or aspirations of citizens is not known, though what is clear is that many have been removed from existing housing to make way for glossy new developments (Watson, 2013).

Any award for dystopian development would need to include a long and increasing list of contenders. High on the list must feature the new city of Neom in north-western Saudi Arabia. Launched by Saudi Crown Prince Mohammad bin Salman at the Future Investment Initiative conference in Riyadh in October, 2017, with a budget of US$500 bn, the city will be fully automated and totally powered by renewable energy, making it the ultimate 'smart' city. Influenced by the design of a project in Singapore, Neom is intended to help Saudi Arabia transition from its dependency on oil to becoming a tourist and entertainment hub, with flying cars, robot workers, beaches with glow-in-the-dark sand and an artificial moon, not to mention facial recognition technology (Sheck et al., 2019). It even includes plans to create 'a new way of life from birth to death reaching genetic mutations to increase human strength and IQ' (Eastman, 2019).

Another category for dystopian development should include projects developed as extensions or replacements for existing cities. Africa and Asia present no less than eight contenders in this category.

The first contender is an extension of Tanzania's largest city, Dar es Salaam. In order to relieve the city of congestion and land shortages, the government commissioned Korean consultants to prepare plans for New Kigamboni City, an eco-city on the edge of the existing city. Mono-functional zones for business, industry, education, residences, and tourism are separated by a road hierarchy oriented towards a car-owning population in a country where car ownership is extremely low. The project has the support of Anna Tibaijuka, formerly head of UN-Habitat, and a strong promoter of inclusive cities (Watson, 2013). However, the 80 per cent of Dar es Salaam's population living in informal settlements are unlikely to be welcome in New Kigamboni City, except as construction workers or domestic staff.

A second contender is provided by proposals for the Urban Pole of Diamniadio in Senegal. Located 40 kilometres from the capital Dakar, the project is the brainchild of the President who considers it a key expression of his Plan for Emerging Senegal (PES) strategy, an ambitious set of initiatives 'aiming at getting Senegal onto the road to development by 2035' (Sala, 2018: 1). Developed on government-owned land, proceeds from the $2 bn investment project will be used to provide enough housing for 350,000 people with luxury, middle-class, and affordable housing near one another. Although the new national strategy seeks to create a dynamic, cohesive, equal, and well-governed nation, the grandiose scale of the new city plan and its florid architecture is so alien to the local culture and climate that the existing residents of Dakar could be forgiven for concluding that the new city is intended only for the affluent minority. Sala cites Cheikh Cissé, urbanist and researcher: 'The majority of the population in Senegal is poor: even the so-called economic housing is going to be too expensive for them', adding that the ambition of building a city for the middle class is misplaced as this represents 3 per cent of the population. According to Cissé, 'Diamniadio has been planned without inhabitants in mind'. The President is not the only person promoting a utopian vision of the urban future. Inspired by the fictional city of Wakanda in the film *Black Panther*, the Senegalese music mogul Akon is raising $6 bn to create the third contender, 'Akon City', a real Wakanda near a coastal village 100 kilometres from the capital Dakar. He claims this will be a 100 per cent crypto-currency based, solar-powered city, and has so far raised a third of the funding needed. He also plans to export the approach to other African countries and the Ethiopian government has also announced a $3 bn tech city promoted as a 'true Wakanda' in the city of Bahir Dar (Diallo, 2018).

On the Moroccan north coast of Africa, the fourth contender is the Port of Tangier, where development has a sound economic basis as the largest port on the continent, but is being undertaken with Chinese investment of $10 bn over ten years, raising questions about the degree to which the repayments will be justified by the returns to the local people. Further south on the coast of Nigeria, the Eko Atlantic project is the fifth contender, intended as an African version of Dubai (Dou, 2018). Built on an artificial island near Lagos, it is intended as a tourism and business centre for up to 250,000 people. The decline of oil revenues has resulted in development being suspended, leaving the area covered in roads and subdivided, but with empty plots apart from two tower blocks (Maya, 2019). With starting prices for a two-bedroom apartment at around $150,000, this is not for the average Nigerian.

Similar issues arise when examining details of the New Administrative Capital (NAC) for Egypt, the sixth contender. This is being promoted as an escape from the congestion of Cairo, to a 'state-of-the-art smart city' some 40 km to the east. With a new airport, hundreds of medical facilities, cultural hubs, administrative centre complete with new presidential palaces, parliament building, embassies, and ministerial buildings, a central park larger than that in New York, a central business district with the highest building in Africa at nearly 400 m, a theme park four times larger than Disneyland, and housing for young professionals and the middle class (Egypt Real Estate Hub, 2019), the NAC represents all that a political, social, and economic elite could want. Strong government support and a proposed monorail link to Cairo are intended to make it an ideal opportunity to invest in real estate. However, a basic two-bedroom apartment, complete with a maid's room, starts at around $60,000, making the development affordable to only the top 10–15 per cent of Egypt's households. However, they are not the only ones finding it difficult to meet the costs. With a budget of $58 bn, the government is struggling to raise funds after a key Chinese investment fell through only a year after the project was launched (Lewis and Abdellah, 2019) and key elements are behind schedule. The devaluation of the currency in 2016 did not help and the new project will not only suck scarce resources out of the existing city, but will even siphon off already-scarce water from nearby satellite cities.

Elmouelhi (2019) cites Sims' (2014)[3] disclosure that the 21 new desert cities the authorities have established since 1976 have attracted less than a million people compared to the 20 million projected. Indeed, these 20 million people are in the greater Cairo area, whose population is expected to hit 23 million by 2030. Clearly, this does not augur well for the success of the NAC. According to Sims (2015), rather than invest in improving Egypt's existing urban areas where 30 million people live, the government invests 750 times more in new cities where only 1 million people live. By withdrawing from the convivial congestion and cultural wealth of Cairo to a development that reflects their socio-economic aspirations, the political, social, and economic elite will further weaken the ability of Cairo to function efficiently and will not provide for the needs of the lower strata of Egypt's social pyramid. Elmouelhi (2019: 23) argues that 'The NAC project is a good example of how the state imitates private real estate developers and competes with them for a share in the real estate market, with no clear or transparent vision for socio-economic development'. He concludes (2019: 25) 'Neither the social aspects nor their impact have been considered during the processes of decision-making and management of the project. On the contrary, exclusiveness is used as a marketing tool to attract customers who prefer to be separated from the lower classes'. With the national population projected to increase to 180 million by 2050 (Soliman, 2021), the country urgently requires a more balanced and equitable form of urban development.

The list of cities in Africa and in other regions that see the future as reflecting international norms of high-rise, high-density, high-tech – and high-price – housing developments is almost unlimited. With their large scale, a focus on digitally crafted visual images, claims to 'modernity', unclear governance structures, and a lack of reference to any kind of participation or democratic debate, these developments meet the conditions described by Watson (2013) for being examples of Africa's urban fantasies.

A seventh contender for the dystopian city award must be the new capital city for Myanmar, Naypyidaw, being developed under the watchful eyes of the oppressive military government. Myanmar is not, of course, the only country to have relocated its capital city. Brazil, Tanzania, Kazakhstan, and Turkey all relocated their capital cities to more strategic locations, and Indonesia has also announced a similar move, though more because large parts of Jakarta are sinking below sea level. However, another likely reason in this case is that the political elite has become so segregated from the mass of the urban populations for which they are responsible that they prefer to create new cities that reflect their own aspirations and expectations, leaving others to cope with the consequences of their failure in the cities they leave behind. This could well explain the proposal to abandon Yangon and start again with a new city reflecting the military requirements of order. With 20-lane highways devoid of traffic, vast empty shopping malls, and housing projects arranged in military fashion, the government is intent on imposing spatial control over society as interpreted from a military perspective. This is not a place for diversity or conviviality.

Of all the examples cited, and the many others that exist, it is difficult to see any candidate for a prize for dystopian development beating Ashgabat, the capital of Turkmenistan. The city was completely redeveloped following the 1948 earthquake, which killed an estimated 110,000 residents and made many more homeless. It has been rebuilt to an extremely high standard, with no concern for costs, or for the needs of people, since every aspect of living is controlled closely by the government. The authoritarian president has closely overseen the development of over 450 high-rise apartment blocks clad in white Italian marble tiles that have already led to the city entering the Guinness Book of Records for the world's highest concentration of white marble buildings (State Bank for Foreign Economic Affairs of Turkmenistan, 2013) (Photo 6.4). How this would affect the population in the event of a future earthquake was clearly not a concern.

Photo 6.4 Typical apartment blocks and villas in Ashgabat, Turkmenistan
Credit: Geoffrey Payne

In addition to the gleaming white towers, rows of identical villas straddle each side of impeccably clean multi-lane highways. Every car has to be washed on entering the city at one of a myriad of washing stations, with heavy fines levied for any dirty vehicle stopped by the vigilant police. The new international airport terminal is roofed in the form of a falcon and even boasts a smaller version for a second terminal for the exclusive use of the president. As an example of grandiose development, it is impossible to beat, though the small towns and villages surrounding the city remain in a sad state of poverty and neglect. Concentrating so much money in the capital city has not made life easier for the local population and the country is listed by Human Rights Watch as 'among the world's most repressive and closed countries, where the president and his associates have total control over all aspects of public life' (Human Rights Watch, 2019). Things are also difficult for immigrant workers since Ashgabat has become the most expensive city in the world for expatriate workers, according to one assessment (Chapman, 2019).

It is a fanciful notion that the prospect of winning an award for dystopian development might deter those in power from continuing along their present paths. While beauty may be in the eye of the beholder, and image is increasingly important in determining value, there can be no doubt that globally pervasive and increasing inequality has resulted in utopia for a few being at the expense of dystopia for the many. For many, Singapore and Dubai represent the image of urban living to which they aspire, but 40 per cent of Singapore's population and 80 per cent of the United Emirates' population are migrant workers, many of them poorly paid and living in substandard, overcrowded housing with limited rights. The social divisions that neoliberalism has engendered are now expressed spatially within existing urban areas in the form of gated communities, dormitories for migrant workers, and informal settlements for the majority.

The formal grandeur and social atomization that many utopian visions project expose a fundamental failure in understanding what makes cities successful and congenial places in which to live and work. Yet they reflect an increasingly common tendency as the gap between those in power and everyone else increases to the point where society itself is in danger of fragmenting, and the order that such developments seek to impose becomes the very means of its collapse. The examples reviewed above substitute style for place and are designed to provide individual gratification, and not to create collaborative communities. In doing so, they often dispossess existing occupants of land and deny them their political rights (Watson, 2013).

This process has now reached the point in many countries where the affluent and powerful minority live like colonialists in their own countries, dependent upon the services provided by the majority that they are happy to exploit. Such forms of development project a comfortable way of life that has since been snapped up by many developers so that those with adequate resources can live in comfort, yet still enjoy access to the social, cultural, and economic benefits of the major cities and avoid both the pollution and payment of the taxes needed to make the cities themselves more liveable. Yet it is the populations of the neglected cities that will invariably end up paying the bills.

The French Revolution, Cambodia's Khmer Rouge, Peru's Shining Path, the Middle East's Isis/Daesh, all demonstrate that utopian plans ultimately create dystopias. A better option is, therefore, to accept that society, and successful towns and cities, involve embracing a degree of natural disorder. Sendra and Sennett (2020) argue that the urban environment has been over-designed in ways that reduce the spontaneity and opportunities for improvisation and innovation that are an essential element in making cities stimulating places in which to live and work. They contrast the forms of order imposed by a globalized real estate industry with the informal and often unruly areas that have developed to meet diverse needs and have evolved over time. They advocate city forms that encourage social and economic diversity, ambiguity, and innovation, rather than centrally planned and self-contained environments as personified by the gated communities of self-selected homogeneous groups. At a time when technology can enable state authorities to monitor every action of citizens and impose penalties for non-conformity to imposed norms, such controls are incompatible with long-term development.

The challenge of reconciling elitist and popular visions of a shared urban future has never been more urgent. Continuing urban population growth will require existing towns and cities to be expanded and new settlements developed. However, these need to be undertaken in a far more participatory manner, and with active roles for the representatives of those who will live in them. As anyone familiar with settlements developed by the residents can attest, they are always vibrant and put available land areas to maximum social use, whereas many officially developed projects impose norms and forms of development (often designated under the euphemism of 'beautification') based on the interests of those in power. The larger the social gap between policymakers and local communities, the greater this gap will be. Neoliberal economics has forced the poor out of high value locations but, as Harvey (2008) concludes, establishing democratic management over the urban deployment of surplus value is essential in achieving the right to the city for all, irrespective of income.

At a time of increasing social inequality, political instability, and economic volatility, the role of built-environment professionals is coming under increasing scrutiny in terms of whose interests are being served. The developments reviewed above pose serious challenges to the role and responsibilities of the built-environment professions concerning social justice, shared prosperity, and environmental sustainability. With public sector resources increasingly limited, relative to the needs of the majority, employment opportunities are increasingly linked to serving the interests of a privileged elite. If this becomes the norm, then the vocational function of the professions providing a public service will be lost, paving the way for a dystopian future.

Fortunately, there are many groups and organizations seeking to meet the needs of the under-privileged. NGOs such as Habitat International Coalition, Asian Coalition for Housing Rights, Slum Dwellers International, Habitat for Humanity, Architects, Designers and Planners for Social Responsibility, ARC-PEACE,[4] and many others, all operate to meet the needs of those outcast by neoliberal policies and all deserve more support. Also, a generation of young professionals is ready and looking for the opportunity to address the challenges of existing urban centres that are inadequately resourced, and to help develop new ones that reflect the cultural and social needs of both existing and future populations. This places a large responsibility on the professional establishment to do all in its power to support them and create more sustainable and liveable towns and cities. Working with the majority is the only way forward for a realistic future that may not be utopia, but is as flexible and adaptable to diverse and changing needs as the ideas of the Metabolists and Archigram groups, and puts technology at the service of human needs and the environment.

Notes

1. *Utopia* discussed the idea of a perfect society, though whether it was a serious essay of an ideal world or a satire on politics at the time is unclear.
2. Prime Real Estate and Infrastructure in Africa, Eko Atlantic website <https://www.ekoatlantic.com/> [accessed 15 April 2021].
3. Also, see Sims (2011).
4. Habitat International Coalition (HIC) website <https://www.hic-net.org/>; Asian Coalition for Housing Rights (ACHR) website <http://www.achr.net/>; Slum Dwellers International (SDI) website <http://sdinet.org/>; Habitat for Humanity (HfH) website <https://www.habitat.org/>; Architects, Designers and Planners for Social Responsibility (ADPSR) website <https://www.adpsr.org/>; ARC-PEACE website <https://arcpeaceinternational.org/>.

PART II
How we value urban land and housing

CHAPTER 7
To have and to hold

Land is such a central aspect of where and how we live, work, and play, that the ways in which it is held, developed, used, and transferred exert a major influence over how and where people can find somewhere to live. Given that the majority of urban land globally is not formally registered and is occupied under a wide range of customary, religious, statutory, non-statutory, and uncertain categories, it is vital that urban managers have an objective basis for policy formulation and practice.

Land tenure and property rights

The way an issue is defined influences how it is managed. Given the centrality of land tenure in social and economic development, definitions are important, though the range of historical, cultural, and political factors mean that a range of definitions is inevitable. For example, land tenure is variously defined as referring to 'the rights of individuals or groups in relation to land' (Durand-Lasserve and Royston, 2002: 7), or 'the relationship, whether legally or customarily defined, among people – as individuals or groups – with respect to land' (Food and Agriculture Organization, 2002: 3.1). However, these conflate tenure and property rights, an issue addressed in the UN-Habitat (2008a) definition which makes an important distinction between tenure status and property rights. For example, it is possible to have a high degree of tenure security, but restricted rights and vice versa. This is illustrated in the case of the British sovereign, who has ultimate ownership of vast areas of land but is not permitted to sell or alter any of the palaces or royal estates without the express will of the British Parliament and approval of the electorate. Conversely, many residents of land and modest houses in the urban areas of rapidly expanding urban centres may not enjoy any formal or legal status to their land or property, yet be free in practice to use, develop, amend, expand, or transfer it as they see fit. In this respect, many low-income households in poor countries may have more de facto rights regarding property than wealthy households in rich countries (Payne, 1979). It is therefore important to clarify what these terms involve. Identifying and classifying the full range of tenure categories existing in a city and the degrees of security they afford, is not sufficient to provide a proper understanding of the issues involved. It is also important to assess the rights associated with them and how these are perceived by different stakeholders.

UN-Habitat (2008a: 5) defines land tenure as 'the way land is held or owned by individuals and groups, or the set of relationships legally or customarily defined amongst people with respect to land. In other words, tenure reflects relationships between people and land directly, and between individuals and groups or people in their dealings in land', while property rights are defined as 'Recognised interests in land and property vested in an individual or group and can apply separately to land or development on it. Rights may apply separately to land and to property on it (e.g., houses, apartments or offices). A recognised interest may include customary, statutory, religious, or informal social practices which enjoy social legitimacy at a given time and place'. Rights may include a wide range of interests, including those listed in Figure 7.1.

The key factor in any system of land tenure and property rights is therefore the relationship of an individual to a group, and of different groups to each other and the state and their collective impact on land. From this, it follows that concepts of land tenure are an expression of the values to which a society adheres or aspires. As such, they may vary enormously from those at one end of the spectrum that regard land as a sacred trust, to be protected for future generations, to those at the other end that regard it as a commodity to be enjoyed or exploited like any other. Tribal, feudal, colonial, capitalist, socialist, and religious societies have all evolved distinctive concepts concerning the occupation and use of land. Countries that have been subjected to colonialism have particularly complex tenure arrangements; indigenous and imposed tenure systems coexist at the same time and location, creating legal plurality and causing widespread land disputes. In addition, legal plurality undermines public support for legal tenure regimes if the imported concepts do not accord with social and cultural values and norms in a given context. This poses major challenges for policymakers and urban managers in recognizing the status of individual land parcels and ensuring the equitable and efficient management of land, especially given the potentially substantial variations in land value.

In addition to statutory or formal regimes, a wide range of semi-legal, unauthorized, or informal tenure categories exist in most cities around the world, each serving the needs and interests of different groups and providing different options for accessing land for housing. Each comprises a vital part of the overall urban land and housing market and policies affecting any one tenure category have a 'knock-on' impact on the others. Furthermore, as urban centres expand into adjacent rural areas, these legal complexities pose major challenges for policymakers. As if this were not complex enough, the inability of formal land supply systems to meet increasing demand has increased the proportion of informal developments. In cities where these constitute a high proportion of total supply, they will inevitably include a wide range of sub-categories, many of which may be partly legal, such as when land is legally purchased, but developed in an area not zoned for residential use, or when it is developed in ways that do not conform to official procedures, standards, or regulations. Finally, a property might meet all these official requirements, but the residents may not possess the required documentation. The fact that these categories have existed continuously for many years also suggests that they have acquired a degree of formalization at a time when formal processes are increasingly informalized.

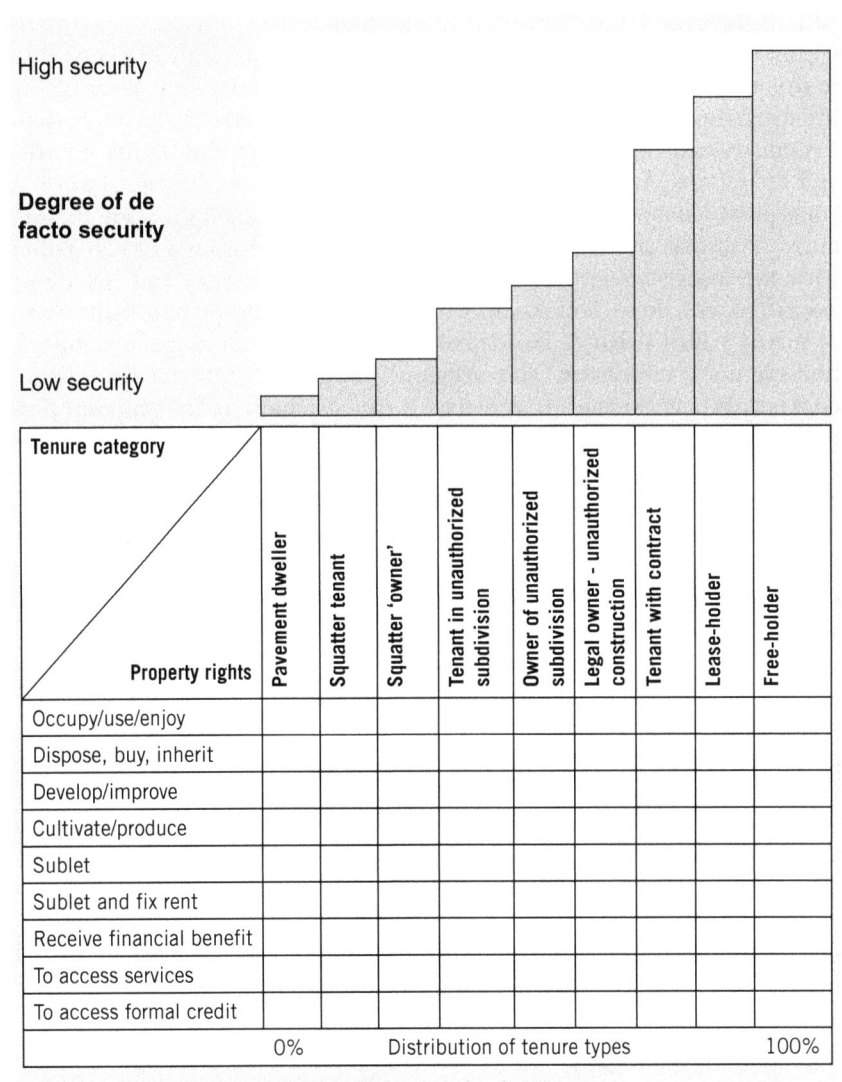

Tenure category / Property rights	Pavement dweller	Squatter tenant	Squatter 'owner'	Tenant in unauthorized subdivision	Owner of unauthorized subdivision	Legal owner – unauthorized construction	Tenant with contract	Lease-holder	Free-holder
Occupy/use/enjoy									
Dispose, buy, inherit									
Develop/improve									
Cultivate/produce									
Sublet									
Sublet and fix rent									
Receive financial benefit									
To access services									
To access formal credit									

0% — Distribution of tenure types — 100%

Notation: The availability of rights by gender can be shown as:
\\ Right available to men only
/ Right available to women only
X Right available equally to men and women

Figure 7.1 Notional typology tenure categories, degrees of security, and associated property rights
Source: Reproduced from 'Introduction' in Payne, 2002: 8

Assessing tenure security and property rights

As noted in UN-Habitat reports (2004, 2008a) and the New Urban Agenda (UN-Habitat, 2020a: clause 29), UN member states commit to 'promote increased security of tenure for all, recognizing the plurality of tenure types, and to develop fit-for-purpose, and age and gender responsive solutions within the continuum of land and property rights, with particular attention to women's land security of tenure as key to their empowerment'. Recognizing the diversity of tenure regimes and categories, UN-Habitat (2004: 8) provides a summary of major tenure systems, their characteristics, and relative benefits and limitations. Adopting a similar approach, I proposed (Payne, 2002: 8) a conceptual framework (Figure 7.1) that makes it possible to include the full range of formal and informal tenure categories existing in a city, together with the associated level of tenure security each provides and the rights associated with them. This modifies the continuum concept, making it a form of matrix which needs to be adapted to include the full range of statutory, non-statutory, customary, and religious categories applicable in specific contexts. Where evidence is available, it can also indicate the proportion of the total represented by each tenure category by adjusting the widths of each column. Finally, it relates the property rights associated with each tenure category and the extent to which these are gender neutral.

The matrix enables a great deal of information to be provided on tenure and property rights in a single chart. In countries where a high proportion of all housing or land development is considered informal, it is likely that will include sub-categories, each serving a different social group. The more categories that exist, the more chance households will have of finding an option that meets their needs, so an objective understanding of the full range is essential for effective intervention. As we will see in Chapter 15, the matrix provides an efficient basis for carefully targeted, evidence-based, policy interventions. Its main limitation is that it retains the notion of a continuum, implying that individual ownership is the ultimate to be aimed for, even though this may only apply to those with secure and above-average incomes. It also omits perceptions of tenure security, a key factor influencing residents' willingness to invest in home improvements. A means of addressing perceptions of security in a non-linear way is provided by Lahoti (2021) using a series of spider charts as shown in Figure 7.2.

The need for legitimacy

When a significant proportion of the population routinely breaks a set of laws, this suggests that the laws in question have lost social legitimacy and are not relevant for the situation for which they were drafted. In the case of informal or unauthorized urban land and housing development, the reason is largely failure by the state and private sectors to meet the needs of people on terms and conditions to which they can conform. Such legal and regulatory frameworks lose their legitimacy and become impossible to enforce without coercion or market-distorting subsidies.

The only way to regain legitimacy and increase conformity with the laws, rules, and procedures involved in accessing land and housing in urban areas is to undertake a systemic review of the terms and conditions of entry to

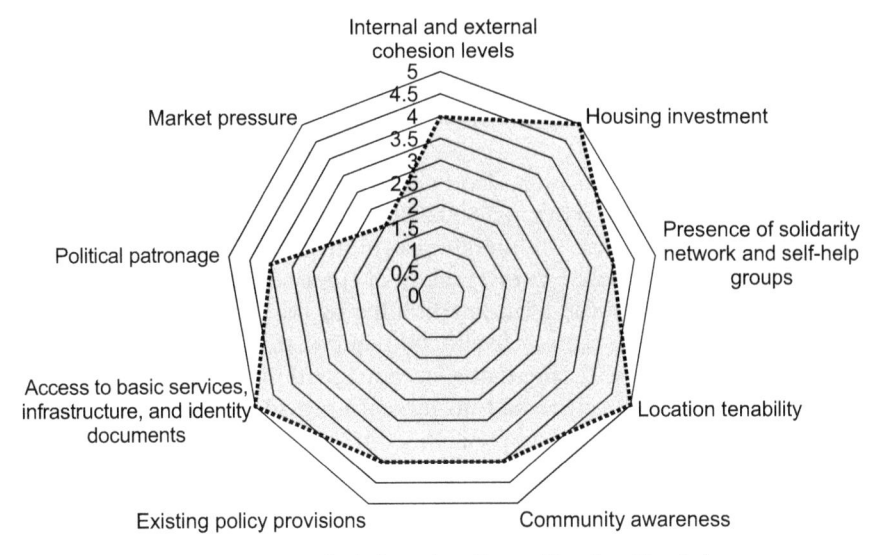

Figure 7.2 Perceived tenure security in Sarvodaya Nagar, Bhandup, Mumbai
Source: Lahoti, 2021

legal forms of land and housing. This should include a review of all existing categories of land tenure and property rights by which people occupy land and housing, including non-formal or unauthorized categories. The coexistence of these different tenure systems and sub-markets within most cities creates a complex series of relationships in which policy related to any one category has major, and often unintended, repercussions on the others. To further complicate matters, many settlements and even dwellings within settlements, move between one category and another.

The impact of cultural and historical factors demonstrates that land and property, while increasingly seen as exclusively economic resources, are more complex in that they also attract strong emotional attachments. In addition, each piece of land is unique in terms of its location, quality, and other attributes, so that generalizing about it is more difficult, yet effective urban land tenure policies can only be developed if they take these factors into account.

In many cities, various forms of informal or unauthorized land and housing developments now represent the largest single channel of supply. As they have expanded, so they have diversified in terms of the level of security provided and the social groups served. Local terms such as *gecekondu*, *bidonville*, and *favela* may now subsume multiple processes of land settlement, development, and exchange which embody significant differences in perceived tenure status not recognized by outsiders. For example, an area classified as unauthorized or illegal may consist of squatters who invaded the land and built without permission. In some cases, they may not be considered a threat to the locality and in India can be classified as 'notified' or 'non-objectionable' meaning they have more de facto security than those defined as 'objectionable'. The level of de facto tenure security in the 'non-objectionable' settlements will be higher than in the 'objectionable' settlements and it would be logical to assume that these would command a higher entry price and encourage a higher level of local investment.

The most basic form of urban land occupancy in any city is that of street dwellers. In Mumbai, an estimated 500,000 people live on the streets near the city centre as this is where livelihood opportunities are greatest. In 1981, the state government proposed to evict many of these settlers and some shacks were demolished. However, a landmark ruling by the Indian Supreme Court in 1985 found that the right to livelihood required that the city corporation must provide settlers with alternative accommodation before they could be evicted. Since the authorities had no funds to provide alternative housing, the vast majority were allowed to remain, even though some demolitions and evictions continue occasionally (Tellis, 2015). A further consideration was probably that even if alternative housing was provided, land costs in Mumbai were so high that alternative housing would have been too far away from livelihood opportunities so recipients may well have sold them and returned to the street to repeat the process.

Street dwelling and other unauthorized or informal tenure categories are not restricted to rapidly urbanizing countries in the Global South. In the UK, an increasing phenomenon is the growth of 'beds in sheds', whereby legal home-owners convert existing garden sheds to provide rental accommodation for migrant workers or poor families.

The wide range of settlement processes existing in cities throughout the world requires that before preparing any policy interventions concerning non-formal or unauthorized settlements, it is vital to undertake a detailed, objective assessment of the different categories and sub-categories that exist in an area. Experience shows that a failure to understand the likely outcomes of a policy guarantees that they will be different from those intended.

The evolving debate on land tenure and property rights policy

International focus on urban land tenure and property rights was first provided by the United Nations' comprehensive report (1973), which established a sound foundation for the 1976 Habitat I Vancouver Declaration on Human Settlements. This proposed measures to ensure land tenure security for unplanned settlements where appropriate and programmes for regularizing tenure, though without defining the means to be used. The World Bank (1993: 5) housing sector policy paper ignored customary and religious tenure systems and stated that 'In low-income countries, priorities are to develop market-oriented systems of property rights' and 'In centrally planned and formerly centrally planned countries, priorities for reform are property rights'.

As one of the world's largest development funding agencies, policy papers by the World Bank carry considerable influence. The 1993 report was therefore hugely significant in that the Bank effectively tied its flag to the neoliberal agenda of promoting the interests of markets. Yet for others trying to improve access to land and housing for those the markets ignored, the concept of enabling was based on the ideas of Abrams (1966), Mangin (1970), and Turner (1967, 1976), all of whom had demonstrated since the 1960s that people were quite capable of building both houses and complete settlements. For them, the role of government was to enable such creativity and investment; to enable people and communities, *not* markets.

Three years before the Bank published its housing policy paper, Turner (1990) demonstrated that just by offering three options for his seven listed variables in supplying land – finance, building maintenance, and other components of a housing development – a total of 2,187 different courses of action were possible. However, Bank policy during the 1990s and for several years after was based on the assumption that the best way to meet the land and housing needs of the urbanizing countries to which it was lending, was to focus its resources on just one option, maximizing the role of the private sector to achieve market efficiency. This was interpreted as best achieved through individual land and property ownership and the Bank soon after launched the first of many national land titling programmes.

The 1993 Bank policy ignored the rich diversity of customary and religious forms of land tenure and property rights. It also overlooked the vital aspects of cultural values and social needs that influence patterns of demand, despite McAuslan (1985: 19) warning that there are almost as many forms of land tenure as there are nations and 'Whatever the deficiencies of existing practices and policies in any country, land tenure reforms ignore culture and tradition at their peril'. The Bank's report was published during a period of Western triumphalism following the collapse of the Soviet Union and the publication of Fukuyama's paper 'The end of history' (1989) which reinforced neoliberal claims that a free market economy was the universal future. However, the most triumphalist publication was by de Soto who argued that 'capitalism triumphs in the west and fails everywhere else' because the West developed individual property ownership that can be used as collateral for credit and 'by this process, the West injects life into assets and makes them generate capital' (de Soto, 2000: 6). This reinforced the attitudes and assumptions of ideological superiority of capitalist forms of market-driven development and the fact that they were published by an economist from the Global South must have been music to the ears of the Reagan administration in the USA and the Thatcher government in the UK, since both had been avid supporters of neoliberal economics and both had appointed Milton Friedman as an economic adviser.

It is difficult to avoid the impression that a major reason for the considerable influence of de Soto's book on tenure policy globally was that it was telling the leaders of the West what they wanted to hear – and expressing it far more convincingly than they could themselves. He claimed that property ownership provided the foundation on which capitalism itself flourished and that if the Third World was to develop, it would need to follow the path laid out by the West. As previously discussed (Payne 2002: 10-12), de Soto fails to provide a causal relationship between Western affluence and property ownership and even denies the role of slavery and colonialism in enriching the West and impoverishing the rest of the world.

The gap between de Soto's claims and reality have been exposed by many other reviewers. In Bogotá, Gilbert (2002) found that formal finance was not available to households after they had received titles and they continued to rely upon freely available informal finance; furthermore, there was little sign of a secondary housing market following legalization. He concludes (2002: 22) that 'de Soto is dangerous insofar as he is conjuring up a myth about popular capitalism. He is fanning the delusion that anyone, anywhere, can become a fully-fledged capitalist. Although he offers little or no empirical evidence in support of his assertion, that has not stopped Washington from, once again, rallying to his call'. Home (2004: 22) argued that de Soto's optimistic language in favour of formal property systems concealed, however, the likelihood that 'converting oral into written, informal into formal, local into national– will not be uniformly benign, neutral or free of power relationships and exploitation ... Integrating plural and informal property rights into one unified system under State control may facilitate the spread of global capitalism'. He concluded (2004: 27) 'The value of customary, more flexible and localized land rights systems is being increasingly recognised'. Similar conclusions were reached by other researchers such as von Benda-Beckmann (2003) who found that the idea that formal property and a free market can work under conditions of great economic and political inequality to the benefit of the poor is wishful thinking. In assessing the impact of titling in South Africa, Kingwill et al. (2006: 2) reported that 'Titling does not necessarily increase tenure security or certainty; in many cases it does the opposite. Formalisation of property rights does not promote lending to the poor. Rather than turning their property into "capital", formalisation could increase the rate of homelessness'. Mitchell (2007) records how de Soto persuaded the son of Egypt's president to strengthen the powers of private property by passing laws to that effect. However, farmers were not ignorant of the implications of private property and successfully resisted the laws, fearing it would expose them to the predations of outside interests.

Of all the critical reviews of de Soto's claims, the most damning are those focusing on his home country of Peru, where he had persuaded the World Bank to support a national land titling programme. By 2002, this had granted formal titles to 1.2 million urban households and was being heralded as a great success and the basis for application in other countries. However, Cockburn (2002: 7), a Peruvian researcher found that 'In general, and despite the increase in the number of properties regularized between 1998 and 1999, access to loans decreased during that period, coinciding with the economic recession and related problems affecting private banks'. He concluded that 'there is no direct relationship between the number of title deeds handed over to informal dwellers and their subsequent access to loans from private banks'. A similar finding was reported by Kagawa and Turkstra (2002) to the effect that the majority of mortgages provided to newly titled households was by the public sector Banco de Materiales, which then suffered 25 per cent defaults by borrowers who were either unable or unwilling to repay. At the same time, Field and Torrero (2006: 1) could find 'no evidence that titles increase the likelihood of receiving credit from private sector banks, although interest rates are significantly lower for titled applicants regardless of whether collateral was requested'. Although Field reports in another paper (2005: 279–80) that significant levels of investment in residential improvements followed the granting of titles, she acknowledges that 'The bulk of the increase is financed without the use of credit', undermining claims that titles would lead to the use of property as collateral for loans'. She also acknowledges that 'The nature of investment is limited to small renovations as opposed to housing additions', suggesting that the key factor was a perception that improved tenure security encouraged small-scale improvements rather than major investments. All empirical evidence on tenure shows that there are many other options than ownership for achieving this objective. In summary, claims that titles turn property into collateral, collateral into credit, and credit into increased income lack substance.

Analysis into action

Recent experience confirms the limitations of land titling and individual property ownership. Analysis of the informal settlements in Colombo, Sri Lanka (Redwood and Wakely, 2012) concludes that universal freehold to land may be the desired aim of public policy, but it is not realistic. Rather than attempting to launch a citywide titling programme, it was preferable to start with tenure security by acknowledging occupancy in the under-serviced settlements. However, the mantra of individual ownership has remained the cornerstone of government policy in many countries, noticeably the UK and USA, where governments led by Thatcher and Reagan and their successors fully subscribe to the neoliberal theories of Milton Friedman.

In the UK, the electoral motivation driving property ownership generated an economic imperative to hold an asset whose value would increase at least as rapidly as any other commodity. 'Getting on the property ladder' became a popular means of increasing wealth and personal security and increasing prices came to be regarded as highly desirable, at least for those already on the ladder. This tempted others to join on the bottom rung, pushing prices up for those higher up the ladder and stimulating an ever-increasing, and self-sustaining, spiral of demand and price inflation. As a result, home ownership in the UK increased from 32 per cent in 1953, to 75 per cent in 1981, reducing slightly to 70 per cent in 2007. With house prices reflecting ever-increasing demand, it was possible for one's wealth to increase more rapidly by lying in bed as one's home increased in value than it was by going out to work!

The same approach was adopted in the USA under President Reagan and later by President Clinton. Republicans were following the neoliberal approach of individualized ownership of assets under a 'light touch' regulatory regime, while the Democrats were keen to show that the benefits of ownership were also available to lower-income communities. As a result, real estate agents, banks, and other mortgage providers generated substantial revenues from increased demand and rising prices. However, once the proportion of people in stable employment able to service long-term loans had been satisfied, the only source of commissions was from those moving home. To expand the market, real estate agents and banks started to allow those on lower incomes to self-certify that their incomes were sufficient to enable them to repay a loan on the clear understanding that asset values would continue to rise, enabling them to sell at a profit if they ran into difficulties with repayments.

To further stimulate demand for home ownership, US banks created a secondary mortgage market to sell on mortgages using complex financial contracts that enabled them to securitize risks and even make profits through 'special purpose vehicles' and 'credit default swaps'. This made it much easier to fund additional borrowing and proved extremely profitable for the banks, which earned a fee for each mortgage they sold on. Accordingly, mortgage brokers were encouraged to sell more and more of these mortgages. As demand for home ownership was artificially increased, so prices rose, further adding to demand. This in turn led to abuses as banks no longer had the incentive to carefully check the mortgages they issued.

By 2005, one in five US mortgages was to 'sub-prime' borrowers, that is, those with poor credit histories, or limited evidence of income, usually because they were poor. To sustain demand, agents were offering loans for home ownership to 'Ninjas' or those with no income, no jobs, and no assets. Initial payments were fixed for two years, and then became variable and much higher. Consequently, a wave of repossessions started to sweep America as many of these mortgages were reset at higher interest rates.

As with any market, when demand exceeds supply, prices tend to rise. However, once the short-term subsidized interest rates expired and commercial rates applied, low-income homeowners found that monthly repayments increased dramatically and many decided to cash in by selling. Such was the scale of sales that suddenly supply started to exceed demand, resulting in massive falls in property prices across the country, extensive repossession of properties by the banks, and the destruction of communities. It is thought that as many as 2 million families may have been evicted from their homes as their cases made their way through the courts.

Once it was realized that the 'sub-prime' mortgages were worthless, banks such as Fannie Mae and Freddie Mac sustained colossal losses and were put into 'conservatorship' at vast cost to taxpayers, and Lehman Brothers bank collapsed on 15 September 2008. The crisis could have been confined to the USA had British and other international banks not sought to expand by buying heavily into the international bond market. The British bank of Northern Rock had invested heavily in US bonds and was only saved from collapse by being nationalized by the UK Government, this time at vast cost to UK taxpayers. Although privatized again in 2012, the public ended up subsidizing the losses incurred by private organizations, triggering the economic crisis of 2008 from which the global economy has still not recovered.

The facts of this crisis are well known, and even became the subject of the 2015 Hollywood film *The Big Short*. However, they bear repeating because the lessons do not appear to have been learned. Despite initial outrage in the form of the 'Occupy' movement that railed against the greed of the bankers and their weak regulation by governments, others who suffered from the crisis blamed the political establishment, electing populist leaders who promised to restore national pride at the expense of international collaboration. Those who caused the crisis have not only escaped punishment but continue to prosper, while the global recession has resulted in massive cuts to public services for the majority.

How long people are prepared to tolerate such situations remains to be seen. However, the crisis is not accidental. As Klein (2007) demonstrated just before the crisis, economic shocks were identified by economic theorists such as Friedman as great opportunities to impose policies that would promote their ideas. While unrestrained and under-regulated market capitalism has succeeded beyond the dreams of its advocates, its manifest failure to meet the basic needs, let alone reasonable aspirations, of the poor and the young poses a challenge that requires new ideas from those concerned with challenging the status quo. As the following examples demonstrate, the need for lessons to be learned is urgent.

Cambodia's land management and administration project

Before the limitations of the Peruvian tilting programme became evident, the World Bank supported the approach with funding for a mainly rural land titling programme in Thailand which was broadly successful, having allocated approximately 13 million titles over 20 years from 1984 to 2004. Buoyed by the success of the Thai programme, the World Bank agreed to support an even more ambitious Land Management and Administration Project (LMAP) in Cambodia. Many of the key staff from the Thai programme moved to implement this and work commenced in 2002 with co-funding from the German (GIZ) and Canadian (CIDA) international development agencies. Following the harrowing experience of the Khmer Rouge regime whereby between 1 and 2 million people were executed or died under one of the most repressive regimes in recent history, together with all property rights being declared null and void, and maps and title records destroyed, people were naturally grateful to receive documentary evidence that the state recognized their tenure rights.

Progress was initially smooth and 1.124 million titles were issued at a modest unit cost in rural areas throughout the country. However, the limitations of land titling were to be quickly exposed when the programme moved into urban areas. The LMAP project included the area around and within Boeung Kak Lake in central Phnom Penh. This was publicly announced in January 2007 and in the same month, a 99-year lease agreement was signed between the municipality and a private developer to fill the lake and develop a massive commercial development. The area had a population of about 18,000 people, some living around the 90 hectare lake and others on houses raised on stilts within the lake itself. The total area was approximately 130 hectares right in the heart of the city. Residents were offered three options: relocation to a site 25 kilometres from the city centre; move to a similar relocation area for four years, after which housing would be provided in the Boeung Kak area; or accept cash compensation of US$8,500. Given that land prices in the area were between $2,000 and $3,000/m^2 at the time, this was modest in the extreme.

On 24 September 2009, the Inspection Panel (IP) at the World Bank received a request for an investigation. It is to the Bank's enormous credit that in the same year its housing policy was committing the Bank to promote markets, it also established an independent complaints mechanism for people and communities who believe that they are adversely affected by a Bank-funded project. As such, the IP exists to ensure that all Bank projects adhere to its standards, regulations, and procedures, one of which is an operational policy known as OP4.12 on involuntary resettlement. The organization requesting an investigation alleged that some residents had been forcibly resettled and others were under pressure to leave the area, and that their land claims for protection had been denied. Following a proposed joint suspension of the project, the government cancelled the whole project. The investigation took place and eventually concluded that the Bank had failed to comply with its obligations under OP4.12, since the residents had been denied due process in not having had the chance for their claims to be adjudicated. Attempts by the Bank to stop the evictions and resolve the issue were unsuccessful (World Bank, 2011b), at which point the Bank cancelled all loans to Cambodia, renewing them only five years later in May 2016 (Paviour, 2016). This painfully illustrates the risks that titling poses in urban areas.

National land titling in Rwanda

An ambitious land titling programme was undertaken between 2007 and 2012 in another country that has also suffered terribly, the small, landlocked, African country of Rwanda. In 1994, an estimated 800,000 Tutsi men, women, and children, as well as some moderate Hutus and Twa, were slaughtered in just 100 days by Hutu extremists.

As part of efforts to rebuild the country, the UK Department for International Development (DFID), other donors, and the government established the National Land Tenure Regularisation Programme (NLTRP) to build on a land policy that had been developed from 2004 onwards. It benefited from strong political support from the government of President Kagame and was perhaps the most far-reaching outcome in terms of significance and impact. This is partly because Rwanda is the most densely populated country in Africa and, as Bruce (2007) shows in an authoritative review, competition for land was a factor in the events leading up to the conflict. As the population increased from 3 million to 10 million between 1960 and 2010, the average size of a family farm holding fell from 2 hectares in 1960 to 1.2 hectares in 1984, and to just 0.7 hectares in the early 1990s. Furthermore, in 1984, it was estimated that 16 per cent of the population owned 43 per cent of the land, while the poorest 43 per cent of the population owned just 15 per cent (Musahara and Huggins, 2005: 298–307; Bruce, 2007: 6).[1] Bruce considered that the politicization of land along ethnic lines was critical to the events that unfolded in Rwanda and that it made land policy a central basis for reconciliation and the building of a peaceful nation. However, other priorities had to be addressed first, such as finding employment and places to live for the waves of post-conflict returnees.

It was to resolve these issues and provide clarity and security for both ethnic groups that the NLTRP was launched. Its objective was to identify and demarcate land parcels, issue titles and leases, and establish nationwide and support institutions in charge of land management and administration, all within five years. The project required both the active participation of the population and the coordinated interventions of several institutions at central and local levels. They aimed for the adoption of an appropriate legal and regulatory framework, the exhaustive inventory of land holdings and landholders at national level, the timely delivery of land titles or land leases to identified landholders, and the maintenance of the land information system, especially the registration of land transfers following tenure regularization.

Over a seven-year period, multi-donor support contributed to the development of a national land policy which in turn formed the basis for the Land Law approved in 2005. Among the provisions of the Law was that all land belongs to the Rwandan people, is managed by the state, and is classified as either a) public domain (land strictly for public purposes, specifically defined in the Law to include wetlands), or b) private domain (land which the state can alienate or lease out to private users). The government makes land available to private users under leases of between 3 and 99 years through local land commissions. An extremely progressive requirement is that gender discrimination is prohibited and in fact women have been appointed to key positions in both government and other organizations nationally. However, the requirement that land parcels cannot be sub-divided below a 1-hectare minimum has caused considerable problems as this is well above the average parcel size nationally. As a result, de facto subdivisions are frequent, so that all members of a family can have access to a small piece of land for food production. This practice is pushing people back again into the informality/illegality that the NLTRP was supposed to resolve, thus making micro-landholders vulnerable to expropriation.[2]

UK support for the land sector in Rwanda commenced in 2002 with a feasibility study, followed by field trials during 2007–2008, and by November 2010 over 2.8 million parcels had been demarcated. The programme completed the titling of nearly 4 million land parcels by the end of 2012, an impressive achievement by any standards. However, the number of leases allocated at the time was very small, partly because the number of plots to be demarcated and titled proved to be substantially higher (at 10.9 million) than the 7.9 million originally estimated, and also because the capacity of the District Land Boards (DLBs) was insufficient to manage the process within the tight timetable. A further concern was that the DLBs would not be able to process subsequent transactions, thus quickly making the land register out of date and prejudicing the certainty that titling was intended to provide. Although this was considered by DFID and the government to have been resolved before the completion of the programme, anecdotal evidence suggests that a significant number of land transactions are not formally registered, though by definition unregistered transactions cannot be quantified.

The Government of Rwanda and DFID deserve considerable credit for undertaking such an ambitious programme and for supporting a strong and stable government that has shown great determination in rebuilding the country, society, and economy. The challenges of land management are considerable in any country, so international donors understandably look for examples of success, particularly at a time when reactionary domestic pressures seek to undermine international development funding. Both the Government of Rwanda and DFID therefore have strong reasons to consider the NLTRP a model approach and have promoted it as an example for wider application. This has had some success with visits from international delegations. However, it is important to recognize that each case needs to be treated as unique. The conditions that enabled the Rwandan programme to make progress – generous donor support to a small country with a strong, committed government which discourages dissent – would be difficult to replicate in larger countries. For example, applying a similar approach to the whole of Nigeria could involve a budget in the region of $800 m–900 m, place heavy demands upon implementing agencies, and involve similar risks of subsequent unregistered transactions.

Land titling in South Africa

The final case study reviews the experience of land titling in South Africa, one of many countries in which European settlement has had a negative impact on the indigenous population. Under the apartheid (segregation) policy of the nationalist government, the non-white majority of the population was denied any rights to vote or own land. The 1913 Natives Land Act decreed that the white population was not allowed to buy land from the indigenous population and vice versa. This would not have been so disastrous for the majority had they possessed most of the land. However, they had been confined by the white minority to a small proportion of the land designated as native reserves or homelands to be held under traditional customary tenure. The discovery of gold and diamonds in 1895 had led to massive expansion of the mining industry, attracting foreign investment that boosted the economy but leaving the indigenous population in poverty. The non-white population was forced into working in the mines, on farms owned by white landowners, or living in townships outside the expanding urban centres where tenure was at best public rental (Napier, 2009). Opposition to the oppressive white minority government was ruthlessly repressed for many decades, though the end of apartheid came surprisingly peacefully and suddenly. A combination of local opposition and international pressure forced the resignation of the nationalist government, and the national elections of 1994 that entitled all adults to vote resulted in a landslide victory for the African National Congress under Nelson Mandela.

In 1994, the Reconstruction and Development Programme (RDP) was launched to improve living conditions in the townships and led to the construction of over 2 million houses. However, the majority of the new developments were located well outside the urban centres, not because of racial segregation but as a result of continuing economic inequality: the land on the urban periphery was cheaper and therefore the housing provided was more affordable. Social segregation has therefore continued, based on economic and spatial grounds. Of course, the spatial location of the townships cannot be physically changed, though improved transportation has helped. The Development Facilitation Act 67 of 1995 was enacted to increase security of tenure for people living in informal settlements by creating a form of tenure known as 'initial ownership' (Marx and Rubin, 2008: 118).

It was in this context that the land reforms sought to provide for the poor majority the same legal rights of land ownership that had been the exclusive preserve of the white minority for over a century. After all, if individual ownership is good enough for the rich minority, why should it be denied to the poor majority, especially if international policy had claimed that ownership was the route out of poverty? However, in a detailed study of the land titling programme in an area east of Johannesburg, Marx and Rubin (2008: 118) found no evidence of titling having any financial or economic impact on poor households. Cousins et al. (2005: 1) also report that 'Formalisation through registered title deeds creates unaffordable costs for many poor people: registered properties become subject to building regulations, boundaries must be surveyed, services must be paid for, and rates must be paid to local government'. In addition (2005: 4) lower-income households 'are unlikely to get access to formal credit using land or housing as collateral, whether or not they hold title deeds to their homes and land'. Most people already enjoyed a degree of de facto tenure security and the possession of a title deed has had little effect on access to formal credit, home improvements or household investment, with most funding coming from the state in the form of subsidies and improved infrastructure. Although the RDP programme produced more than a million houses, they were of a standard design and variable quality, and the peripheral locations led to many people selling (despite rules preventing this) and moving into informal settlements or overcrowded tenements in the urban centres. Napier (2009) reports that few low-income households can afford to participate in the land and housing market and despite the election of the African National Congress Party and the end of apartheid in 1994, inequality remains extremely high. The resilience and innovation that township residents were forced to develop under apartheid continue to be necessary.

Reflections and next steps

It is perhaps no coincidence that the most comprehensive land titling programmes have been undertaken in post-conflict countries and each of the examples cited in this chapter are cases in point. Peru suffered the violence of the Maoist revolutionary army known as the 'Shining Path' during the 1970s, while Cambodia and Rwanda suffered genocide that left deep scars from which they are still recovering, and the non-white majority of South Africa were herded into reservations or townships and denied justice for a century. In each of these cases, land was a key factor in denying people their rights, so policies to make secure forms of land holding available are an important element in building more equitable and stable societies. In such cases, the promotion of titling after prolonged periods of extreme conflict and insecurity could be justified as offering the prospect of total legal protection from eviction and the opportunity for a future in which people can invest with confidence. This is particularly important in urban areas where demand for land and housing is intense and competition favours those in power or with influence. However, experience has shown that even in these extreme cases, outcomes are significantly different from projections, suggesting that a more nuanced approach is needed.

None of the criticism of land titling or home ownership summarized above, either globally or in the case of individual countries, is intended to deny that individual property ownership represents an attractive option for households with reasonable incomes and in stable employment. However, it is not appropriate for the poor, the young, or possibly even the old. In most societies, these groups represent at least one-third of the total population, suggesting that any country that allows home ownership rates to exceed approximately 67 per cent of the population is promoting ownership to excess. This suggests that it is highly dangerous to prioritize ownership over other options, especially at the present time, when land registries are so incomplete and inaccurate that moves to provide titles in urban or peri-urban areas may encourage or intensify disputes over who has the primary claim. The best approach to meeting diverse and changing demand is to provide diversity of supply, as any advocate of efficient markets should acknowledge. The overwhelming findings of the research community and examples from practice provide no evidence to support claims of titling liberating the poor from their poverty and turning them into dynamic entrepreneurs, removing any basis for claiming that land titling is a universal, or even local, solution to global poverty. The key issue is to what extent titles are *the only* means of addressing global poverty? As we will show in Chapter 15, the answer is that a wide range of options exist to meet this objective.

Notes

1. Bruce (2007: 6) cites Musahara and Huggins (2005) as summarizing the relevant data very effectively at pp. 298–307.
2. Personal communication with A. Durand-Lasserve (2006).

CHAPTER 8
The global move to market

The ways that land and housing are valued involve balancing social, cultural, and legal, as well as economic, aspects. As discussed in previous chapters, the globalization of market capitalism has increasingly prioritized economic values over all other aspects. It has also prioritized individual ownership over other forms of tenure, with negative consequences for countless households to the point that even the conservative journal *The Economist* has published a special issue (*Economist*, 2020) on 'The horrible housing blunder' acknowledging that home ownership has become a harmful obsession. Yet despite the 'sub-prime' crisis of 2008, the global financial crisis it generated, and the mass of evidence exposing the limitations of a market-driven approach, land and housing have remained major vehicles for international investors and speculators, driven by increased urban populations competing for what is a finite resource. The global penetration of market forces into land management and housing provision has been supported by many governments and international development agencies, a process that has increased prices and intensified global inequality.

The price inflation generated by the excessive promotion of home ownership and land titling programmes has risen to the extent that even middle-income households in cities throughout the world are now finding it difficult to become home-owners. While this has generated substantial wealth for some people in a single generation, it has been at the expense of prospects for the next, to the point where those born since Reagan and Thatcher promoted home ownership are now known as 'Generation Rent'.

The result of these ownership and land titling policies, even in rich countries like the UK and USA, has been a dramatic increase in overcrowding and homelessness. In both countries, households relying on welfare support are being relocated to other cities where housing is more affordable, destroying social support networks and causing widespread suffering, bad health, and social alienation. This is the exact opposite of the outcome claimed by proponents of the capitalist dream of enterprise lifting millions out of poverty and into the sunny uplands of middle-class affluence. More seriously, the lessons of the global crisis that was caused by the mismanagement of the housing sector in just one country, the USA, have still not been fully acknowledged or acted upon by political leaders. None of those who caused the crisis have been held to account in the USA, and Iceland stands out as one of few countries where justice for key actors in the crisis was meted out by the courts (Noonan et al., 2018). If ever a theory of economic management has been shown to have failed on its own criteria, let alone criteria that place a greater value on wellbeing and social coherence, neoliberal policy on land and property is a prime example.

To understand the range of challenges facing different countries, it is necessary to appreciate that although most countries have either embraced market-driven capitalism, or had it imposed upon them, they are in a process of transition from different forms of economic management, at different stages of the transition, and sometimes heading towards diverse forms. For example, the UK has embraced feudal, social, and neoliberal approaches, while China has followed a state-driven form of capitalist development in which land and housing investment has been a major means of reducing poverty, though not without difficulties in social and cultural terms. Cuba, Ethiopia, and Vietnam provide examples of countries retaining socialist controls while seeking foreign investment, and Mongolia, Albania, and Cambodia have moved from socialism to embrace market-based forms of economic development and land management. A final range of countries, including Lesotho, the Solomon Islands, and Vanuatu, are in the process of adapting customary forms of development to embrace market systems.

Although generalizations pose obvious limitations, these distinctions can help to illustrate broad trends and identify major differences between ways of valuing land and housing. The examples provided in the following chapters are intended to illustrate the key differences and provide a framework for evidence-based policy formulation and evaluation. However, it is important to acknowledge that a wide range of customary, statutory, and informal land tenure and property rights categories coexist in many countries, of which India and Indonesia are major examples. The outcomes of policy interventions in such complex contexts are therefore extremely difficult to predict.

The political economy of land and housing

Throughout history, urban centres have been the basis for social development, technological innovation, political change, and economic growth. The mere physical proximity of large numbers of people stimulates creativity and the demand for improved access to services, which in turn generates high value employment opportunities. It is this quality that has resulted in sustained, high levels of urbanization and urban growth globally during the last two centuries. However, it also generates competition for preferential access to land and housing which, while beneficial within reason, can exclude vulnerable groups if inadequately regulated.

Global cities like London, New York, and Paris offer luxury and a rich cultural life, attracting a highly mobile global elite unable to enjoy such benefits so freely at home. A London estate agent recently claimed that 80 per cent of all houses valued at more than £10 m (US$13.7 m) were being snapped up by foreign buyers (Scanlon et al., 2017). Much play has been made of the £140 m ($192 m) paid for a two-floor apartment at 1 Hyde Park in central London by a central Asian businessman. Such dwellings are not the permanent homes of most owners, but temporary watering holes. However, by removing their dwellings from the stock available to the local population, they are adding to the housing shortage, and increasing housing prices to a level that excludes all but the most affluent locals. For those not able to meet the costs of either purchase or inflated private rental accommodation, the only options are to accept ever-smaller dwelling units, move out to less expensive cities where employment opportunities are fewer, or commute at high cost.

As urbanization has increased in parallel with the globalization of market-driven economic management, the cost of access commanded by land in urban and peri-urban areas multiplies in price increases over rural land, occasionally by up to 100 times more. Management of the wealth generated from the expansion of urban land and housing markets around the world has fundamental implications for society, as demonstrated by the 'sub-prime' housing crisis in the USA. The global economic implications of dysfunctional land and housing markets mean that policymakers in all countries must carefully consider the role of finance in national and international housing policy.

While massive social housing programmes were undertaken during the 20th century, home ownership rates also increased steadily in many countries. The collapse of the Soviet Union triggered a dramatic transition in ownership from state to private sector land and property owners, both in Russia and what then became independent countries in eastern Europe and the Commonwealth of Independent States. Individual home ownership now accounts for 96 per cent of the housing stock in Estonia, 77 per cent in Slovenia, and more than 80 per cent in China (UN General Assembly, 2012: 4). According to Jordá et al. (2014a: 2):

> The share of mortgages on banks' balance sheets doubled in the course of the 20th century, driven by a sharp rise of mortgage lending to households. Household debt to asset ratios have risen substantially in many countries. Financial stability risks have been increasingly linked to real estate lending booms which are typically followed by deeper recessions and slower recoveries. Housing finance has come to play a central role in the modern macroeconomy.

While the costs of labour, construction materials, services, and finance are relatively inelastic, the increase in housing costs is increasingly due to inflationary pressures on land in prime locations and particularly in peri-urban areas, where land use changes from rural to urban can generate many multiples in land values.

These processes have accelerated rapidly since the 1980s, when the financialization of land and housing became global, and has continued unabated since the 2008 financial crisis. However, much of this investment is misallocated and speculative in nature, being spent on luxury properties that do not address affordable housing needs. As a result, housing has become a means of increasing inequality and reducing economic stability.

For the increasing proportion of people living in the ever-expanding cities of the Global South, and even many in the Global North unable to afford legal access to land and housing, the only option is to live outside the formal system. Many of the world's megacities have large informal populations. The world's largest unauthorized settlement – Neza-Chalco-Itza, in Mexico City – has over 4 million residents, and in Cairo a large number live in the 'City of the Dead' between or above the tombs of the deceased residents of a large cemetery complex. Even cities like Lisbon, Athens, and San Francisco have all seen major increases in unauthorized development, including people living out of their cars in San Diego (Pollard, 2018), largely because entry to the formal land and housing market has become unaffordable.

In these situations, informality is often formalized. The Mathare Valley settlements in Nairobi offer an example of how the residents of what is regarded as an illegal and impermanent settlement have responded to the lack of official governance over the settlement by creating their own economic and informal governance mechanisms. Alongside booming African cities like Nairobi and Addis Ababa, various types of unofficially developed settlements are illustrating the governance capacities of local communities. The bestselling novel *Shantaram* by Roberts (2003) provides an excellent example from India of how governance operates in areas considered disorganized.

While financial speculation in land is an ancient preoccupation, the scale of global investment in housing as an asset class is a relatively new trend. According to the UN Special Rapporteur (UN, 2017: 3–4) 'Housing and commercial real estate have become the "commodity of choice" for corporate finance and the pace at which financial corporations and funds are taking over housing and real estate in many cities is staggering. The value of global real estate is about $217 trillion, nearly 60 per cent of the value of all global assets, with residential real estate comprising 75 per cent of the total.' The financialization of housing is defined as 'structural changes in housing and financial markets and global investment whereby housing is treated as a commodity, a means of wealth and often as security for financial instruments that are traded and sold on global markets'.

Privatization and investor subsidy programmes have included the sale to sitting tenants of public rented housing through right-to-buy policies and an aggressive sale of public land to property developers with little public benefit, as in the United Kingdom; property transfers to not-for-profit actors as in the Netherlands; and in some cases, transfers to commercial actors, as in Germany and the United States (Abood, 2018). Yet this process has not been universal. When Singapore attained self-government in 1959, only 9 per cent of Singaporeans resided in public housing. Today, 80 per cent of Singaporeans live in a government-built apartment (*Economist*, 2017) and the government retains ownership of most of the land, enabling it to adjust supply in line with demand and thus restrict inflationary risks. With about 90 per cent of all land owned by the state, all flats and most high-rise private condominiums are sold on a 99-year leasehold basis (Phang and Helble, 2016). Singapore's approach is supported by strong regulations, with public sector land assets protected as past reserves under the constitution, which precludes sale below objectively assessed market value (Navaratnarajah, 2017). The Government of Singapore legally binds developers into completing and selling the housing they build on sites sold by the public sector within a 5-year period. Development rights expire after 5 years. India and other countries have ambitious targets for the creation of more public rental housing, though previous performance has proved difficult to maintain and maintenance has been poor.

The role of global capital in transforming land and housing markets

Despite conventional economics acknowledging the dangers of yawning inequality, housing wealth continues to increase across advanced economies (Berg and Ostry, 2011; OECD, 2018). Investor speculation on housing is not limited to developed country markets, however (Zhu, 2014), and the use of land administration powers as a political tool for evicting the poor is common in the cities of rapidly urbanizing countries. Access to land and affordable housing for all remains an aspirational goal (Amirtahmasebi et al., 2016).

Prior to the advent of mortgage-backed securities in the 1980s, the provision of credit for housing purchase was generally an individualized contractual relationship between a single lender, usually a bank or a savings and loan institution, and a single creditor or home-owner. However, global financial integration transformed the political economy of housing, especially when central banks drastically reduced interest rates after the 2000 stock market crash, which added more available credit to the economy, pushed up asset values, and improved profitability for mortgage lenders (JCHS, 2011). From this time up until the global financial crisis in 2008, mortgage-backed securities were promoted as a means of attracting additional lenders into the mortgage market by reducing the reliance on local financial institutions. The use of residential mortgages as a securitization tool for the financial sector slowed following the 2008-09 financial crisis but has since recovered.

The size of mortgage markets varies between countries. For example, mortgages represent less than 5 per cent of GDP in Brazil and over 30 per cent in Malaysia. Analysis by Green and Wachter (2005) shows that these differences can be traced to differences in legal systems; in particular, legal systems that provide little protection for lenders result in fewer loans being made. The relative strength of credit information systems, how onerous the property registration process is, and the country's history of macro-economic instability are additional factors that impact on the availability of mortgage finance.

In developed markets mortgage finance is readily available, typically accounting for 50 per cent or more of national GDP (OECD, 2017), though it is significantly less than this in most emerging markets. For commercial providers of debt finance, this discrepancy represents a huge opportunity to lend more money and build a new suite of securitized financial products in emerging markets. Total mortgage debt outstanding in the Netherlands, Australia, and the United Kingdom is equivalent to around 85 per cent of GDP, whereas it amounts to less than 1 per cent of GDP across many low- and lower-middle-income countries in Asia and Africa (Badev et al., 2014).[1] Whether the growth of housing mortgage finance to the same scale as exists in the OECD markets is healthy for these economies and societies remains open to question.

The International Finance Corporation (IFC) has a well-established housing unit, whose goal is 'to help clients seize opportunities in housing finance, which has an estimated global investment potential of as much as $700 billion' (IFC, n.d.). The IFC runs mortgage finance programmes including a corporate partnership with the world's largest cement company to support lending to low-income households, as well as high-interest micro-finance mortgage lending in markets like Afghanistan (IFC, 2005: 30). The ingenuity and flexibility of private markets in providing housing finance is clear.

The global financial crisis demonstrated that alongside ingenuity, robust housing finance requires well-regulated housing markets. Indeed, robust regulation and the range of creative financial instruments linked to urban land and housing are vital to national and international economic health and political stability. The global response to the housing crisis, and the ability of key players in the problematic financial engineering of land and housing markets to re-enter the sector, suggests there are still important lessons to learn. In Spain, more than half a million foreclosures between 2008 and 2013 resulted in over 300,000 evictions, while in Hungary there were almost 1 million foreclosures between 2009 and 2012 (United Nations, 2017). Recent attempts to privatize the public land registry in the United Kingdom are symptomatic of prevailing attitudes among the world's wealthy, who consider land and housing primarily as private assets rather than a public good (House of Commons, 2016). Despite variations in land supply politics, policies, and planning, not to mention cultural, legal, and tenure norms, housing finance products increasingly serve global capital.

Promoting property ownership with subsidies

Demand subsidies linked to mortgage finance or savings usually do not target the poor, and in effect benefit the better-off segments of society. Income tax deductions of interest payments or a broad-based interest rate subsidy for mortgage loans tend to be regressive, as they increase with the amount of the loans and benefit those who can afford larger loans more than those with smaller loans. In urbanizing countries, mortgage markets are still in development, but follow a similar pattern of supporting relatively affluent households (those in the 40–60 percentile income groups) to access additional credit. If the world is to meet ambitious targets for housing provision and land administration in the public interest by 2030 as envisioned in the Sustainable Development Goals, developing and developed financial markets must learn from past lessons and encourage more rational investment in accessible housing to meet the needs of all social groups.

A more pernicious use of housing subsidies is the example of the 'Buy to Let' policy introduced in the UK in the late 1980s, ostensibly to meet the increased demand for private rental housing due to the unaffordability of ownership and limited supply of social housing. The number of investors expanded rapidly from 1996 when low-interest mortgages became widely available and investors could claim tax relief on mortgage finance costs to the basic rate tax level, as well as a 'wear and tear' allowance. Sustained criticism that the policy contributed to property price inflation resulted in the introduction in 2016 of a sales tax on such properties, after which many investor landlords sold out. Scanlon and Whitehead (2016) report that although only 7 per cent of landlords owned multiple properties, they accounted for 40 per cent of the total private rental dwellings, indicating the extent to which the rental sector had been inflated for commercial, not social, benefit.

> **Box 8.1** A tale of two housing subsidies – Chile and the Philippines
>
> In Chile, the majority of housing built through a national subsidy scheme between 1978 and 2000 has been concentrated in peripheral locations, lacking adequate infrastructure, schools, health facilities, and access to employment opportunities (Trivelli, 2010). Poor public transport and road quality further impairs residents' ability to access services and employment.
>
> In the Philippines, interest rate subsidies account for 90 per cent of the value of housing subsidies; however, the vast majority of the country's population cannot afford a formal-sector loan even at subsidized interest rates (UN-Habitat, 2008b: 39–40). Part of these subsidies may also leak out to benefit others in the housing market and raise the value of existing dwellings and land.
>
> These examples indicate the challenge for governments seeking to use supply-side incentives to address housing market failure without adequate consultation.

Housing subsidies can take many forms, both direct and indirect. An example of an indirect subsidy can be found in the reduced rate of council tax levied on second homes in the UK. Although details are determined by local governments, it is common for owners of second homes to pay a reduced rate of council tax of up to 50 per cent (Gov.UK, n.d.). Invariably, these are located in attractive holiday resorts where affluent households seek a holiday home. While this attracts inward investment, the resulting price inflation reduces access to affordable land and housing for the local population and, more seriously, undermines commercial activity out of season, reducing the viability of public services such as schools and social amenities. As so often, the benefits for a few come at a price for the many.

Citizenship and land rights for sale

The complex interaction of land and housing policy with global capital markets and domestic politics are embodied in the proliferation of 'golden visa' schemes (Lee, 2018; Salewski and Johannes, 2018) that offer residency visas to individuals who invest, most often through the purchase of residential property, a certain sum of money into the issuing country. Portugal launched one of the world's most successful golden visa schemes in 2012 where, for a minimum investment in real estate of €500,000 ($580,000), a non-EU buyer would receive a residency visa and, longer term, a route to national citizenship and a European passport. More than 1,500 visas were issued in 2014 alone (Savills World Research, 2015: 27) and by June 2015, the scheme had stimulated around €1.5 bn ($1.7 bn) in new investment into Portugal, primarily into housing. Such was its popularity with Chinese investors that it has spawned an industry specializing in the sale and investment of Portuguese residential and commercial property to Chinese clients. Cyprus, Greece, Malta, Spain, and the UK all offer similar programmes.

The popularity of housing as an investment for the purposes of obtaining citizenship has distorted local markets in Europe and elsewhere, sparking concern over the setting of false price floors in a number of urban property markets. The entry price point for housing becomes linked to the investment amount required for the golden visa. Properties worth less are artificially priced to the investment minimum as the number of international investors expands. As golden visa holders, investment banks and other private sector actors are increasingly asked to play a more proactive, socially responsible role to recognize and support the legitimate land rights of communities affected by land-based investments. However, more information is required to support responsible investment decision-making and to better understand the complexity of land tenure risk (USAID, 2018).

Rental housing

In any urban area, public investment in infrastructure or facilities raises property values, making home-owners wealthier without spending a cent. However, it almost inevitably increases rents for tenants, thereby making them poorer and increasing inequality. This trend of increasing asset values has been exacerbated further by the global tendency to reduce the availability of public or social rental housing during the last four decades. In many cases, private sector tenants are paying 40 per cent or more of their net incomes on housing rents, so when they retire and their incomes are halved, this will become 80 per cent, forcing many into crisis. For the millions currently excluded from formal land and housing markets, things are even more challenging.

Even in Germany, where rental housing represents almost half of total housing, the protections accorded to tenants in private rental housing are coming under increasing pressure from commercial interests. Berlin has been a haven for artists and young professionals due to its traditionally low rent levels on housing built during the communist period. However, rents rose by 20.5 per cent in 2017, faster than in any other city in the world, partly due to incremental reforms of tenancy laws under which private landlords were able to pass on part of the costs of modernization. While landlords need to recover

> **Box 8.2** Airbnb as a case study in adaptive regulation
>
> In countries as diverse as the UK and Cuba (Harpaz, 2015; Manthorpe, 2018), Airbnb has challenged housing policymakers and raised key social justice themes in housing markets globally. The issue of how to regulate the short-term rental market will continue beyond the coronavirus disruption. In existence since 2008, Airbnb is a peer-to-peer marketplace that allows individuals to 'list, discover, and book' over 3 million accommodations online in over 65,000 cities across the world (Sheppard and Udell, 2018: 1). It has expanded so fast that in some locations popular with tourists, a significant proportion of the total housing stock is registered with the platform.
>
> While Airbnb has enabled many people to supplement their incomes, it has also encouraged others to purchase properties specifically to rent, creating a class of 'rental-preneurs'. Concerns over the impact of Airbnb on rental markets have prompted piecemeal investigations by market regulators, most notably in New York City by the Office of the Attorney General (Schneiderman, 2014). Paris, Amsterdam, and London have all imposed restrictions on the use of Airbnb lettings due to the inflationary pressures they have exerted on housing costs. Barcelona fined Airbnb €600,000 ($696,000) in 2017 for continuing to advertise unlicensed properties on its platform. However, the company's lobbying power and a lack of coordination between municipal authorities means that there is no public data on the global implications of this business model.

the costs of improving the housing stock, many tenants are now spending a disproportionately large share of their incomes on rent.

Private equity investors such as Blackstone, an American private equity corporation with a global portfolio valued at over $500 bn, are expanding from investments in property ownership into private rental housing, spending $10 bn in purchasing repossessed properties at courthouses and in online auctions, and emerging as the largest rental landlord in the USA (Abood, 2018). As home ownership becomes increasingly unaffordable to even middle-income households, this increases demand for private rental housing at a time when non-market options, such as public rental or other forms of social housing, are no longer a viable option. In many countries, 'generation rent' is increasingly becoming exposed to prices that are unaffordable and this is forcing even middle-income people into sharing. A World Bank report (Peppercorn and Taffin, 2013: x) finds 'Rental markets also play a key role in enhancing the market value of housing assets and in generating revenues from an unlocked housing wealth'. The need to maximize the social value of housing and enable tenants to access affordable housing is clearly subordinate to the interests of landlords and investors.

Competition for investment capital and the distortion of public policy

Cities competing for inward investment to create employment opportunities for their increasing urban populations are in danger of creating a race to the bottom. For example, secondary cities in Vietnam's Mekong Delta are establishing large industrial estates on environmentally sensitive agricultural land without an adequate assessment of demand and in ways that fail to nurture its ecological assets, making the region more vulnerable to climate risks (World Bank, 2020: 12). Of the 14,787 hectares of industrial zones developed by 2016, only 3,688 hectares have been occupied (Vietnam Investment Review, 2016), providing potential investors with the opportunity to drive a very hard bargain and thereby reducing the potential revenues to local and national governments who enabled the land conversion. A similar approach is being applied in Ethiopia, where the government is seeking to attract investment capital in manufacturing by developing industrial zones of over 100 hectares outside Addis Ababa and other cities. In a further example of speculative land conversion, the government of Uganda destroyed large parts of a eucalyptus forest to develop the Kampala Industrial and Business Park covering more than 2,200 hectares, forcing the World Bank to withdraw a loan for environmental reasons and leaving the government with a heavy financial cost and a large number of vacant plots, as well as the loss of a productive forest. This craving for inward investment at almost any price enables multinational and even smaller international investors to play one country or city off against another in order to invest in land at minimum cost to themselves but also minimum benefit to the local community. Multinational corporations increasingly make decisions on where to locate headquarters by the nature and extent of tax incentives provided by governments. Part of the responsibility for this situation has to be borne by the World Bank in encouraging cities to do whatever they can to attract private sector investment. The Bank's *Competitive Cities* report (2015a: 40) encourages governments to provide 'free or highly subsidized land' for investors, and although it provided a caveat to the effect of avoiding 'a build-it-and-they-will-come scheme' approach, the message was clear that land was a major means of attracting investment and promoting local economies. Governments must take care in balancing commercial needs, and investor and corporate pressure to subsidize land conversion for private gain, with the long-term economic wellbeing of their citizens and local residents.

The impact of markets on urban form

The pervasive application of market forces on urban land globally has resulted in increasing social segregation and the creation of a 'them' and 'us' society in which people are judged according to where they live. Those who can afford the high costs of prime locations seldom meet less fortunate groups, unless they are providing them with services. Social and spatial segregation is now arguably greater in many cities than it was under colonialism or during the Victorian age when the affluent minority accommodated domestic staff on their land. However, as noted by Lave (1970), the spatial structure of the city will change if the preferences of the rich group change. The point is that in societies where income or other disparities between groups are large, a willingness to live in close proximity to those of different backgrounds or income levels is likely to be severely reduced.

Today, the position for lower and low-income households dependent upon public sector support, in the form of social housing or housing benefit for private rental accommodation, is even more precarious. The UK coalition government (2010–2015) proposed to limit the amount of housing benefit which a household could receive from the state to meet the costs of their rent. This generated an outward migration from central areas to inner suburbs, forcing up private rents there and causing a further outward ripple effect to the outer suburbs and beyond, just as Engels had found happened in the 19th century. Many lost not only their homes as a result of so-called 'social cleansing', but also faced substantial increases in transport costs to get to work. Such punitive processes are widespread in the Global South. Those who cannot afford to pay market rates are forced not just further to the urban periphery, where any savings on housing costs are offset by increased times and costs of transport, but to rural sites many kilometres from transport or other basic services, or even to other cities where land and housing are less expensive, but where jobs are more difficult to find, and where they lose the vital support of family and wider social networks.

As discussed in Chapter 4, private sector initiatives to provide for the needs of middle- and high-income groups in the form of gated communities and private sector cities have exacerbated already significant social divisions. This makes it more difficult for young, creative groups to contribute to the cultural and social life of urban areas, making them less stimulating places in which to live and work. Yet the scale of private development is increasing in almost all countries and not only provides completely self-contained developments within cities, as in the Royal Vinh City development in Hanoi, Vietnam (see Chapter 6, Photo 6.1), but also includes the privatization of public open space (known as POPS). As the number and scale of private sector urban developments increase, so the amount of previously public land becomes effectively privatized. As many people visiting parts of Canary Wharf in London can verify, taking a photograph of the area can quickly arouse the attention of private security guards informing you that this is private land and photographs are not permitted without a permit (Canary Wharf Group PLC, n.d.). London's City Hall, designed by Norman Foster, and the public open space surrounding it, are owned by the Government of Kuwait and charges such high rents that the mayor has moved out to other premises.

The privatized realm of central business districts is a familiar pattern and even many public buildings are owned by international investors. Almost all rapidly urbanizing countries now boast major shopping malls to serve the needs and aspirations of the emerging middle class, and some of these developments occupy so much land that they are effectively reducing the public areas of cities. In some cases, facial recognition cameras are being used to control activity on these sites, raising major issues linked to pervasive social control, and the erosion of privacy and basic human dignity.

While the increasing privatization of public space is cause for concern, market forces have discreetly effected a mass transfer of public land into private hands. Research by Christophers (2018: 1–5) shows that of all the privatizations undertaken in neoliberal Britain since 1979, that of public land is by far the greatest and amounts to some 2 million hectares, or about 10 per cent of the entire British land mass. He estimates that this would be worth approximately £400 bn ($515 bn) at current prices and observes that once government disposes of public land, it disposes of the public power associated with it. There surely cannot be many government decisions that matter more in a democratic society. Christophers cites research by Ludewigs et al. (2009: 1357) to show that in Brazil, the proportion of northern Amazonian land under public ownership declined from 30 per cent in 1970 to just 7 per cent in 1996, while in Kenya, he cites research by Klopp (2000) showing how, in the 1990s, public land was used by the government as a source of patronage and an instrument to maintain socio-political control through a process of corrupt 'irregular privatization'.

Claims that the private sector puts land to more efficient use are based on the assumption that private developers do actually develop land they own. However, Harvey (1973: 139) argues that housing markets function under conditions of scarcity and that 'We therefore find a paradox, namely that wealth is produced under a system which relies upon scarcity for its functioning. It follows that if scarcity is eliminated, the market economy, which is the source of productive wealth under capitalism, will collapse. To resolve this dilemma many institutions are geared to the maintenance of scarcity'. Extensive personal experience provides evidence to support the findings of Harvey and Christophers that developers fail to develop land for which they have planning permission and hoard it to force up prices. This creates a systematic, manufactured shortage of residential land. The tendency towards land hoarding and speculative investment in vacant land has proved resistant to public attempts to force developers to 'use it or lose it'. Even in cases where private sector developments are completed, they often under-provide the social facilities essential for an acceptable quality of life.

Another consequence of the ideologically driven push to put prime urban land to its most economically efficient use – as a high-yielding investment – is that it has resulted in forced evictions and market-driven displacement on a massive scale in rapidly urbanizing countries throughout Africa, Asia, and Latin America (Durand-Lasserve, 2006). Even when occupying unused land that nobody else wants, such as along roads, railways lines, or in environmentally vulnerable locations on steep slopes or floodplains, low-income residents are often evicted as commercial interests take precedence over social needs and they are forced to move to areas far from where they can earn a livelihood.

As land ownership becomes increasingly concentrated in the hands of the capitalist class, it is clear that the interests of citizens have become increasingly constrained, posing a threat to access, use, and control by elected bodies and democratic governance. Land has become a means of institutionalizing inequality globally.

The role of international development agencies

International agencies have invested many billions of dollars in improving land administration throughout the world, though the amounts are small compared to the resources required and the resources generated by urban land markets. In this sense, the influence that donor agencies exert through the legitimacy they give to forms of land administration may be as important as the funding itself. Thus, the World Bank family and the Global Land Tool Network in UN-Habitat are in a powerful position to promote approaches that make urban land markets more equitable and efficient. The World Bank in particular has supported market-based policies that have exacerbated rather than resolved the problems facing the urban poor and 'deeply undermined the right to adequate housing around the world' (Rolnik 2019: 21). However, this has recently changed in some key respects and now approaches are more soundly based on improving equity as well as efficiency in land administration. The Bank's ability to realize this potential depends, of course, on having partners in client governments willing to endorse codes of conduct and related policy recommendations for improving interaction with, and opportunities in, pro-poor urban land management. Unfortunately, experience has demonstrated that positive interventions have intervening in the urban land sector has proved far more challenging for the World Bank than providing loans for mortgage finance to lower-middle income groups.

The issues of land and housing are being increasingly considered in financial terms and this has led UN-Habitat to publish a series of reports on 'land-based finance', including non-market options, to explore ways to maximize public benefit (see, for example, Walters, 2016, 2020; UN-Habitat, 2021). This involves exploring options by which central and local government agencies can generate a financial surplus through enterprising and efficient land management. Of course, it is vital to ensure that housing is not only affordable, but adequate and this would not be the case if dwellings are located on cheap land many kilometres from city centres, as happens in many countries, which only increases the costs of transport and associated stress. Furthermore, housing provided through subsidies invariably ends up being reintegrated into the market at inflated prices, reducing its availability for future generations of households in need. It is therefore vital that financial revenues generated from state actions should be allocated, at least in part, to non-market forms of housing, such as various types of social tenure, such as communal lease or ownership, in order to protect residents from market-driven displacement or gentrification.

Implications and next steps

The last decade has provided humanity with a much needed wake-up call. Not only have we failed to learn the lessons from the 2008 economic crisis, but even mainstream media (Constable, 2019; Plender, 2020) are forecasting that the global economy is in such poor shape that the next crisis already looks overdue. A principal cause of the 2007–08 meltdown – an excess of debt – has become worse. Despite governments' austerity policies, particularly in Europe, global debt now stands at about $250 tn, 75 per cent more than when the Lehman Brothers investment bank collapsed. A further indication of the fragility of the global economy is that global debt now equals three times more than global GDP. The Covid-19 pandemic has ushered in a new era of unconventional fiscal and monetary policy from which the global economy will take years, and probably decades, to recover. The irony is that although market-driven economic policies have lifted hundreds of millions of people out of absolute poverty, relative poverty shows no sign of reducing. Global GDP in 2013 equated to $17,300 per person, a sum that large sections of the populations in poor, and even some in rich, countries can only dream of. This is the first time in living memory that younger people cannot assume their lives will be more comfortable than that of their parents. For those in the Global South, the prospects are even more challenging.

The current global economic crisis coincides with an increased acceptance that human activity has accelerated climate change. It is widely recognized that the prospects for averting an irreversible 'tipping point' – beyond which parts of the world will become uninhabitable and the remainder is put under even greater pressure than today – are dwindling. The implication of both the economic and environmental crises is that we need a fundamental reappraisal of what we mean by development and how to achieve it. We will discuss the options for achieving this in later chapters. However, we first need to consider how the current processes of valuing land and housing apply in countries undertaking the transition towards market-driven forms of economic management from very different starting points, since this will influence the potential for constructive policy interventions.

With housing now at the centre of a historic structural transformation in global investment, national and municipal governments around the world have a window of opportunity to address the profound consequences of this trend for those in need of adequate housing.

Note

1. In Badev et al. (2014) the World Bank refers to Mortgage Depth as the outstanding mortgage debt relative to GDP, and gauges the depth of mortgage markets by focusing on the total volume.

CHAPTER 9
From feudal to market in the UK: A property-owning democracy?

When the sixth Duke of Westminster was asked what would be the best way people could become as rich as he was, he recommended 'Make sure they have an ancestor who was a very close friend of William the Conqueror'. This was not just witty, but accurate. The example of the UK is relevant to the assessment of land values and wealth distribution globally for two reasons. Firstly, it illustrates how the concentration of land and property in a small elite, whether aristocratic landowners as in history or the global elite of today, can enable the use of land and housing as a means of perpetuating and reinforcing their social, economic, and political power. Secondly, the UK was the first country in the world to urbanize as an industrial market economy in which property ownership was used as a means of reinforcing a regressive division of national wealth. The patterns of land ownership and concentration of wealth enabled by the Industrial Revolution have been accentuated through the application of neoliberal economics in the late 20th century, and continue to the present day.

The story starts as long ago as the 11th century, when William the Conqueror invaded the UK and allocated vast estates to his supporters who became barons of the realm. Punitive demands by William's successors led to the barons' revolt of 1215. This resulted in the Magna Carta agreement which limited the powers of the king relative to the landed gentry but did nothing for the ordinary citizen. In 1432, King Henry VI determined that only male owners of property worth at least 40 shillings, a significant sum, were entitled to vote. In the 1530s, Henry the Eighth redistributed another enormous area of land to his favourites after the dissolution of the monasteries. As a result, by the start of the Industrial Revolution in the 18th century, the UK was still a feudal agricultural society with a mere 189,000 families owning two-thirds of the total land area of the country, most of it productive agricultural land. Over the next century, large estates and mansions were also created by merchants made wealthy from the slave trade or from service in the colonies. These estates mostly remain in the same families and account for 60 per cent of all land in the British Isles, including large swathes of what has become prime land in London. The Duke of Westminster's estates included 40.4 hectares (100 acres) of the 95.1 ha (235 acres) that constitute Mayfair in central London, which alone were valued at £3.35 bn in 2001 (Cahill, 2001: 148)[1] and probably much more since. In a major survey of landholdings in the UK, Cahill concludes (2001: 208) that in 2001, fewer than 157,000 families, 0.28 per cent of the population, owned 64 per cent of the land area of the country, a situation largely unchanged from the 18th century. Not only do such landholdings generate vast rental and leasehold incomes, but also income from farming subsidies. They also force up prices and rents, inhibiting efforts to improve access to land, services, and livelihoods for the majority of the population, especially the urban poor. To make matters even more regressive, such properties are not necessarily taxed at anything like their market values.[2] The situation has become so regressive that revenues generated from incomes from workers are used to subsidize rural landowners, including the most wealthy.

Until the end of the 18th century, tax was paid to the monarch on such landholdings, though this was financed by the tithes and other incomes generated from the land. However, in 1799 additional taxes were levied on incomes by William Pitt the Younger to finance the war with France, and the proportion of tax revenues generated from incomes has increased ever since. Not only did this allow the landed gentry to minimize their tax liabilities (Lindert, 1987: 25–51; Cahill, 2006: 243), these same people also comprised the majority of members of both the House of Commons and Lords, as well as holding key positions of authority on behalf of the monarch. As Cahill (2006: 242) observes 'This was a totality of control such as dictators might have prayed for but never got. That it was in the main, exercised benignly, was all that saved Britain from revolution'.

The aristocracy is not the only form of land concentration in the UK. Greenwood and Adams (2018) report that Oxford and Cambridge universities collectively own 51,000 hectares (126,000 acres) and it is said that it is possible to travel from St John's Oxford to the city of Cambridge on land entirely owned by the college. The recent proposal to develop a 'Brain Belt', including five new 'garden towns', between Oxford and Cambridge would enable the universities to dramatically increase the value of their property portfolios even more. Whether such concentration of landholdings within elitist educational institutions is in the public interest (and whether they would be adequately taxed on the uplift in land values for such developments) is more than doubtful.

It was the Industrial Revolution, however, and trade resulting from its colonies that changed the face of the country during the 1800s and led to the UK rising to a position of global dominance. This did not start in London, the centre of power, but in the industrial centre of Manchester. Technological innovation enabled the cotton factories there to produce and transport vast quantities of finished textiles efficiently, and provide workers with higher incomes than they could earn in agriculture. Manchester's great public and commercial buildings reflect a massive sense of civic pride and the city was seen at the time as the symbol for a new age (Briggs, 1963, rev. 1968)[3] and even generated its own economic philosophy – the Manchester Free Trade School.

Manchester's population increased more than 10 times from 22,481 in 1773 to 235,507 in 1841 as the economy boomed. Yet not all sections of society reaped the benefits. Wages for children were one-tenth that of adults, so it made economic sense to employ as many children and as few adults as possible. Children as young as six were employed as 'scavengers' to crawl beneath active machines to collect loose cotton, which killed many. Industrial pollution and the lack of public sanitation, or even safe drinking water, took its toll on life expectancy. Even for the merchants or industrial barons, life expectancy was a modest 38 years, while for the factory workers and their families it was a mere 17 years (Briggs, 1963, rev. 1968: 101). Sewage disposal consisted of ashpits and communal cesspits, which overflowed into the cellars where many workers lived. However, it was the airborne diseases that accounted for the greatest mortality figures and pulmonary tuberculosis was among the top causes of death, while major cholera outbreaks finally produced the Public Health Act of 1875.

The living conditions of workers in Manchester attracted the interest of many social observers, notably Friedrich Engels, who spent nearly two years studying the lives of working people and published his seminal *The Condition of the Working Class in England* in 1845 at the young age of 24. Although the son of a wealthy industrialist, Engels was committed to social progress and contributed with Marx in drafting the Communist Manifesto, published just three years later. He later wrote *The Housing Question* which argued that 'In order to put an end to this housing shortage there is only *one* means: to abolish altogether the exploitation and oppression of the working class by the ruling class' (1975: 18).[4]

Throughout much of its history, the UK has effectively been a feudal society in which the housing deficit was matched by a democratic deficit and very few people had the right to vote. A survey conducted in 1780 revealed that the electorate in England and Wales consisted of less than 3 per cent of a population of approximately 8 million (UK National Archives, 2005), and in Scotland a mere 4,500 men, out of a population of more than 2.6 million people, were entitled to vote in 1831. Large industrial cities like Leeds, Birmingham, and Manchester did not have a single Member of Parliament between them, whereas 'rotten boroughs' such as Dunwich in Suffolk (with a population of 32 in 1831) were still sending two MPs to Westminster.[5]

Pressure for reform increased after the French Revolution in 1789. Influenced by Thomas Paine's *Rights of Man*, radical reformers demanded that all men be given the vote. During 1819, at a peaceful gathering in St Peter's Field, Manchester, demanding parliamentary reform, local yeomanry attacked the crowd, killing 11 people. After the 'Peterloo Massacre' the government passed a series of repressive measures and progress was not made until the Reform Act of 1832 which lowered the property qualification for voting. As John Stuart Mill stated in his address to the Land Tenure Reform Association in 1871:

> Land is limited in quantity while the demand for it, in a prosperous country, is constantly increasing. The rent, therefore, progressively rises, not through the exertion or expenditure of the owner, to which we should not object, but by the mere growth of wealth and population.

> The incomes of landowners are rising while they are sleeping, through the general prosperity produced by the labour and outlay of other people. (Land Tenure Reform Association, 1871: 183; Lindert, 1987: 27)

The issue was picked up soon after by Henry George (1881: 29) who argued that:

> The great cause of inequality in the distribution of wealth is inequality in the ownership of land .... [T]o relieve labour and capital from all taxation, direct and indirect, and to throw the burden upon rent, would ... counteract this tendency to inequality, and, if it went so far as to take in taxation the whole of rent, the cause of inequality would be totally destroyed ... But more than this. Taxes on the [rental] value of land not only did not check production as do most other taxes, but they tend to increase production by destroying speculative rent.

Of course, a precondition for introducing and enforcing a land tax is the availability of reliable evidence of land values. This has proved a stumbling block every time the issue has risen up the political agenda, and in the early 1900s land taxes yielded so little revenue that they barely covered the cost of collection (Lindert, 1987: 30). However, the 'People's Budget' of 1909 argued for a 20 per cent land tax to be levied on future unearned increase in land values. Later that year, Winston Churchill (1909) gave a speech in which he argued that:

> It is quite true that land monopoly is not the only monopoly which exists, but it is by far the greatest of monopolies – it is a perpetual monopoly, and it is the mother of all other forms of monopoly. It is quite true that unearned increments in land are not the only form of unearned or undeserved profit which individuals are able to secure; but it is the principal form of unearned increment which is derived from processes which are not merely not beneficial, but which are positively detrimental to the general public.

Unsurprisingly, landowners successfully resisted this proposal and following the First World War, the momentum was lost and land taxes remained low. Despite interest in land value taxation (Plimmer and McGill, 2003), little progress has been made.

The British often boast of living in a 'property-owning democracy' as though this had been the case since the Magna Carta in 1215. In fact, the term was coined by conservative politicians in 1923 seeking, unsuccessfully, to prevent the first socialist Labour government that came to power the year after. The reason for establishment concern was that property ownership was a precondition for being eligible to vote until as recently as 1918, and the 19th century building society movement was founded largely to enfranchise ordinary citizens by enabling them to buy their own dwelling. It was only after the 'war to end all wars' that all men over 21 and women over 30 were given the right to vote without the condition of being property-owners. This was also a year after the Russian Revolution and establishment fears of unrest from unemployed returning soldiers may have promoted change. However, it was not until 1928 that women over 21 were eligible to vote without the precondition of owning property. Britain can therefore really only claim to have become a fully fledged democracy relatively recently, and this may help to explain why home ownership became inextricably linked with the development of popular democracy.

Promoting the social value of land

During the latter part of the 19th century, a range of initiatives on land development helped to make the UK a leading source of urban planning theory and practice, though progress was not uniform and took different routes. Manchester committed itself to global free trade and spent lavishly on great public buildings and parks. Birmingham, however, adopted a more pragmatic approach based on small-scale engineering industry and a powerful sense of civic pride, in which the gap between those in power and the population was much smaller. Housing conditions across the UK were also far better and 'the benefits of the age of improvement were felt to be shared, if unequally' (Engels, 1975: 18).

As the new industrial aristocracy joined with the landed aristocracy to acquire estates and mansions of their own, social movements increased pressure for more rights and better living conditions. Partly out of self-interest (to improve the views from their mansions, or the productivity of their workers) and also genuine concern for less privileged groups, some landowners and industrialists developed what became known as 'model villages' to accommodate their workers. Port Sunlight was planned and built by William Lever of Lever Brothers, Bournville was built by the Cadbury brothers, while Sir Titus Salt developed Saltaire. These were effectively company towns and about 400 of them were developed during the 19th century (Patoway, 2017), providing good quality housing and a healthy environment, though often on land owned by the employers. By this means, both patronage and goodwill benefited the providers as much as the residents.

Other initiatives helped improve not only the living conditions of the urban poor, but also enabled them to live in prime locations near to employment opportunities and social amenities. The pioneering social and spatial maps of different income groups in London produced in 1898 by Charles Booth (1892–97) revealed there was a remarkable mixture of income groups in many parts of central London. This was at least to some extent thanks to the large-scale affordable housing developments funded by philanthropists such as George Peabody, a London-based American banker. Peabody loved the city and launched his 'Model Dwellings Company' in 1859, followed three years later by a donation of £150,000 which he increased to £500,000 just before he died in 1869. The Guinness Trust was another enterprise with similar objectives and was founded in 1890 by Edward Guinness, to help homeless

Photo 9.1 Guinness Trust social housing projects were of a high standard and in prime locations
Credit: Geoffrey Payne

people in London and Dublin. He donated £200,000 to set up the Guinness Trust in London, the equivalent of £170 m in today's money. These philanthropic initiatives enabled a series of medium-high-density housing projects to be developed in several central London locations in which those on low incomes, but providing essential services to the city, were able to live. Together, they contributed to the cultural, economic, and spatial diversity that is the bedrock of all successful cities, something that is currently at serious risk across the world.

During the 20th century, the UK developed a global reputation for socially progressive and economically efficient land and housing management, based on a combination of social pressure, enlightened industrialists, and professional thinkers. Chief among these were thinkers such as Ebenezer Howard (1902)[6] who started the garden cities movement, and Patrick Geddes (see, among other works, Geddes, 1915) who pioneered the concept of 'conservative surgery' for urban regeneration. In 1918, when granting all men over the age of 21 the right to vote without the precondition of owning property, the government also announced a policy of 'Homes Fit For Heroes' that formed the basis of their ambitious 1919 Housing Act. The 1919 Act aimed to help finance 500,000 new homes within three years (although only 213,000 were actually completed). In addition to improving existing urban areas, the garden cities of Letchworth and Welwyn Garden City built on the precedent of the 19th century model villages. They also provided the foundation for the New Towns Movement launched after the Second World War, providing another disturbing link between major disasters as a basis for social progress. What enabled the New Towns programme to expand successfully was that the land required was acquired at existing, mainly agricultural, use value and with low interest government finance. This was to prove a major foundation in the way that land was valued for realizing social development objectives.

From that time onwards, governments of both main political parties competed to see who could build the most houses, with annual targets of up to 300,000. A high proportion of the new housing was developed by municipalities for public rental and resulted in large-scale estates of basic, but well-designed houses in landscaped settings. In 1963, the Parker Morris Committee published its influential 'Design Bulletin 6 – Space in the Home' that established space standards for all public housing, eventually resulting in tenants enjoying higher space standards than more expensive privately owned housing. A generation of architects demonstrated innovative ways of creating egalitarian land developments in central urban locations, such as Neave Brown, who refused to design multi-storey housing and focused on high-density terraces; Lewis Womersley, who designed 'streets in the sky'; William Reed, whose 'street enveloping scheme' comprehensively upgraded the buildings and environment of complete residential districts in Birmingham starting in 1978; Darbourne and Darke, who designed high-density, medium-rise projects in central London (see Photo 9.2) (Municipal

Photo 9.2 Lillington Gardens Estate in Pimlico, London. One of the architects was only 26 years old
Credit: Geoffrey Payne

Dreams, 2014); and Kate Macintosh, who included communal facilities and individual balconies in social housing. More recently, the prize for the best architecture for 2019 was awarded to a rare modern example of a public rental housing project which provided every home with direct street access, confirming that medium- to high-density does not require high-rise solutions.[7]

Progress reversed

All the progress achieved during the 19th century and the major part of the 20th was systematically and intentionally destroyed by the neoliberal policies of the Thatcher government and its successors, in favour of privatizing land and housing and asserting their financial value over their social value.

An obsession with home ownership was also promoted by the Thatcher government, which offered tax relief on the first £30,000 (£60,000 for joint owners) of mortgage plans. Getting on the 'property ladder' massively distorted the housing market in favour of ownership at the expense of other tenure options. Naturally, the increased demand for home ownership resulted in massive price inflation and created such strong popular support that it was possible for the government to abolish the subsidy in 2000, when price inflation had made it insignificant. However, council taxes remain based on property values established in 1991 even though prices have risen many times since. These taxes have also become increasingly regressive as the owner of a luxury mansion in central London may actually pay a smaller amount than the owner of a modest house in a provincial city.

However, the 'Right to Buy' policy introduced by Thatcher in 1980 to privatize public housing assets was the main catalyst that reversed all the progress in prioritizing the social value of land and housing. At the time, public rental housing represented 32 per cent of all dwellings in Britain, but by the mid-2000s about 2.8 million homes, half the total stock, had been sold at discounts of 33–50 per cent (Disney and Luo, 2014: 4). In one case known personally, the tenant of a public rental home purchased it for £34,000, and sold it for £340,000 just 10 years later. The policy represents a massive and unprecedented transfer of public wealth built up over many years into private hands.

As the subsidies from both the tax relief and the 'Right to Buy' policy encouraged more and more people to become property-owners, so prices continued to rise, often by greater amounts than annual salaries. The decoupling of property values with wage growth in key UK cities reinforced the perception of housing as primarily a good investment, rather than a place in which to raise a family and be part of a community. Thatcher had demonstrated the power of the state in economic management, but ironically put it at the service of markets, and created a population who had a vested interest in maintaining high property prices in order to protect the value of their newly acquired assets. The promotion of home ownership since 1980 has resulted in millions more people becoming home-owners. As a result, political support for increased land or property taxes has been successfully reduced. The slogan that 'every man's home is his castle' has proved highly effective as a political trope, even if the size and quality of such 'castles' has diminished to being among the poorest in size and quality in Europe.

Inflationary housing prices have made the UK a very attractive investment location, as noted in Chapter 8, leading to more and more luxury apartments being constructed. In the few cases where local authorities managed to stipulate that a small proportion of the homes should be affordable to local people, the entrances were often concealed out of sight of the target buyers, spatially segregating the different social groups. According to UN-Habitat, home ownership is considered affordable if the price is not more than three times gross annual household incomes, and rental is affordable if rents consist of no more than 25 per cent of household incomes (Acioly, 2019: 16). However, in the UK, the ratio of house prices to annual household income levels for first-time buyers rose from an affordable 3:1 nationally during the 1980s and 1990s to over 5:1 nationally (and over 10:1 in London), making home purchase well out of reach for all but the affluent or those with affluent parents – the famous 'Bank of Mum and Dad'. Central government restrictions limiting the ability of municipalities to replace housing privatized under the 'Right to Buy' policy reduced public rental housing from 30 per cent of the total housing stock in 1970 to a mere 7 per cent in 2017. This contraction has forced those unable to buy into the weakly regulated private rental sector, forcing up prices so that even rental has become increasingly unaffordable and insecure.

London's status as a global city with a wide range of cultural amenities and social diversity has always attracted people and investment. However, the relaxed regulatory framework and low property tax levels have made the city a magnet for overseas investors looking for somewhere to park their money. The fact that they do not even have to declare the ultimate ownership status of investment property means that land and property has become a major vehicle for money laundering by foreign investors, to the extent that an expert witness to the UK Houses of Parliament Home Affairs Select Committee (2016) reported that the London property market was the primary avenue for the laundering at least £100 bn of illicit money a year (House of Commons, 2016). A recent report by Action on Empty Homes claims that the combined numbers of London's long-term empty homes, second homes, short-term-let investments, and a possibly smaller stock of genuinely foreign-owned buy-to-leave-empty investments are likely to exceed 125,000 residential properties. All of these are unavailable to Londoners and either totally empty or significantly underutilized (Trust for London, 2020: 6). With local authorities starved of resources by central government, many have partnered with international investors to generate revenues, thereby producing developments locals do not need or want.

Eventually, the excessive promotion of home ownership backfired spectacularly and failed even on its own terms, as inflationary prices made ownership completely unaffordable to all but an affluent minority by the early 2000s. While the proportion of British households owning their homes rose from 52 per cent in 1971 to a peak of 70 per cent in 2002, it had reduced to 64 per cent by 2017 (Minton, 2017: 102) as ownership became more and more unaffordable. This is despite even more subsidies such as the 'Help to Buy' policy that ended up benefiting housebuilders rather than households. In fact, one housebuilder made a profit of £1 bn (US$1.4 bn) in 2018 from building a mere 16,000 houses, while its Chief Executive Officer was handed a *bonus* of £75 m, despite the company receiving widespread complaints of poor quality construction (Young, 2019).

As Shrubsole (2019) notes, the price of housing has not increased because the price of bricks and mortar has suddenly become incredibly expensive, but because the value of land in the UK has increased fivefold since 1995 and over half of the UK's wealth is now locked up in land, dwarfing the amounts invested in savings. One reason for the high profits to be made from housing is that an avowedly market-driven government should consider it appropriate to recommend that 15–20 per cent represents a 'suitable return' on investment for property developers (Gov.UK, 2014), at a time when many are grateful for 2–3 per cent. By influencing the market in favour of housing suppliers not households, the government is largely responsible for the inflationary prices of all housing.

Even as the evidence increased that land and housing policy was benefiting developers and investors, not households, the government failed to get the message and introduced yet another subsidy to benefit investors at the expense of households. This was the 'Buy to Let' policy providing mortgage interest relief to investors to increase the private rental stock, presumably hoping this would make rental housing more affordable. In practice, investors purchased properties as a better return than was possible from the banks or bond markets, forcing up prices due to increased demand, and taking advantage of tenancy conditions that exposed tenants to poor housing standards, minimal tenure security, and increased rents. Although the subsidy was dropped in 2015 following widespread complaints, it led to massive investments, giving investors a handsome return. At a time when average, inflation-adjusted wage increases have been lower than for the past 300 years, and one woman complained on television that she is only ever four paydays away from being homeless, increases in rental costs have resulted in overcrowding and even the illegal construction of 'beds-in-sheds' as home-owners found an opportunity to exploit the need of low-income households for somewhere to live.

All these developments are a product of the increasing financialization of land and housing in the UK and globally. As Aalbers (2016: 81) observes, this has led to 'the increasing dominance of financial actors, markets, practices, measurements and narratives, at various scales, resulting in a structural transformation of economies, firms (including financial institutions), states and households'. Proposals by the government's housing and planning special advisers (Airey and Doughty, 2020) to rethink the UK planning system for the 2020s include a presumption in favour of new development and that 'market conditions' should be the basis for development and planning decisions, drastically reducing the control local councils are able to exert over local development.

Meanwhile, the financialization of urban land and housing has not only corroded the basis of government policy, it has also changed the way that non-financial organizations think when valuing land and housing (Sammon, 2019). According to Wargent et al. (2020: 194) 'By the turn of the century private sector activity reached into more aspects of the planning process, creating long-range plans and strategies, designing and implementing public engagement strategies, providing technical studies and undertaking development control functions'. They report how private actors now co-construct the regulations they are later subject to and how local authorities have entered into a relationship of critical dependence with the private sector. This fundamentally undermines the ability of the public sector to operate on a basis that protects the wider public interest and particularly the most vulnerable sections of the population. While many private-sector consultants provide high quality expertise, the scale of their involvement inevitably raises questions about the ethos of the planning profession as a public service.

A similar process to planning applies in the case of housing. A study of rental housing in London reports how councils have resorted to creating private companies to deliver housing in ways that mimic the private sector objective of maximizing returns, rather than improving the provision of affordable housing (Sammon, 2019: 29). While putting public resources to efficient use is a sound objective, it has now reached the stage where central government policy forces local councils to adopt increasingly commercial approaches. Financial viability and revenues from land have become key priorities and households are considered as customers, not residents. With ownership out of the question, the private rental market is ripe for picking.

For more than 4 million people living in the UK, access to housing is dependent upon receiving housing benefit (UK DWP, 2018: 3), while 32 per cent of all adults under the age of 34 are living with parents (UK ONS, 2019a) and multi-generational households look set to increase. Households dependent upon housing benefit are routinely accommodated in converted office blocks and even shipping containers, while over a million households were on the waiting list for local authority housing in April 2018 (UK MHCLG, 2018). As if this were not enough to demonstrate the abject failure of UK government land and housing policies, 80,270 families and individuals were registered as homeless in 2018, an increase of 66 per cent since 2011 (UK ONS, 2019b: fig. 3a).

For some years, government responses to independent assessments of its housing policy were hostile and ignored the evidence (Rolnik, 2013; Gentleman and Meikle, 2013), even when a UN report on poverty in the UK found that a fifth of the population live in poverty. This largely explains why, for the first time in decades, young people expect to be poorer than their parents (O'Connor, 2018).[8]

Yet even this is not the end of the story. Since the 1980s, half of all public land in the UK, about 2 million hectares, has been privatized. The value of this land far outstrips the £40 bn of the privatized public housing stock and amounts to about £400 bn ($515 bn) of public assets transferred into private hands. Speculation and investment have resulted in the value of British homes being estimated at four times the national economy at £9.2 tn ($12.6 tn) in 2021 (Osborne, 2021). Even many so-called public open spaces are, in fact, privately owned public spaces (POPs) and at any of these locations, private security guards can remove you for protesting, taking photos, or just looking too scruffy for comfort. For one of the most affluent countries in the world, and one which had previously been a global leader in providing decent and affordable housing for all social and economic groups, the current situation represents an abrogation of government responsibility for protecting the public interest. Throwing taxpayers money at home ownership has inflated prices to the benefit of those who have already paid off their mortgage, but trapped others into high levels of debt, and inflated rental charges for those unable to afford ownership. Home-owners cannot be expected to vote for a party that would reduce the value of their newly acquired asset, or increase taxes upon it, trapping home-owners in the neoliberal agenda. However, cancelling subsidies must be the first step in correcting market distortion, and a second step must be to make rental more secure and ensure that rogue landlords are penalized. This can pave the way for a more diverse range of tenure options to meet diverse needs.

Mending a broken system

The fact that the authorities now accept that the housing system is broken provides a pre-condition for structural change and a number of policy options could be applied without delay. These include: 1) strengthening the ability of local governments to generate a greater public benefit from private investments through various forms of land-based finance, some of which are already in place but not adequately enforced; 2) significantly increasing tax rates on second homes, or homes kept empty for more than three months a year; 3) requiring developers to develop land for which planning permission has been granted on the basis of 'use it or lose it' to deter private land banking and increase supply; 4) increasing the tax bands and tax rates applicable to all residential properties, particularly within the upper price range; and 5) reducing the stranglehold that volume house-builders have on housing supply. All of these proposals have been widely circulated, so the only constraints are political will and the capacity of local authorities. The Covid-19 pandemic has generated a surge of social networks addressing local issues that can harness local knowledge and energy and create a more inclusive and participatory form of democratic decision-making and resource allocation. Until these issues are addressed, access to adequate housing in the UK will remain hooked to the feudal society as represented by the landed gentry and other wealthy land and property-owners. Change need not involve revolution, but it will certainly require that such groups pay a far greater contribution than at present in creating a fairer society and sustainable economy.

Notes

1. Cahill claims that the aristocracy gained control of UK land through three or four major land grabs: the Norman conquest, Henry VIII's dissolution of the monasteries, Cromwell's Republic, and the enclosures and clearances.
2. For example, council taxes in the UK are based on 1991 property values, even though average prices have increased many times, particularly in prime districts of London. Property values in London increased 3.5 times in just 16 years between 1995 and 2011, and in Westminster, central London by 45 per cent in just five years to 2012, providing existing property-owners with a large indirect subsidy they are unlikely to forgo without a fight.
3. Briggs compares the boom and bust cycles of Manchester with the more pragmatic, mixed economy of Birmingham which never enjoyed the same booms – but never suffered the busts.
4. The original texts were published in a German newspaper during 1872–3. These were combined and published with amendments in 1887. The work was republished in English in 1975 by Progress Printers, Moscow.
5. The term 'rotten boroughs' referred to depopulated election districts that retained their original political representation through the 19th century, up to the 1832 Reform Act.
6. Howard's book *To-Morrow: A Peaceful Path to Real Reform* was published in 1898. It was published again in 1902 under the title *Garden Cities of To-Morrow*, by Swan Sonnenschein & Co., London. The book has been reprinted several times since, by various publishers, and most recently in 2016.
7. Royal Institute of British Architects (RIBA) Stirling Prize website <https://www.architecture.com/awards-and-competitions-landing-page/awards/riba-stirling-prize> [accessed 1 April 2021].
8. Average house prices in the UK rose by 152 per cent in the 20 years to 2015–16, while net family income for 25–34-year-olds only grew by 22 per cent.

CHAPTER 10
State land and housing management in China, Cuba, Ethiopia, and Vietnam

China, Cuba, Ethiopia, and Vietnam are prime examples of socialist countries that have adopted market-based forms of economic development but in which the state still exerts a high degree of control over land. This pre-eminent position places a major responsibility on the political and technical leadership to balance the changing nature and extent of housing needs as part of wider economic management, though each has adopted different approaches and with varying outcomes.

China

Among the countries in which urban land is strictly under state control, China is pre-eminent. With the urban population increasing by 640 million since the economic reforms of 1978 (Liang, 2018), demand for urban land and housing has also increased dramatically (Textor, 2021). Unlike many other countries, China embraced urbanization as a key part of its economic development strategy and the country became more than 50 per cent urban in January 2017. Urban development accelerated to the point where the planned provision of urban housing and facilities vastly exceeded demand and resulted in the emergence of 'ghost cities' in which the only occupants were security guards and maintenance workers. However, many of these cities eventually attracted residents and business investors and have become functioning conurbations, such as Pudong near Shanghai.

Major cities account for a large proportion of total urban growth and Shanghai's population increased by 50 per cent between 2000 and 2019 to 24.28 million (Shanghai Municipal Public Security Bureau, 2020). However, this includes an estimated 9.59 million migrant residents living in the urban and peri-urban areas of the city without a local registration permit, or *hukou*. Since access to health and education facilities, obtaining marriage certificates, or ID card renewals are tied to the area in which a person is born, urban residents without a local *hukou* are forced to make expensive journeys to meet such needs. Despite these constraints, many millions of predominantly young or middle-aged migrants leave their children back in the village to be brought up by their grandparents and move to the cities for the employment opportunities and the incomes that they can obtain to support their families.

The need for housing to accommodate migrants without *hukous* has generated a massive unofficial response in the form of what are known as Small Property Rights (SPR) housing. This is not officially sanctioned development, since although rural land is owned collectively by the villagers, they have no land development rights. However, SPR developments provide an efficient and mutually beneficial means of housing migrants and providing essential urban services. The ability of municipal governments to expand urban land supply is constrained by strict farmland preservation requirements and when the state does acquire land for urban development, compensation is based on agricultural production values, so many villagers find it far more attractive to subdivide their land. Migrants also benefit as SPR housing is 40–60 per cent cheaper than formal housing. Although evidence on this is inevitably limited, research by Sun and Liu (2015) suggests that an estimated 70 million housing units, or more than a third of all urban housing in China, is illegal in that it is developed without official approval (Li, 2014, cited by Sun and Ho, 2018).

Occupants of SPR housing prefer to buy rather than rent and the cultural priority for security is illustrated by the fact that the Chinese term for 'family' (*jia*) is literally the same as for 'home' (Sun and Liu, 2015). While reform of the *hukou* system has been considered for many years, it is likely that SPR housing will continue to accommodate a large proportion of residents in the major cities for some time to come.

To make it easier for registered households to become legal home-owners, the government introduced the Economically Affordable Housing (EAH) programme in 1998 as part of the introduction of market reforms. This improved the quality of housing, but also increased prices and was not popular with private developers as it squeezed profits. By 2009, this option only accounted for about 1.1 per cent of total urban housing. In 2010, a national Public Rental Housing (PRH) programme was launched to meet the needs of those whose incomes are not the lowest, but also not high enough become owners. However, it proved difficult to confirm the incomes of applicants and the system was prone to fraud and abuse.

In Shanghai, PRH has a high vacancy rate, yet the overall housing deficit has been estimated at 2 million units (World Bank, 2014). While the *hukou* system was intended to control rural-urban migration and permit the planned development of urban centres, it has manifestly failed on both counts, since migration has continued and people have been forced into the informal settlements that the government was seeking to prevent. In another attempt to attract the sort of migrants that government hoped would enhance local economic development, the *hukou* system was adapted and PRH, together with *hukous*, was provided for 'talented' professionals, especially those with higher degrees. Cities therefore ended up competing with each other for such 'knowledge migrants' and provided them with heavily subsidized housing, even though many of them could afford market prices.

Income from land sales has been a key source of revenues for local governments throughout China to finance their policy objectives, especially in urban and peri-urban areas where they routinely account for up to 45 per cent of all municipal revenues (Tian, 2014; Sun and Liu, 2014).[1] This has a number of serious consequences. In peri-urban districts, the authorities are able to force the collective owners of land to sell at low agricultural prices, so that they can sell the land to developers for the maximum profit. Displaced households are provided with an apartment in a medium or high-rise development and a disturbance allowance. For older households this represents a traumatic change of lifestyle as well as providing extremely poor compensation. It also involves a massive public capture of land and property values by the state at the expense of peri-urban landholders. In one case in Chengdu, for example, peri-urban land was acquired from its owners at a price of 9 yuan/m^2 ($1.4) and sold to developers for 640 yuan/m^2 ($99), with the resulting apartments costing 6,900 yuan/m^2 ($1,071). In this way, peri-urban landowners are effectively funding urban development.

Since inner-city authorities have no empty land to sell, many have taken to relocating households to peri-urban developments (see Photo 10.1) and redeveloping the cleared sites with high-rise luxury apartments. This destroys well-established communities and forces relocating households to make long journeys to their places of work, imposing high commuting times and costs as well as contributing significantly to air pollution.

The radical reforms to introduce market practices into the land and housing sectors have not fully replaced old statist attitudes and central government retains the power to set targets and delegate responsibility for their delivery to

Photo 10.1 Public rental housing project in Shanghai
Credit: Geoffrey Payne

local levels without any assessment of the extent to which targets reflect social needs or effective demand. Despite institutional weaknesses and regulatory failings (Cao and Keivani, 2013), central government establishes targets for all local and district authorities, for example requiring that 36 million affordable housing units be developed within the 12th Five Year Plan (2011–2015) with each district authority allocated a target. When I asked how the target for his district related to demand, one official responded by saying 'Demand? We are required to increase supply by this number'. The implication was that he had to deliver the target, or else. The needs of local residents were of no official interest or consequence.

Investment in land and housing has contributed significantly to China's economic growth. However, the supply-driven approach has resulted in a massive gap between demand and supply. There was, and remains, a gross shortage of genuinely affordable housing appropriate to the needs of lower income groups, and an excess of luxury apartments, leading to extremely high vacancy rates. An estimated 21.4 per cent of all dwellings in China, amounting to 50–80 million dwellings, are kept empty as investments (Says, 2018; Janda, 2019; McIntyre, 2019). Anecdotal evidence suggests that owners are reluctant to rent units out as a 'second-hand' apartment would fetch a much lower price, and in case the previous occupants had had bad luck that could be passed on to them. In a context in which government diktat determines so much, it is almost reassuring to hear that cultural considerations exert such influence.

There is an estimated deficit of 2 million housing units in Shanghai despite the increased supply and the gap is being met by the SPR informal settlements. However, SPR housing cannot be formalized as it is not built in accordance with the terms and conditions of the planning regulations (Sun, 2015). In a recent study, Sun and Ho (2018: 889) conclude that 'China's SPR housing fulfils a critical function for its owners – not as a marketable asset, but as a form of social security. For one, as its average price is only half that of formal, commercial housing, it might not come as a surprise that over two-thirds of the respondents indicated it was one of their motivations for buying'.

China has succeeded in lifting more than 500 million people of out of poverty during the last three decades, an amazing achievement. However, the paternalistic, top-down, centrally determined, and supply-driven approach to land and housing interventions has absorbed vast resources yet failed to respond to the nature and extent of demand. Rather than seek to identify what people need and can afford, the government has stamped down ruthlessly on protests by farmers on the urban periphery over unfair compensation when their land is commandeered for sale to private developers (Branigan, 2012), though there are also cases where protests have produced positive results for both sides (BBC, 2012; World Bank and Development Research Center of the State Council, The People's Republic of China, 2014). Defaults on bond repayments by the developer Evergrande have increased speculation that the urban land and housing sector poses major risks of a property bubble that could adversely affect China's, and therefore the global, economy at a time when the risks are already high (Bloomberg News, 2022). However, the government has been quick to clamp down on speculative tendencies by preventing transactions when the market becomes overheated and offering incentives when investment declines.

As noted in the World Bank and Development Research Center report (2014: 38) on urban China, new arrangements are needed 'for the transfer of collective land for urban construction purposes and rural land expropriation; developing mechanisms for the better sharing of land value, integrating urban-rural land use planning and land allocation and the redevelopment of "urban villages"; and modernizing urban planning and land management'. However, the proposal in the Bank's report to implement a more market-driven approach raises serious questions, given the supply-driven approach adopted to date. What is needed is a more sensitive and transparent approach to assessing needs and effective demand, in order to ensure that the land and housing markets achieve inclusive and sustainable development.

Recognition that the *hukou* system has failed to control rural-urban migration, especially since the urbanization policy promoted rural-urban migration, has led to regular calls for reform. This has been addressed in the 2019 National Urbanization Plan which requires that cities with populations between 1 and 3 million scrap all restrictions on household registration. This should significantly help to increase the urban population by a further 100 million, reduce the concentration in the mega-cities and make it easier for families to stay together if prices are lower in the smaller cities. Meanwhile, the population of cities such as Shanghai can be expected to continue growing.

Cuba

For years after the end of colonialism, Cuba was the playground of foreign investors who owned vast sugar plantations that produced most of the country's exports, leaving the local population impoverished. Following the revolution in 1959, these plantations were taken under state ownership and allocated to local residents to be managed by *campesinos* (farmers), providing the foundation for Cuba's egalitarian approach to development. Universal education and healthcare, together with strong cultural traditions in music and the arts, enabled the country to score highly in terms of welfare. Housing was a high initial priority for the revolutionary government, and legislation in 1960 ended the free market in residential property, extended home ownership, and reduced rents in the remaining rental sector. Mass building programmes also helped to reduce the pre-revolutionary slum conditions and in 1984, the General Housing Law allowed Cubans to rent, sell, and buy housing. However, this was reversed just two years later and was replaced by participatory, self-help construction with state support and subsidized materials (Anderson, 2009). These policies enabled the vast majority of Cubans to enjoy secure housing at low cost, irrespective of social status or spatial location.

For many years, state control of the economy focused on maintaining equality rather than promoting growth, and housing was considered a social need, rather than a commodity. However, this restricted revenues to finance social housing programmes or improve the existing stock. While there was no speculation on land or housing, since everyone had a home, there was no incentive to put it to the most productive use and for many years, much land was unproductive. However, everything changed after 1990. A long-term trade embargo imposed by the USA had made Cuba's socialist government dependent upon the Soviet Union, so when this collapsed, Cuba suffered an economic crisis known as the 'Special Period'. With the economy under intense stress, people used their housing plots to produce food and former sugar plantations were cultivated, providing essential food for workers and residents. After 1999, Cuba was helped economically by Venezuela and also maintained close relations with Russia. To promote investment, the government diversified the economy by investing in biotechnology and pharmaceuticals, and allowed many doctors, engineers, and other professionals to work overseas. Tourism provided valuable foreign currency and many Cubans sought employment in the more lucrative tourist industry as taxi drivers or guides where they could receive tips in foreign currencies. However, this resulted in increasing economic inequality despite government attempts to restrict it and inevitably led to frustration and resentment among the country's highly educated younger population.

The government responded to this challenge with a series of reforms to promote local enterprise. In 1997, people were allowed to rent out rooms in their houses or apartments as homestays to tourists in what were known as *casas particulares*. The abundance of traditional vernacular houses proved

Photo 10.2 Rooms for rent in the historic centre of Havana
Credit: Geoffrey Payne

highly attractive to tourists and enabled many households to significantly increase their incomes (see Photo 10.2). The government also allowed private farmers and cooperatives to lease unused land and loosened regulations on farmers selling directly to consumers. In 2011, the *Lineamientos* reforms package allowed Cubans to buy and sell homes, rather than just exchange them, as had been the case previously. An informal market developed and this enabled people with funds to obtain good quality housing in popular locations, so that the housing sector began to reflect the emerging economic inequality. In addition, the expansion of demand for homestays caught the attention of Airbnb and more than 22,000 rooms have been listed on the platform since it began operating in Cuba in 2015, generating at least US$40 m (Anderson and Serpa, 2018). As in other countries attractive to tourists, Airbnb tends to force up prices, displacing local residents.

While self-help construction was common and provided extensive employment opportunities, the lack of state resources has resulted in a shortfall in new housing. This in turn has resulted in overcrowding and the poor state of repair of much of the older urban housing stock. While some major buildings in the historic centre of Havana are being painstakingly restored, others are held up by scaffolding (see Photo 10.3), and in 2008 an average of three buildings in Old Havana collapsed daily (Mathéy, 2021). Given that about 76 per cent of the country's population live in urban areas, this represents a major challenge.

Photo 10.3 Building in need of refurbishment in Havana
Credit: Geoffrey Payne

While land is available for urban development, economic constraints restrict the import of key building materials, and the extremely limited public transport system is imposing long journeys for people going to work.

While women enjoy equal rights in Cuba, the elderly often have problems in maintaining their homes and cultural aspects are not considered important. Mathéy (2021: 27) reports that 'Design standards for mass housing in Cuba are very similar to those from Eastern Europe of the 1960s to 1980s, when those countries were still socialist'. He proposes a form of 'a self-financing social housing program. Rent pooling, revolving fund and cooperative investment schemes regenerate the initial investment cost of housing by spreading the expense over more heads and a longer period'. Should future resources permit, public bicycles and energy efficient mini-buses offer attractive options to help people get around.

Despite the difficulties imposed during the 'Special Period' by the USA embargo, Cuba has maintained its impressive commitment to social programmes and environmental sustainability. The increase in urban agriculture, including eco-farms (González-Couret and Payne, 2020), has improved food security, though economic constraints have prevented redevelopment of the historic centres of Havana and other cities. Now that Cuba has four historic urban centres designated as World Heritage sites, their unique characteristics will be preserved, though many remain in desperate need of repair. One option for funding this could be to invite bids from foreign investors seeking to open commercial premises in Havana's historic centre. Selected investors could then be offered leases of 25–30 years in return for completely refurbishing a building and providing the upper floors for social housing administered by the state.

Its long-term focus on health and welfare and its low ecological footprint (González-Couret and Payne, 2020) has helped Cuba score highly in the Human Development Index (Loh and Wackernagel, 2004). Homelessness does not exist and literacy levels and life expectancy are on a par with the most economically developed countries, a major achievement with lessons for other countries. Urban agriculture has contributed significantly to sustainable food production and Cuba has an exemplary prevention and response civil defence system for protecting people from the hurricanes that ravage the region.

Cubans are incredibly resilient and enterprising and opportunities for local enterprise have increased through relaxations in private investment rules and trading agreements with European and Latin American partners. Inevitably, expectations are high and the opportunity now exists for formulating and implementing measures to increase domestic and foreign investment to stimulate growth, increase incomes, put land to more productive use, meet the need to provide new housing, and improve the existing older stock. However, political reluctance to commercialize land and housing has constrained the investment needed to increase supply and improve the existing stock. At the same time, land available for development has not been fully developed due to the absence of an economic incentive to use it (Mathéy, 2021), though opportunities exist to expand land value capture options, (see Chapter 14), as introduced in some tourist areas. Decision-making on all potential initiatives also remains extremely centralized and opaque. The country has had to cope with a prolonged embargo and until this is lifted, it is likely that resilience will continue to be needed. However, recent anti-government protests suggest that the USA embargo is not the only barrier to progress.

Ethiopia

Ethiopia occupies a special place in human history as possibly the location from which *Homo sapiens* emerged. A further claim for importance is as the location in which coffee was first produced, a product which has helped to sustain us ever since. However, one attribute that is relatively new in the country is democracy. Emperor Haile Selassie's autocratic rule left the country in poverty, then followed a major famine, while conflict with Eritrea also constrained progress. This was followed by the military dictatorship of the Derg and another major famine that brought the country to international attention. Following extensive campaigns by regional and ethnic groups, a democracy was established in 1991 and a new constitution was approved in 1995.

While all citizens have the right of ownership of property, Article 40.3 of the constitution states that 'The right to ownership of rural and urban land, as well as of all natural resources, is exclusively vested in the State and in the peoples of Ethiopia'. Despite the plethora of political parties and establishment of a Human Rights Council, this has led to policymaking and resource allocation continuing to reflect elements of the previous centralized power structure.

With an estimated population of 109 million, Ethiopia is the second most populous country in Africa and is estimated to be increasing at over 3 per cent annually, one of the highest rates in the world. If this continues, the population will double within 30 years. In addition, the country is urbanizing at an even faster rate of 5.4 per cent a year, so that the urban population could nearly triple from 15.2 million in 2012 to 42.3 million by 2032 (Eshete et al., 2010; World Bank, 2015b). This presents major challenges in providing jobs, land, services, and housing. In 2010, 80 per cent of the population of the capital, Addis Ababa, were living on low incomes in substandard, insecure settlements (Keffa, 2014), and informal development continues (Abagissa, 2019). Water scarcity is another issue, while an earthquake could be devastating given limited enforcement of building standards.

The literature on urban land and housing in Ethiopia is expanding almost as fast as the demand for land and housing itself. This reflects the national ambition to become a middle-income country by 2025, a goal which is on target, though the recent conflict has had a major adverse economic effect. A number of large industrial development zones have been established, though all the evidence shows that land for housing is short of demand, resulting in high prices and allegations of corruption.

Photo 10.4 Typical inner-city settlement in Addis Ababa
Credit: Geoffrey Payne

A twin approach was adopted to address this challenge. Land for housing was provided in two ways: first, by converting agricultural land to urban residential use and compensating the farmers for the investment they have made or the possibility of land elsewhere; and second, by relocating residents of older, substandard inner city housing to new units on the urban periphery and redeveloping the sites under an 'urban renewal' programme. Leases on registered plots were introduced in 1993 and are governed by the Lease Proclamation of 2011 which means that 'a lessee of urban land cannot claim to collect the market value of the land use right he has acquired through lease' (Abdo, 2014: 180–1). Some land has been sold at auction to generate revenues. However, the amount of land auctioned has been extremely limited, forcing up prices to levels unaffordable to the majority of the population, while land allocated to developers, small-medium enterprises, and for industrial zones has been made available at the official benchmark rates, which are well below market prices. According to Kaganova and Zenebe (2014: 41), the disparity between the benchmark and auction prices for both commercial and residential land in 2013 was between 'two to dozens of times' in different cities. They also report that approximately 94 per cent of land transfers in Addis Ababa are through allocations that lack transparency.

The manner in which this twin approach has been implemented has severely disadvantaged both the farmers and the inner-city residents, most of whom are poor. The compensation received by farmers is restricted to the financial investment that they have made over the years, or with an alternative plot of land elsewhere, but the sums involved are generally far lower than the implied market value of their land. As a result, many farmers pre-empt the possibility of government acquisition by illegally subdividing their land for residential development from which they can generate a more acceptable return. Inner-city residents are similarly disadvantaged by being forced to abandon their homes in reasonably well-located areas and relocated to government projects in the urban periphery where access to employment, social facilities, and even transport systems are limited. Anecdotal evidence suggests that many sub-let their new apartments and return to living in informal settlements. By failing to recognize and meet the reasonable needs of both farmers and inner-city residents, the ability to implement land and housing policies is severely impeded and the outcomes are more, not less, informal development and unregistered transfers within the formal land and housing markets.

In Addis Ababa, a mass housing programme known as the Integrated Housing Development Programme (IHDP) was launched in 2004 and 314,000 apartments were completed by 2018 to accommodate the city's increasing population and those relocated from inner-city settlements, though this is far short of total housing requirements (World Bank, 2019a). Apartment blocks of ground plus four or ground plus five floors in the urban periphery have been developed along suburban roads and ground plus 12 floors in inner city

Photo 10.5 IHDP housing in Addis Ababa
Credit: Geoffrey Payne

locations. However, they are without any sense of place, variety, or community. Having spent all their lives living at ground level, many people have also found it difficult to adapt to living in high-rise condominiums, especially as the quality of construction frequently requires internal retrofitting. The units are also very small and ill-suited to Ethiopian culture.

Since land is a state asset and is allocated according to a centrally determined objective irrespective of the social implications, widespread resentment has been aroused that has in turn weakened the social support networks on which people depend. It also ignores the personal attachment that both farmers and well-established inner-city communities have to their particular location as a home. On one occasion, an official I encountered was forced to concede that moving farmers from an area where they had lived all their lives and where their parents and grandparents were buried, failed to acknowledge the deep personal attachments people have to land. I also met a group of young men chatting in an area of demolished houses in the inner city who explained that they had been relocated to different suburban locations and this was still the area they regarded as home. Such indifference to the social, cultural, and psychological attachments that people have to the places where they live and work has not made it easy for the government to identify or meet the needs of different social groups. Options for enabling both farmers and inner-city residents to remain in their existing locations as part of redevelopment or new housing projects were not adopted. However, a recent World Bank project has strongly supported the creation of an inter-Ministerial Task Force to draw from international best practice and promote land pooling/land readjustment projects as a means of converting rural to urban land without the need to resort to expropriation (World Bank, 2019a: 27).

Land can provide a powerful means of financing the provision of infrastructure and other public needs, especially under conditions where land is publicly owned and where local authorities have the authority, as in Ethiopia. However, as Berrisford et al. (2018) note, the requirement that land can only be released for development once the state has serviced it, and the state's limited ability to realize this, severely constrains land production in Addis Ababa, which in turn constrains options for generating revenues for infrastructure provision. With demand unmet, prices of formally accessed land have escalated beyond the reach of many households and Haregewoin (2007: 6) claims that 'the informal sector is the largest residential land and housing supplier, which is an indication of the formal market failure'.

The Addis Ababa City Structure Plan for 2017–2027 (AACCPO, 2017) proposes a polycentric urban form and mixed land uses, both of which will facilitate access to social and economic opportunities for the city's population. Cooperatives are also being promoted, which will help in diversifying supply and making it more responsive to diverse demand. However, the key issue that the plan does not address is the need for institutional reform in order to make the land and housing sectors more demand-sensitive. The multiplicity of central and local government agencies involved and the concentration of their powers in terms of the scale and forms of supply place a great responsibility on them to be seen to operate efficiently and in the public interest. However, technical and financial constraints inhibit this and have resulted in widespread allegations of corruption in land administration (Plummer, 2012; UN-Habitat, 2017) that have undermined the social legitimacy necessary for success. While control over land was for many years subject to feudal, then imperial, control, followed by the Derg military regime, the current government is struggling to introduce market-based reforms, but without diversifying supply systems to make provision sensitive to demand.

The reluctance of Oromia State to release land for urban development around Addis Ababa has prevented some of the benefits of development accruing to that state and the relief of some of the pressure on Addis Ababa. Land production is overly reliant on expropriation and this has met with great resistance, while only a small proportion of land parcels are auctioned for private development. The majority of land is allocated for government-led programmes, leaving many households to find housing in the informal sector (World Bank, 2019a: 7). Even if households win an IHDP flat in the lottery, they will probably rent it out and find an informal dwelling for themselves. Sadly, neither social needs nor economic efficiency are currently being realized and the UN-Habitat report (2017: 2) notes that although commitment to improving urban governance is genuine, it 'heavily suffers from inappropriate and sometimes even corrupt practices as well as weak institutional capacity for planning. This is especially the case in such critical areas as urban land, basic urban services and housing'. The peace treaty with Eritrea demonstrated the government's ability to resolve international disputes, though the internal conflict in Tigre confirms that progress is urgently needed on domestic issues. Recognizing the needs and interests of citizens by more inclusive policies and diverse supply options on urban land and housing would be a good place to start.

Vietnam

To say that Vietnam has had a turbulent history is an understatement. An agricultural society for centuries, it has been engaged in regional conflicts that have prevented economic development. It was subject to colonial rule by France between 1859 and 1883 and was part of France's control of Indo-China until 1945. Following its occupation by Japanese forces during the Second World War, France sought to recapture the country but was defeated in 1954 and the country was divided between North and South at the Geneva Conference on Indochina, with the North governed by the Communist Party led by Ho Chi Minh and the South under a government supported by the USA. In 1961, the Viet Cong initiated a campaign to reunite the country and conflict with the USA escalated into a full-scale war, ending with the defeat of American forces and the reunification of the country as the Socialist Republic of Vietnam in 1976. Having successfully liberated itself from American influence, Vietnam helped to liberate Cambodia by invading it in 1978 to topple the repressive dictatorship of the Khmer Rouge regime and its four-year war of terror on its own people. This led to an American-led embargo against Vietnam, though gradually a more constructive relationship was established and diplomatic relations with the USA were established in 1995.

Since the introduction of the *Doi Moi* reforms in 1986, when the Communist Party introduced the goal of creating a socialist-oriented market economy, Vietnam has been transformed from one of the poorest countries in South-east Asia to a lower-middle income country and the latest country to be labelled one of Asia's 'tiger economies'. The economy grew at an average of 7.5 per cent during 1991–2000 and 6.8 per cent between 2000 and 2018, enabling poverty levels to fall from 58 per cent in 1993 to 17 per cent in 2012 (World Bank, 2013a). Market reforms have stimulated investment (particularly foreign investment) in land and housing, and increased supply. However, this has not delivered housing solutions accessible to the poor or near-poor and approximately 4.8 million of Vietnam's 24.2 million households live in poor conditions. Growth spurred by foreign investment and speculation led to significant dwelling price increases in the high-end segment that eventually resulted in a real estate bubble from 2009 to 2012 (World Bank, 2015d). Since then, legal reforms and the 30 Trillion Dong Stimulus Package have helped to reorient developers and lenders toward the affordable middle-income housing sector with real home ownership needs.

With the urban population increasing by nearly a million a year, much of it concentrated in the two main cities of Hanoi and Ho Chi Minh City (HCMC), demand for land and housing is increasing more rapidly than the overly bureaucratic formal supply systems can match, despite major policy and legal reforms to enable the transition from valuing housing as a social good to a market-oriented system. As a result, the gap is being met by informal subdivision of peri-urban land and self-built or organized housing construction and this continues to represent the largest proportion of new housing supply, especially in the rapidly expanding suburbs. Non-state investments are neither facilitated nor appropriately regulated (UN-Habitat, 2014a). However, many of the informally developed areas are highly efficient in terms of land use, with narrow (less than 4 m) frontages and several floors with commercial activity on the ground floor (see Photo 10.6), popularly known as 'Tube' houses. For the landholders subdividing their land, the builders and the home-owners, this represents a financially attractive and efficient way of meeting their needs. It has also helped Vietnam avoid the development of urban slums.

Full individual land ownership is not permitted in Vietnam as the state remains the ultimate owner of all land, with responsibility for its management. The government issues Land Use Rights Certificates (LURCs) which can then be amended to the Building Ownership Land Use Certificates (BOLUCs) to provide formal tenure rights.[2] In this way, the state retains the principle of state ownership while seeking to promote private investment. However, it has so far proved unable to regulate the markets in ways that reflect the nature

Photo 10.6 Typical 'Tube' housing development in urban Vietnam
Credit: Geoffrey Payne

and extent of demand. This is to some extent a result of public institutions being granted policymaking and advisory roles, but ultimate power is still being held by local people's committees of the Communist Party. These institutions set land valuations and pricing policy annually for land leases and other fees, but they are routinely well below market-based prices, fuelling more informal development.

The legislative framework for land management is confusing and enforcement is weak. This is partly due to overlapping and competing ministerial responsibilities which have proved resistant to change. The low official land valuations create fears of possible forced land acquisition that reduce tenure security and investment in land and housing. However, private developers are able to hold land with development permission for protracted periods, despite rules requiring them to develop land within specified periods.

Similarly, the bureaucratic hurdles for obtaining a BOLUC, together with high transaction costs for registering transfers, combine to discourage people from completing the registration process. Incomplete and unclear information about administrative procedures was made available to the public and the processes for issuing property rights and certificates were complicated and lengthy, providing opportunities for corruption (World Bank, 2011c). At the same time, land tax rates are low and based on the official rates, while the dramatic increase in land values resulting from state action in land use changes is not being captured. The failure to enforce regulations on these issues has undermined the effectiveness of government agencies in land management and severely constrains the revenues needed for meeting a range of policy objectives. As the World Bank notes, the market price of land is often 10 times higher than the official price, transferring huge benefits to developers (often State-Owned Enterprises (SOEs)), investors, and speculators and 'is significantly forfeiting the creation of public benefit by undervaluing one of its most valuable assets' (World Bank, 2011a: xix). Thu and Perera (2011) argue that the government is trapped by a peculiar two-price system that favours the developers over the public at large. Based on a survey of land prices in HCMC, they find that, even though the government price is updated yearly, the market asking price ranges from 3 to 11 times the government-set price.

Attempts to require developers to generate a public benefit from private investment have achieved limited success. For example, the 2005 Law on Housing requires that developers of new urban areas of over 10 hectares allocate 20 per cent of the land assigned to them for the construction of social housing, which they must then transfer to local housing management agencies (Labbé and Musil, 2014). Unsurprisingly, many development projects are said to have registered with just below 10 hectares to avoid this requirement. According to UN-Habitat (2014a: 10) 'The current planning and investment framework for cities, partly a hold-over from a past grounded in state-directed economic management, is inadequate to guide and control urban development in a market economy. Non-state investments are neither facilitated nor appropriately regulated'.

A key driver of urban development in Vietnam is the administrative system which classifies urban centres into classes, based on factors such as size and economic activity. The higher a city's ranking, the greater its level of autonomy in revenue generation and the salaries of its civil servants. This naturally encourages authorities in Class III cities to adopt measures that will achieve Class II status and for Class II cities to achieve Class I status. This results in a 'build it and they will come' approach, to expand the population and built-up area, as illustrated in the Mekong Delta Province, where master plans provide serviced land for housing and industry on the assumption that this will attract in-migration and justify official promotion. Thus, administrative boundaries have been expanded and large swathes of fertile, low-lying agricultural land transformed into industrial and residential developments outside the built-up area. However, plans were not based on market assessments of potential demand, leaving a high proportion of industrial sites undeveloped. Plans also specify that no more than 44 per cent of the available land is developed and 30–35 per cent is allocated for roads and circulation, leading to urban sprawl and imposing long-term maintenance costs. Such low-density urban development represents a fundamental change from existing forms of urban development which put available land to intensive use. The obvious conclusion is that urban managers are seeking to impose a vision of valuing land that ignores the wider environmental implications. Such criteria show flagrant disregard for the fact that most of the province, and much of HCMC, is less than a metre above sea level (Atkinson, 2007), posing existential threats to their viability as the climate crisis exposes the area to flooding and saltwater penetration (see Photo 10.7).

Local officials have been extremely enterprising in developing ambitious tourist, residential, and industrial developments as a logical response to incentives, though these have proved inappropriate. The dynamism of existing

Photo 10.7 Urban housing in the low-lying Mekong Delta Province, Vietnam
Credit: Geoffrey Payne

urban centres is difficult to recreate in these planned cities and the over-provision of industrial sites enables potential investors to play one city off against others to drive a hard bargain. More positively, Vietnam has undertaken major initiatives on land and housing, such as land pooling and encouraging local builders to provide a high proportion of housing. This generates massive employment in forms that reflect changing local needs and resources despite ever-increasing demand. These approaches to valuing land and housing deserve wider application.

The real estate industry in general, and housing in particular, has contributed significantly to Vietnam's economic development (UN-Habitat, 2014a). Self-help housing remains a dominant form of supply for the majority of the population, helping the country to avoid the emergence of urban slums (World Bank, 2011a), while the formal sector meets the needs of higher income groups. The 30 Trillion Dong Stimulus Package introduced in 2013 is essentially an interest rate subsidy and has faced disbursement issues and poor targeting. According to UN-Habitat 'While most of government regulations focus on development of formal housing projects, self-help or "self-reliant" housing, which accounts for at least 75 percent of urban housing production, has been neglected' (World Bank, 2011a: 24).

Most houses in urban Vietnam do not have legal title and in the face of housing shortages, buyers are willing to buy houses without full property rights. This helps to explain the prevalent perception that buyers and sellers may prefer to transact completely outside the official property registration system, so that the seller may avoid the transfer of ownership tax (which can be as high as 20 per cent of the official land price), and the buyer can continue to avoid the BOLUC registration fees. In Hanoi, Gough and Tran (2009) also note widening inequality in the housing sector, as housing ownership and other sources of wealth are passed down through generations, excluding the families and youth of less well-off and lower status groups from the possibility of accessing or buying their homes or apartments. They also claim that despite moving towards a market-oriented economy, the housing system is still built on old ideologies and supports the old hierarchy. Assessments of progress in the way that land and housing are managed and provided in Vietnam therefore suggest that the transformation from a 'command and control' system of urban management to a more demand-sensitive approach requires greater public involvement as well as improved institutional capacity to assess and meet changing needs.

Common threads

These case studies illustrate the difficulties governments face when transitioning from a long-standing approach based upon state control towards one in which market forces exert an increasing influence. The ideological assumptions that have been the basis of paternalist approaches for many decades are clearly in need of major change if cities are to meet needs in ways that are more socially, environmentally, and economically sustainable. While a strong role for both central and local governments is needed, the form this takes needs to be reconsidered and greater autonomy will be required at local level to respond effectively to diverse and changing needs for land and housing.

While China has adopted a quasi-private sector monopoly approach to maximizing public revenues from land at the expense of rural landholders, Cuba has sought to maintain the social value of land and housing, though failed to promote its economic potential. Vietnam has applied an institutional framework that encourages urban sprawl and increased environmental vulnerability, though it does allow a dynamic informal housing sector to thrive. Together with Ethiopia, each country exhibits an overly bureaucratic approach to land development and housing supply that fails to acknowledge the personal attachment people develop to where they live. Moving people from one location to another without taking the social aspects of housing into account is extremely disruptive socially and can produce outcomes as soulless as any produced by private developers.

None of the countries has managed to meet the extent or nature of their housing needs. Unmet demand is commonly a means of increasing the profits for providers within a market economy, and it can be a means of maintaining or increasing bureaucratic power when the state is responsible, thereby increasing the risk of abuse, inefficiency, and corruption. However, both Cuba and Vietnam have done well to enable low-income groups to live in inner-city areas close to employment locations and social amenities. Vietnam in particular has stimulated a vast number of small-scale builders to meet local needs.

Greater oversight and transparency, combined with a more inclusive approach that involves local communities and civil society organizations, is needed to ensure the efficient and equitable management of land and housing as vehicles for achieving social, economic, and environmental development. Change to a more demand-sensitive approach will not be easy. However, if convinced of the need for change, governments that are confident of being in power for the foreseeable future can afford to take more short-term risks to achieve longer-term benefits.

Notes

1. According to Sun and Liu (2014), 'The national total revenues from land concessions increased dramatically from RMB 51 billion in 1999 to RMB 4.3 trillion in 2014, which was as much as 45 per cent of the municipal revenues from taxes and inter-governmental transfers'.
2. In October 2009, the government issued Decree 88 which unified the Red Book providing the BOLUC and Pink Paper providing the LURC into one unified document called Land Use Rights, House and Assets Attached to Land Ownership Certificate.

CHAPTER 11
From state to market in Mongolia, Albania, and Cambodia

Many countries have transitioned from centralized, authoritarian backgrounds to market-based systems of economic management. They include those managed under communist ideology that regained independence following the collapse of the Soviet Union and others that experienced it independently. Most have embraced Western market economics to boost their economies and make up for lost time. Western powers and international development agencies were quick to realize the potential for supporting these processes, though not always adequately taking into account that senior policymakers in the emerging countries were poorly equipped to manage the transition in a way that was conducive to the broader public interest. In fact, Western support focused as much on the opportunity to penetrate new markets as on generating local benefits. The experience of three such countries illustrates the difficulties and challenges of making the transition and the ways in which land and housing sector management reflect broader developmental issues.

Mongolia

For the millions of households crammed into small housing plots throughout the world, Mongolia's capital of Ulaanbaatar would appear to provide unbelievable luxury. Each officially registered urban resident, including children, is legally entitled to a free *khashaa* (residential plot of land) of up to 700 m^2, making the city the most generous in the world in land provision. However, even free benefits can come at a high price.

There is no shortage of land for Mongolia's population of just over 3 million. With 1.3 million living in the capital of Ulaanbaatar, the average density of population in the rest of the country is well below two people per square kilometre. Climate change has led to drier summers producing less vegetation for sheep and cattle, while harsher winters known as *dzuds* lead to many animals starving to death, making nomadic pastoral life more difficult to sustain. Extreme climatic events that previously took place once a decade now occur far more often and in more extreme form, forcing many pastoralists to move to urban areas.

During the socialist period of 1924–91, the state owned all the land and controlled many industrial enterprises. All land transactions took place in accordance with centrally prepared master plans, some of which were prepared in Moscow without regard to local conditions, though a limited form of market operated even under Soviet influence. The period produced a large amount of housing in the form of three and four storey earthquake-resistant apartment blocks that occupy what is now a central part of Ulaanbaatar and a key part of its architectural heritage (M.A.D., 2014). Following the end of the Soviet Union, Mongolia rejected communism and the 1992 constitution established a multi-party democracy. The country opened its doors to a market economy approach, resulting in the mass privatization of state-owned industries, apartments, and land (Batbileg, 2007), though this only directly affected a small proportion of the population for some years. Restrictions imposed by the communist government were replaced by freedom of movement that stimulated rapid migration into the capital. Later attempts to prevent migration into Ulaanbaatar failed, though many migrants still find it difficult to register as residents and access social services.

Migrants arriving in Ulaanbaatar have to adapt quickly within the evolving market economy. The high demand for land makes the adjustment more challenging since few unregistered migrants have the funds to purchase a plot on the open market. The main initial option is to erect a *ger* (yurt) within the plot of a registered relative or rent rooms in a *ger*-district house (see Photo 11.1). Migrants seeking a free *khashaa* need to obtain a document from their original *aimag* (district) and apply to the city authorities; the authorities then assign them an area where they have to submit another application. In this sense the Soviet-era paternalistic approach has continued within the market-based economy, creating a parallel system of land management as well as opportunities for abuse. This can be partly explained as 'a result of limited

Photo 11.1 Typical *ger* settlement in Ulaanbaatar
Credit: Geoffrey Payne

awareness and understanding by the general public, as well as by policy makers, of the public costs of their actions on land management. Also, many supporting mechanisms, including land valuation and taxation, have not yet been properly developed' (Kamata et al., 2010: xv). Anecdotal evidence suggests that many migrants are reluctant to lose the benefits to which they are entitled in their original *aimag*, so prefer not to register and settle on an empty plot of land on the city outskirts, and either pay some officials a bribe to register their claim or simply fail to register.

As part of the move to transform the country into a market economy while maintaining a semblance of control, a plethora of legislation relating to land and property was passed and amended during the 1990s and early 2000s within a complex and frequently changing administrative system. In 2008, another initiative involved the US-funded Millennium Challenge Corporation (MCC) establishing the Property Rights Project to 'increase the security and capitalization of land assets held by lower-income Mongolians' (Innovations for Poverty Action, 2015: 5). People were quick to appreciate the increasing financial value of property and a market developed within the newly privatized areas, a process that intensified as the expanding mining sector stimulated investment. The MCC intended to survey and register 75,000 plots in the *ger* areas of Ulaanbaatar, though this was later reduced to 53,000 (ibid: 8) and eventually they were only able to title half the number intended.

The Ulaanbaatar Master Plan 2020 and development approaches for 2030 were prepared on the Soviet-era assumption that people would do what planners told them. However, many senior officials trained under the Soviet system had no experience of land management in a market economy and were therefore in a weak position to manage the city's growth efficiently. The Plan proposes an extremely low density city, imposing prohibitively high infrastructure costs, especially since pipework needs to be several metres below ground level to prevent freezing. The Plan designates an extremely small proportion of the total urban area as mixed land use and is far below the UN-Habitat recommendation of at least 40 per cent. This discourages future commercial investment in predominantly residential areas, insulates existing commercial activities from future competition, and has proved economically ineffective. More corrosively, segregation of land uses minimizes the opportunities for social interaction which is the hallmark of any successful city. Further, there is little evidence that the plan was based on an assessment of housing needs or the funds available to implement it.

The rapidly changing legal, regulatory, and institutional framework for managing urban land complicates matters for households and investors and puts officials responsible under great strain. Further adding to the confusion, different international donor agencies have tended to have their own procedures for assessing the impact of their policies. International support from agencies such as the Asian Development Bank (ADB) and the World Bank helped to strengthen central and local government capability to meet basic demands. However, rather than focusing on meeting the basic needs of the population, the government has adopted increasingly grandiose projects without sound evidence of need. These include: a new airport 50 km from the city on the other side of a mountain range costing over US$500 m (equivalent to $600 for each household nationally, if the loan from Japan is ever repaid); proposals to relocate universities to a site two hours from their existing urban locations; and the proposed decentralization measures to relocate many people to satellite towns more than 50 km from the city at densities as low as 4–14 persons per hectare. These proposals impose heavy capital costs yet provide minimal social facilities or employment opportunities, further increasing costs and air pollution levels from private transport. This has proved particularly problematic as Ulaanbaatar is reputed to be the coldest capital city in the world, with winter temperatures permanently below freezing and often lower than −30°C. Combined with climatic inversions that trap pollution from factories and coal-burning stoves in *ger* settlements, air pollution poses a serious public health threat.

Citizens and businesses are required to navigate a mass of rules and procedures for managing land. For example, while only Mongolian citizens can own land, firms and legal entities must apply for possession licences for periods from 15 to 60 years, with the possibility to extend for 40 years, and foreign applicants are only able to obtain five-year land use certificates, with each option involving different authorities. The short duration of the land use option, especially given the uncertainty over extensions, has been a major deterrent to foreign investors. Similarly, 'The quality of service to the public of various land-related offices varies substantially across the city: some offices provide clear guidance through one-stop-shops while others may have absent or unqualified staff and require applicants to visit multiple times' (World Bank, 2015e: xii).

Unlike China, where local governments generate a substantial proportion of revenues from land, revenues from land fees are based on official valuations established in 1997 and are so low that the cost of collection exceeds the revenues generated. As a result, they are not collected from *khashaa* plots in *ger* areas. This changing and complex administrative framework makes it difficult for the urban authorities to assess and respond to demand, reducing public support for policy implementation.

The one policy that has resisted change is the legal entitlement of all registered citizens to a free plot of land of up to 700 m^2, even though most plots are smaller in practice. This generous area is understandable given the vast expanse that the population have been accustomed to occupying and using freely for centuries. *Ger* settlements now accommodate more than half the city's population and cover a majority of the urban area. Most residents have built permanent structures, retaining their *gers* to accommodate household members and visiting relatives, or possibly renting to the next wave of in-migrants. Transactions on land are increasingly common, though the municipal authorities struggle to keep pace with demand and unauthorized subdivisions continue to proliferate. Reliable data on land prices is difficult to obtain partly because some transfers take place unofficially, or because contracts include two prices, only the lower of which is registered in order to avoid the sales tax (World Bank, 2015e: 62).

In an attempt to make all land transactions transparent and provide a common platform for information about land sales and leases, the government and municipality launched the Land Exchange in 2019 (Baljmaa, 2019) as a digital platform for conducting auctions of land for acquisition and tendering. It remains to be seen if encouraging all transactions of both possession and ownership rights to be formally registered through the Exchange will prevent under-reporting of property transfers in what is already an active land and housing market, even in the *ger* areas. After all, why would people voluntarily pay a fee to the Land Exchange in addition to that of a broker? The alternative option of making it mandatory to transact land through the Exchange would have added another cost and layer of bureaucracy with no benefit to those exchanging land (World Bank, 2015e: 66). A more effective means of raising revenues from land and property would be to improve the land registration system and increase the land fees in *ger* areas.

Despite its dispersed development, 40 per cent of Ulaanbaatar's population lived in fully serviced apartments in 2010 and the Master Plan proposes to increase this to 79 per cent of the housing stock by 2030. Progress has, however, been extremely slow. Despite significant subsidies, most developers lack funding and experience to reach agreements with the high proportion of currently unapproved *ger* residents in areas designated for upgrading. Also, while *ger* residents would welcome the facilities and comforts provided by apartments, their small floor areas are unattractive compared to the spacious standards the *ger* residents currently enjoy and which provide opportunities for home-based economic activities. Options to facilitate improvements could include encouraging *ger* residents in prime locations to negotiate directly with developers (as applied in Ankara, see Chapter 15) or to form residents' associations to pool their land plots and negotiate en bloc with developers on terms that enable them to exert more control. Another constraint on moving people into apartments relates to the impact on water supply. Access to water in the *ger* areas is almost entirely from a network of local kiosks and requires residents to collect it in containers, so per capita consumption is far lower than in the apartments where it is freely available at a cost far lower than that paid by *ger* residents (Kamata et al., 2010). Increasing the numbers of people living in apartments will dramatically increase the demand for water. As a landlocked country dependent on rainfall and local aquifers for its water supply, Ulaanbaatar is in an extremely vulnerable position given the rapidly escalating climate crisis.

The generous provision of free land has had serious negative outcomes in terms of poor sanitation, air pollution, long journey times, a lack of easily accessible social services, and limited opportunities for social interaction. While compact forms of land development and housing are the most effective way of reducing infrastructure costs and improving the urban environment,

Photo 11.2 Terraced inner-city housing and communal gardens in Ulaanbaatar
Credit: Geoffrey Payne

apartments do not have to be high rise in order to achieve adequate densities. Medium-rise developments, such as the Soviet-era 40K apartments developed in the late 1950s (see Photo 11.2) provide a basis for more flexible and congenial forms of urban development and deserve greater consideration (M.A.D., 2014). A proposal for such a medium-rise and energy efficient mixed-use and mixed-income development, known as Ulaanbaatar Village (Roberts, 2019), offers an approach deserving of wider consideration.

Outside the main urban area, *ger* settlements are managed increasingly on the basis of relatively low, albeit unclear, market prices, and the majority of residents use land as a natural resource, rather than a market asset to be bought and sold. The pride that all Mongolians have in their cultural traditions provides a good opportunity for the proposed decentralization to draw on water resources over a wider area and for a network of relatively self-sufficient, compact settlements to evolve, allowing families to retain *gers* on their plots and maintain cultural traditions, a form of 'urbanization with Mongolian characteristics'. This could provide the basis for reducing dependency on travel to employment locations in central Ulaanbaatar and its attendant environmental impacts, but would require the dispersed provision of basic health, educational, and social service facilities to compact settlements of up to 10,000 people, developed by local people with technical support and with higher order facilities in the main city. Costs for these facilities could be met by grants, mining sector revenues, increased area-based land fees or property taxes, development charges, and renewable energy supplies such as solar power. Another initiative that helps incoming residents to the city adapt to urban living is the GerHub centre, a modern community facility designed to replicate the sense of shared space provided in *ger* areas (Wainwright, 2020). Such hubs could provide a valuable social asset in well-designed, semi-autonomous settlements.

While many residents have been quick to realize the financial benefits of holding land, creating an active market even in the *ger* areas, urban governance is still heavily influenced by the previous state-driven forms of land and housing management and has struggled to regulate a market-based approach. The administrative structure remains complex and lacking in transparency, while legislation has been introduced to provide short-term solutions to long-term issues. Secondary legislation and regulatory provisions are either lacking or are changed frequently, undermining investor confidence. However, some elements of the state-controlled system, notably the medium-rise apartment complexes, have proved to provide a more human-scale, flexible, and popular form of development and deserve to be retained.

The resilience demonstrated by Ulaanbaatar's population has enabled the supply of land and housing to keep up with demand, though not as yet in a form that is consistent with official plans or socially, environmentally, or economically sustainable. As a result, Mongolia continues to exhibit state-based, paternalistic approaches of preparing master plans that promote a market system which is poorly regulated. The population is having to make massive adjustments to the way it values land and housing and options for maintaining cultural values are proving hard to maintain. This challenge can be expected to take some time to resolve.

Albania

Mongolia's experience of communism was benign compared to that of Albania which was under communist rule from 1944 to 1992. The dictator Enver Hoxha was so repressive that he even cut ties with the Soviet Union and China, both of which he considered had gone soft on the principles of Marxist-Leninism, leaving Albania isolated as the poorest country in Europe. All land was nationalized, but when the communist period ended, laws were prepared to return land to its original owners. At the same time, the State began to sell parcels of 300–500 m^2 for token amounts (equivalent to $1/$m^2$) to farmers outside the urban boundaries who had been working it under the collective system. The 1993 law[1] was intended to return all rural land to the original owners, though many could not be identified, creating uncertainty and discouraging development.

Rural-urban migration following the end of the communist regime saw the population of the capital, Tirana, grow during the 1990s by 35 per cent, dramatically increasing the demand for land and housing. However, the

National Housing Agency, established in 1993, was primarily responsible for completing unfinished multi-apartment buildings that had been started late in the 1980s and were left unfinished due to changes in the system, not meeting the needs of the increased population. As a result of high demand and institutional corruption, supply was well short of demand, contributing to people seeking informal channels to obtain land and housing. This resulted in the evolution of a 'dual city' (Pojani, 2010), with new high-rise, high-density developments in the inner city and unauthorized settlements on agricultural land outside, closely based on family and ethnic links (Bardhoshi, 2011). The lack of public space and infrastructure, combined with poverty and social segregation, led to extensive distress.

Original landowners within urban areas were unable to receive restitution of agricultural land since it had been built upon. Instead, they were to receive financial compensation based on current market values. According to Law 9482, occupants of urban land are required to pay for the land they occupy and the money paid into a special fund towards compensating the original landowners, but according to Kelm (2009: 25) the funds collected through the legal process administered by AKKP[2] were unlikely to be sufficient to fully compensate the original landowners. The cost of such is unknown but under the standard of compensation at full, current market value, it is estimated to reach into the billions of euros. For a country that has a GDP of approximately $22 bn, accepting a compensation bill many times that amount does not make sound economic sense (Kelm, 2009: 35) even if repaid over many years, though other steps could have been taken, such as to offer original landowners shares in developments.

Initial efforts to restrict unauthorized development proved ineffective and were dropped after 1995 in the face of massive – and occasionally violent – public pressure (Urbaplan, 2008: 91). This gave an incentive for landholders to build rapidly, even when the legal status of the land was unclear or disputed. The understandable inability of public sector agencies responsible for land administration to cope with the dramatic changes and pressures accelerated opportunities for developments to take place without obtaining, or even seeking, formal approval, so that a large and increasing proportion of all urban development is considered informal or extra-legal. It has been estimated that there are approximately 400,000 illegal constructions and the informal settlements cover more than 300,000 hectares nationally, many of which are in Tirana (Kelm, 2009: 22). To maximize security for such investments, developers constructed substantial structures and numerous villas appeared throughout the urban periphery, though most had limited services or access roads. Albania is therefore a prime example of households and communities taking advantage of political change to develop land informally, driven initially by the needs of migrants to locate near employment opportunities and later by speculation, corruption, and links with politicians. Amendments to the law providing opportunities to legalize such developments only served to enhance informal development further.

Given the extensive nature of unauthorized development and the energy with which landholders and developers were exercising their new-found freedoms, a comprehensive approach to formalizing the urban land and property market was formulated and approved in 2006, following recommendations from the economist Hernando de Soto. This was embodied in the Law No. 9482 On Legalization, Urban Planning and Integration of Illegal Buildings, and was intended to legalize all informal land development and provide for compensation to the original landowners at market rates based on land use categories (urban, agricultural, tourist, etc.). This compensation would come from additional revenues which were anticipated as a result of economic growth generated through enlivening 'dead capital' from the informal into the formal economy (Kelm, 2009: 33).[3] The agency to implement the provisions of this law, ALUIZNI,[4] was founded in 2006, based on the Commission for the Formalisation of Informal Property (COFOPRI) established in Peru for the same purpose. As part of this process, an original landowner was expected to sign his or her agreement, at which point the existing occupant of land would be entitled to receive the formal title to his or her parcel on completion of relevant formalities and payment of a token amount, normally €3,000 ($3,480) for a plot of less than 300 m^2, though the rate increased significantly for areas in excess of 300 m^2.

Implementation of the law proved problematic for several reasons. Many existing occupants failed to pay the €3,000 charges to ALUIZNI, since they had effectively already become owners without having to pay anything. The only limitations experienced by these newly entitled owners are that they cannot use their newly formalized asset as collateral for a formal loan as it is not registered, and they cannot realize the formal land market value if they intend to sell. However, they retain the right to do either on payment of the fee. This gives major benefits to new owners yet denies ALUIZNI and the original landowners the income to which they are entitled in law. The lack of secondary legislation on compensation schemes and procedures, issued only in special cases such as for coastal areas or touristic zones, has contributed to the failure of the compensation process (Bejtja and Bejtja, 2013: 295).

As of 2014, ALUIZNI reported that only 6 per cent of the 350,000 informal buildings had been legalized, despite having a national staff of about 800, a generous budget, significant political support, and a strong technological base (Kelm, 2009: 26). The possibility of legally issuing the permit, even in the case of non-payment of the building parcel, generated a peak of successful applications. In this case, ALUIZNI issues the permit and keeps note for the legal mortgage (Petanaj, 2018). This has enabled the agency to issue 190,000 legalization permits as of 2019 (Vanelli, 2019: 107).

By promising full land ownership titles to existing informal occupants for a token amount and restitution or compensation at full market rates to original landowners, the State has entrenched the vested interests of both parties and stalled cases in which existing and original landowners were in the process of coming to a mutually agreeable compromise. Experienced local officials privately acknowledge that the current impasse is of the government's own making. However, this was largely as a result of accepting the 'shock therapy' recommendations of de Soto in 2006 to provide titles to informal residents without considering the interests of the original landowners or the social impact of massive increases in the financial values of land. This privatization process went hand in hand with rapid market liberalization, generating corruption tendencies and ineffective governance (Bandelj, 2016: 90).

ALUIZNI has recently completed the transfer of land ownership and field surveys for a large number of land parcels nationally, so has largely fulfilled its functional role. Following an electoral promise in 2013, the process of legalization was virtually free of charge. However, the small income generated from new owners was insufficient to compensate the original owners, leaving them no recourse except to appeal to the European Court of Human Rights, many of which were decided in favour of the claimants, leaving the government facing large compensation bills and penalties. In 2015, another attempt was made to balance the legitimate interests of both the original landowners and the current occupants of land in and around Tirana. Law 133 states that compensation be based on the value of the land at the time of the expropriation in 1945, irrespective of its approved use. This is dramatically lower than current values, so the priority of the law is to provide compensation in the form of land, for which a land fund has been allocated to ALUIZNI. If that is not possible, the next step is to grant 20 per cent financial compensation and 80 per cent land compensation. A sum of 100 per cent financial compensation is the last resort in cases where the first two options are not acceptable.

The problems facing original landowners are complex, partly because many have died or emigrated, so that claims of ownership are difficult to prove. More importantly, informal settlers have more political influence with those politicians who retain a socialist approach and the levels of compensation available are trivial compared to current values. Disputes can only be resolved through the courts, which is an expensive and time-consuming process without any guarantee of practical benefits even if the case is successful. In addition, the surveying processes and techniques applied by IPRO, the agency for property registration, differed from those applied by ALUIZNI, the agency in charge of issuing the legalization certificates, inhibiting the ability of original owners to gain resolution of their claims. To resolve this, ALUIZNI and IPRO were unified in early 2019 into the ASHK, Agjencia Shtetërore e Kadastrës (the State Agency of Cadastre).

A final constraint on the prospects for enabling original landowners to gain compensation or a negotiated agreement with new landowners is that many new owners are unwilling to pay the higher unit rate of land for all areas over 300 m^2. For example, a new owner occupying a plot of 450 m^2 may offer to allocate 150 m^2 to the original owner in order to reduce the cost of fees, but do so in a way which produces an unusable area, as shown in Figure 11.1.

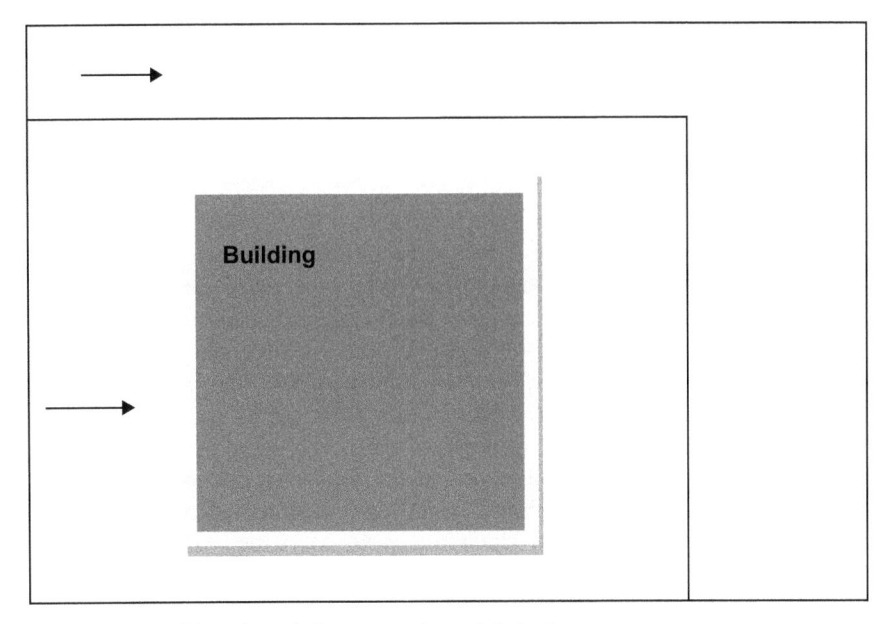

Figure 11.1 Possible unintended outcomes from plot sharing

The difficulties in addressing the challenge have been reinforced by a lack of political stability at both national and local levels and frequent tensions between central and local government. As developers have continued to invest according to their own interests and with little recognition of the impact of individual actions on the wider community, the role of the public sector has continued to shrink despite the intentions embodied in the 2006 law. Now, even formal institutions, such as the Bank of Albania, are undertaking major building works and extensions without planning or building permission. However, access by the new landowners to formal credit has failed to materialize or generate economic development as envisaged and, as a result, government revenues have failed to increase nearly enough to compensate original owners.

In this political panorama, informality has risen as a secondary economy, while the lack of trust towards public institutions and social-spatial fragmentation are major consequences (Bandelj, 2016: 90). Land conflicts account for episodes of violence and social disruption, while the length of administrative procedures causes social tensions among those with stronger claims. The geographical fragmentation of informal settlements hampers the creation of community cooperation prior to and during the process of getting title (Vanelli, 2019). Limited institutional capacity in land registration and administration have also provided opportunities for corruption, with anecdotal evidence of multiple claims for land resulting in extensive litigation. Moreover, these processes have also possibly fuelled a land and property bubble in that both domestic and diaspora investors have found land and property to be an ideal vehicle for channelling assets from the informal into the formal economy.

In summary, Albania has replaced one of the most extreme forms of state control with one of laissez-faire capitalism, which quickly evolved into monopolistic capitalism controlled by oligarchs. Unauthorized land occupation and development has now become the norm in Tirana and other urban centres. Had the government adopted a 'Post-Keynesian' approach balancing economic, social, and political relations as advocated by Scrieciu and Stringer (2008), or facilitated negotiations between the original landowners and existing occupants of land, a more pragmatic and cost-effective solution may have been achieved. Despite these constraints, there are highly visible, if superficial, signs of progress. Between 2000 and 2011, the previous mayor of Tirana, Edi Rama, literally brought colour into citizens' lives (Photo 11.3) by painting the grey communist blocks in a riot of colours which stimulated civic pride, improved the local environment, and even generated increased revenues (Rama, 2012). A General Local Plan, established in 2014, drove the strategic development of the city; some informal settlements were demolished and replaced by parks (though original landowners remain in dispute over their rights). Proposals were also made to undertake a City Development Strategy, though this sadly ceased when a new mayor was elected. However, Rama was later elected Prime Minster in 2013, showing what local leadership can achieve.

Photo 11.3 Repainted official apartment buildings in Tirana, Albania
Credit: Geoffrey Payne

It is perhaps inevitable that after decades of repression, the pendulum would swing to the other extreme. While Tirana has yet to resolve the tensions between social and financial forms of valuing land and housing, it now enjoys a rapidly improving environment and public facilities attractive to tourists. However, many historic buildings have been lost in the process and the key to future success will be to ensure that benefits are based on the needs of residents.

Cambodia

Of all the countries that have transitioned from repressive state control to market-based forms of development, few have had such a traumatic experience as Cambodia. Under the Democratic Kampuchea regime led by Pol Pot between 1975 and 1979, the entire urban population was evicted and relocated to the countryside, where between 1 and 2 million were executed or starved to death. The regime was toppled in 1979 by the Vietnamese army which withdrew in 1989, paving the way for the Paris Peace Accord and international funding to rebuild the country. People returned to the cities on an ad hoc basis, with the first and most powerful claiming the best properties and the others occupying what was left, eventually being forced to build huts on the banks of canals or alongside railway tracks (Photo 11.4).

Photo 11.4 Residents of unapproved settlements in central Phnom Penh, Cambodia
Credit: Geoffrey Payne

Soon after the withdrawal of the Vietnamese army, the government reinstated a measure of private property rights, although not complete ownership rights, with a constitutional amendment that permitted citizens to have full rights to hold and use land as well as to bequeath land rights through inheritance. Socialist policies were officially abandoned and a market economy introduced under the tutelage of the United Nations administration, the International Monetary Fund, the World Bank, the ADB, and other development institutions. Policies promoting private sector development and foreign investment, including the formalization of land ownership, were adopted. The 1992 Land Law re-established that all land belonged to the state, though also allowed for temporary possession to become a basis for individual ownership of residential land if certain conditions were met. An active urban land market soon developed, even though formal registration was lacking and insecurity was common for most people.

The 1993 Constitution confirmed the right of all citizens to own property, which cannot be acquired by the State except in the public interest and with the payment of fair and just compensation in advance. The government also ratified human rights treaties as a basis for the provision of housing. This represented a major step forwards for a society that had literally lost everything and needed a tangible and legally recognized form of security. Initially, benefits were relatively easy to achieve in rural areas since land availability was more than adequate for the predominantly rural population. However, the demand for land by an increasing urban population, particularly in Phnom Penh, combined with the introduction of market forces, led to a sudden increase in urban land values and presented opportunities for land grabbing. As Rabé (2009: 93) notes 'Even as high-level officials from government, the police and the armed forces (in their private capacity) were stimulating squatting through their ties with informal brokers, and even as politicians were encouraging squatting for political gain in the run-up to the national elections in 1993, the Municipality of Phnom Penh and local authorities embarked on a violent forced eviction campaign'.

The 2001 Land Law defined two main categories of land ownership in Cambodia, namely public and private (Khemro and Payne, 2004). In the public domain, land is further classified as state public and state private land. Only the land area clearly required for a specific public use is recognized as the former category and is held and managed by the state for public purposes. However, the latter comprises all other state land, which can be placed in the hands of private interests for productive activities either temporarily, by economic concession, or permanently, through alienation.

At the same time as the population was valuing land as a means of obtaining legal security following the depredations of the Khmer Rouge regime, the government saw the opportunity to use land as a means of attracting domestic and foreign investors to promote economic growth. As discussed in Chapter 7, a multi-donor national Land Management and Administration Project (LMAP) was also launched to survey, title, and register all land parcels in the country and establish a functioning land market. While the project was successful in rural areas, it resulted in forced evictions of low-income households in parts of Phnom Penh and demonstrated that land titling in itself cannot be expected to realize such diverse social and economic policy objectives in a range of contexts. The government cancelled the project in late 2009, though it continued without World Bank support.

As part of the 2001 Land Law to promote inward investment into Cambodia, another proposal was introduced soon after the LMAP commenced in 2002. This was the concept of Economic Land Concessions (ELCs), the subject of a controversial sub-decree of the Law passed in 2005. ELCs generated large-scale commercial land acquisitions in rural and forest areas that prompted extensive reports of land grabbing by commercial interests. Many households had their land taken from them by powerful individuals and some foreign investors withdrew as a result. Widespread protests by villagers whose land had been taken from them by ELCs forced the government to issue Order 01 in May 2012, not long after the LMAP project had been cancelled and replaced by the Land Administration Sub-Sector Programme (LASSP). This proved to be highly successful by issuing 610,000 titles between June 2012 and December 2014 on state private land and many ELCs were cancelled (Grimsditch and Schoenberger, 2015). However, given the speed and scale of the programme, many people found that not all of their land was titled due to surveying issues and others did not receive any titles, especially if they were in dispute with powerful actors (ibid: 3).

Order 01 was applied mainly in rural and forest areas. Within Phnom Penh, forced evictions and relocations were a common practice before, during, and after the World Bank's LMAP involvement. Scurrah and Hirsch (2015) cite several sources, including Amnesty International, who found that an estimated 11,000 families were forcibly evicted from the city between 1998 and 2003 and a further 30,000 people were evicted between 2003 and 2008. They conclude that 'Land reforms in Cambodia have taken place in a post-war political economy where resource extraction and state-building are mutually reinforced by patrimonial networks that benefit political and economic elites' (Scurrah and Hirsch, 2015: 21).[5] Further evidence continues to be reported of Cambodia's poor being coerced into parting with their land in order to repay a microloan that would otherwise move into default following large-scale land titling and the use of land as collateral (Bateman, 2020: 31).

On a more positive note, the Urban Poor Development Fund (UPDF), supported by the Asian Coalition of Housing Rights, launched a programme of community-based development programmes in Phnom Penh that expanded to other urban areas after 2008 (Phonphakdee et al., 2009). Although only operating at very small scale, UPDF provides vitally needed small loans to community associations to improve living conditions for poor households, though its main contribution is in promoting partnerships with local governments to enhance more equitable urban development.

In another positive move, in 2010 the Prime Minister signed Circular 03 on the Resolution of Temporary Settlements on State Land Temporarily Occupied in the Capital, Municipal and Urban Areas (Royal Government of Cambodia, 2010). This provided temporary and limited occupancy rights for residents of informal settlements while surveying and classifying the extent to which the settlements could be upgraded with community participation or needed to be relocated if considered unsuitable. Such a pragmatic and incremental approach had been recommended in research carried out in 2003–4 (Khemro and Payne, 2004), demonstrating that research can contribute to improvements in practice. The 2014 National Housing Policy built on the progressive steps announced in 2010 by providing a framework to identify future needs and encouraging a wide range of public, private, and civil society groups to help meet housing demand. It also strengthened the incremental approach to upgrading unauthorized settlements where possible by announcing a moratorium on forced evictions, as proposed in the 2004 research, with relocation a measure of last resort, as well as measures to ensure that implementation responded to changes in demand (Khemro, 2014).

Cambodia's economy has performed well in recent decades, making the country one of the fastest growing in South-east Asia (Fung and McAuley, 2020) and enabling Cambodia to become a lower middle-income country in July 2016, with plans to become an upper-middle income country and eventually a high income country by 2050 (Cambodia Urban Forum, 2019). However the rate of growth was adversely affected by a failure to upgrade or diversity the garments industry (World Bank, 2019b: 3–51) and it remains to be seen what impact this will have on the ability of the urban population to access land and housing on affordable terms.

In adopting a free market economy approach, the government has allocated a major role for the land and housing sectors, particularly in and around Phnom Penh where land is valued primarily as a commercial asset to attract inward investment. The real estate market has expanded dramatically following the allocation of thousands of licences for the provision of condominiums and more recently the development of gated communities, known locally as *Boreys*, containing a range of villas with names like King Villa, Queen Villa, and Prince Villa. With prices for both condominiums and *Boreys* in the range of $1,000 per m^2 or more, and investors from South Korea, Thailand, Japan, and even the UK, units are clearly targeted at the country's emerging upper-middle class, not the average or below average income groups. Although foreigners are legally prohibited from owning landed property, it appears that investors are able to pay additional fees to bypass this requirement and protect their investment. Whether or not the scale of such investment will result in a property bubble bursting remains to be seen. Meanwhile, residents of areas designated for redevelopment have been provided with cash compensation that may not be sufficient for finding alternative accommodation.

Following the excessive brutality of the Khmer Rouge regime, it is easy to understand the attraction of a legal system that protects individual rights to land and housing. Cambodia has made rapid progress over recent decades and, despite increasing economic growth, levels of inequality are low and decreasing – an impressive achievement. However, by valuing land and housing primarily as a commercial asset, there is a real danger that the poor will continue to be pushed out as the real estate market expands. In addition, all state public and state private land in and around Phnom Penh has now been exhausted, so state agencies seeking land for new facilities, such as a centre for tourism development, are having to acquire private land at considerable expense.

Although policies on urban land and housing have become far more progressive, the question now is the extent to which this has succeeded in balancing powerful commercial interests with those most in need. It has also exposed the danger of relying on land titling to resolve problems of tenure insecurity and land market management, especially since competition favours those in power or with influence.

Conclusions and implications

As with people, a country's past influences the way it addresses the future. Transitioning from repressive state control to market-based forms of economic management poses threats and opportunities to those in power and these are physically expressed in the ways of valuing urban land and housing. When those previously in power remain, the paths are different than when new forces take over.

All three case study countries have experienced decades under the influence of centralized power, decision-making, and resource allocation in which financial efficiency was a secondary consideration. A major benefit of this was that affordable mass housing was provided in prime urban locations, but land was not always put to the most efficient use. Built environment professionals, including planners, were expected to meet centrally determined targets, rather than to balance needs and resources based upon independent assessments. Subsequently, all the countries were encouraged by international donors to adopt Western market-based approaches to economic management for which they had no experience and limited capacity. Mongolia experienced a rush of foreign investment when a massive deposit of copper and gold was discovered in the south of the country in 2001. Foreign investment and expectations of sudden wealth for the country's small population led to a dramatic increase in GDP to the point where Mongolia recorded the highest economic growth rate globally in 2012. However, limited experience in extracting the maximum public benefit from foreign mining corporations ended with an equally dramatic reduction in growth and limited resources to finance increasing social needs, including housing. Despite this experience, the continued application of a centralized approach to urban development and land management has resulted in dramatic proposals that have failed to take financial viability into account.

Albania and Cambodia both experienced extreme forms of repressive, authoritarian government that denied their populations even the most basic rights. However, this was not imposed by outside powers, but by local ideologues intent on imposing classless societies using brute force. In each country, many key personnel from the previous regimes remain in positions of influence (Quackenbush, 2019).

The trauma experienced by the populations of all three countries with similar experiences has cast a long shadow from which they are only now emerging and the siren voices of simple solutions to complex problems proved attractive but required frequent legislative and regulatory changes that remain unresolved. In each country, allegations of corruption resulting from limited democratic accountability have inhibited progress, though the strengthening of civil society through social media is reducing the number of forced evictions and improving the institutional capacity to generate investment. What needs to be done now is to strengthen the ability of the state to negotiate with skill and determination to ensure that the benefits of inward and local investment are shared more equally.

Notes

1. Law No. 7698 of 15 April 1993, On Restitution and Compensation of Properties to Former Owners, revised by Law No. 9235 of 29 July 2004, On Restitution and Compensation of Property.
2. Agency for Property Restitution and Compensation (Agjencia e Kthimit dhe Kompensimit të Pronave)
3. Kelm (2009) cites information that between 2005 and 2008, compensation has only been paid to original owners for 6.6 per cent of the area claimed.
4. Agency for Legalisation, Urbanisation and Integration of Informal Areas and Buildings (in Albanian: Agjencia e Legalizimit, Urbanizimit dhe Integrimit the Zonave dhe Ndertimeve Informale)
5. Scurrah and Hirsch (2015) cite evidence from: 1) Amnesty International (2008); 2) Centre on Housing Rights and Evictions (2011: i–viii, 1–33); and 3) Mgbako et al. (2010: 39–76).

CHAPTER 12
From customary to market: Lesotho and Vanuatu, with lessons from part two

Of all the systems by which land is valued, used, and developed, by far the oldest is that of customary practice. Originally applicable throughout North America, sub-Saharan Africa, and Australasia, it remains common in rural areas and is a sensitive issue as urban areas, developed under various statutory forms of land management, expand into areas held under the traditional regimes. The following examples highlight some of the challenges posed. Lessons from these and the other country case studies in Chapters 9, 10, and 11 are summarized at the end of this chapter.

Lesotho

Carved into the rock at the mountain pass that leads down into the plain of Malealea, in the mountainous, landlocked country of Lesotho, is a sign that reads 'Pause a-while, ye traveller, and gaze upon the gates of Paradise'. Such an injunction is well justified, given the view that opens up of an unspoilt mountain landscape, home to Basotho villagers, and a retreat for visitors seeking exercise and calm after the hectic life of the capital, Maseru. Although classified as a lower-middle-income country, 70 per cent of this small country's population live in rural areas as subsistence farmers under harsh conditions. These conditions are becoming even harsher as a result of climate change, with drought, flooding, and extreme temperatures threatening already vulnerable livelihoods and food security. In recent decades, many men migrated to work in South Africa and remittances from workers has been a key source of income. However, it also contributed to Lesotho suffering one of the highest HIV rates in the world and an associated AIDS pandemic. Poor health and poverty have severely constrained national population growth and estimates of life expectancy vary between 40 and 52 (Kingdom of Lesotho, 2015; UN-Habitat, 2015). Other migrants moved to the urban areas, particularly the capital Maseru, established by the British administration in 1869.

Land in Lesotho is vested in the Basotho nation and is held in trust by the King, who has the power to grant lease titles for a maximum period of 90 years (UN-Habitat, 2015: 53). Until 1980, village chiefs, acting on behalf of the King, allocated land without payment using a Form C. The principle of equity is central to traditional land allocation practices, so plot sizes in rural areas tend to be generous, allowing for privacy and small-scale farming. When arriving in urban areas, rural migrants accept that they have to pay for land, but still expect plot sizes to be generous (Hall, 2004: 27). This is reflected in the official minimum residential plot area of 375 m^2, though this is frequently exceeded and one urban resident told me that anything less than 600 m^2 was too small.

An amendment to the 1979 Land Act in 1980 removed the land allocation role of the chiefs in urban and peri-urban areas. However, rapid urban growth, combined with competition and overlapping responsibilities between central and local government departments, meant that neither the State nor the market was able to meet increasing needs, so chiefs have continued for many years to simply back-date the Form C documents to a date before their authority ceased. Customary tenure was abolished under the 2010 Land Act, and responsibility for allocating leases was delegated to the Director of Lease Services at the Land Administration Authority (LAA) for a modest cost. However, the majority of Maseru's population continue to occupy land with a traditional Form C and it is even possible to transfer a plot held under a Form C into a lease, even if not acquired legally. This disadvantages women as, under customary practice, they are prohibited from owning land. Although the 2010 Land Act overruled customary barriers to women owning land, discrimination continues because of cultural attitudes. In addition, the State proved unable to allocate anything like the number of leases required to increase the proportion of formally developed land and housing, and the official government report to Habitat III acknowledged that the role of chiefs in land allocation remains unresolved and 'the management of urban land remains chaotic' (Leduka, 2012; Kingdom of Lesotho, 2015: 19).

Until recently, the cost for an allocated lease was lower than the cost of surveying the plots and completing the administrative procedures, an issue that severely reduced the number of leases allocated, though this has increased significantly under the LAA. However, even in the gazetted areas, the 2010 Land Act entitles any citizen to occupy one plot for his or her own residential use free of ground rent (UN-Habitat, 2015), so revenues from land and property have been extremely limited, constraining the ability of the authorities to finance infrastructure provision and meet other basic needs. Consequently, the city council budget has rarely been sufficient to cover recurrent expenditure, let alone undertake capital works or investment. Furthermore, the lack of clear policies and effective governance has resulted in sporadic, low-density development and encroachments onto fertile agricultural land (see Photo 12.1). Endemic corruption, weak land administration, and low-density development have resulted in urban sprawl and made the costs of providing infrastructure prohibitive. This in turn makes public transport uneconomic and many people have to walk long distances to get to work, or even to a bus stop, while the traffic from the wealthy minority and government employees with car allowances combine to increase pollution and congestion in the city centre.

To improve institutional capability, USAID funded the Millennium Challenge Corporation (MCC) to prepare a land administration reform

Photo 12.1 Housing on land allocated by a local chief in Maseru, Lesotho
Credit: Geoffrey Payne

project (Leduka, 2012). This introduced 'one-stop shops' and simplified procedures, which dramatically reduced the time and cost of registering leases. However, the transition from a customary to a statutory approach has proved challenging, and attempts to reconcile the interests of customary practices of land management in peri-urban Maseru with the need to put available land to efficient use have yet to bear fruit. A land pooling/land readjustment project was proposed in 2000 on the southern edge of Maseru to enable existing landowners to remain in the area, benefit financially from urban development, and also ensure that newly urbanized land would be put to efficient use. The proposal was abandoned, partly due to institutional reservations and limited expertise in negotiating with leaseholders and private corporations on managing land in ways that balanced the needs of all concerned while maximizing public benefits. However, the concept has since been revived under the Maseru Urban Planning Project (MUPP). It is hoped that the widespread institutional inertia and risk aversion within the public sector that was observed during the earlier study has been replaced with a more enterprising approach to land administration, as this is essential for progress to be made.

Efforts at land reform under the 2010 Land Act had mixed outcomes. The most significant change was the introduction of systematic land titling which permitted the retrospective legalization of informal land allocations. Unfortunately, this was undertaken without adjustments to frequently irregular plot layouts, making subsequent upgrading more difficult and expensive.

This reflects an ambiguous approach by government and the population to the core objective of the Act which was to 'modernize land administration, regularize peri-urban land and settlements, facilitate investment, including foreign investment and create land markets, and abolish customary land tenure in rural areas' (Leduka, 2012: 9). The cultural traditions which had enjoyed social legitimacy for generations were to be replaced by 'modern' systems of valuing land and housing that even senior ministers were ambivalent about supporting.

The role of the chiefs in land administration has had a major impact on outcomes. One might expect that as demand for reasonably well-located urban land increases, leaseholders would be incentivized to redevelop plots at higher density to realize the potential incomes or increment in capital values. However, this outcome seems slow to appear, possibly due to the competing interests of chiefs representing the customary values and a government seeking to impose what are seen as alien statutory systems. Hall (2004: 63) reports a general sense of inertia in government, 'resulting in *any reforms in any sector* taking years to implement', a fear of 'rocking the boat' and creating resentment from those opposed to change, and in doing so putting their own jobs in jeopardy. These attitudes and a long period of political instability have severely constrained the government's progress. In this respect, it is perhaps significant that in the 1998 riots that damaged many government buildings in central Maseru, the offices of the Chieftainship that held land records were untouched.

The division of responsibilities for land management between different government ministries and departments has constrained institutional capability in the application of progressive approaches that can reconcile customary and more market-sensitive approaches to land and housing provision. The combined efforts of the MCC and the state-owned Lesotho Housing and Land Development Corporation failed to provide more than a small amount of land or housing, and much of what was provided was for middle-income owner-occupiers. This forced many households and predominantly single female factory workers into the private rental sector in *malaenes* (rows of single and double rooms with shared latrines and water supply, in informal settlements). Some affluent investors are even reported (Leduka, 2012: 23) to have obtained land on which to provide *malaenes* as an investment. Opportunities exist to make money through land allocations for personal benefit that undermine the social legitimacy of the customary system, to the point where it has been considered neo-customary (Leduka, 2012: 22).

Key stakeholders created the Lesotho Vision 2020 in 2004 to provide a long-term perspective for the country, and this has now become official policy (Kingdom of Lesotho, 2004). However, proposals to enhance the contribution of urban areas, or clarify the sensitive issue of land tenure and the role of the chiefs, were omitted. The key role Maseru had been playing in national development was recognized in the 2010 Maseru Urban Planning and Transport Study. This proposed to throw a cordon around the urban boundary to prevent further urban sprawl and develop 80,000 new dwelling units at higher density. A range of measures were proposed to achieve this, including a complex range of reduced plot sizes and plot development options down to a minimum of 150 m^2. However, little action was taken; the official minimum plot size area of 375 m^2 remains in place and the delivery of land by government and its agencies has been minimal compared to other actors in housing delivery. As a result, 53 per cent of households in Maseru have acquired land from customary chiefs and only 13 per cent from government agencies (UN-Habitat, 2015: 59).

More than 5,000 new urban dwellings a year are needed to meet demand linked to population growth and to reduce overcrowding (UN-Habitat, 2015). A National Housing Policy was formally adopted by Cabinet (Kingdom of Lesotho, 2018) to address this and contains abundant commitments to increase, expand, improve, and facilitate a functioning land and housing market though, as with the Vision 2020, the policy is noticeably short on specifics. One positive achievement has been to improve the construction permit process by moving from a manual to an electronic and automated system, thereby reducing the time and cost of issuing permits.

The announcement in 2019 of the MUPP or 'Maseru2050' project supported by the Private Sector Competitiveness and Economic Diversification Project (PSCEDP), a government initiative backed by the World Bank, promises to inject new momentum into urban development policy. The thrust of the plan is to promote sustainable urban development in Lesotho through a variety of coordinated and integrated community, public, and private sector interventions. According to one press release, this involves systematically curing 'the haphazard nature of Maseru's settlements that have hindered the city's growth and stifled its potential' (PSCEDP, n.d.). However, this can be expected to cause concern to the majority of the city's population currently living in unapproved settlements since international experience shows that, when inward investment is encouraged, market-driven evictions and displacement are a common outcome (Durand-Lasserve, 2006).

Another recent proposal that will need careful handling is the plan to establish a number of special economic zones. Had these been adopted when originally proposed two decades ago, Lesotho could have become an international leader. However, it was not until 2018 that the Lesotho National Development Corporation incorporated the option in its strategic development plan, and commissioned a feasibility report that was published in December 2019 (Vivid Economics, 2019). While this report is welcome, the approach has by now been adopted in many cities worldwide, raising concerns that the extent and nature of demand will need to be carefully calibrated to avoid over-provision. Experience shows that competition between cities to attract an unpredictable amount of private investment reduces the public benefit and could easily result in expenditure exceeding revenues. It will also be vital to ensure that investors are not given priority over the needs of local people when the country is recovering from a bad harvest that is leaving many people on the edge of starvation. Fortunately, the Lesotho National Dialogue and Stabilization Project launched in 2019 acknowledges the need for such an inclusive approach and offers hope for a change in policy and practice. The MUPP has also initiated an extensive stakeholder engagement plan involving more than 50 people, including chiefs, who had been actively involved in the planning process until the Covid-19 pandemic intervened. It includes a professional communication strategy and a civic capacity-building programme for the development of affordable housing and densification. This work will include publishing and promoting simple brochures advising leaseholders how to put their plots to the most effective use by increasing housing density. It is hoped that public support can be generated and maintained throughout the course of the project by closely engaging the community in the design of the plan.

Hopefully, the government will commit to detailed policies and a clear timeline for their implementation. With statutory systems well-established in urban areas and customary practices even more deeply ingrained in rural areas, the peri-urban areas are the stage upon which the different actors are seeking to establish a new modus operandi. This suggests that the chiefs and the state will have to come to a shared understanding on how to value and manage land and housing that is economically efficient, but also reflects local needs, resources, and cultural traditions. After a politically volatile period, the people of Maseru deserve no less. However, it will likely need time for the Basotho nation to regain Paradise.

Vanuatu

The island republic of Vanuatu has the distinction of being ranked as having the highest disaster risk of any country in the world (Birkmann and Welle, 2016), exposed as it is to sea level rise, active volcanoes, earthquakes (due to its location on the Pacific 'Ring of Fire'), and tropical cyclones that regularly cause widespread destruction. By what measure can we therefore begin to understand how it is also designated by the Lonely Planet guide as the happiest place on earth?

A large part of the answer lies in the strong sense of community in the predominantly rural areas of the various islands. Small island populations with a customary system of governance enable people to feel involved in decision-making and imposes minimal pressure on non-renewable resources that reduce the ecological footprint, while the environmental threats have made people extremely resilient. The strong sense of community is well-expressed in the traditional architecture of different cultural traditions, as shown in the design of a chief's meeting house, or *nakamal* (see Photo 12.2). These structures consist of an ovoid plan shape and face away from the sea to avoid cyclones, and also function as community centres for meetings, weddings, and funerals (Christian and Salong, 2018). Under the customary system of governance,

Photo 12.2 Traditional *nakamal* in Nguna Island, Vanuatu
Credit: Geoffrey Payne

chiefs play a key role in establishing and maintaining the rules by which each community is organized, but in each case active participation is normal.

Rural housing is typically constructed using a timber frame with horizontal bracing and a covering of coconut palm leaves or whatever other materials are locally available. Such buildings are lightweight and can be oriented to minimize exposure to the elements. When Cyclone Pam struck in 2015, and Cyclone Harry in 2020, villagers took advantage of the national climate monitoring system to move themselves and their valuables to a safe building such as a school or church and waited until the storm had passed before venturing out. Invariably, the wind had removed the houses' covering, leaving the exposed structure. However, people also found other materials had been blown down from the trees so were able to re-cover their homes and continue as before. Such is the strength of community cohesion in some villages that residential plot boundaries may not be clearly defined or enforced, and it is not uncommon for the graves of deceased family members to be scattered between homes, so that the dead remain as members of the living community. Both land and housing are valued exclusively as social assets with the adjacent land sufficient for subsistence agriculture. Unfortunately, the increasing intensity of cyclones is threatening the future availability of materials to maintain *nakamals*, threatening the future of Vanuatu's vernacular heritage (Christie, 2017).

It would therefore be naïve and incorrect to conclude that the lives of ni-Vanuatu are free of problems. The population of 300,000 is spread over half of the country's 83 islands, limiting the provision of health and education facilities for the rural communities on the smaller islands. Gender inequality is high, with bride price contributing to a situation in which 60 per cent of women in a relationship have experienced physical or sexual violence. These factors help to explain why Vanuatu is ranked 140 out of 189 countries in the Human Development Index (UNDP, 2020). Approximately 75 per cent of the national population live in rural areas, though migration to urban areas is increasing, and an estimated 114,000 people live in the capital, Port Vila, and the adjacent peri-urban area. The city's population is increasing by more than 4 per cent a year, requiring at least 1,000 new housing units to be provided annually, excluding the replacement of older or substandard stock. As a result, land has become a key resource in enabling the existing and incoming urban populations to find somewhere to live and build a better future. However, this is not simply a matter of finding and paying for a plot on which to build a house.

Nearly all rural, rapidly growing peri-urban, and non-declared urban land in Vanuatu is held under customary or *kastom* landholding. The remainder is held by government in gazetted physical planning/urban areas, including in Port Vila and Luganville. The 1983 Land Lease Act allowed for land held under customary tenure to be leased for a period of up to 75 years for investors. As Port Vila's population increased, the area of public landholding rapidly proved insufficient to accommodate the urban population and so pressure increased on the urban peripheries of Port Vila and Luganville where land is held under *kastom* tenure. It was alleged that leases were being approved by government that were opposed by members of local communities, and in 2006 a National Land Summit was held to address concerns.

A key resolution of the summit was that 'the ownership of land by groups and *not* individuals was a "rule of custom" described in article 74 of the *Constitution*' (Regenvanu, 2008: 67). This illustrates the conflicting systems of valuing land between customary and statutory systems of land governance and the need for the former to protect the interest of future generations. A secondary consideration is that, while individual interests in land are not relevant in small rural communities, they become central in urban areas where plots are occupied by individual households that need legal protection, especially as leases become increasingly expensive. Land governance in Vanuatu, therefore, exemplifies the challenges facing countries where land has been held, managed, and valued for an extended period under customary rules in which commercial interests are absent and even alien. As noted by Stefanova et al. (2012), land leasing practices in Vanuatu have failed to take into account the customary principles of group landholding, leading to inequitable outcomes for landholders.

Although the area had been settled by Melanesian communities for centuries, Port Vila was only declared the national capital in 1906, when it was the home to British and French commercial settlers, and ni-Vanuatu were prohibited from living there unless employed locally. When the country became a tax haven in 1971, a construction boom provided better conditions for the small, mainly foreign, population, and residential plots of 1,000 m^2 or more were the official norm. Such generous provision of land was understandable when the city's population was extremely small. However, it became difficult to justify when population growth and an increasing proportion of new development began to take place in the urban periphery on land held under the customary tenure system.

In most contexts globally, the local authorities would finance the provision of basic services to new developments from a wide range of revenue sources. However, Vanuatu's tax haven status has deprived the government of the revenues needed to provide essential services, and no taxes are levelled on incomes or capital gains. The country has also attracted the attention of international regulators following the publication of the Panama Papers, and the local authorities have acknowledged that money laundering and drug trafficking have to be addressed. The government is reliant on regressive revenue-raising schemes such as value-added tax (VAT) and other taxes on goods and services, while a scheme enabling foreigners to acquire 'golden passports' for $130,000 accounted for 42 per cent of all government revenue in 2020 (Ward and Lyons, 2021). The other major contributor to the economy and to government revenues is that of tourism, with cruise ships arriving regularly. The Economic Citizenship Programme, by which foreigners can obtain a residential lease for a single payment of about $50,000, has helped the economy, but at the price of denying the local population access to prime coastal areas increasingly occupied by gated communities. A third of Port Vila's population live in high-density, substandard housing with limited security or access to public services (see Photo 12.3). Since they are not able to obtain materials from the local environment as they could in the villages, people obtain what they can from local hardware stores and build basic shelters on spare land left over from formally planned developments.

Photo 12.3 Typical low-income housing in Port Vila
Credit: Geoffrey Payne

To ensure that available urban land was put to optimal use under increasing pressure from a growing population and the climate crisis, the government approved a National Land Use Planning Policy in 2013 promoting inclusive and resilient development. However, this had a largely rural focus and did not provide the necessary parameters for urban land subdivision and development. As a result, development applications were being reviewed and approved in a piecemeal, slow (approximately 2 years), and opaque manner, including in highly hazardous areas such as coastal zones. Once applications were approved, land developers were not responsible for providing or maintaining roads, drainage, or other services. This resulted in 1) sprawl into increasingly hazardous areas, and inefficient use of land; 2) the absence of infrastructure and service standards resulting in residential subdivisions without basic services such as water, sanitation, power, road access, and drainage (exacerbating flooding); 3) lack of environmental, social, and disaster risk considerations in the subdivision designs; 4) unclear institutional roles and responsibilities for regulation; and 5) lack of affordability considerations, particularly for low- and middle-income earners.

In 2014–15, the World Bank undertook a rapid needs assessment of housing in consultation with central and provincial government staff, customary chiefs and landowners, representatives of private sector groups, civil society organizations, and service providers. The study indicated that Port Vila would need an additional 10,000 residential plots by 2025 and that, to avoid developing particularly vulnerable areas and ensure housing was affordable to all in need, plot sizes would need to be reduced from the then-current minimum of 600 m^2. Following Tropical Cyclone Pam, the Public Works Department, UN agencies, the Red Cross, NGOs, and local civil society organizations formed the Shelter Cluster to coordinate assistance in reconstruction and disaster preparedness. Assistance encouraged the self-help concept and promoted the communities' adoption of effective preparedness measures, enabling the self-recovery process to commence immediately after the cyclone had passed. That they have had to start all over again following the destruction wreaked by Cyclone Harry in April 2020 and the Covid-19 pandemic, which has badly affected incomes from tourism, is further evidence of both Vanuatu's vulnerability and the resilience of its communities.

A later Bank mission in 2017 collaborated with key government stakeholders to address the need for affordable and resilient housing settlements in both the upgrading of existing settlements and new developments in Port Vila. In the absence of a spatial plan for Greater Port Vila, and with a zoning plan that was restricted to the municipal boundary, the study estimated that plot sizes of 350 m^2–500 m^2 and efficient land use planning would require an area of greater than 11 km^2 to meet housing needs for the next 15–20 years. However, the National Land Subdivision Policy (NLSP) (Government of the Republic of Vanuatu, 2019), announced in April 2019, stipulates minimum plot areas for residential development as 1,000 m^2 for low-density, 500 m^2 for medium-density and 400 m^2 for high-density developments, and applies on both *kastom* and public land. On-site or off-site sanitation systems are required in the absence of a city-wide reticulated network, though it would be sensible to plan new areas with this possibility in mind.

The NLSP raises a number of concerns. A combination of the stipulated plot sizes would require an even larger area of land to meet projected needs than estimated by the 2017 study, encroaching further into rural areas and leaving large sections of the population, few of whom have their own transport, facing expensive and polluting journeys to centres of employment and social amenities. It does not appear to be based upon any assessment of social, cultural, economic, or environmental considerations and will make it difficult for Vanuatu to meet Sustainable Development Goal 11, Target 11.3.[1] If a policy does not reflect local needs and resources, it is likely to remain on paper. If imposed through the regularization of existing settlements, it could well result in involuntary resettlement despite intentions to the contrary. Finally, by placing the planning and financial burden on developers without reliable evidence of the financial implications of these norms, the policy may fail to attract interest from both developers and households at the scale required. This suggests that a more holistic approach is needed that links plot size standards, infrastructure provision, transportation costs, and social considerations within an urban development strategy that provides easy access to commercial and social amenities and promotes a sense of community.

Fortunately, the government's Vanuatu Enabling Affordable and Resilient Settlements (VEARS) initiative announced in 2019 (World Bank, 2019c) presents the prospect for progress. It was the fruit of three years' intensive study with World Bank support and applies on both *kastom* and public land. It includes proposals that encourage a multi-pronged approach to the development of land to meet housing needs, and the upgrading and regularization of existing informal settlements within the context of managing and reducing disaster risk. It also provides the opportunity to undertake detailed socio-economic studies of the residents in existing primarily low-income settlements to understand how people relate to each other in the use of private and communal open space, their priorities and resources for the future, and what lessons this offers for the planning of new settlements. If the study were to suggest that new developments would benefit from the provision of different plot sizes, group landholding, multiple-occupation of plots, the provision of communal open space, and rental accommodation, it would provide a sound basis for updating the NLSP and developing innovative approaches to planning new settlements. These developments need to be integrated with neighbourhood centres to provide essential services and amenities. After all, a land subdivision policy is no substitute for a planning strategy that facilitates community development in ways that build on Vanuatu's unique cultural heritage, in the same way that protecting the *nakamals* is recognized as important. The VEARS initiative offers the opportunity to develop innovative demonstration projects that can be applied at scale, and also build local institutional capability; hopefully, the opportunity will be taken.

As Vanuatu moves from a primarily rural and agricultural society, in which land is regarded as a communal asset and people are trustees for future generations, to an increasingly urban society, in which land is allocated to individual households and managed partly by the state and the *kastom* system, imagination and perseverance will be required to both maintain a sense of social cohesion and meet people's need to have easy access to opportunities for social and economic development. Maintaining the ethos of community within the city will present a major challenge and will require close collaboration between *kastom* owners, developers, the state, and community groups.

A custom-made approach

The experiences of Lesotho and Vanuatu have one major element in common. Each is struggling in its own way to reconcile vastly different, and in some respects incompatible, concepts and practices of valuing land and housing. Transition from a system in which each generation is a trustee for the future and lives within modest means to one in which land is a tradeable asset like any other resource cannot be managed quickly or painlessly.

In seeking to promote economic growth, international support has focused on helping countries to attract inward investment. This invariably involves foreign investors seeking access to land that meets their need for security of tenure, where statutory arrangements are their priority as they are the only form of arrangement they know. How can these needs be reconciled with the needs of customary owners to retain the principle of trusteeship? At the same time, how can exploitation of the increasing competition for urban and peri-urban land by traditional authorities seeking to extract maximum personal benefit at the expense of their communities be minimized? The evidence also shows that, while many migrants from rural areas find statutory land tenure systems incomprehensible, some adapt quickly to their personal advantage, undermining the ethos and social legitimacy of the customary system.

Many other countries are experiencing these challenges. In Ghana, for example, Gillespie (2015: 70) reports that 'Prior to 1957, land was acquired to enable rational town planning and provide facilities essential to the functioning of the colonial enterprise, such as bungalows for civil servants. Following decolonization, land was expropriated by the developmental state for projects considered to serve the national interest'. He concludes that:

> The state land system in contemporary Accra functions as an instrument of accumulation by urban dispossession that expropriates land historically used as a communal means of social reproduction ('commons') and transforms it into a factor of production for an emerging luxury real-estate market. When interviewed about the state land system, government officials argued that the role of the state was to enable private-sector-led development by facilitating access to land for

developers who would otherwise be discouraged by the complexities of the customary land system.

At the same time that the state is eroding the customary system in favour of a small elite, so the customary leaders themselves are undermining it for personal gain. According to a study by Nyasulu (2012: 2) of Kasoa, a peri-urban area of Ghana's Central Region, 'The chiefs within this institution have exhibited special interest in increased land value that is not necessarily in line with those of the people in the local communities'. Another study of land development in Yendi municipality by Leyawdeen (2017) found that brokers had become a major factor in enabling customary chiefs to raise land prices at the expense of the local population. They have now become so effective and efficient in this role that most land buyers acquire their lands through the brokers, undermining the ethos of customary tenure. In another case, Yaro (2009) finds that the customary system seems to be crumbling, leading to growing inequalities in access, control, and ownership.

Similar processes apply in Uganda, which has established a system of land tribunals to resolve frequent disputes over land as the customary system is replaced by a statutory regime of land governance. While the tribunals can adjudicate cases within months, decisions can be appealed to the regular Court of Appeals system and beyond to the High Court and, given the backlog, this process can take considerably longer. As a result, conflicts over land are likely to increase. National NGOs, such as the Land Equity Movement of Uganda, argue that privileging purely legal approaches to land tenure, which require an educated grasp of English and a familiarity with the concepts of European statutory law, only helps those interested in large-scale commercial land development, while effectively disenfranchising millions of poor people in urban and rural areas (UN-Habitat, 2010).

With customary tenure applying in rural areas and statutory tenure in the urban areas of many countries, a major problem arises when urban areas expand. Naturally, residents who claim they acquired their plot by payment or through a relationship with a customary owner are unlikely to want to pay again to a system that is not understood or regarded as fair. In addition, procedures for allocating land under colonial administrations still cast a long shadow over the allocation, development, and transfer of land, leading to widespread allegations of corruption.

While the customary system is, therefore, under strain in all countries, it remains a powerful cultural influence and will exert pressure on those in power to make concessions in order to balance the need for economic growth and social stability. Experience suggests that key elements for making progress are dialogue and time. There are encouraging signs of these being adopted in both Lesotho and Vanuatu. Remaining open to the possibility of new forms of land management that can combine the clarity of statutory tenure with the principle of trusteeship could help in the development of new forms of tenure that reflect local needs in all countries moving from customary to market-based systems of land management. What would be truly progressive is that the ethos of customary practice permeates market-based approaches.

Lessons from Part Two

The case studies in Part Two demonstrate that the global path to loosely regulated market-based land management and housing provision is not only difficult, but is also not what most people need or want. This is most clearly shown in the example in Chapter 9 of the UK, where market forces have been virtually unrestrained during recent decades. Yet the notion of a 'property-owning democracy' has been exported, and even imposed, on countries throughout the Global South, forcing them to compete for inward investment on terms dictated by foreign investors and speculators, and not to meet local needs. This has inflated urban land and housing prices to unsustainable levels and increased the burden of private debt. Home-owners are highly unlikely to vote for a political party that threatens the market value of their hard-won assets, so prospects for major change are unlikely unless pressure from the disadvantaged younger generation, or external factors such as increased inflation, lead to market failure.

It is also clear from Chapter 10 that strongly centralized state management of the supply of urban land and housing, as in China, Cuba, and Ethiopia, is no guarantee that the varied and changing needs of local communities will be met. Although the Communist Party in Vietnam has ultimate responsibility for land and housing policy nationally, local governments have been more pragmatic in stimulating a wide range of local developers to provide land and housing in ways that are both highly efficient economically and responsive to needs socially and culturally. Vietnam therefore offers valuable lessons to other countries in similar situations.

For countries that have already transitioned from state-controlled forms of economic management to market-based systems, Chapter 11 records how the limited understanding of how land and housing markets operate, and the failure to develop appropriate institutional frameworks to manage markets in the public interest, has resulted in a tendency for elites from previously state-managed regimes to maximize the benefits for themselves. In such contexts, progressive change is likely to be best advanced if it is in the interests of those in power as well as the majority.

The final group of case studies in Part Two addressed the ways countries transitioning from customary forms of managing land and housing towards market-based systems are faring. Chapter 12 showed that, in these cases, the change is not only one of management but of the ethos in which land is conceived socially. Instead of maximizing economic value, customary practices prioritize social benefit and the concept of trusteeship, so change has undermined the social order, forcing individuals to fend for themselves. Prospects for progress may depend upon introducing communal forms of land and housing ownership and management that can combine the benefits of social and economic value. Fortunately, as we will see in the following chapters, many examples already exist that offer exciting possibilities for progress. If successful, these could even provide lessons for other countries suffering from the limitations of market-based approaches.

The need now is to increase the political will and institutional capability to manage markets in the public interest and also promote the concept of trusteeship as represented by the ethos of customary tenure. After all, we only occupy land and housing for a few decades and have a responsibility to leave it in better shape than we find it. Effecting change will take time and determination, and the reduced role and capacity of the state under neoliberalism has made it more difficult to analyse, oppose, and respond to the approaches advocated by commercial interests. Some might argue that people have become used to having free access to land under customary systems and now they will need to get used to having to pay market rates. However, the greatest achievement of neoliberalism is perhaps the way it has persuaded states and other non-commercial organizations to adopt 'value for money' criteria in the administration of public assets in place of social or environmental benefits. People who have inherited land and property through feudalism have thrived under neoliberalism. Others will be happy to exploit opportunities for personal gain. However, many brought up under socialist or customary values that enshrine land as a shared societal asset, including to be cared for and passed on in good shape to future generations, will struggle to accept its commodification and conversion into a product to be competed for by whoever can pay the most. The resolution of these differences will prove challenging for policy-makers at all levels of government, especially because those from previous regimes who still exert influence are likely to resist change.

Another key point is that it took countries which urbanized in the 19th century about 200 tumultuous years to formalize systems of land management that enjoyed social legitimacy, even though their populations were small. In the case of many Western European countries, this period was also defined by massive out-migration from countries like Ireland and Italy to North and South America, which relieved pressure on their overcrowded cities. They also enjoyed greater economic autonomy than is available to countries currently undergoing the same socio-economic and environmental transformation, many of which have been fully independent for only a few decades, have far larger numbers of people in need of land, housing, services, and employment. Many of these have to cope with the legacy of legal and institutional systems imposed upon them during the colonial period. It is therefore unrealistic to expect such countries to quickly evolve new ways of governance, land management, and tenure systems based on locally applicable social, cultural, institutional, and political realities.

While change will inevitably take time, the international community and built-environment professionals must determine whose interests they intend to serve. A start can be made by identifying objectively those systems of land management, tenure, and property rights that currently provide affordable access to adequately secure land with basic services and the opportunity to build housing that can be improved over time. This approach of learning from the poor and building on what works has enabled millions of people to assimilate into the urban economy and make a positive contribution. It does, however, require a major change in the mindset of those in positions of power and influence. It will also require governments to cease subsidizing individual ownership, and improve the security and attractiveness of other options, such as rental and non-market options.

The growth of urban populations will see intense competition for land in urban and peri-urban locations in almost all countries. Progress will depend largely upon how the struggle between competing interests and concepts of valuing land and housing is managed. Ongoing dialogue between key stakeholders, especially at local government level, will be essential to reconciling options that are culturally, environmentally, and economically sustainable, and could lead to innovative approaches that reflect local circumstances.

Having progressive and practical policies to meet these needs is a necessary, but insufficient, precondition. Skills in advocating policies and presenting proposals that reflect the legitimate concerns of different stakeholders will be as important as the policies and proposals themselves, and arguments that might appeal to policymakers whose careers flourished under socialism may not be applicable to those brought up under customary practices. It is to explore these aspects that we move to Part Three.

Note

1. 'By 2030, enhance inclusive and sustainable urbanization and capacity for participatory, integrated and sustainable human settlement planning and management in all countries' (United Nations, 2015).

PART III
What needs to be done

CHAPTER 13
Growth and sustainability

The previous chapters have considered some of the challenges facing international development from the basic consideration of finding somewhere to live that is decent and affordable. But after 50 years in the field, I find myself asking a very simple question: What do we mean by development? Is it the elimination of extreme poverty as proposed by the World Bank? Achieving universal happiness as advocated by Layard (2005)? Realizing capabilities or achieving freedoms as advocated by Sen (1999, 2009), who inspired the Human Development Index (Barder 2012)? Reducing inequality? Protecting the planet and other species? For anyone engaged in some form of social, economic, or environmental development, these are questions that require answers.

In recent decades, international and national development policies, including housing programmes and projects, have focused almost exclusively on the objective of increasing economic growth, giving 'value for money', getting a good return, and making a profit. At a global level, the evidence suggests this has been achieved for large sections of the global population, at least on paper. Economic growth during the last two centuries, and particularly recent decades, has succeeded in lifting hundreds of millions of people out of poverty. However, this has come at a heavy price. Market capitalism succeeded largely by pitting companies, countries, and individuals against each other in a 'survival of the fittest' approach. While those who succeeded under this system understandably considered themselves the 'fittest', the system itself has been exposed as creating a world that is not only grossly unequal, but economically and environmentally unsustainable to the point where it is driving humanity rapidly towards disaster.

Moving out of extreme poverty clearly improves living conditions and quality of life, as does moving out of relative poverty. However, for many in the Global North, and a minority in the Global South for whom economic growth has met their basic needs, we should ask to what extent more of the same is needed or appropriate. Has growth in incomes and assets become an end in itself rather than a means to an end?

With economic policies designed to promote growth, the richest in the world have every reason to feel successful. All they have done is to exploit the opportunities made possible by the current economic system. But is the achievement of material comfort all there is to development? Material comfort and success have clearly not made people better or happier. Pressure to succeed and meet ever-increasing expectations has triggered a rise in mental health problems, while anti-social behaviour shows little sign of declining as incomes increase. There is powerful evidence that, as incomes increase beyond the level sufficient to meet basic needs, the correlation between increased happiness and wellbeing declines to the point where it ceases altogether. As such, growth in incomes ceases to be a useful indicator of the quality of life, or provide a meaningful definition of progress. Perhaps it is time to focus on reducing excessive consumption.

What we need and what we want

If the Covid-19 pandemic has taught humanity anything, it is the value of people we usually take for granted: teachers, doctors, nurses, street cleaners, sewage workers, the police, supermarket workers, and other people who sustain public services. On a well-managed planet, one would assume that these people, on whom we all depend for our health and welfare, and whose work was designated by government as 'essential' during lockdowns, would be well respected and rewarded. Yet, as we found in Chapter 4, it is those who speculate with other people's money using increasingly creative financial instruments to bet on various market outcomes who are the most richly rewarded. Investors who use private equity and hedge funds to 'short' options and hedge their bets in the casino capitalism that we currently live in are the ones who reap the financial rewards promoted by neoliberal economics. All they are doing is playing by the rules of a game that has long ceased to follow any discernible norms of transparency, fair play, or equity.

So, at this unique moment in human history, what do we mean by development? Some years ago, a visiting ex-student introduced me to a book she was reading on happiness that got my interest. Visiting the local bookshop, I forgot the full title, but was surprised to be told that there was a complete section on the subject downstairs. Amazed, I found *Happiness: Lessons from a New Science* (Layard, 2005) among a large collection of books on wellbeing and self-help. Certainly, policies that make people happy are preferable to those that don't but, as Layard acknowledges, happiness needs to be seen as part of a more holistic approach to development. After all, despite being depressed to the point of considering suicide, Beethoven composed some of the greatest music in history, and Van Gogh created some of the most popular paintings. Both found an outlet that elevated them to greatness and made millions of other people happy in the process. Perhaps the definition of development should include the improvement of the wellbeing of the vulnerable as a measure for those of us living in relative comfort to lead meaningful lives?

This is the essence of the conclusions reached by the renowned epidemiologists Wilkinson and Pickett (2010: 8) following decades of research, who found that,

> whether we look at health, happiness or other measures of wellbeing, there is a consistent picture. In poorer countries, economic development continues to be very important for human wellbeing. Increases in their

material living standards result in substantial improvements both in objective measures of wellbeing like life expectancy, and in subjective ones like happiness. But as nations join the ranks of the affluent, developed countries, further rises in income count for less and less [on the happiness scale].

They acknowledge that 'In poorer countries, it is still essential to raise living standards and it is most important among the poorest. In those societies, a more equal distribution of resources will mean fewer people will be living in shanty towns, with dirty water and food insecurity, or trying to scrape a living from inadequate land-holdings'. Both across countries and over time, they found that high levels of depression, infant mortality, crime, drug abuse, and other negative social indicators were consistently higher in unequal societies than in more equal ones and that the situation improves if a country moves towards greater equality. As a result, they conclude (ibid: 29) that 'reducing inequality is the best way of improving the quality of the social environment, and so the real quality of life, for all of us [including] the better-off'.

So, for those living with a degree of financial security and in adequate housing, what is the point of spending more and more valuable, irreplaceable time, earning more and more money, for no apparent additional benefit? The economist John Maynard Keynes (1930: 5) predicted that technological innovation would be such that his grandchildren's generation would be able to meet all their needs working for about 3 hours a day, or 15 hours a week, enabling them to live 'wisely and agreeably and well'. Keynes was writing just after the Great Depression of the late 1920s when capitalism was under threat, and he sought to demonstrate that it could lead humanity to the promised land in which (ibid: 7):

> There will be ever larger and larger classes and groups of people from whom problems of economic necessity have been practically removed. The critical difference will be realized when this condition has become so general that the nature of one's duty to one's neighbour is changed. For it will remain reasonable to be economically purposive for others after it has ceased to be reasonable for oneself.

Not only have Keynes' predictions signally failed to materialize, levels of happiness are lower, and those in employment tend to be working even longer hours and with less job security than decades ago. In explaining what went wrong, Skidelsky and Skidelsky (2012) point out that he focused on the ability of technology to meet human needs, which are finite, whereas capitalism has succeeded by focusing our attention on *wants*, which modern advertising and marketing turn into an infinite source of consumer demand by creatively exploiting technological innovation to promote a constant stream of new wants that did not previously exist. 'Creative disruption', as discussed by Schumpeter (1942), building on the work of Marx, repeatedly replaces one technology with another, albeit to meet the same needs. Thus, the reel-to-reel tape recorder was replaced by the cassette, then the CD and more recently streaming in an endless cycle to meet the same need for recorded music. The regular releases of Apple iPhones and the worship of designer consumer goods are constant reminders of society's collective myopia. The aim of advertising is to make people feel the need to be in fashion even though this entails more time at work and less time for living wisely, agreeably, and well.

Skidelsky and Skidelsky (2012: 211) propose that preventing businesses from writing off advertising as a business expense would cut at the root of the advertising industry. As they note (ibid: 69), 'Capitalism rests precisely on this endless expansion of wants. That is why, for all its success, it remains unloved. It has given us wealth beyond measure, but has taken away the chief benefit of wealth: the consciousness of having enough'. They also point out that education aims to fit pupils for the job market by providing them with merely useful knowledge and skills. They envisage a future in which education will be informed by the understanding that the 'jobbing' part of a person's life will be a decreasing fraction of his or her waking life and that one of its main tasks will be to prepare people for a life of fulfilment outside of the job market.

The extent to which markets have penetrated all aspects of life and corrupted moral values is rigorously analysed by Sandel (2012: 8–9), who points out that 'in a society where everything is for sale, life is harder for those of modest means. The more money can buy, the more affluence (or the lack of it) matters'. He continues, 'Putting a price on the good things in life can corrupt them. That's because markets don't only allocate goods; they also express and promote certain attitudes towards the goods being exchanged'. It was the extension of this approach to even treating other people as commodities to be bought and sold that led to slavery. While it was the extent to which markets had lost all morality and had captured financial regulators that led to the 2008 financial crisis, Sandel points out that it discredited governments more than the banks. Serious debate about the role of markets, governments, and the economic infrastructure that triggered the crisis is still lacking.

Sandel (2020) follows his critique of the moral limits of markets by targeting the concept of meritocracy as a means of reducing inequality, which he argues hung the Western working class out to dry, with disastrous consequences for the common good. He demonstrates the fallacy of assuming that those who work hard and play by the rules will rise to the top. This theory fails because it assumes that everyone starts from a level playing field, which is clearly not true. Even though education can help compensate for unequal starting points, it is not a sufficient means of redressing this inequality. Sandel's main concern is that the concept of a meritocracy has been used to enable those at the top to claim that they got there by their own efforts, and implies that those who do not succeed have no one to blame but themselves. This dominant theory of meritocracy thus exempts elites from any responsibility for addressing underlying social and economic factors that lead to the inequality of opportunity.

The main conclusion from the research by Skidelsky and Skidelsky, Wilkinson and Pickett, Sandel, and numerous other researchers is that, while capitalism has reduced poverty and massively increased global wealth, it has failed to provide for a better quality of life, and promoted competition over collaboration. These dual shortcomings have led to social insecurity and economic inequality. All the evidence shows that community life is stronger in more equal societies, people become more public spirited and trust each other more, and are also more aware of the common good (Wilkinson and Pickett, 2020). This suggests that governments have a simple choice: spend time, effort, and resources on reducing inequality, or spend far more time, effort, and resources coping with the social and health consequences of inequality. Since the Covid-19 pandemic has exacerbated already high levels of inequality, Wilkinson (2020) concludes that 'The picture could hardly be clearer: almost all the problems that we know are related to social status within our society get worse when status differences are increased. If we want a less dysfunctional society and a healthier population, building back better means addressing the scourge of income inequality'. This advice comes with a warning from the Nobel Prize winning economist Joseph Stiglitz (2012: 288) who notes that:

> Throughout history the top 1 percent have [always had] the best houses, the best educations, the best doctors, and the best lifestyles, but there is one thing that money doesn't seem to have bought: an understanding that their fate is bound up with how the other 99 percent live. Throughout history, this has been something the top 1 percent eventually do learn. Often, however, they learn it too late.

Another dimension of inequality is reviewed by de Rivero (2010: 13–4) as applying to nations and their ability – or inability – to achieve development targets as have been understood by the Bretton Woods institutions, the World Bank and the International Monetary Fund. He argues that global economic conditions make it very difficult to enable the majority of the population in so-called developing countries to enjoy both a high living standard and personal freedoms, to the point where the very notion of development is a myth:

> The underdeveloped countries' elites, through a variety of national projects, have pursued the myth of development. This myth took on the shape of state intervention or of a socialist revolution and is now in the guise of a neoliberal capitalist revolution. In all these cases, the authorities have exacted mountains of social sacrifice without managing to eliminate poverty and establish a true civil society ruled by law and by democratic institutions. The cost of the Soviet model was shortages and lack of freedom; today, that of the neoliberal, capitalist variant is unemployment and social exclusion.

But de Rivero focuses his main concern on the environmental burden of what he calls the California Model of development. Based on a calculation of average lifetime resource consumption in different locations, he claims (de Rivero, 2010: 121–2) that, 'A baby born in California represents double the environmental burden for the planet caused by one in Sweden, three times that of an Italian baby, thirteen times that of one born in Brazil; thirty-five times that of a baby born in India; 140 times that of one born in Bangladesh; and 280 times that of one born in Chad, Rwanda, Haiti or Nepal'. This suggests that it is not the numbers of people globally that is putting the environment under pressure, but the levels of consumption by the wealthiest. The only way to achieve a sustainable future is, therefore, for the rich to consume significantly less and enable the poor to consume more. Experience also shows that fertility levels decrease as incomes and education levels increase (Fullerton, 2013), so improving incomes in the Global South can only help further to reduce overall consumption. Of course, as citizens in poor countries escape from poverty, individual consumption will increase, reducing the gap if citizens in rich countries consume less.

An additional barrier for poor countries to achieving the same level of material consumption as Californians is that, apart from oil-exporting countries, most rely for growth on exporting raw materials to rich countries that process them and capture the added value, often by exporting finished products such as petroleum or textiles back to the same countries that produced the raw materials. The decision to prolong an economic structure based on the export of raw materials is both a domestic political choice and the product of an unfair international trade regime that prioritizes the interests of wealthier nations, and the spread of Western-style democracy has failed to generate the economic benefits and freedom that it promised. As Bates (2010) demonstrates in the case of Africa, authoritarian governments benefitting from abundant natural resources were suddenly faced with organized opposition, and frequently resorted to predatory actions to remain in power in partnership with large global mining and oil and gas companies. Similarly, Hawksley (2009) draws on years of experience as a foreign correspondent to show that the promotion of liberal multi-party democracy by the West has resulted in increased violence and the impoverishment of masses of farmers in countries as diverse as Côte d'Ivoire, Argentina, Bosnia, and Iraq.

On the grounds of both environmental sustainability and social equity, the current model of development is clearly inappropriate and unsustainable. Even Keynes' recommendation that the road to recovery from a crisis is to increase consumption is not applicable at a time when we have already exceeded the planet's carrying capacity. The need to develop holistic criteria for assessing development in its social and environmental, as well as economic, dimension was recognized in 2011 when the United Nations General Assembly (2013) adopted a resolution which included happiness as a fundamental human goal. It called for a more inclusive, equitable, and balanced approach to economic growth that promotes happiness and wellbeing. This was followed in 2012 by the first UN High Level Meeting called *Wellbeing and Happiness: Defining a New Economic Paradigm*, which was jointly chaired by the UN Secretary-General and the Prime Minister of Bhutan. It produced the first World Happiness Report which has been published annually since. The UN General Assembly adopted a resolution at the 2012 conference that decreed that the International Day of Happiness would be observed every year on 20 March (United Nations, n.d.). It was celebrated for the first time in 2013.

Some governments are now beginning to move in the direction of accepting the need for new definitions of development and measures of progress towards it. While Finland and other Scandinavian countries regularly top the annual Happiness Index, soon after being elected in 2017, the New Zealand Prime Minister, Jacinda Ardern, announced that the government budget would be founded on the idea that financial prosperity alone is not a sufficient measure of the quality of life. The budget treats public policies as investments and applies over 60 indicators within the New Zealand Treasury's Living Standards Framework (Mintrom, 2019). Key components of the budget are to create new frontline services for mental health, reduce child poverty, reduce inequalities faced by Māori and Pacific Island people, expand digital services, and transition to a low-emission, sustainable economy.

New Zealand is perhaps the largest country, and the most affluent, to implement a national budget based on a new approach to development. However, it is not alone. The UK Office for National Statistics has begun to collect data on societal and personal wellbeing, looking beyond what is produced to areas such as health, relationships, education and skills, what people do, where they live, their finances, and the environment.

In formulating and applying new ways of measuring progress towards a broader definition of development, these affluent countries are learning from the experience of other, less affluent countries. Bhutan and Vanuatu, both of which are classified as lower-middle income countries according to the World Bank (2019e), with per capita gross national income (GNI) of around US$3,000, compared to GNI in the UK and New Zealand of around $40,000, have both prioritized happiness and wellbeing. Bhutan has even adopted Gross National Happiness instead of Gross Domestic Product as its main development indicator; Cuba scores highly in the Human Development Index (Loh and Wackernagel, 2004); while Vanuatu has topped the rankings of the wellbeing and environment Happy Planet Index (2021), despite being the most environmentally vulnerable country in the world due to its exposure to rising sea level, hurricanes, tsunamis, and earthquakes. It scores highly because its people are satisfied with their lot, live to nearly 70 and do little damage to the planet (Campbell, 2006).

Seeing more clearly

The Covid-19 pandemic has enabled us to see the world, and a possible better future, more clearly. That the Himalayan mountains could be seen from New Delhi because of the improved air quality made citizens aware of how bad the situation had become. The pandemic has provided compelling evidence of the benefits of structural change in development policy. With cities being major contributors to pollution, the scope for urban planning, development, housing, and land use policies to contribute to change is equally compelling.

So, if growth for its own sake is unsustainable and, beyond a certain level, even undesirable, where should investment be targeted? According to Stiglitz (2012: 283), investment and innovation should be redirected from saving labour to saving resources. Of these, land is clearly key in that it is undeniably finite and subject to increasingly intense use and competition.

Progressive wealth taxes can help, both in practical terms by reducing inequality, and by repaying public debt generated by the Covid-19 pandemic. They also send a signal to both the rich and poor that the concentration of wealth in a few hands is bad for all, including the rich. A more equal global distribution of wealth would enable all to have a basic income level, access to basic services, and adequate housing. Progressive wealth taxes are common in several European countries, including Portugal, Italy, Netherlands, Norway, and Switzerland, while Spain imposes taxes on assets above €700,000 and France raises €2 billion a year from wealth taxes paid by the 150,000 richest households.

Bregman (2017) takes the idea a stage further and proposes a universal basic income for which the only condition is that people have a pulse. He records that it was first proposed by Thomas More in 1516 in his book *Utopia*, and it has been tested in countries as diverse as Canada, Kenya, Malawi, Namibia, and the United Kingdom. It was even proposed by President Nixon in 1970 under the title of the Family Assistance Plan (Zelleke, 2019), only for it to founder years later in the Senate despite being considered within the country's economic and fiscal capacity. Trial runs of the policy demonstrated how concerns that a basic universal income would make people lazy were not justified as paid work barely declined, and people were able to spend more time on personal development such as education, contributing to a rise of 30 per cent in high-school graduation rates for children of participating families. Bregman argues that the policy would meet the political left's demand for fairness and give the political right a more limited government than ever by reducing the layers of bureaucracy associated with state welfare payment and monitoring of beneficiaries.

His proposal has been introduced to some extent in some rich countries where governments undertook to pay the majority of workers' wages during the Covid-19 pandemic. Allocating the money to individuals directly, extending this approach indefinitely, and allowing it to include a shorter working week, would free people to find more viable forms of economic activity, and pursue activities that reflect their interests and skills, generating new and socially meaningful economic opportunities. This, combined with the provision of basic services, could be funded by the introduction of progressive tax policies on wealth and land ownership, environmental pollution charges on both organizations and individuals, and the closure of tax havens. The launch of the Patriotic Millionaires movement (Gabbatt, 2019) and the Fight Inequality Alliance demonstrate that even some of the world's most wealthy individuals recognize the need to curb excessive concentrations of wealth and pay more tax. US President Biden's proposed global minimum tax on multinational corporations reflects increasing recognition of the need to prevent a 'race to the bottom' as countries compete to attract inward investment at any cost, while also ensuring corporations cannot evade tax responsibilities. The combined revenues from corporate and individual wealth taxes would help transform global and domestic economies in ways that improve the health and wellbeing of all, especially those who make the greatest contribution to society but were taken for granted until the Covid-19 pandemic struck. As always, of course, the devil is in the detail, and both accountants and tax lawyers have decades of experience in helping individuals, corporations, and even governments to avoid their social obligations.

Addressing the climate crisis

The Covid-19 pandemic has also helped us see that markets are completely ineffective in resolving major issues like the climate crisis. Never before have we had a demonstration that, ultimately, democratically accountable governments are the best means of determining how resources, costs, and benefits are most effectively allocated. Although each financial crisis forces us to realize how important the role of government is, the climate crisis represents a systemic risk many magnitudes greater than the cyclical collapse of financial markets. As Mazzucato (2013) has eloquently illustrated, many of what are considered the results of private sector investment and initiative are, in fact, the outcome of massive public investments in long-term research. While private corporations have reached historically unprecedented asset valuations (Apple shares reached $2 tn in 2020), much of the technology they employ was developed as a result of high-risk state research and investment, yet the state has not received anything like the recognition or return on its investment compared to that of shareholders. In fact, the state is often blamed in right-wing media outlets for wasting resources and taxpayers' hard-earned money on investment in research and public education systems.

While Mazzucato admires the innovative achievements of tech corporations, she argues (ibid: 176) that 'Key to the future of the green revolution taking off will be the building of innovation ecosystems that result in *symbiotic* public-private partnerships rather than parasitic ones'. Gore (2006) also proposes a new relationship between the state and market capitalism in which state policies and business practices take into account their impacts on the environment – both positive and negative – rather than regarding them as 'externalities'. Focusing on redistribution rather than growth in the Global North will also reduce demand on non-renewable energy sources until renewables are able to meet projected needs.

The drumbeat for action on climate risk has intensified recently and only powerful vested interests in the high emissions energy and transport sectors, or those governments in hock to them, can explain their wilful ignorance in the face of overwhelming scientific evidence explaining the severity and urgency of the crisis. Other political leaders have responded with fine words in the hope of appeasing public pressure but without committing to specific actions. However, unprecedented storms, fires, droughts, and high temperatures since 2000 have combined to create a rare example of leaders being led by the people. Prompted by the Swedish school strike by the teenager Greta Thunberg in 2018, 1.6 million young people covering 125 countries attended youth strikes the following year demanding action on the climate crisis. Mass movements such as Extinction Rebellion and the Sunrise Movement in the USA also reflect increasing public demand for change, and political leaders are beginning to respond. The Urgenda campaign in the Netherlands even took the government to court and forced Royal Dutch Shell to reduce its emissions.

As one of the world's largest total producers of carbon emissions, China experienced a dramatic reduction during the pandemic and announced an ambitious pledge to reduce carbon emissions to net-zero by 2060, which will require a major restructuring of its economy, with a focus on the energy and transport systems. Also, in 2020 the European Commission announced a radical Green Deal regulatory package that would channel more than a trillion dollars towards making Europe carbon neutral by 2050 and restructure national economies to align with the same target. The Intergovernmental Panel on Climate Change report (IPCC, 2021a) provides a clear policy warning, and campaigners at the COP26 global climate change conference make abundantly clear the extent of change needed to prevent a global catastrophe. However, announcements on global and national policies are the easy part, even if all countries commit. The real test is what governments, businesses, and citizens actually do. While the costs of change will be high, the costs of inadequate action will be far, far higher and irreversible.

Government commitments made at the 2021 COP26 conference held in the UK failed to restrict average global temperature to 1.5°C above pre-industrial levels and discussions continue. The scale of the challenge means that even the full implementation of radical government plans will not be sufficient on its own to prevent a climate catastrophe. Individual and corporate investors, including pension funds, have a key role in ensuring that investment is made exclusively in companies that accept their social and environmental responsibilities, and have a demonstrated purpose other than returning all profits to their shareholders and boosting executive pay. Enormous and sustained public pressure will be needed for the foreseeable future if fine words are to be followed by action on the ground – and in the air and sea. As with the Sustainable Development Goals, progress will need to be monitored in every country and published in relevant United Nations agencies and the

IPCC. Indeed, the publication of Nationally Determined Contributions (NDCs), as committed to by all countries in the Paris Agreement, requires this (UNFCCC, 2016), and many private companies are committing publicly to similar targets (UNFCCC, 2020). Every community, household, and individual will also need to change behaviour.

Consuming less and wasting less need not, however, be as hard as it may appear to those already enjoying the fruits of economic growth. Striving to make the most of what we have, especially time, creates ample opportunities to be creative and find fulfilment. Incentives that recognize and reward cycling rather than driving, for example, such as introducing a personal carbon allowance with progressive tax rates on higher emission levels, can help to curb excesses, and GDP could be replaced as a measure of development with criteria that promote human wellbeing and long-term environmental sustainability over consumption.

Migration

Even partial implementation of the measures outlined above would help dramatically to reduce inequality, globally and nationally. It would give those in the Global South less need to endure the enormous risks of migrating to the Global North for a better future since prospects would be improved at home. This would, in turn, reduce pressure on communities receiving large numbers of migrants and refugees.

The current global economy is organized to enable money to be transferred anywhere in the world within a nanosecond, though people are prevented from moving to areas of greater opportunity in the Global North, which has effectively become a vast gated community with increasingly militarized borders. The only effective way to reduce migration is to reduce global inequality through a massive redistribution of wealth. Clearly, those in power under the present system are unlikely to accept this. However, present trends are in danger of creating such high levels of inequality that change will be forced upon the incumbent political classes. Surely, it is better that this be a peaceful and organized transition, especially if it makes the world a better place for everyone. The challenge is how to make this change look as attractive as possible so that political leaders across the ideological spectrum will take action.

One option that could help both migrants and the local economies of the Global North is to encourage those approved for entry into Europe to settle into, and help rebuild, the vast number of small towns and villages in France, Italy, Spain, UK, USA, and other countries that have been abandoned by local populations, who themselves moved to urban areas. Many of these towns are in a bad state of decay, yet have enormous potential for creating socially and economically viable communities if the process is managed so that the needs and interests of existing, predominantly older residents are well protected (Nadeu, 2016; Harris, 2019; Jones, 2019; Hall, 2020; Ling, n.d.).

This has already been achieved in the case of the Italian town of Sutera, where the mayor took in survivors of the devastating Lampedusa shipwreck in 2013. In the years since the initial arrivals, more refugees have settled here, giving new life to a once-depleted town. According to Needleman (2017),

> Sutera's population had dwindled from 5,000 in 1970 to just 1,500, and the mayor recognized the humanitarian and economic opportunity the migrants could provide for his moribund town. To help the refugees, most of whom are from sub-Saharan Africa, integrate into the community, they are paired with local families, and required to take Italian lessons, given to them by the town's citizens. (The European Union provides funding for food, clothing and housing, which can spur the creation of jobs for both migrants and locals.) Initially, there was some resistance, but that has disappeared with the energy these newcomers have brought to the area. Today, one can find young Nigerians taking their morning espresso alongside the old men, and local children kicking soccer balls in the street with their new playmates. And each summer the town hosts a daylong festival featuring the traditional food, music and dance of the immigrants.

If local leadership can achieve this level of success in one town, why could it not be replicated elsewhere to the mutual benefit of both migrants and local people? After all, it was inbound migration of a mixture of diverse social and ethnic groups that helped make America great in the first instance and built cities like New York and Buenos Aires through the 19th and early 20th centuries.

Towards a new economic future

Both the climate crisis and the immediate effect of the Covid-19 pandemic have shown the power of state action when it chooses to apply it. However, instead of using state power to prop up an outdated economic system, that power needs to be applied to creating a truly sustainable one. This new system would take proper account of social, environmental, and economic drivers of human wellbeing through a more effective and symbiotic partnership between public, private, and civil society sectors. An important place to start would be to transfer state subsidies from fossil fuel companies to those promoting renewable energy, a stated policy at the G20 (University of Toronto, 2009). As Klein (2019: 17) notes, 'trillions have been marshalled for endless wars, bank bailouts and subsidies for fossil fuels, in the same years that coffers have been virtually empty for climate transition'. If such resources are redirected, and taxes are levied on multinational corporations in the countries where they generate their sales, as currently proposed by the Organisation for Economic Co-operation and Development (OECD) (Reuters, 2020), this could finance new jobs and build out renewable energy infrastructure. Governments have already been forced by the Covid-19 pandemic to act in ways that were unthinkable until recently. Now is the time to capitalize on the current reality to create a new, more sustainable one.

As discussed in Chapter 3, it is nearly 50 years since the Club of Rome published the *Limits to Growth* report, yet economic policy appears even more addicted to increased growth and consumption than ever. This addiction is finally being challenged even by economists. Widespread recognition that the global economy cannot return to 'business as usual' after the pandemic provides the foundation for replacing the current linear form of economic management characterized by 'make, take, and dispose' with the circular economy model to eliminate waste at the local, national, and regional levels, as advocated by a number of groups and individuals (Geissdoerfer et al., 2017). In 2015, the European Commission adopted the EU Circular Economy Action Plan as one of the main blocks of the European Green Deal (European Commission, 2020), while the Port City of Rotterdam has built on this by focusing on the construction, consumer goods, agri-food and green flows, and healthcare sectors in the transition to circular systems. For the construction sector, the plan is to reduce material consumption by 50 per cent by 2030 by building houses and offices in a way that allows for easy disassembly or renovation instead of demolition, using sturdy, long-life materials, and reusing materials and components in a way so that construction and demolition is connected in a closed loop of recycled materials.

Doughnuts are a common treat in many Western countries. They may be good for wellbeing, but three are enough to account for a total healthy daily calorie intake. However, doughnuts may be good as another alternative basis for economics. In promoting the concept of the 'doughnut economy', Raworth (2017) offers a guide to the goal of economic activity as meeting the core needs of all but within the means of the planet. The inner ring of Raworth's doughnut (or a larger American donut) sets out the minimum we need to lead a good life, as set out in the UN's Sustainable Development Goals and agreed to by world leaders of every political stripe. It ranges from food and clean water to a basic level of housing, sanitation, energy, education, healthcare, gender equality, income, and political voice. Anyone not attaining such minimum standards is living in the danger zone of the doughnut's hole (Figure 13.1). The outer ring of the doughnut (where the sprinkles go) represents the ecological ceiling drawn up by earth-system scientists. It highlights the boundaries across which humankind should not go to avoid damaging the climate, soils, oceans, the ozone layer, fresh water, and abundant biodiversity. Between the two rings is the good stuff: the dough, where everyone's needs, and that of the planet, are being met and people are able to thrive. The approach has been adopted by the city of Amsterdam where plans are in place for new housing to use recycled or bio-based materials as much as possible. Other cities, including Brussels and Cali, are adopting the same approach, and interest is increasing.

Another illustration of the need to reform economic policy is that of de-growth, as advocated by Kallis et al. (2020). Addressing a primarily Western

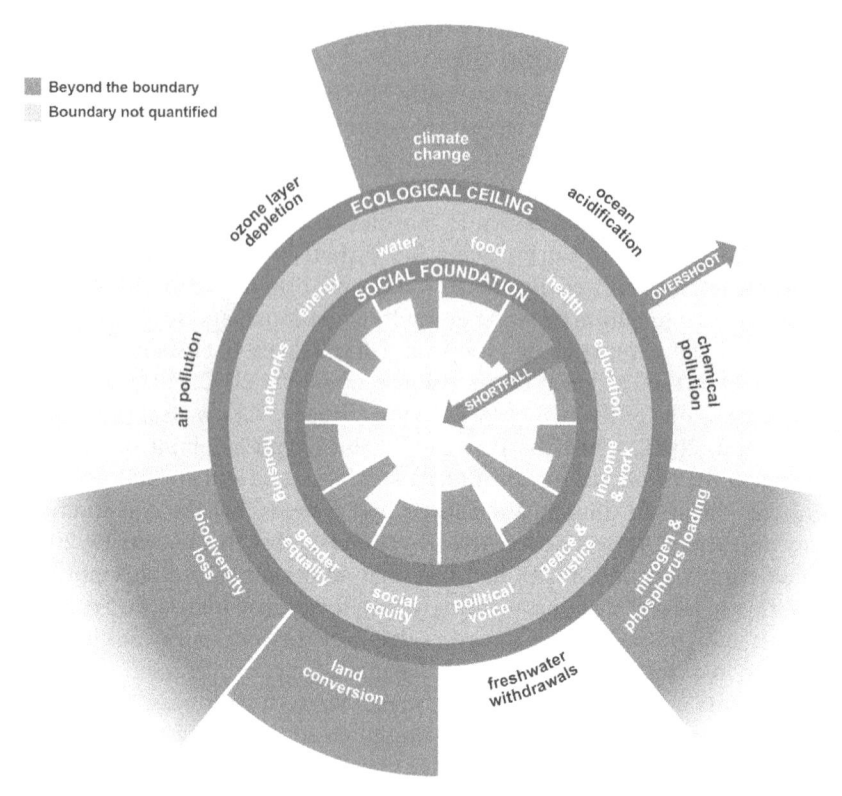

Figure 13.1 The doughnut of social and planetary boundaries
Source: Kate Raworth and Christian Guthier. CC-BY-SA 4.0

audience disenchanted with materialism, they draw on a wide range of sources and examples to demonstrate the benefits to wellbeing by living well with less and prioritizing equity and sustainability. In the same way that Layard's book, *Happiness*, is part of an expanding literature, so other writers, such as Callaway (2009), Nelson (2011), Nelson and Schneider (2018), Nelson and Edwards (2020), and Liegey and Nelson (2020) propose a range of 'postgrowth' policies to reshape how we work, live, and care. Their work also explains how de-growth policies can also enable investment strategies that avoid exploitative and environmentally unsustainable practices.

The need for economic theory and policy to change was highlighted when undergraduate economics students at Manchester University rebelled against their academic curriculum. Complaining that their course assumed the primacy of free markets as the optimum means of balancing demand and supply, they established the Post-Crash Economics Society (Inman, 2013) and demanded that the course include a wide range of theory from the far left as well as orthodox liberalism, which put excessive focus on equation-heavy mathematical models and discouraged critical thinking of social and environmental considerations. Other groups of students and scholars have founded a similar movement, Rethinking Economics, with similar aims.[1] However, it is not just educational curricula in economics that need a fundamental rethink; the scope of education itself has focused excessively on imparting information rather than stimulating curiosity and preparing students for a more equitable future that even they can see may not exist unless major changes are made. Finland leads the world in providing education for life, striving for equity over excellence, and requiring such high standards of teachers that external oversight is unnecessary (Colagrossi, 2019).

Taxing wealth, especially land and property, would encourage investment in renewable energy, education for life, and biodiversity. A massive reorientation of development policy can promote and reward the concept of trusteeship over natural resources, including land, rather than individual ownership, since our individual occupation of this planet is counted only in decades and anyone living to the age of 80 has only experienced about 4,000 weeks. The issue was eloquently expressed by Nemonte Nenquino (2020), cofounder of the Amazonian indigenous non-profit organization Ceibo Alliance, who complains that, for years, Western civilization has been 'taking, taking and taking from our lands' resulting in the 'climate crisis, species extinction and, driving it all, spiritual poverty'. Shrubsole (2019: 289) addresses this issue by advocating a proposal by Aldo Leopold to foster a new 'land ethic' that embeds the concept of stewardship, to make a cultural change to the treatment of land so that '*all* land ownership titles, when sold on, contain a simple, basic clause – an obligation on the part of the land-owner to *leave the land in a better state than they found it*'. Options for achieving this include leasing government or customary owned land and promoting communal ownership or leases.

Evidence and experience suggest, therefore, that the basis for a new definition of development and a good quality of life is now within reach. The Covid-19 pandemic has forced us to re-examine and change, not only our behaviour, but also our values. It has even helped us to redefine what we mean by value; we need to be more systematic in considering all aspects of our life, not just in material terms, but also in personal terms. Because these are not easy to measure or put a financial price on does not mean they are less important. As anyone who has experienced life at the brink of extinction knows, money is a peripheral consideration, unless, of course, you don't have any. Creating a world in which poverty no longer exists also requires that extreme wealth, and associated distortions in political priorities, no longer exist. Achieving this change will present the major challenge to realizing real development and a decent quality of life for all. The Covid-19 pandemic has shown that, when we are forced to change, human nature can rise to the occasion. In fact, the pandemic or the Ukrainian crisis may prove to have been more effective than any political oratory or scientific evidence in forcing humanity to realize that there are things other than materialism that are core to creating a good quality of life.

To aid and abet?

The considerations presented above are a luxury for the global majority struggling from day to day to feed themselves and their families. This makes the role of international development assistance key to achieving change. In assessing the nature and extent of rich-world responses to poverty and the need to improve incomes and living conditions in the Global South, Bregman (2017) notes that, although the sums of money committed for international development by rich countries are large, they are minute compared to what these countries spent on subsidizing domestic agriculture in 2009, or on arms purchases. He also cites Gurría (2008) who reports that poor countries lose three times as much to tax evasion as they receive in foreign aid, concluding that measures against tax havens, for example, could potentially do more good than well-meaning aid programmes ever could. This is not an argument against aid but does demonstrate how it needs to be seen in the context of inequitable wealth transfers globally that inhibit development in the Global South.

In 1970, the world's rich countries agreed to give 0.7 per cent of their GNI as official international development aid annually, though few actually did so. Instead, the average amount of aid has been around 0.2 to 0.4 per cent, some $150 bn short each year (Shah, 2014a). As a result, OECD estimated in 2014 that the shortfall amounted to nearly $5 tn (Shah, 2014b), a figure that will have increased even more since the financial crisis of 2008. Furthermore, aid has often come with a price of its own for the recipient nations:

- 'Tied aid' comes with conditions that the recipient country must use the funding on overpriced goods and services purchased from donor country companies.
- Most aid does not actually go to the poorest who would need it the most.
- Aid amounts are dwarfed by rich-country trade protectionism that denies market access for poor-country agricultural products, while rich nations use aid as a lever to open poor-country markets to their manufactured products and foodstuffs.
- Aid channelled into large infrastructure projects or massive, grand strategies often fails to help the vulnerable as money can often be embezzled away via opaque legal structures and weak procurement rules.

Predictably, many donor countries have used these limitations as an excuse to reduce their aid budgets still further or impose conditions that enable them to use aid as an extension of foreign policy to further their own interests. Even the UK, one of the few countries to commit to the 0.7 per cent rate, opted to abandon this legal commitment in 2021, integrating the Department for International Development (DFID), which had performed well in addressing global poverty, into the Foreign and Commonwealth Office. A significant proportion of the aid budget has also been reallocated to other departments where there is little transparency and funds often come with strings attached that benefit British institutions and companies (Elliott, 2019).

So, what should be done? The announcement by US President Biden of international collaboration on corporate taxation is a positive first step, though far more is needed on debt relief and prioritizing the needs of the poor. However, commitments at the UN Forum 2021 to strengthen international collaboration since the pandemic – especially in the areas of debt and taxation, which were priorities for the Global South – were massively diluted and weakened (Ellmers, 2021). It may also be time to consider a more radical option of extending the policy advocated by Bregman to provide free money directly to everyone to create a truly *universal* basic income. Of course, this would entail unprecedented operational challenges to minimize abuse, but the times are also unprecedented and justify exploring radical approaches. If the World Bank Group, for example, is happy to finance the rollout of biometric identity cards across West Africa with support from European governments (Burt, 2019), surely they could consider a similarly ambitious basic income programme. Funding such a policy could be achieved by a combination of measures including: the cancellation of debts; taxation of multinational corporations on turnovers in the countries where they operate; the closure of tax havens; progressive wealth taxation;[2] no longer treating advertising as being tax deductible; introducing and enforcing personal carbon allowances; and the implementation of progressive increases in land and property taxes globally. With even a portion of these fiscal policy measures in place, a significant increase in international aid could be agreed by donor countries, to be monitored and reported on annually by the United Nations. If ever humanity has faced a time for thinking big, it is now. As we will see in the following chapters, managing urban land and housing has a vital part to play.

Notes

1. Rethinking Economics website <https://www.rethinkeconomics.org> [accessed 28 April 2021].
2. Wealth taxes already apply in Belgium, France, Italy, the Netherlands, Norway, Portugal, and Switzerland and have been proposed for the UK.

CHAPTER 14

Managing urban land markets: From problems to progress in land management

While it took millennia for the human population to reach 1 billion in 1804, it took only another 123 years to reach 2 billion, 32 years for another billion, and then almost another billion every decade, reaching 7 billion in 2011 (McGinty, 2011). Although the growth rate is projected to slow and eventually to decline, the total world population is expected to reach 8.6 billion by 2050 and 11.2 billion by 2100. Most of this growth will happen in cities.[1]

The global urban population has grown rapidly from a baseline of 751 million in 1950. By 2008, more people were living in urban than rural areas for the first time in human history, and in 2018 this included 4.2 billion people (United Nations, 2018). Furthermore, 68 per cent of the global population is projected to live in urban areas by 2050, an increase of 1.6–2 billion in the 32 years between 2018 and 2050, at an annual average increase of 83–85 million people a year. This rapid and sustained increase in urban populations puts pressure on available land in and around urban areas, especially as the globalization of market economics has raised access costs to levels well beyond the reach of large swathes of the population in countries at all levels of economic development. Those unable to meet these costs have been forced into various forms of unauthorized or informal settlements that are invariably insecure, substandard, and provide minimal access to essential services.

While the spatial extent of urban areas and the rate at which they are expanding is open to dispute (given different approaches to measurement), urban areas are swallowing land at a rapid rate (Seto et al., 2011) with an observed increase of 58,000 km^2 from 1970 to 2000. Applying typical urban densities of 15,000 people per km^2, this indicates approximately 5,500 km^2 of rural land is being urbanized annually. Between 2010 and 2030, global urban land cover will increase by between 430,000 km^2 and 12,568,000 km^2, with an estimate of 1,527,000 km^2 – an area the size of Mongolia – considered more likely (Seto et al., 2011: 8).

India, China, and Africa have experienced the highest rates of urban land expansion over the past decades, though variations in growth rates point to differences in national and regional socio-economic environments and political conditions (Seto et al., 2011). This is particularly evident in the case of China, where annual rates of urban land expansion vary from 13.3 per cent for coastal areas to 3.9 per cent for the western regions (Seto et al., 2011). On the other hand, the range of urban growth rates in North America is more evenly distributed between coastal and inland areas, suggesting more even economic opportunities across different cities on the continent (Urban Institute, 2017). Cultural factors also influence urban densities and therefore the amount of land needed to accommodate expanding urban populations. For example, residential densities tend to be lower in sub-Saharan Africa, so urban growth is likely to encroach on larger areas of peri-urban land than in more established, higher density urban areas in East Asia (Deuskar, 2015). In many cases, such as the Mekong Delta in Vietnam, urban expansion is encroaching on environmentally vulnerable, and agriculturally productive, rural land (World Bank, 2020). The challenges faced by coastal cities in Asia and Africa will increase as they expand beyond the natural land base onto reclaimed surfaces, similar to Singapore and Hong Kong. The scale of urban areas and their ongoing expansion also poses major difficulties in accessing places of employment and the social facilities needed to sustain a reasonable quality of life. Some people living on the outskirts of major cities already spend up to three hours travelling to and from work every day, resulting not only in vast increases in air pollution from vehicular transport, but an equally vast waste of valuable time.

In a well-regulated market, an increase in demand would result in increased supply. Such a balance would ensure that prices remained affordable and the market diversified to meet changing needs. However, the 2008 'sub-prime' crisis revealed the extent to which land and housing markets, and markets in general, have been manipulated through financialization (United Nations, 2017) and the rise of oligopolies in housing production (Cosman and Quintero, 2019), often with the support of governments, to serve the interests of suppliers, rather than those in need. It has also resulted in the loss of valuable public land as found in Uganda (Mukwaya et al., 2018) and many other countries. Examples of intentionally constrained supply designed to maintain and inflate high prices are common in countries at all levels of economic development. Markets have been shown to be inherently unstable and result in concentrations of wealth and gross inequality if unconstrained by effective regulation.

The fact that land and housing have become a physical manifestation of the crises facing people everywhere does, however, suggest that if managed efficiently and equitably, land and housing sectors can be part of the solution in reducing inequality, addressing the climate crisis, and providing a good and sustainable quality of life for everyone. The Covid-19 pandemic may prove to have been the catalyst that reminded humanity that we are not masters of the universe and need to adopt ways of living that are in closer harmony with nature. A key element in this is to regulate land markets in ways that retain the best elements of market behaviour – initiative, flair, investment, responsiveness, and efficiency – with the equal need to achieve social legitimacy, accountability, and an equitable distribution of benefits. It also means putting land to the most effective use in cultural, social, environmental, and economic terms.

The need for a more holistic approach to development provides unparalleled opportunities to develop urban areas that can provide access to land, housing, and a good quality of life for all. Throughout history, urban centres, from villages and towns to cities and vast conurbations, have provided humanity with the means of realizing social and economic development and enhancing progress. They put land to efficient use in accommodating and assimilating the increasing global population, leaving approximately 97 per cent of the world's land area for agriculture or nature. According to one study, 'In 2010, [the administratively defined] urban land was close to 3 per cent, the global built-up area was about 0.65 per cent, and the global impervious surface area was merely 0.45 per cent, of the world's total land area (excluding Antarctica and Greenland)' (Liu et al., 2014: 1; see also Schirber, 2015). But even this relatively small percentage of the built-up global land area with an impervious surface has impacts on hydrology, weather, and greenhouse gas emissions due to the intense levels of consumption and emissions that they produce as centres of economic activity. The environmental impacts of land use change and resource consumption driven by cities are increasingly felt at the regional, continental, and global scales (Brown de Colstoun et al., 2017; Intergovernmental Panel on Climate Change, 2019).

The scale and nature of urban growth is now such that many local and national governments understandably feel overwhelmed. Some have sought to restrict urban growth, either by investing in rural development programmes, or by failing to make life tolerable for those already in urban areas to discourage further rural-urban migration. While rural development is certainly needed, international experience has shown that urbanization is irreversible and a key feature of economic development. It therefore makes sense to manage it in ways that help the poor as much as other groups, since it is the revenues generated by successful cities that provide the resources to improve rural areas.

In an increasingly integrated world economy, countries and cities are struggling to meet existing, let alone projected future needs in a changing economic and political environment. Success in securing the necessary investment and revenues will therefore be influenced by the ability to respond creatively to changing opportunities. The challenge facing policymakers at all levels of government is to devise strategic responses that are market sensitive, socially responsive, and environmentally sustainable. This requires that land and housing markets are regulated in ways that serve society first and not, as is presently the case, where society serves financial markets. Fortunately, governments are in a potentially powerful position to achieve this shift to prioritizing societal needs, since land and housing cannot be physically relocated to tax havens.

The challenge for governments and other stakeholders in the land and housing sectors requires a 'twin-track' approach. First, there is a need to improve the living conditions of people living in substandard housing and various types of unauthorized settlements. This can best be achieved by providing basic services and protection from eviction, rather than providing formal tenure that exposes areas to market-driven displacement. Second, urban land assessments are essential in planning future developments to meet the needs of all sections of urban society, especially the poorest and most vulnerable, to prevent the need for *future* slums and unauthorized settlements. Prevention is also far simpler and less expensive than post facto upgrading. Both these objectives need to be achieved in ways that provide adequate levels of security and access to livelihoods, services, and credit.

The good news is that between 2000 and 2014, the proportion of the world's urban population living in slums declined by 20 per cent (from 28.4 to 22.8 per cent). However, the number of people living in slums actually increased from 807 million to 883 million over this period (United Nations, 2018: 3–4). While the rate of increase is slowing, the numbers are vast and by 2050, sub-Saharan African cities will need to accommodate an additional 790 million people. This is more than the current total urban population of the European Union, UK, USA, and Mexico combined (Durand-Lasserve et al., 2018) and equates to the need to provide new housing for more than 100,000 people every working day over three decades.

The increase in market-driven development strategies is changing the options available for governments to manage the process of urban growth and development. It is not possible in today's rapidly changing world for governments to simply prepare master plans or zoning plans to be implemented over future decades and assume that investors, developers, or landowners will be willing to invest in accordance with the plans. In fact, countries and cities are all competing within a global market economy for increasingly fluid resources and trillions of dollars are moved around the world every day (Bank for International Settlements, 2016). Attracting a share of such fluid and fickle investment is taxing the imagination and skill of politicians, administrators, professionals, and communities worldwide. Traditional approaches to meeting policy objectives, such as subsidizing home ownership, have also proved ineffective. Once financial speculation dominates a national or local housing market, the economic gains from successful policy interventions are difficult to protect from capture by different groups from those intended.

Fortunately, the potential for innovative approaches to land and housing market regulation is immense. At a structural level of urban management, the broad aim of planning and urban management should be to create pluralistic systems of supply which can respond to variations in demand and needs. This can be demonstrated by comparing the 'closed or restrictive' and 'open' supply systems shown in Figures 14.1 and 14.2.

Any household in need of a home needs to overcome four hurdles, those of obtaining land, finance (mortgage or rent and deposit), services, and materials. While there may be many options for obtaining materials, this is not helpful if options for access to land, finance, and services are highly restricted. Irrespective of whether supply is state or market based, such a system does not incentivize suppliers to be efficient or respond to changing needs,

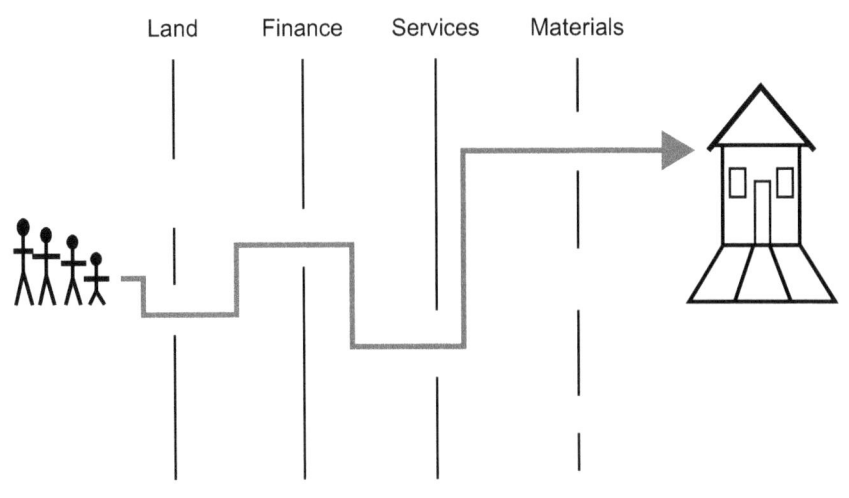

Figure 14.1 Closed or restricted housing supply system
Source: Based on Turner, 1990

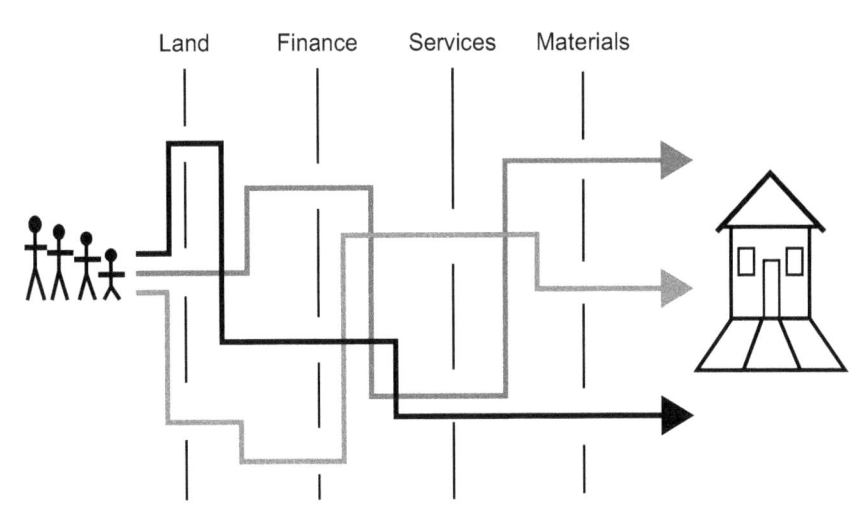

Figure 14.2 Open housing supply system
Source: Based on Turner, 1990

since they effectively exercise monopoly power. This suggests that an open supply system, as shown in Figure 14.2, is far more effective in stimulating competition between suppliers, particularly in terms of land and finance, in order to reflect the diversity of demand. In this context, the priority is to identify which element of the supply system is in need of additional options to meet the assessed needs of different social groups, and for urban authorities to stimulate new supply options to meet such needs. The range of innovative approaches celebrated at the annual World Habitat (2020) awards, in the

Dubai Best Practice database,[2] or at the World Bank (2019d) annual land policy conferences all demonstrate the wealth of innovative examples that policymakers can draw upon.

The key to success is therefore for urban authorities and planning agencies to promote innovative approaches to meeting currently unmet needs for accessing land and housing on terms and conditions appropriate to different social groups. Since households with good incomes can be reasonably expected to look after themselves within existing supply systems, priority will need to be given to stimulating and supporting options that focus on the needs of low- and very-low-income households.

As Turner proposed (1990), simply by providing three new means for addressing each of the elements, the options for meeting needs increases exponentially. The role of the public sector in this context will be to create and maintain a 'level playing field' in which different suppliers of land, services, credit, and building components can compete on equal terms. This in turn suggests that subsidies need to be carefully considered in terms of their market impact. For example, subsidizing capital costs or interest rates may result in inflationary pressures which only serve to raise prices overall and require even more subsidies, creating a vicious spiral. However, subsidies on health, education, or clean water have minimal price effects and improve the wellbeing of society as a whole.

Within this context, individual projects cannot address the limitations of inefficient and inequitable land or housing markets. However, they can serve as experiments capable of testing innovations in costs, management, design, standards, regulations, and procedures for possible wider application. The need is to involve all key actors in the process – public authorities, landowners, developers, civil society groups, and communities – in order to incorporate the legitimate needs of each. A key component of successful urban planning will therefore be to identify and build on those things that people do well already. Planning needs to be innovative as well as socially and environmentally responsible and local political leadership and elected officials are key to ensuring that all land is put to the most socially efficient use in accordance with local norms.

In addition to stimulating a range of supply options, governments also possess several policy instruments to regulate urban land and housing markets to meet both existing and future needs. These range from land and property taxes and user charges, direct intervention through land acquisition, to a wide range of land value capture or land value sharing measures, and include the options discussed below.

A taxing issue

A key element in policy formulation needs to be based on sharing the increments in land value that accrue when officially designated land uses change from rural to urban and from residential to commercial. In some cases, these increments can be as much as 1,000 times the original value of the land parcel. Since they are based on the granting of development permissions or investments made by government, the practical and moral basis for the state capturing a reasonable proportion of this increment for allocation in the public interest is undeniable.

Governments have many policy instruments at their disposal should they choose to apply them. In most countries around the world, land and property taxes are among the oldest forms of all taxes (Bird and Slack, 2004), though they are not always efficiently applied. Property tax functions as a progressive tax on capital since, as a rule, income from land and capital constitutes a relatively higher share of income for wealthier people. Others consider the portion of the tax that falls on land as being paid out of economic rents and find it inherently equitable to tax such unearned increments arising from public actions, for example the provision of roads and other essential infrastructure. In most countries today, the state is required to pay compensation for reductions in the value of private landed property as a result of eminent domain and public works, but cannot always recover the betterment it creates via the systematic application of land value taxation. Of course, the increasing emphasis on private wealth as a means to gain power in market economies means that any changes are challenging powerful and deeply entrenched vested interests, often the very people and organizations seeking to avoid their responsibilities by hiding or facilitating the hiding of property wealth in tax havens (Zucman et al., 2015).[3] Shaxson (2019: 7) estimates that 'Tax havens collectively cost governments between $500 bn and $600 bn a year in lost corporate tax revenue, depending on the estimate' and that 'offshore capital tends to drain from poor countries to rich ones'.

The Panama Papers and Luxembourg Leaks revealed the extent of the nefarious use of tax havens and prompted the Organisation for Economic Co-operation and Development (OECD) to launch the Common Reporting Standard (CRS) to exchange information between tax jurisdictions. Shaxson lists many loopholes, though the CRS did share information on 47 million accounts worth €4.9 tn with national governments seeking to recover taxes. He also notes how financial sector growth has reached the point where it can be considered as a financial curse, similar to the resource curse afflicting many countries dependent upon commodities such as oil. He argues that financial sector growth long ago passed the point of promoting development and is harmful to economic growth and that 'shrinking the financial sector to remove harmful financial activities should boost prosperity' (Shaxson, 2019: 10). Christine Lagarde also made progress in exposing and correcting the abuse of tax havens during her time at the International Monetary Fund, when she argued for a fundamental policy rethink. As President of the European Central Bank, she has indicated that the European Union should show leadership on this issue (Shaxson, 2020) through the Covid-19 recovery period. Shaxson concludes that more than a decade of cuts to public sector expenditure following the 2008 financial crisis provides a major impetus for such change, since taxpayers in both rich and poor countries are being denied the resources to meet their basic needs, and that countries that unilaterally act to rein in offshore financial sectors will not only help poor countries, but also their own citizens. If that case was strong in 2019, it is far stronger following the economic crisis brought on by the Covid-19 pandemic.

Requiring that land records identify the ultimate owners of land and property so that registers are transparent is therefore a prerequisite of effective land governance and any strategy to make land markets both efficient and equitable. Yet taxes on land and property are relatively minor sources of revenue at the national level in most parts of the world. For urbanizing countries, land and property taxes accounted on average for only about 0.4 per cent of GDP and about 2 per cent of total tax revenues through the 1990s, as large tracts of land in many countries are not even surveyed, let alone registered for tax purposes. Figures are slightly higher for OECD countries. Although property taxes are marginal at national level, they constitute important sources of local or municipal revenues in many countries, particularly in the Global South. In the 1990s, property taxes accounted for 40 per cent of all subnational taxes in lower-income countries, and 35 per cent in developed countries. In the same period, property taxes financed more than 10 per cent of subnational expenditure in developed and developing countries (Bird and Slack, 2004: 5). Governments must therefore take care in crafting municipal and state land and property tax regimes in order to maintain an important source of revenue. This is particularly important if central government funding is unreliable or absent. In such cases, creative local government fiscal policy and land administration are both important tools for realizing progressive urban development, reducing social and spatial segregation, and providing adequate housing.

Assuming that urban land available for housing is in limited supply (the supply of land offered for development is unresponsive to price changes), a tax on land falls on landowners and cannot be shifted to others. Increased site value taxes will thus be capitalized into lower property values. Since the tax is borne proportionately more by owners of land than is the case with a tax on both land and improvements, and since landownership is unequally distributed, such a tax should be more progressive, that is, borne relatively more heavily by high-income taxpayers than low-income taxpayers. According to Bird and Slack (2004: 13) 'site value taxation thus scores well in terms of both efficiency and equity. One problem with taxing land alone, however, relates to the administration of the tax'. In both developed and under-developed markets, accurate land valuation presents a challenge to assessors because most urban real estate sales combine the value of land and improvements (Netzer, 1998).

Whether levied as a tax on land or property (land and the buildings on it), the potential for taxing such unearned wealth and generating significant revenues for hard-pressed local governments is self-evident. This is especially so since land and property is soaking up more investment globally than stock markets thanks to neoliberal economics and the promotion of individual ownership, even to those who can least afford it and may not need it. The very fact that so many people now own property, or are in the process of acquiring ownership through the use of a mortgage loan, poses the greatest source of opposition to property taxes. It may also deter people from completing registration in countries where the proportion of registered land is small. As all the examples above demonstrate, land and property taxes have become marginal sources of revenue generation and do not reflect current property values. Further, the global promotion of home ownership has frustrated all attempts at increases.

This may be about to change as the house price to income ratio makes ownership increasingly unaffordable, especially to the young. Many people I met during international research have indicated that this needs to change and would be willing and able to pay more, so the opportunity exists for imaginative leaders to make the case and win public support. Increasing land and property taxes, and applying land taxes on the basis of its officially approved use, whether developed or not, would deter land hoarding and enable the state to increase the provision of non-market, social housing that can overcome the spatial segregation that market values have created.

A key consideration is therefore the rates at which taxes are levied and updated. In the UK, council taxes are based on property values determined in 1991, though the average value of a home has increased more than four times (HM Land Registry, 2021a), effectively reducing the value of the tax collected to a quarter of the original value. Updating the tax and adding more bands to allow for the concentration of taxes on high value properties resulting from increased inequality could not only generate much needed revenues for meeting social needs, but considerably reduce the role of land and housing as institutionalizing inequality. For those with high property values but low incomes, the tax can be collected on the sale of the property instead of annually. Policies that include a land or property sales or transfer tax need, however, to be carefully calibrated, since a high transfer tax rate has been shown in many countries to result in substantial under-reporting of sale prices.

Another tax-based instrument that can help reduce inequality and improve access to affordable housing is a tax on empty property or second homes. The intention of the tax is to discourage owners from treating land and property primarily as an investment, forcing up prices to locally unaffordable levels. Steps would need to be taken to prevent households from registering properties in the name of family members to avoid the tax. When restrictions on the purchase of second homes were introduced in China in 2010, it triggered an increase in the divorce rate by couples seeking to avoid the tax (Guppy, 2010). In Denmark, it is illegal to keep a property empty for more than 180 days (Hallmann, 2021), while the city of Vancouver, Canada introduced a tax on empty properties of 1 per cent of their 2019 assessed taxable value (City of Vancouver, 2020). Net revenues from the city's Empty Homes Tax are being reinvested in affordable housing and these have increased since first being introduced, with the province of British Columbia applying its own 'speculation and vacancy tax' to homes in Vancouver (Brolich, 2021). The UK has a more regressive approach to empty homes and, as noted in Chapter 8, actually provides a discount of up to 50 per cent on second homes. This has resulted in more than half of all homes in many popular holiday resorts being empty during the winter, rendering the provision of essential community facilities such as schools, libraries, and other facilities unviable. Levying a 100 per cent surcharge instead of a subsidy would deter such activity.

As discussed in Chapter 9, the issue of land and property taxation has a long history. Following proposals by Henry George, it was proposed in the UK by Winston Churchill as a key element of the 1909 People's Budget (Moore, 2021).[4] Unsurprisingly, this generated a hostile response from the large estate owners controlling the House of Lords and led to a constitutional crisis. Eventually, the First World War resulted in the proposal being abandoned, though the Covid-19 pandemic and high levels of inequality suggest that its time has finally come.

In addition to a basic land value tax, a recent review (UN-Habitat, 2021) of the role of land in improving access to adequate and affordable housing identified several policy instruments, including the option of a land value *increment* tax as an effective option for increasing state revenues. The tax is assessed as a percentage of the increase in land value resulting from state actions or general market trends and has been widely applied in Argentina and Colombia, where it was used to meet the need for affordable housing in the New Usme project in Bogotá (Smolka, 2013).

In summary, tax policy can guide development to areas where it is most needed and generate revenues for a wide range of public needs. However, its application is dependent upon political will to pass the necessary legislation and the institutional capability to enforce it. Where either of these is lacking, land or property taxes are unlikely to be a practical option. Among the reasons that make it a highly sensitive issue are the following:

- Those most liable to payments of such tax are those in middle or higher income groups, or with higher value properties. These groups have the most to lose and are often able to exert influence over the political process to inhibit such policies from being passed or implemented. In many countries, tax evasion and elite capture of tax policy impacts public welfare and the timely provision of essential urban infrastructure.
- Assessing tax liability is fraught with technical considerations of property valuation.
- If taxes are based on property values, they may unfairly penalize residents on low incomes who own or occupy properties which were not high value when initially acquired.
- If taxes are based on the ability to pay, collection costs may actually exceed revenues collected for a significant proportion of the population.

However, in some Brazilian cities, such as Porto Alegre, property taxes are structured on an 'ability to pay' basis, effectively protecting poorer members of society from over-taxation (De Cesare, 1999).
- While some of these concerns can be remedied by levying taxes on transfer, sale, or inheritance, any perceived excess in the level of taxes levied may encourage under-reporting of such transfers, creating or reinforcing a 'black market' land economy. However, inheritance taxes can help reduce inequality over time, but need to be progressive.
- The introduction of a vacant land tax is another means of discouraging property speculation and obtaining government revenue from wealthier segments of society (Lam and Tsui, 1998).[5]

Key policy choices affecting land use must be properly addressed if taxation regimes, and land market regulation more generally, are to be successful. These include: decisions over what is included and excluded from the tax base, how property value is defined for different classes of property, what percentage of value is taxable for each class, and how effective tax rates vary within and between classes of property (Bird, 2006).

Fee-based instruments

The most common form of fee-based instrument is the sale of development rights.[6] This takes the form of a charge assessed as a percentage of the increase in land value due to public actions such as rezoning, or general market trends. Rights may either be sold at auction or at a fixed price by developers, transferred to other locations, or resold.

The policy has been widely applied in India, where landowners can be granted an addition to the permitted floor area on condition that the additional profit is allocated to provide free housing for households who had been living on the land for some years without permission. In Brazil, the approach took the form of CEPAC bonds (Certificados de Potencial Adicional de Construção or Certificates for Additional Construction Potential) issued by municipal governments as additional development rights in areas that need redevelopment. The bonds are offered both through public and private auctions and are openly traded on the stock market (Smolka, 2013: 53).

The sale of development rights is a simple and efficient instrument for generating local government revenues. However, it has been criticized for causing displacement and increasing spatial inequality (Durand-Lasserve, 2006). Revenues generated from sales may also be allocated to a range of sectors other than housing.

Development-based instruments

A wide range of development-based instruments have been implemented in one or more countries and, as with all policies, they have both strengths and limitations, making it vital to assess the context in which they may or may not be applicable. Key considerations in reviewing their potential applicability are summarized below.

Developer charges and impact fees

Developer charges, or exactions, are required private sector contributions to either build or pay for additional public services, such as water supply and sewerage, required by new developments (Smolka, 2013). Local governments levy these charges as a one-time, up-front charge and receipt of payment is a precondition for public approval to develop land. They are applied in several countries, and have helped fund thousands of affordable housing units in San Francisco, where they are charged to any new (market rate) development projects in the city. An important consideration is to set the fee level high enough to generate the funds required to build new affordable housing in the same city, but not so high as to discourage development.

Land sales and leases

This involves the sale or lease of public land to developers who pay a fee for the right to occupy and develop. They have been applied in China to generate a substantial proportion of total revenues from land requisitioned from existing peri-urban landholders at well below market values and then sold to developers. It has proved extremely contentious and increasing resistance has made it difficult for new projects to break ground. Land leases are the most common forms of accessing land for housing in countries as diverse as Ethiopia, Mongolia, Singapore, and Tanzania where the government owns or controls the supply of land, and have proved to be a valuable tool for urban land management. This places the responsibility for matching demand and supply on central and local government authorities and on the integrity of land administrations to ensure that revenues generated are transparently and fully accounted for and put to the intended use. Leases have been successfully adopted in the historic centre of Havana, Cuba, which is under the control of the Office of the Historian which restores buildings to rent, lease, or sell and also offers special services. Lease payments are paid into a revolving fund which supplements property taxes. As Cuba opens up to international collaboration, such leasing arrangements could help to finance the provision of affordable social housing.

Land pooling or land readjustment (LP/LR)

LP/LR is a technique for managing and financing urban land development in which privately owned peri-urban land parcels are assembled and comprehensively developed. Some plots are sold to recover costs and the remainder distributed to the contributing landowners. It was first applied in 1791 by George Washington to acquire the land to develop Washington, DC (Deuskar, 2013), but has since been applied widely throughout Asia, as well as Australia

(Archer, 1999). In India, LP/LR projects are known as Town Planning Schemes (Sanyal and Deuskar, 2012) and were the basis for a new capital for the state of Andhra Pradesh. This is a self-financing means of urban development that enables the benefits to be shared between the public authorities and landholders, and may also enable some plots to be allocated for affordable housing or other social purposes. However, given the need to maximize support from landholders, the scope for generating land for allocation to affordable housing may be limited. Large-scale applications require a clearly defined legal framework.

Guided land development

Guided land development (GLD) is a technique for guiding the conversion of privately owned land in the urban periphery from rural to urban uses. It uses the provision of infrastructure as a mechanism to guide urban development and has been implemented widely in Pakistan. GLD is undertaken in partnership with landowners who pay for the cost of servicing their land through the donation of land for public infrastructure and payment of a betterment levy, after which the infrastructure development plan is prepared, ensuring that roads and infrastructure follow existing plot boundaries. GLD is less costly than outright land acquisition and more equitable than land banking and can use infrastructure investment to guide efficient land development. However, it cannot be applied in areas with fragmented land ownership. The benefit over LP/LR is that the government does not need to decide on the amount of land to be returned to the landowners at the end of the project.

Mandatory allocations or inclusionary zoning

These approaches link the construction of low- and moderate-income housing to the construction of market-rate housing. Local governments encourage or require developers to preserve a percentage of housing units to be sold or rented at below-market prices and to promote socio-economic, ethnic, and racial integration (Calavita and Mallach, 2010). The policy has been applied in many European countries, the Philippines, India, and the USA. If a developer knows in advance what proportion of costs will need to be allocated for a social benefit this can, in theory, influence the market value that a land parcel commands. If a developer or investor acquires land in the hope of a change of use for more profitable development, the state should not be required to take this 'hope value' into account when negotiating the financial viability of a development. Experience suggests that this policy instrument is limited to contexts in which the land market is buoyant and prices are increasing.

Requests for proposals (RFPs)

RFPs are invitations to suitably qualified developers to submit proposals for a specific site, generally on publicly held land. They specify a number of mandatory requirements, plus a number of additional optional elements. Qualified developers are invited to submit proposals that meet all the mandatory requirements and include additional elements. It is a means for realizing a public benefit from a private development. RFPs have been widely implemented in Eastern Europe and Russia (Lynch et al., 1998) and are particularly appropriate in countries transitioning from socialist to market-based forms of economic management which have large reserves of state-owned land. However, the need to maximize the revenues may reduce the potential provision of affordable housing.

Site development briefs

These are statements by public sector land agencies specifying the minimum social, financial, and environmental requirements which need to be included in a proposal in order to obtain planning approval. A good brief will be just that – brief. It should also be clear and based on criteria that can yield an acceptable return on investment by developers in return for the reduction of risk involved. The benefit of this approach to a developer (whether commercial or not-for-profit) is that it eliminates risk by specifying in advance the conditions required. Preparing a brief requires the ability to place oneself in the mind of a reader who may not share the same assumptions or objectives. It is therefore important that a site development brief:

- is based on a realistic assessment of the likely development costs (including short-term finance), selling prices, and potential profit margins for each project component;
- specifies the social and environmental requirements for maximizing public benefit;
- concentrates on aspects of particular public concern;
- distinguishes between those elements which are mandatory and those which are optional;
- focuses on information which potential developers need when preparing proposals.

Once a brief has been published, a wide range of interested parties can be given a reasonable time to prepare and submit proposals. Time taken at this stage can result in considerable savings later, and enables the successful proposal to begin without delay, reducing costs and therefore prices.

Transfer development rights (TDR)

TDR is a tool for enabling developers to purchase rights in areas where development is restricted and transfer them to designated reception areas. It applies to owners of private land on which non-remunerative uses are prescribed in the development plan and has been widely applied in the USA, Brazil (Acioly, 2000), and the Indian city of Mumbai (Adusumilli, 1999).

By separating development rights from the ownership of land, TDR seeks to guide development from areas where it is discouraged to those where it is considered desirable. The options available to the landowner are to use the TDR on any remaining area of land owned, use it on any other land, or sell it to others who can use it elsewhere. While TDR can originate from anywhere in the designated areas, it can be consumed only at designated receiving zones, which exclude sensitive and congested areas. However, TDR programmes are very complex and can be difficult to administer. Smart developers can usually gain extra density through variances or other means, and will have little incentive to purchase development rights unless the zoning process is relatively inflexible and incorruptible. Preconditions for success are a stable and growing property market, an adequate receiving base, and an effective land administrative framework for applying TDR in a way that is consistent yet also market sensitive.

Land banking

Land banking involves the acquisition and aggregation of a number of land parcels at their existing use value for future development. It may be undertaken by public entities primarily to acquire land at existing values for future development for public benefit or by private entities to provide affordable housing for employees or for profit. A land bank was managed in Colombia by MetroVivienda, a state-owned land bank (Gilbert, 2009), and in India by the Delhi Development Authority. In both cases, the social benefits were well below those intended. In the UK, the approach was employed to acquire land at existing rural land prices for a series of 32 new towns to be developed by government-funded New Town Development Corporations and included a wide range of attractive and affordable housing. More recently, it has been widely applied by private developers seeking to maximize profits by constraining land and housing supply to force up prices. Another possible outcome is that rural landowners may be tempted to pre-empt land banking procedures by selling to informal developers who then subdivide the land and create unauthorized settlements, as in Ethiopia. The approach requires long-term financial commitments and a strong and effective form of land governance within a well-defined and enforced legal framework. Where these conditions do not apply to the acquisition, management, and development of land, land banking is unlikely to be successful.

Non-market-based instruments for enhancing equitable land markets

The role of land management in facilitating or constraining access to affordable and adequate housing has been widely acknowledged for many years. Since the value of land is created by society, it is inevitable that as market forces have become the dominant form of economic management globally, so its market value has become the strongest determinant in allocating, transferring, or developing land. However, as we have seen in previous chapters, market forces have failed to meet the legitimate needs of a large and increasing number of people and communities in countries and cities at all levels of economic development. As such, there is a need to recognize and support the provision of non-market options for allocating land for housing. Examples are illustrated in Chapter 15 and are an effective means of ensuring that high priced land can remain available in the long term for lower-income groups.

Dealing with disorder

Experience shows that the systemic and entrenched limitations of formal land and supply systems globally reflect differences in the distribution of power, wealth, and opportunity. Unless these structural imbalances are addressed, the symptoms of inequality, as reflected in limited access to land and adequate housing, will remain and grow even more acute, increasing corruption and disputes over land and property. These disputes represent the largest single basis for litigation in the civil courts of most countries. The issue is even more challenging in regions such as sub-Saharan Africa, where no more than 10 per cent of all land is registered (HM Land Registry, 2021b).[7] This does not necessarily mean that land is undeveloped, or that exchanges do not take place. In fact, the demand for land has led to a mass of unofficial or non-formal mechanisms to enable people and organizations to access, transfer, use, and develop land for housing and other uses. These involve a range of social networks, dealers who subdivide public land illegally, or private landlords providing rental housing. In some contexts, these systems are so widely applied that they have become highly structured at the same time that formal, officially recognized systems have failed and have themselves become 'informalized'. A good example is Cairo, a conurbation of 20 million people, which Sims (2011: 268) describes as out of control, but which has succeeded due to the application of informal processes 'all of which are proscribed by law. It is the informal urban development that has created the high densities that the metropolis enjoys'. He concludes that despite all the challenges, the city continues to function quite well.

Of course, *all* cities embody a degree of disorder and chaos. In fact, as discussed in Chapter 6, Sendra and Sennett (2020) argue that this is to be welcomed as encouraging the spontaneity and opportunities for improvisation and innovation that makes cities stimulating places in which to live and work. Sennett proposes 'incomplete form' as a means of encouraging spontaneity and improvisation and in this sense endorses the ideas of the British Archigram group and Japanese Metabolists as discussed in Chapter 2, to create urban environments that are continually evolving.

Building bridges

The need for governments to move from attempts at controlling urban growth and development towards managing land and housing markets suggests that for the foreseeable future, city administrations will have to work with the grain of different mechanisms for regulating land that recognize the social, as well as the market, value of land. This will, in turn, require different ways of relating to local communities and diverse interest groups, including private sector developers, civil society groups, and landowners.

Since neither public nor private sectors have been able to meet the need for land and housing in expanding urban centres, efforts need to be pursued to develop and apply innovative partnerships to guide investment in ways which meet social, economic, and environmental policy objectives. A range of multi-stakeholder partnerships have been developed in different countries between public, private, and civil society sectors that can help countries to meet their obligations under the UN's Sustainable Development Goals and New Urban Agenda. An earlier publication (Payne, 1999) provides a wide range of examples in which public sector agencies have become more market sensitive, and private sector actors have become more socially responsive. These include joint venture companies in which the relative contributions of the parties are valued as a proportion of the total proposed development and benefits are allocated accordingly. Collaboration between civil society organizations has also yielded benefits that could not have been achieved independently. In Asia and parts of Africa, civil society organizations such as Asian Coalition for Housing Rights, Slum Dwellers International, and ARCPEACE have contributed to participatory approaches to improving existing urban areas, while in Europe the Transition Towns movement (Hopkins, 2008) is also pressuring, and working with, local governments. Partnerships will only flourish if they can demonstrate an ability to satisfy the primary needs and interests of *all* key stakeholder groups, especially the potential beneficiaries. The best way to introduce and expand such partnerships will be to create pilot projects in areas where there is local support. Local success will help build confidence in tackling more varied contexts in land management and other sectors. Decentralizing decision-making to local levels will also help will be important in this process.

International experience shows that no single policy instrument or agency can meet diverse needs within dynamic land and housing markets. It will be essential to develop a diversified set of options and a suite of tools, and build programmes around these to better regulate land and housing markets in the public interest. Success in meeting the needs of both existing and future urban residents for somewhere to live that enables them to enjoy a decent quality of life will require policymakers and urban managers to adapt assumptions and attitudes regarding progress to include those of the people they seek to serve. It is likely that the greatest opportunities for progress will occur under conditions when expectations and roles are open to change and local leadership rises to the opportunity. The stakes are high and we will explore the issues and options on the basis of this broader definition of value in the coming chapters.

Notes

1. This chapter draws upon a number of previous publications including UN-Habitat (2021).
2. All winners of the Dubai Award, established in 1995, are set out in UN-Habitat's Best Practices Database (UN-Habitat, n.d.).
3. Approximately $7.6 tn in assets are hidden in offshore jurisdictions; this represents around 8 per cent of total global wealth, which is valued at about $95 tn. Much of this is invested in land and property.
4. The 1909 People's Budget included the introduction of a Super Tax on the wealthy and duty of 20 per cent on the Unearned Increment (broadly capital gains) on land value, payable on transfer of the property title (ownership) (see Moore, 2021).
5. For a discussion of Taiwan's experience with land value taxation and taxation of vacant land see Lam and Tsui (1998).
6. This and the following two sections provide a summary of UN-Habitat (2021).
7. In the United Kingdom, by comparison, around 87 per cent of all land is registered (HM Land Registry, 2021b).

CHAPTER 15
Promoting tenure security and diversity

At an annual housing lecture by a distinguished British official, the professional audience was asked how many owned their home. As the majority raised their hands, it was noticeable that they (actually, *we*) were nearly all grey-haired. When younger members of the audience were asked how many owned their own home, one woman in her mid-30s disputed whether it was even a sensible question as the option was so far over the horizon for her generation as to be unthinkable. Everyone who had raised their hands looked extremely uncomfortable, and with good reason.[1]

Despite the 2008–09 'sub-prime' mortgage crisis and the global recession it triggered, land and property remain the asset class of choice for many investors, especially given low rates of interest on other investments. In fact, one estimate values residential property globally at a staggering US$220.2 tn (Barnes, 2018) and, in 2015 alone, Chinese investments in Australia amounted to $18 bn (Thurlow, 2016). The financialization of land and housing mean that these sectors have now become central to the global economy with mortgage markets accounting for an ever-growing share of national GDP in G20 countries. Increasingly desperate efforts to prop up the system of individual home ownership by pumping resources in the form of subsidies to enable households to 'get on the property ladder' only serves to further inflate the cost of housing and benefits developers. Lack of adequate access to affordable housing now threatens both economic and political stability and even middle-income households in rich countries, especially the young, find it increasingly impossible to buy, or even rent. However, it may be that this is the trigger needed for fundamental change.

Just after presenting a paper reporting on the limitations of land titling programmes at a World Bank conference, a senior Bank official approached me and said he recognized that the Bank had 'put too many eggs in the omelette' by excessively promoting land titling. Although the Bank continues to provide loans and grants for land titling programmes, as discussed in Chapter 7, it has also recognized the need for more pragmatic, intermediate and context-sensitive, demand-led options for managing urban land markets. It was on this basis that I was invited to contribute to a number of Bank-funded projects in a range of countries. This revealed that it was not only the Bank that needed to change, but also national and local governments.

The complex range of formal, semi-formal, and non-formal tenure categories that exist in most cities, and particularly throughout the Global South, all form part of the overall market serving the needs of different groups. Each category has its own terms, conditions, and entry costs, so any policy intervention will have both direct and indirect impacts on the others. Failing to recognize this can be reliably expected to result in outcomes different from those intended. For example, the promotion of land titling as a universally applicable instrument to promote tenure security and economic growth was demonstrated to have failed in all the case studies reviewed in Part Two. In fact, the push for land titling often made matters worse, as in the case of Albania, by adding another basis for dispute between different stakeholders. As shown in Figure 15.1, providing land titles to one of the non-formal categories, such as squatter settlements, distorts land markets dramatically by granting the residents equal legal status to existing households with freehold tenure. This naturally encourages investors with inside knowledge of land markets and residents higher up the tenure continuum to try to acquire properties within the newly legalized settlements, especially if in prime locations, leading to market-driven displacement and also encouraging others to create the very non-formal settlements that titling programmes are intended to resolve by occupying vacant land in the hope of repeating the process.

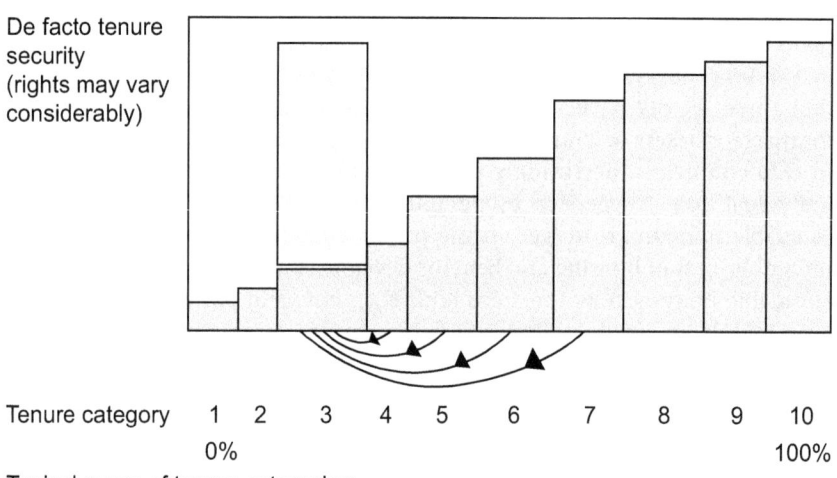

Typical range of tenure categories:
1. Pavement dweller
2. Squatter tenant
3. Newly legalized freeholder of squatter house or plot
4. Tenant in unauthorized subdivision
5. Squatter 'owner' – regularized
6. Owner – unauthorized subdivision
7. Legal owner – unauthorized construction
8. Tenant with contract
9. Leaseholder
10. Freeholder

Figure 15.1 Likely consequences of providing titles to 'owners' of squatter houses
Note: For simplicity, this illustration excludes customary and Islamic tenure categories

An objective analysis of the full range of non-formal, semi-formal, customary, religious, and statutory tenure categories existing in a city, together with the range of rights available, as provided in Chapter 7, provides a gender-sensitive basis for formulating carefully targeted policy interventions. Despite the limitation of a continuum in implying that freehold is the ultimate goal, the key to success is to assess the degree of ease with which households are able to move from less to more secure forms of tenure, and the wider the range of options available, the easier this will be. Where the level of de facto tenure security between categories is significant, this transition is likely to be impeded, suggesting that this is where a policy intervention could be most effective. Adopting a targeted, five-step approach to improving tenure security as described below offers the prospect of making the land and housing market more diverse and efficient at minimal cost and market distortion.

The five steps towards enhancing tenure security and diversity

Step one: assessing degrees of legality

In preparing a matrix for a given city, local terms such as *barrio, bidonville, bustee, favela, gecekondu,* and *katchi abadi* should be avoided, since they frequently include a wide range of sub-categories. Instead, the nature of each category should be assessed in terms of the level of security it provides, the entry costs and the social groups served, including the rights of women and ethnic or religious minorities.

The degree of tenure security that applies in a given context and at a given time will exert a major influence on the ability and willingness of residents to invest in improvements to their homes and neighbourhood. However, extensive research in 16 countries (Payne, 2002) demonstrates that security of tenure often depends not so much on legal status as on residents' *perceptions* of past and present government policy. Priorities for tenure and property rights vary between sub-groups of the urban poor. For example, the priority for the poorest is to achieve easy access to places in which they can obtain a livelihood. Since these are invariably inner-city locations where land prices are highest, they are generally forced to accept insecure accommodation as a price of such access. Those on low, but less uncertain, incomes are able to accept slightly longer travel distances to employment areas and afford a more secure form of tenure, though probably not at full market rates. For the upwardly mobile or less poor, distances to work are less critical than the need for longer-term and more formal tenure. Similarly, tenure needs vary with age, with young adults prioritizing short-term security in order to pursue career opportunities in different cities or even countries, those with young children needing medium- to long-term security, and the elderly in need of short- to medium-term security. When cultural and gender considerations are added to the mix, the need for a wide range of tenure options is self-evident and helps to explain why such diverse tenure categories exist already – albeit without official endorsement or even recognition.

Before considering tenure policy options, three further issues deserve serious consideration. The first is the common existence of legal plurality, for example when indigenous customary or religious forms of tenure coexist with imported or imposed statutory tenure regimes. Navigating the complexities that have remained unresolved for decades or even centuries is not an issue that can easily be resolved simply through changes in the law since each will have its constituency of supporters and vested interest groups. The second issue is the related one of cultural aspects, by which land contributes to an individual and collective sense of identity. Third, it took the West two centuries to develop and institutionalize systems of tenure and property rights when countries were masters of their own destiny, so it is hardly surprising that urbanizing countries with more complex situations, less autonomy, and larger populations have yet to resolve this issue in ways that reflect their legal, cultural, economic, and political circumstances. For these reasons alone, the most effective approach is to find out what works in a given context and build on it with a range of intermediate, incremental options. Such highly targeted forms of intervention can facilitate the continual evolution of land and housing markets in ways that are socially responsive and impose minimal burdens on urban authorities.

Step two: selecting settlements for regularization

The primary objective of tenure policy should be to ensure protection for all households from forced eviction and provide short-term security of tenure while the attributes of different settlements for relocation or regularization are assessed. This need not involve public sector agencies losing control, or private landowners losing their land, but that people in areas not considered appropriate for medium-term regularization are given due notice and reasonable options for alternative accommodation that protects their existing needs. The secondary objective involves improving access to livelihoods, services, and credit, usually in that order.

The first priority is to survey all semi-legal or non-legal settlements and identify those that are causing major strategic or environmental threats to the residents or surrounding areas and therefore need to be relocated as soon as possible, and those settlements that are providing shelter without causing such problems. Distinguishing between the two will not be easy since it will depend upon the criteria adopted and the interests and priorities of those making the decision. Decisions on settlements considered unsuitable for regularization should therefore be subject to review and appeal to independent experts. The number of such settlements also needs to be considered and can indicate the number of people for whom alternative accommodation may be needed. Providing a moratorium on forced evictions for a specified period of at least a few months, would in itself provide short-term security and enable people in such settlements to plan their lives.

Step three: forms of indirect intervention

A simple means of improving tenure security and promoting local improvements is to install basic public services in settlements that are not causing any significant public health or strategic planning problems. This also reduces social and environmental inequality without distorting the land and housing market. For poorly resourced government agencies, an added benefit is that it imposes minimal costs, especially if residents are encouraged to contribute their labour as community contractors. The accretion of utility bill receipts can also be sufficient to promote investment and enhance living standards and, in Egypt, documents relating to property taxes, utility charges, voter registration forms, ration cards, and so on have all become an effective means of stimulating substantial levels of investment in homes and businesses.

A variation on the representation in Figure 15.2 of this generic land tenure continuum is provided by UN-Habitat (2016), and distinguishes between tenure categories at high risk of eviction (red zone), categories that may be

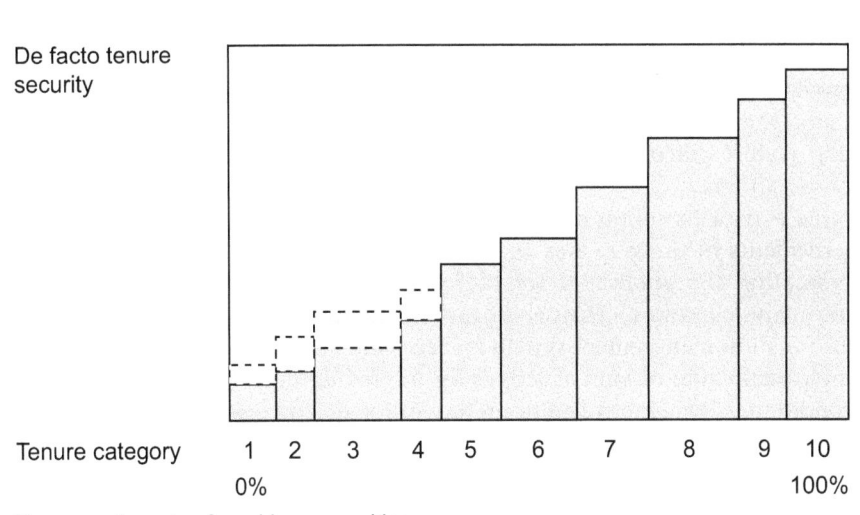

Tenure categories found in many cities:
1. Pavement dweller with approval to remain
2. Squatter tenant with protection
3. Squatter 'owner' – regularized
4. Tenant in unauthorized subdivision – with protection
5. Squatter 'owner' – regularized
6. Owner – unauthorized subdivision
7. Legal owner – unauthorized construction
8. Tenant with contract
9. Leaseholder
10. Freeholder

Figure 15.2 Likely consequences of improving property rights in unauthorized settlements
Note: For simplicity, this illustration excludes customary and Islamic tenure categories

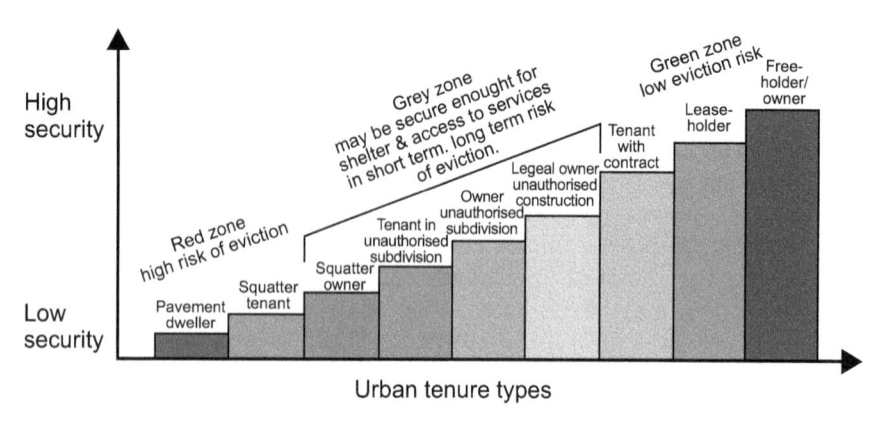

Figure 15.3 Urban land tenure levels of risk
Source: UN-Habitat, 2016: 2

secure enough for shelter and access to services in the short term, but with a long-term risk of eviction (grey zone), and categories with a low eviction risk (green zone). These variations are illustrated in Figure 15.3. The report also provides a framework of four categories for evaluating different levels of tenure status, those that explain the relationships between different categories, those that predict outcomes, and those that evaluate outcomes against predetermined criteria.

As part of its commitment to improving tenure security for residents of settlements in the grey area as shown in Figure 15.3, UN-Habitat has been promoting the application of the Social Tenure Domain Model (STDM) in many countries. This is a participatory and gender sensitive land information management system for recording information on residents and their occupation of land as a basis for improving tenure security and living conditions. Given that a significant proportion of land in urban and peri-urban areas of rapidly urbanizing countries is not included on land registries, STDM provides a simple form of recording rights, claims, and restrictions based on close community involvement. The system has been applied in several countries, including Iraq, Kenya, Uganda, the Philippines, and Zambia, and allows for the recording of all possible types of tenure, including customary, statutory, and semi-legal categories.[2]

India has adopted a pragmatic approach towards incremental regularization. Unauthorized settlements, or colonies, are designated as either 'non-objectionable' or 'objectionable' in some states and 'notified' or 'non-notified' in others. The former enjoys a quasi-legal status, allowing the residents to feel that modest investments are justified and entitling them to receive heavily subsidized public services. Such de facto security and access to public services is not available to the latter category and implies that residents may need to move in the near future. Additional options include the provision of No-Objection Certificates (NOCs) and a major NGO-organized

Slum Networking Programme (SNP) in the city of Ahmedabad. The SNP has two components: first, improvements in the physical environment which enhances social protection and, second, a community development and social infrastructure component. The entire programme is community-driven, with local government and the Ahmedabad Municipal Council providing a ten year 'no eviction guarantee'. More than 60 settlements have benefited from the programme. An additional indirect form of de facto tenure security was also inadvertently provided through the decision to collect property taxes in all settlements receiving public services, so receipts for payment increased perceived security the longer the taxes were paid (Mahadevia, 2010). This final option indicates a potential means for local urban governments around the world to enhance tenure security while strengthening public finances.

One of the largest examples of enhanced tenure security resulting from indirect intervention is that of the Orangi Pilot Project (OPP) in Karachi, Pakistan. Situated on the urban periphery at the time, the predominantly low-income residents of Orangi were unable to afford conventional public services. From its launch in 1980 by Akhtar Hameed Khan, the OPP developed a community-based means of installing sewers street by street under the leadership of Arif Hasan and later Perween Rehman. Despite the assassination of Ms Rehman in 2013, the vast majority of the population of nearly 2.5 million benefited from connections to a fully functioning sewer system. This contributed to a strong sense of tenure security to the point that when the residents were offered 99-year land leases, it is estimated that no more than 20 per cent of households applied (Hasan, 2020). Presumably, the provision of de facto security made the payment for a lease document, together with the probable requirement to pay property taxes, unattractive.

Another example is that of Ankara in the 1970s and 1980s when the city population was doubling every decade or less and the authorities were unable to impose conventional planning norms. Migrants took advantage of the 1858 Ottoman Land Act that entitled citizens to occupy unused public land on condition that they put it to good use. Settlers applied traditional concepts of self-help and communal solidarity to construct houses and develop settlements on such a large scale that it amounted to a community-led form of urban development (Payne, 2007).[3] Over time, large swathes of unauthorized settlements were incorporated into the formal land and housing market to the benefit of all parties: the low-income residents acquired full legal ownership of two or even three apartments free of cost, the developers made a reasonable profit, and the city generated increased revenues, all without any market-distorting subsidy. Many of the originally low-income residents now enjoy a standard of living they could not even imagine decades ago. The key to success was allowing the process to be undertaken over time and with residents in a strong negotiating position.

By ensuring that land and property held under such tenure systems cannot command the full price which formal tenure would entail, low-income households are able to live in locations that would otherwise be unaffordable. At the same time, settlers that occupied private or public land peacefully and without challenge for many years may even be eligible in some countries for full ownership claims under adverse possession legislation.

Step four: intermediate tenure options

In cases where settlements are considered eligible for tenure regularization, a wide range of intermediate tenure options exist that fall short of providing full titles, but increase security, stimulate local investment, and facilitate access to livelihoods and services. Some of these can be upgraded to full ownership over time; some offer improved rights to individual families; and others provide communal forms of tenure. All enable households to retain housing in certain areas in order to improve their economic situation without adversely affecting the operation of urban land markets.

While local conditions need to determine final policy choices, the following options may be considered appropriate for moving incrementally towards a more formal tenure system which improves the equity and efficiency of land and property markets:

Tolerance-based interventions:

- *Security through documentation (Egypt, India, Colombia)*. Tenure security is achieved over time through the accretion of various documents relating to property taxes, utility charges, voter registration forms, ration cards, and so on. This form of de facto tenure is extremely common and can significantly increase perceived levels of security, promoting investment in homes and businesses.
- *Temporary occupation licences (TOLs) (Kenya)*. TOLs promote investment in small businesses and the efficient use of idle public land in strategic locations. Licences are allocated annually on a renewable basis for a land rent and entitle licensees to construct semi-permanent structures. Typical uses include pavement restaurants and kiosks, although some people also live on their sites. The system is simple to administer, payment can be spread, building standards are flexible, and the authorities retain control of the land.
- *Constitutional protection (Colombia, India)*. The Colombian Constitution entitles all citizens to access public services on the sole condition that they can pay for them; tenure status is not relevant. As a result, residents consider themselves sufficiently secure to invest what they can in improving their homes and pay for the services they receive. Many display utility meters outside their houses as evidence of their semi-official existence and no public subsidies are required. In India, a Supreme Court decision in 1985 determined that pavement dwellers in Mumbai could only be evicted if the authorities provided alternative accommodation. Since this was impractical, the settlers have obtained de facto security.

- *Certificates of Comfort (CoC) (Trinidad and Tobago)*. The CoC is the first tenure instrument gained by squatters being regularized by the Land Settlement Agency in accordance with the 1998 State Land Act. It gives the holder a right that he or she will not be removed from the plot that their dwelling stands on unless it is deemed necessary to relocate and an alternative plot is made available. It is therefore an assurance of somewhere to live, either on the spot occupied, or on an identified alternative. Since the state has not been able to provide alternative housing, the CoC provides effective de facto tenure security.
- *Usucapiao rights, Zones of Special Interest and the Right to the City Statute (Brazil)*. In 2001, the 'City Statute' was passed to implement the urban policy introduced by the 1988 Constitution. The City Statute set the basis for a new legal-political paradigm for urban land use and development control: the right to urban property is ensured, provided that a social function is accomplished. Municipalities are tasked with formulating land use policies balancing the interests of landowners with the social, cultural, and environmental needs of other groups, and the city as a whole. The Statute enables municipalities to promote land tenure regularization programmes through a combination of individual and/or communal adverse possession rights on private land and leasehold rights on public land.

Proactive interventions:

- *Slum upgrading Baan Mankong (Thailand)*. When the National Housing Authority of Thailand initiated a slum improvement programme in 1977, it decided that all residential areas where land tenure, or physical and social characteristics were problematic, would be considered as potential upgrading areas. One of the key assumptions was that increased tenure security would be the major incentive to encourage home improvement initiatives without requiring formal titles. The experience demonstrated that people will invest what they can in improving their houses and environment if they feel secure. In 2003, an even more ambitious programme known as the Baan Mankong programme was implemented through the Community Organizations Development Institute (CODI). Secure tenure is negotiated in each locality through cooperative land purchase, long-term lease contracts, land swaps, or user rights. In all cases, the emphasis is on communal rather than individual tenure.
- *Kampung Improvement Programme (KIP) (Indonesia)*. The KIP focused on improving infrastructure and circulation within urban *kampungs*, or urbanized villages. Density levels found in many settlements made it impractical to impose the same standards required for new developments. For example, pathways were routinely just 2 metres wide and plot sizes smaller than 30 m2, although in new developments the official minimums are 3.5 metres and 54 m2 respectively. The programme also

Photo 15.1 Improved services and footpaths in a Surabaya *kampung*, Indonesia
Credit: Geoffrey Payne

generated major community development benefits, including multi-sectoral social, health, and educational programmes. KIP did not change the formal tenure status of plots, though payment of land taxes was regarded by most households as an acceptable certificate of ownership, though later trends favoured more formal processes such as leases. In recent years, the government has undertaken a range of other interventions to improve *kampungs*, mostly by focusing on improving infrastructure rather than changing tenure status (see Photo 15.1). This has helped many well located *kampungs* remain reasonably accessible to low-income households.

- *Communal land rental (Thailand)*. Landowners and low-income groups in Bangkok have evolved a mutually beneficial system of land tenure which enables the poor to live for a short to medium period in inner-city areas which would normally be far too expensive for them. This enables the poor to obtain easy access to employment centres and provides landowners with an income until they develop a site for its maximum value. Many arrangements are informal, but the system is increasingly recognized and some agreements are legal contracts. Local authorities provide services according to the rental period, and when this expires the communities are given enough notice to negotiate a similar arrangement with another landowner. In this way, the urban poor are able to move ahead of the tide of urban expansion without detracting from the efficiency of the formal land market.

- *Customary Form C (Lesotho)*. As discussed in Chapter 12, although Form Cs were allocated legally by customary chiefs in rural areas, they continued to be issued long after they ceased to be legally valid due to the failure of legally approved development to meet the housing needs of the population as Maseru city expanded. They are now tolerated as a reality and the majority of the city's population hold land through a Form C.
- *Anticretico ('Against a Credit') tenure system (Bolivia)*. This involves the owner of a house receiving money (in dollars) in advance, in return for allowing a low-income household to occupy the property for an agreed period, normally two years. At the end of the contract period (or any agreed extension), the occupants return the property to its owner and the owner returns the full amount received initially from the occupants. For the owner, this raises capital without incurring high interest rates, while the occupant is able to live at low cost. The occupant is required to return the property in the same condition as it was received and may even be able to purchase the property if the owner agrees. The system is widely used in Bolivia, but depends for its success on a degree of trust between the parties. The government has formalized the system in order to increase security for both parties; however, it has also increased taxes on such agreements, which discourages their use.
- *Certificates of Rights (Botswana)*. This was introduced in the 1970s and provides holders with the right to use and develop land, while retaining ownership by the state and is estimated to have benefited well over 100,000 people to date. Certificates can be upgraded to Fixed Period State Grants on payment of survey and registration fees. One limitation is that it has not been accepted by formal private sector finance institutions as collateral for loans. The administrative work involved is about the same as that for allocating full titles, although computerization has reduced this. The system also has to compete with customary land allocation procedures that are already well known and active in peri-urban areas. Given the limited population growth of urban areas and these alternative options, Certificates of Rights have been discontinued but could be revived if demand increases.
- *Hekr tenure (Egypt)*. This consists of a modest ground rent charged to informal settlers on government, or unclaimed, desert land. It does not grant title, and cannot be transferred, but ensures that if households have to be displaced, they will receive compensation for the buildings they have erected on their plots. Such an arrangement distinguishes between the ownership of land and the ownership of property and facilitates access by the poor to plots which would otherwise be unaffordable.
- *Occupancy certificates (Kenya) or licences (Zambia)*. Rights are acquired following the application of the STDM approach that records the relationship between individuals, the community, and the land they occupy. In Zambia, it has provided 30-year occupancy licences for residents.

Step five: innovative formal options

- *Communal ownership or lease.* Under communal tenure, land is vested in the tribe, group, or community. It may also include statutory recognition of collective or communal land ownership or lease. Communal landholding has been in existence for thousands of years and remains widely applicable in a large number of countries throughout the world, particularly in sub-Saharan Africa (Wily, 2018) and in this sense is not innovative. However, a number of statutory forms of communal ownership or lease have evolved, such as within the CODI programme summarized above and as part of Thailand's Communal Land Title regulation issued in 2010 (Pobsuk, 2019: 10). To function efficiently, communal forms of tenure require a strong sense of community solidarity and cohesion.
- *Community land trusts (CLTs).* CLTs are locally based, democratically run, not-for-profit membership organizations that own land and property in trust for the benefit of a defined community. A CLT captures the value of land and employs innovative development finance and equity sharing solutions in order to address local housing needs and encourage social enterprise. Land without planning consent has limited value, but once it receives planning permission, the uplift in the value of the site can be significant. CLTs aim to capture the uplift in land value to generate the capital for development, reducing the call on the public purse. They can then ensure good value for money by locking in the value of government subsidy in perpetuity and reusing it for the benefit of successive generations. With the communal ownership of the land as a secure asset base, a CLT can ensure long-term affordability as it prevents land from being subject to market penetration. By doing so, low-income households are protected from relocation and neighbourhoods from gentrification. A pioneering example was developed in Georgia, USA in 1969 by leaders of the Civil Rights Movement seeking to ensure access to land for African American farmers. Since then, the option has been applied widely in the USA, Canada, and the UK. The first example in a rapidly urbanizing country was in Kenya (Yahya, 2002) and in 2015 a CLT in Puerto Rico won a global award (World Habitat, 2015). A CLT requires first and foremost a thriving community with strong roots to the land and a shared desire to remain together. This is increasingly rare in urban areas. Second, it requires political will, available land, a legal framework, and effective land administration for its enforcement. This could explain the limited application to date in rapidly urbanizing countries, though the success of the Puerto Rico example provides a model on which other countries may wish to build.
- *Cooperative ownership (various countries).* Cooperatives (or co-ops) are democratically run or controlled legally recognized enterprises whose

objective is to pool resources to make investments in housing projects for the benefit of members. Housing cooperatives provide access to affordable housing to low-income groups that cannot afford traditional mortgages to acquire and develop land and housing. They also enable groups to access finance and reduce construction costs. They exist in every continent and come in many different forms: some are resident owned while others are rented; dwellings can be either townhouses, small buildings, or large buildings with hundreds of units (UN-Habitat, 2021). They can be structured in many ways, including land-only, equity, or leasehold and exist throughout urbanized and urbanizing countries. Approximately a quarter of all housing in Zurich, Switzerland, consists of cooperatives and they play an important part in many African countries, particularly in Kenya. In 2012, approximately 1 billion people in 96 countries had become members of at least one cooperative, while the turnover of the largest 300 cooperatives in the world reached $2.2 tn (Kumar, 2012). Co-ops need a legal foundation, external financial support, and a large enough community. As land prices and construction costs increase, low-income households also need external support to afford land acquisition and bulk infrastructure provision and this severely constrains their application for this social group.

- *Co-housing (New Zealand, UK, USA)*. A co-housing development is one in which the residents own or lease individual dwellings, but are co-owners of the shared, communal areas, including gardens and buildings for social activities, such as children's play spaces and areas for indoor exercise. In this respect, co-housing provides the best of individual and community forms of tenure though, as with the other community-based options, depends for success on establishing and maintaining effective local governance. In an award-winning project in the UK, Marmalade Lane, residents wishing to sell a property are required to give the co-housing company of which they are members eight weeks to offer it to those on the waiting list at full market value before it may be sold on the open market.[4]
- *Pattas and short-term leases (India)*. Pattas are given after 5 years of occupation if government considers an area is not required for other purposes and is not under a court dispute. There is an income qualification so that low-income families benefit. It is registered for residential use in the name of the woman of the house (they are considered less likely to sell). The *patta* can be inherited, but not sold, though this condition is rarely enforced. A small ground rental has to be paid. Leases are for 30 years.
- *Equity sharing (US/UK)*. A combination of delayed freehold and rental in which residents purchase a stake in their property (often 50 per cent) and pay rent on the remainder. It combines the security and potential increase in asset value of delayed freehold and the flexibility

of rental but requires a legal framework and efficient management. Residents can increase their stake over time, ultimately leading to full ownership.
- *Social rental.* Once so widespread, social housing suffered heavily from the application of market-based policies and much was privatized. However, more than 60 per cent of residents in Vienna live in social housing and it is being revived in the USA under President Biden (Herz, 2021). It deserves a role in any housing policy.

Communal land ownership

Communal land ownership can take many forms and is the dominant form of land tenure in many parts of sub-Saharan Africa, South-east Asia, and the Pacific. It vests land in a tribe, group, community, or family and in many cases enjoys statutory recognition. It applies primarily in rural areas, but as urban centres expand, it coexists with market-based forms of tenure that challenge its efficiency and social legitimacy. However, innovative approaches demonstrate that the principle of communal ownership is highly applicable in contemporary urban developments. For example, in Bangkok, the Community Organizations Development Institute channels government funds directly to poor communities through the Baan Mankong programme. In one project on both sides of the Bang Kaen canal this enabled 3,000 households to remain *in situ* and rebuild their homes (see Photo 15.2) using modest

Photo 15.2 Cooperative housing project with communal land lease on Bang Kaen Canal, Bangkok
Credit: Geoffrey Payne

grants of $2,500 per family and community-based loans of $8,000 (recently increased to about $12,000) at 4 per cent over 15 years. The cooperative adds a further 2 per cent interest annually to cover the costs of community welfare facilities and management costs. Communal leases of 30 years are provided to all cooperatives and the project has resulted in a dramatic level of new investment and improved living standards. It also prevents market-driven displacement of the existing residents. As part of the project, a community library was also developed offering social and educational facilities for all age groups. According to Boonyabancha (2005):

> Secure land tenure terms are negotiated for most communities individually, using a variety of tenure options, such as co-operative land purchase, long-term lease contracts, land swapping, land sharing or long-term user rights. Most of the tenure negotiations happen locally, with minimal legal procedures and minimal involvement of national bodies, but in all cases, the emphasis is on collective – rather than individual – land tenure.

A survey by Archer (2012: 178) found that 'While tenure is regarded as secure in the short term, the long-term situation is not so clear. Homes cannot be sold on outside the community, and therefore Baan Mankong is valued more for improving shelter and strengthening community cohesiveness, rather than as a profit-driven financial investment'. This is the intention of the project, since it prevents the area from entering into an increasingly financialized national housing market. The landholding structure ensures that it will be available in the long term for those in need of a home.

Summary and proposal

Visiting a semi-legal settlement in Jakarta many years ago, I met a man rebuilding his home. When asked where he was living while the work was under way, he pointed to an attractive three storey house on the other side of the lane and said that he had accommodated the owner when his house was being rebuilt and now the favour was being returned. While governments and donor agencies may prefer top-down 'smart' solutions that can improve land and housing sector management, this form of self-managed, pragmatic, incremental approach has proved to be far more responsive to the needs of low-income communities, is market-sensitive and institutionally simple to manage. Systems of land tenure and property rights that encourage social cohesion rather than competition can also accelerate improvements in living conditions and wellbeing for growing urban populations.

Given the global and local diversity of tenure systems and categories, the fact that the legal status of large areas of land in and adjacent to urban areas is unregistered, and the fact that land has immense emotional and cultural importance, the priority of tenure policy should be on short-term occupancy rights and security of tenure, irrespective of an area's legal status. The examples reviewed above provide a wide range of short, medium and longer-term options to meet this challenge and enable societies to evolve locally appropriate responses over time.

Experience shows that there are no quick fixes to create the diverse and demand-sensitive options capable of meeting changing scenarios. While modern surveying technology can be extremely helpful in clarifying claims and rights, it takes time to balance competing interests and resolve disputes. In all countries, interventions should therefore focus on building closer links between municipalities and neighbourhood community leaders or representatives. For countries where the supply of land and housing have been the sole preserve of the state, it is essential that governments quickly acquire a good understanding of how private sector land and housing markets operate so that they are able to ensure the maximum public benefit from a given site. This will require a major commitment to reviewing existing constraints and increasing the skills and working practices of professional staff in central and local government line agencies. Technical assistance is widely available to help develop this institutional capability and should be sought without hesitation. Interventions in such countries should focus on:

- Changing the mindset of politicians and professionals to increase opportunities for more demand-sensitive approaches.
- Increasing the role of local ward leaders and civil society organizations so they act as conduits to identify and channel local needs at settlement level to municipal leaders.
- Creating and supporting residents' associations.

Another priority for policy is the need to promote the concept of trusteeship, or stewardship as manifested in customary forms of ownership and as claimed, but not always delivered, through state ownership. Balancing competition for land with options that strengthen a sense of community, of protecting the long-term public interest in equitable and efficient development, and in being part of something bigger, can be a key part of enabling land and housing to be part of the solution to a more comprehensive form of social, environmental, and economic development. It is, in other words, a way of expressing the social and cultural value of land above its financial value, as part of a wider revolution in values proposed in Chapter 13.

As incremental and intermediate tenure helps households become more secure, some will naturally seek full individual ownership, in the form of cohousing or more conventional forms of individual home ownership either in the development of new housing projects, or in settlements where land is held communally. In both cases, such households should be required to take responsibility for meeting the full survey, legal, and administrative costs.

Notes

1. This chapter draws upon various sources, especially Payne (2020), and the author acknowledges with thanks the permission from publishers Edward Elgar, Cheltenham, to reproduce parts of the original text.
2. Social Tenure Domain Model (STDM) website <https://stdm.gltn.net> [accessed 30 April 2021].
3. Payne (2007) is published in Volume Three of A. Mengi (ed.) (2007) *Kent ve Politika Antik Kentten Dunya Kentine*, a six-volume series in honour of Professor Ruşen Keleş.
4. Marmalade Lane – Cambridge's First Cohousing Community <https://marmaladelane.co.uk/> [accessed 30 April 2021].

CHAPTER 16
Spatial planning and land use for adequate housing

How can spatial planning and land use help to reduce inequality and meet the climate challenge in a post pandemic world? As with most simple questions, the answers are complicated. Parameters for innovation in spatial planning will be set by the policy, legal, and regulatory frameworks applicable at national, regional, and local levels. As advocated in previous chapters, a key factor at each level of decision-making is the need to prioritize the social, cultural, and environmental value of land at least as much as its economic value. All the evidence from settlements planned and developed by their residents shows that every square centimetre of land is always put to locally defined productive use. However, many well-intentioned officially planned developments waste large areas of land by failing to understand the social needs and cultural factors that influence how people relate to each other spatially.

As the examples presented in Chapter 2 demonstrate, the qualities that make a place meaningful permeate our sense of identity and belonging, though they may not be experienced consciously. They are the result of exogenous and endogenous influences that interact and change over time. Thus, planning a settlement or housing project needs to reflect the way people perceive and use space, recognizing that cultures change over time. Creating environments that are responsive to local needs, but also adaptable, is therefore a key element in achieving places in which people feel at home.

The most effective way of planning new developments that reflect social and cultural priorities is by seeing how land is used in developments in which the residents have played an active role. These may appear to be 'unplanned' compared to the visual order created by professionals, but invariably promote mixed land uses and facilitate opportunities for improvisation and innovation. Cities are continually responding to changes in the external environment, so the larger the range of stakeholders, in public, private, and civil society sectors, who are actively involved in planning policy and practice, the more likely a city will succeed. Even newly planned cities, which appear ordered initially, have to adapt to changing needs and these cannot be managed without a high degree of flexibility. Ensuring transparency in the vast quantities of real-time data provided by modern urban management systems and including diverse groups in decision-making also reduces risks of abuse and enhances public support for policies. Under conditions in which market forces are dominant, urban management authorities need to operate in more innovative and strategic ways that promote investment on terms and conditions that can help reduce inequality and address the climate challenge. In this chapter, we consider options that enable spatial planning and land use management to improve access to housing within this context.

Cultural diversity

The need to consider cultural factors when planning new developments was amply demonstrated in the planning of a new state capital for Andhra Pradesh, India when the state was bifurcated in 2014. The then Chief Minister insisted that the Indian concept of *vastu* (see Chapter 2) was included in the master plan (Telgu360, 2016) and the international consultants preparing the plan had to make important adjustments to incorporate this.

Cultural factors apply more critically at the human scale of the neighbourhood, since this is the level at which we perceive and use the immediate environment. This helps to explain why migrant groups tend to concentrate in larger urban areas where economic opportunities are greater and where it is more likely that existing levels of social and cultural diversity makes it easier for them to establish and assimilate themselves. The need to find support from others with similar backgrounds and interests also explains why migrants congregate in the locations where earlier members of their community settled and parts of many major cities have become associated with specific cultural and ethnic groups and the lifestyles with which they are familiar. While this has led to tensions with the indigenous population, migrants invariably make an extremely positive contribution to the social, ethnic, and cultural diversity of the host community, which itself creates innovation and has been a key feature of the success London has achieved over centuries. One could even argue that attracting migrants from a wide range of backgrounds and facilitating their assimilation is the most effective way for a city to flourish. This suggests that layouts and built forms that can adapt to the changing needs of a diverse population will be more successful than those planned for single functions. This is particularly critical in a post-Covid-19 pandemic world where changing work patterns require that the character and function of neighbourhoods and buildings are likely to change. Flexibility will also need to be reflected in the layout and design of the public realm, since public open space provides a vital opportunity for promoting public health, wellbeing, and 'place-identity'. The principle of 'long life, loose fit and low energy' as promoted by Sir Alexander Gordon in 1972 (Langston, 2014), remains highly relevant today and settlements initially planned to reflect cultural values are therefore more likely to adapt to future needs.

Upgrading existing urban areas

The need to improve tenure security and connectivity to places of economic activity and social amenities is central to improving existing urban areas, especially for those on low incomes who are unable to pay for private or even public transport. This inevitably requires access to city centre locations that are likely to be highly expensive, posing the question of how the urban poor can benefit from more equitable planning. The policy instruments reviewed in Chapters 14 and 15 can be applied to achieve access to non-market forms of development by low- and middle-income groups in locations where land prices would otherwise constrain access.

Among the countries that have made great progress in upgrading existing urban settlements, Colombia, Indonesia, Thailand, and Turkey provide valuable lessons. In Colombia, the provision of public utilities by well-managed, profit-making state-owned enterprises, such as the Empresas Pùblicas de Medellin (EPM), contributed 30 per cent of all profits to Medellin's administrative budget in 2011 (Samad et al., 2012: 158). This helped improve the connectivity of the city's semi-legal and non-legal settlements to the central commercial area, improving household incomes and generating local investment in housing improvements. However, while improved connectivity is vital, even innovative developments may not achieve success unless undertaken in a participatory manner. As Cadavid (2011) reports, the installation of a cable car into a *favela* actually *reduced* house consolidation rates since it was perceived by residents as a menace that facilitated access by the authorities who they did not trust. However, in cases where the local population was actively involved, upgrading was highly successful. In fact, one settlement that had been considered the most dangerous area in what was at the time the most dangerous city in the world, was transformed into a dynamic neighbourhood and tourist attraction with roads, a complex system of escalators linking different levels, and footpaths providing an efficient, safe, and child-friendly environment (see Photo 16.1).

Photo 16.1 Improved infrastructure in Comuna 13 settlement, Medellin, Colombia
Credit: Geoffrey Payne

The need for trust between communities and authorities was demonstrated all too clearly when I was contributing to the upgrading of a Palestinian settlement in Amman, Jordan. The settlement at East Wahdat consisted of metal huts scattered across a steep-sided valley and was being upgraded as part of a World Bank-funded project. Naturally, the sight of a foreign planner walking through the site with a large map attracted intense suspicion which was quickly resolved when I asked if I could leave the map overnight with a family that had a smooth concrete floor. I knew that it would be examined intensely overnight, so was not surprised to be met the following day with a large group asking what the plan showed. Realizing that people found reading a two-dimensional map difficult, especially with numerous contour lines, I invited children to find small objects and once these were placed on the spot occupied by houses, everyone started making suggestions for paths and routes for public utilities. The result was a plan that led to the incremental development of the area and an Aga Khan award (Aga Khan Development Network, n.d.).

One of the most ambitious examples of settlement upgrading is that of Indonesia where a national 'Kampung Improvement Program' was launched in 1969 and expanded nationally during the 1970s. Later, the Neighbourhood Upgrading and Shelter Sector Project and the national level Programme for Community Empowerment promoted multi-sectoral community development with a strong focus on improving infrastructure. Community participation was particularly strong in the city of Surabaya, where local committees managed a 10-point programme including physical upgrading, child care, maternal support, and waste management. To improve the sense of identity of *kampungs*, competitions were also held to design entrances, as shown in Photo 16.2.

More recently, an inner-city *kampung* (Kampung Petagogan) in Jakarta was redeveloped with support from the then-Governor, Joko Widodo (who was later elected President of Indonesia). It provided compact, two-storey structures with space for commercial activity along narrow lanes and small public open spaces, allowing low-income households to live in a location that would otherwise have been unaffordable. Elsewhere in Asia, Thailand's Baan Mankong Programme launched in 2003 has been implemented in 200 towns and cities, targeting 300,000 households in 2,000 settlements. External support is provided directly to community organizations that manage and implement the whole process. In this way, not only are settlements improved following local priorities, but local capacity is enhanced in addressing other challenges. The policy has enabled many low-income communities to remain in prime urban locations, demonstrating that sensitive spatial planning can help reduce social segregation.

In Turkey, once the residents of *gecekondu* housing settlements in Ankara had achieved de facto tenure security in the 1970s–1980s, they followed traditional rural self-help practices and campaigned through local *muhktars* or ward leaders for the improvement of their *mahalles*, or wards. For peri-urban

Photo 16.2 Entrance to an upgraded *kampung* settlement in Surabaya, Indonesia
Credit: Geoffrey Payne

areas, the priority was improved road access to the city centre. The municipality would send engineers and surveyors to assess the best route and communities had three options: 1) accept the plan and organize any necessary relocations; 2) make minor modifications; or 3) reject the proposal. Communities naturally tended to adopt one of the two first options and would sometimes even provide labour to complete the project. A wave of local investment would follow and individual houses on the main roads were quickly replaced by apartment blocks, shops, cafes, and other facilities funded by local developers.

For inner-city settlements, or those enveloped by urban expansion during the 1980s and 1990s, land prices increased steadily and there was little difference in price between land with formal titles and the *gecekondu* areas. To facilitate the gradual integration of *gecekondus* into the formal land market, the municipality prepared simple block layout plans. These plans meant that when developers considered a particular area was suitable for redevelopment based on a calculation of adequate profit margins, they would approach residents and negotiate the number of apartments required in order to obtain and redevelop the land (see Photo 16.3). Over time, the *gecekondu* residents learned to negotiate for two or even three apartments in the new development, allowing them to become multiple home-owners, while the developers made a reasonable profit and the city generated additional revenues. These pragmatic approaches to spatial planning enabled Ankara to assimilate vast numbers of rural-urban migrants in ways that were particularly beneficial to the poor. However, during the 1990s, private and state-owned developers asserted a

Photo 16.3 *Gecekondus* being replaced by apartment blocks in Ankara
Credit: Geoffrey Payne

more dominant role in urban development and large areas were redeveloped in less sympathetic ways, generating considerable opposition, particularly in Istanbul. The globalization of neoliberal economics ensured that this outcome rapidly became the norm.

Enabling low-income groups to retain a stake in high-priced inner-city locations is an immense challenge. Enabling them to resist the pressure of market forces after upgrading is even more challenging. The Baan Mankong programme in Thailand succeeded largely by granting communal, not individual, forms of tenure and property rights. In a notable approach in Mumbai, where land prices in the late 1990s were the highest in the world, a similar approach was adopted following regulations introduced in 1995. Development controls (floor space index) were relaxed and profits from the sale of additional dwellings used to finance the provision of 20 m^2 apartments by land owners, developers, or cooperatives of unauthorized settlers. This enabled settlers on a site in Sambhajinagar, central Mumbai, to buy the land and manage the redevelopment with the help of a local architect. Fortunately, the community had good relations with the land owner who was suitably compensated and his daughter even participated in the opening ceremony. The affection shown towards her when they presented her with a sari and the singular dedication with which the scheme was undertaken strengthened an emotional bond. Instead of using the remaining profits to purchase colour televisions, the community resolved to create a fund to finance their children's education. The whole community was therefore enabled to remain in an otherwise unaffordable location, the land-owner was content, and the project was integrated in to the formal city.

The 2020 Covid-19 pandemic has had a dramatic impact pandemic has had a dramatic impact on the way people live and work in cities around the world and provides an opportunity to redesignate some inner-city commercial areas for mixed use, including housing, thereby promoting improved connectivity between work, home, and social facilities. By promoting mixed land use, polycentric urban forms can diffuse land values, improving access to employment opportunities from and within primarily residential areas. Reducing the need for travel, towns and cities can also improve public health and wellbeing, especially if matched by the devolution of powers to the local level, giving people more opportunities to create a locally congenial and biodiverse local environment. Achieving these aims requires political leadership and openness to swift and significant changes from the urban status quo in most large cities.

Planning for expansion

Meeting the needs of existing residents for secure land and affordable housing is only part of the challenge facing urban authorities. As urban populations increase, so does the demand for additional space. Given the need to reduce carbon emissions and promote public health, an equally important factor is to reduce the ecological footprint of urban areas through more compact urban forms, efficient public transport networks, and a focus on human mobility over private automobiles. In this sense, the financialization of land and property has had one benefit of restricting land supply and encouraging denser city centres. But the focus on high-rise residential housing inspired by Hong Kong, Singapore, or New York, has been motivated by the desire by property investors to maximize profits, rather than an interest in adequate housing provision or climate security. The challenge is therefore to address vested interests and ensure that spatial expansion is sufficient to meet reasonable needs, but not so profligate as to encroach unnecessarily on surrounding rural areas. As the examples presented in Part Two demonstrate, urban sprawl and satellite towns increase carbon emissions and reduce social interaction and economic vitality. Peri-urban densification and making satellite towns relatively self-sufficient (as proposed for Mongolia in Chapter 11) can both reduce emissions and reduce inequality by increasing income opportunities for vulnerable groups and reducing over-crowding in existing settlements.

To meet the Sustainable Development Goals (SDGs), it is vital that urban areas minimize their ecological footprint, as proposed by Girardet (1990, 2019; 1996). To achieve SDG 11.3.1[1] (United Nations, 2021), it is also important that the area of land consumed by cities does not increase at a higher rate than their population. However, a global survey of 120 cities (Angel et al., 2011) shows that urban land cover has, on average, grown more than three times as much as the urban population, highlighting the urgent need for more compact urban development models. The rate at which cities consume non-renewable resources became a global issue in the 1980s, prompting a debate on compact urban forms that is even more relevant now. Jenks and Burgess (2000) refer to the need for spatial planning to reduce energy demands but also note that in rapidly urbanizing countries, densification of inner-city areas may result in the unrecoverable loss of built cultural heritage, as in Shanghai, and in 'the break-up of communities, loss of "social capital" loss of important traditional and "informal" low-income services and manufacturing activities, and the destruction of livelihood patterns which are highly sustainable'. In Jakarta, some inner-city settlements have been relocated to cheaper land in the urban periphery, though Indonesia is also a global leader in regenerating high density inner-city areas. The main scope for creating more compact urban development is therefore likely to be through increasing the density of unauthorized peri-urban areas, as applied in Ankara. Given the low densities in most such settlements, considerable progress can be made without the need for high-rise developments, since these will not reflect cultural traditions and the high levels of embodied energy they impose will not be consistent with the need to reduce carbon emissions. By promoting the densification of unauthorized peri-urban settlements, spatial planning can also be a powerful vehicle for improving economic opportunities for local residents, though care will be required to prevent vested interest groups from capturing the largest increments in land value.

Another opportunity exists as a result of the large number of peri-urban industrial estates being developed in countries like Ethiopia, Uganda, and Vietnam. In the capital cities of these countries, lower land prices can make affordable housing an effective means of compact, mixed use development. As the examples of Ismailia, Egypt and Lima, Peru and countless other cities demonstrate, densifying peri-urban areas can also promote self-financed, efficient, and culturally appropriate urban development in which the urban poor can be the primary beneficiaries. While initial stages of self-planned and built housing settlements are low density (Photo 16.4), the priority is to establish road layouts that facilitate road access and the cost-effective provision of public utilities (Photo 16.5). As demand increases, so some households provide additional rooms for rent to new settlers, increasing their incomes and enabling them to expand and improve their homes with more permanent materials (Photo 16.6). Housing therefore becomes a means of steady social and economic development with local businesses opening to serve the increasing population. Even those unable to afford improvements benefit from the enhanced services and property values generated by their neighbours (Photo 16.7). Once the settlement has consolidated, the area is formally established as part of the city and public services are provided.

In Lima and other Peruvian cities, such large-scale, community-led urban developments were developed in the 1960s. Initially, they faced fierce official opposition but were later acknowledged and incorporated into city plans.[2]

SPATIAL PLANNING AND LAND USE FOR ADEQUATE HOUSING 231

Photo 16.4 Initial stage of urban development in Ismailia, Egypt, by settlers
Credit: Geoffrey Payne

Photo 16.5 Stage two of incremental housing development and road layouts in Ismailia
Credit: Geoffrey Payne

232 SOMEWHERE TO LIVE

Photo 16.6 A separate entrance for rental housing enables owners to finance home improvements with permanent materials ready for use in Ismailia
Credit: Geoffrey Payne

Photo 16.7 Investment by some residents also increases the value of other homes in the area
Credit: Geoffrey Payne

The history of these developments should inspire local residents and city planners to consider what innovations might be achievable in the Covid-19 recovery period.

The limitations of master plans

Developing a new city, or major urban development, requires the preparation of a master plan for the spatial allocation of intended land uses and the necessary steps to acquire the land or ensure that the development will conform to intentions. Applying the many policy instruments summarized in Chapters 14 and 15 can help to achieve this. However, it takes many years before new cities become vibrant social and economic centres and outgrow the original plans, while some never achieve this as noted by Sims (2011: 171) in the case of Egypt's new towns.

A not uncommon limitation of master plans is that they are prepared independently of the economic resources required to implement them, or are unresponsive to changes in the economic environment. D'Souza (1989) claimed that during his years as a civil servant in India, he hardly saw a city plan which gave any idea of where the funds for implementing it would be found and globally little appears to have changed since. In market-based economies, a further limitation is that plans make public the areas where investment may be encouraged or discouraged, so that land-owners in areas where official compensation is perceived to be less than reasonable may sell to a developer who will pre-empt the plan by developing an area for more profitable use. Alternatively, developers or speculators (often the same) may acquire land at its existing use value and withhold it from development in order to maximize profits. In countries where planning is a matter of state directive, as in China, Vietnam, and Mongolia, spatial master plans reflect a predilection by both planning officials and those in power for central control that has so far provided very mixed outcomes and lacks evidence of local demand.

While new cities are being planned in many countries (see Chapter 6), the most common issue is how to plan the expansion of existing urban areas. As discussed in the case studies reviewed in Part Two, spatial planning and development control in many urbanizing countries are frequently based on assumptions, interests, and methods inherited or imported from previous periods and external legal frameworks. Unfortunately, the experience of colonialism continues to influence planning policies in many currently urbanizing countries where the urban form was designed to isolate activities and social groups and benefit colonial communities. The implementation of master plans since independence has often remained strongly influenced by this legacy. As a result, housing and settlement patterns have continued to operate to the clear benefit of the social and political elite and to the disadvantage of incoming migrants and the indigenous urban poor who are unable to afford increasing prices or conform to official norms and standards.

The imposition of rigid controls on land use common to many master plans (see the case of Ulaanbaatar, Chapter 11) not only inhibits innovation and investment, but also protects existing commercial activities from competition, which impedes the development of an efficient and demand-driven form of urban development. International experience demonstrates that mixed land use stimulates social interaction and economic development and is a key feature of successful cities. UN-Habitat recommends that while separating incompatible land uses, such as polluting industries and housing is a rational decision, 'monofunctional zoning should be reduced to no more than 10–15 per cent of the overall land' (UN-Habitat, 2014b: 28). Experience also shows that the more stakeholders that are involved in the planning process, the more sound and successful outcomes are likely to be. Finally, the static nature of master plans also means that they are only likely to be appropriate at a specific point in the development of a city; before and after that, they are inefficient and fail to acknowledge that cities are continually evolving organisms.

Structure, or strategic development plans and the participatory planning approach to urban expansion

To address the limitations of master plans, many countries have opted to apply structure, or strategic development, plans. The advantage of these is that they provide a strategic framework, within which local proposals can respond to changing needs and resources through action planning or participatory planning approaches. Such combinations can serve to strengthen good urban governance through the active involvement of civil society in decisions regarding urban development and thereby enhance the legitimacy of government action and the planning process.

For structure plans to succeed, they need public support. One way to achieve this to undertake a City Development Strategy (CDS) as advocated by Cities Alliance (2021). A CDS is a tool that helps a city harness the potential of urbanization and enables a city to develop a coordinated, institutional framework to make the most of opportunities. Most importantly, a CDS gives residents a voice in the future of the place where they live. CDSs have been undertaken for many cities and provide for a holistic approach to strategic development. However, as with any policy approach, they are not without limitations and in a review, Harris (2014) notes the following:

1. The speed of implementation was itself a problem since the stress fell upon producing a product, a plan (even if it was an 'Action plan', not a Master Plan), rather than reshaping the institutional structure of city government, whether to institutionalize economic, poverty, and environmental monitoring, or the participatory underpinning of management.
2. There were rarely the skills available in the city to staff the effort, and no time to encourage the development of those skills for permanent

strategy making. Thus the problem besetting the old city planning exercise re-emerged – a team of planning consultants was dispatched to the city to put together a plan with only rare inputs from the local population and, after completion, even more rare ownership of the plan by the city authorities.
3. In former centrally planned economies (China, Vietnam, Mongolia), there was often a wealth of local economic data (since the central planning procedures mandated the drawing up of local economic plans) but few civic organizations to make participation meaningful.
4. Some cities gave up on attempting an economic strategy, and then, without a strategy for employment growth, had no programme to attack poverty other than local government delivering traditional services.
5. So far as one could see, elements of the full programme of support institutions, as it occurred in Europe and North America – the stakeholders city forum, public-private city development corporations, municipal economic development departments, and city level statistical and monitoring units – rarely appeared.

Another required factor for the successful completion of a CDS as a basis for action, not just a report, is that of political commitment and leadership. Harris reports that a change of mayor in Cali, Colombia, resulted in the report having little effect. Personal experience records the same outcome in Tirana, Albania, though the mayor who commissioned the CDS later became Prime Minister as a result of undertaking popular civic improvements. The key to success in every case is the presence of strong, public-spirited, and innovative local leadership.

Planning new development at local scale

Having considered the ways in which spatial planning and land management can reduce inequality and address the climate crisis at city level, how can it help at the local, neighbourhood level? Secondly, how can adequate housing be provided without the need for external financial subsidies? Within a diverse urban land and housing supply system as proposed in Chapter 14, local level planning can address both issues and questions, even within the constraints imposed by market forces. Successful local level planning requires the state to create and maintain a 'level playing field' in which different suppliers of land, services, credit, and building components can compete on equal terms with clear standards protecting users (Edkins, 2019).[3] More emphasis will also be needed to create and strengthen partnerships between public, private, and community sectors and form multi-disciplinary teams to develop effective proposals. Finally, by applying the discipline of the private sector, including a mix of commercial, light industrial workshops or 'start-up' opportunities, and mixed-income housing, a surplus can be generated that can be reallocated towards the cost of providing basic public services for all households, especially if integrated with policies advocated in Chapter 13. The amount of such surplus a development can generate will depend on several factors, especially the location and type of development concerned, but the objective of maximizing benefits to those in need should be applied in all cases. In developments proposed by the private sector, meeting this objective should be a condition for granting development permission.

While individual developments will not address citywide constraints to better urban governance, they provide an invaluable opportunity to test innovative approaches that can then be expanded if successful. Since every area designated for urban development is unique, feasibility studies are needed to identify the range of social groups and land uses to be included. The larger the site, the more important it is to include a wide range of social groups and land uses, so that a development can create a compact, relatively self-sustained, and diverse neighbourhood. An additional requirement for success is the preparation of site development plans by multi-disciplinary teams, as this enables social, economic, and environmental aspects to be considered within a broad policy context.

A critical factor will be the range of households and income groups for whom the site is being developed. This will determine the type and standard of development which can be afforded initially and over a given period. The first stage is therefore to determine the target groups for whom the scheme is being developed and the mix of uses and standards of initial development. This involves estimating the costs of preliminary proposals and comparing them to resources, or the ability to pay. Realizing the most appropriate combination of levels of provision with affordability is a key feature of pro-poor planning and involves an iterative process of testing and refining in order to achieve an optimal outcome on a given site.

For low-income households, the local equivalent of every dollar by which costs increase will reduce affordability, so the key to success is to reduce initial levels of provision while focusing on providing those elements that people cannot provide for themselves. Thus location, basic security, and services, plus sufficient space, are the key elements required. It will also be necessary to balance costs, many of which are inelastic except for the level of provision selected, against available resources, which may also be inelastic. The skill is therefore to manipulate the types and levels of provision for different components so that a project is viable. In doing this, the first objective is to minimize entry costs to the settlement. The second objective is to do this in ways that stimulate subsequent improvement by residents.

Assessing affordability

This can be done by estimating the range of household incomes and the proportion of net incomes that can reasonably be allocated for housing and related expenditure. UN-Habitat (2019: 6) defines housing affordability as a maximum of 30 per cent of total household incomes for rental and a maximum house price-to-income ratio of 3:1 for home purchase, though an addition can be made if a deposit is provided. Simple discount tables can indicate the monthly amounts that households can afford and a capital sum they can afford to borrow can be generated by assessing the period of repayment at a given interest rate over a period of, say, 25 years (Davidson and Payne, 2000).[4] Household structure will also influence affordability since a large family will have different needs from those of a single-person household, or a retired couple, even if their incomes, and therefore affordability, are the same.

Assessing costs

Any urban development involves a wide range of costs, including:

- *Land acquisition*. The market or opportunity costs.
- *Land development or site preparation, flood protection*, and so on.
- *Services*. The capital and recurring costs of off-site, on-site, and on-plot infrastructure.
- *Construction*. Including materials and labour.
- *Finance*. The market or opportunity cost of borrowing to meet the capital costs of development. This will vary according to the rate of interest charged and the period over which repayment is to be made.
- *Fees and profit*. To cover the design, supervision, and management/administration of the project and contractors' overheads and profit.
- *Maintenance and depreciation*.
- *Contingencies*, especially against default.

Under conditions of high inflation, the greatest single cost will be the money needed to finance the development. In such cases, the most effective way to reduce overall costs is to extend the period over which any loans are repaid. Where inflation is low, the highest single cost is likely to be that of land. In this case, the most effective way to reduce unit land costs at the neighbourhood level is by maximizing the area of private, revenue-generating land uses. Extensive international research (Caminos and Goethert, 1976; Davidson and Payne, 2000) demonstrates that a well-designed development for about 5,000 people requires basic communal facilities, such as a primary school, health clinic, and place of worship, which can be provided on about 15 per cent of the developable area. A larger population will require not only a proportional increase of these facilities, but also the addition of new ones and a higher proportion of the land allocated. For example, a development for 20,000 people will require four primary schools and a secondary school, plus more public services. If the land for public facilities is assumed to be financed by the relevant agency providing them, the unit price of land will be significantly influenced by the proportion of the total area of privately occupied and revenue-generating land. This is illustrated in Table 16.1 where the cost of the 20 per cent public land area in the first case has to be borne by the 65 per cent private area, representing less than a third of the private area. However,

Table 16.1 Allocating land uses by category

Land use category	Percentage of land use	
Private, developable land	65	50
Public areas (roads, etc.)	20	35
Communal areas (schools, health centres, places of worship, etc.)	15	15

in the second case, the cost of the 35 per cent of unproductive public areas has to be borne by the 50 per cent private area, representing 70 per cent of the private area. Where both public and private areas have to be paid for, a modest increase of 15 per cent in the public area more than doubles the unit price of a private plot.

For new developments to be affordable, every effort should therefore be made to maximize the proportion of private land available for productive use, as is done in most settlements planned by their residents. Reducing rights of way standards for roads to the minimum for safe circulation and making sure that all public open space is put to good use can be a highly effective means of reducing unit land costs and providing adequate communal areas. Given the length of roads, even in a relatively small development, reducing road reservations by 1 metre can increase the area of land available for private, revenue-generating uses, reducing land costs. Local rights of way should encourage multi-modal uses, including cycling and walking with options for social use where possible.

A conceptual layout for housing for different income groups, communal amenities, and public rights of way based on proposals by Caminos and Goethert is illustrated in Figure 16.1. By locating the more expensive plots of land on the main roads, where infrastructure is readily available, the additional revenues generated can be reallocated as a cross-subsidy towards the incremental provision of public utilities for lower income groups, even if this requires them to depend upon basic levels of connections, such as public standpipes and pit latrines or septic tanks for an initial period until resources are sufficient to provide connections to full services. Clearly, layouts will need to be adapted to meet site conditions and access points and also reflect local cultural traditions. This can be achieved by studying the way public land and communal spaces are organized and used in existing primarily residential areas where residents have been able to influence the form of development. It also needs to be remembered that where the provision of infrastructure can be afforded throughout an area, the more desirable, and therefore more expensive, plots are likely to be those close to amenities such as open space, rather than facing main roads.

Since water and sanitation connections are normally provided along main roads, this is the logical location for commercial activity and for housing those groups who can afford full services at the outset. This makes it less expensive to extend services to households nearby who cannot afford connections initially. In expensive locations, apartments in four or five storey building offer

SPATIAL PLANNING AND LAND USE FOR ADEQUATE HOUSING 239

Social clustering and housing across the infrastructure grid hierarchy

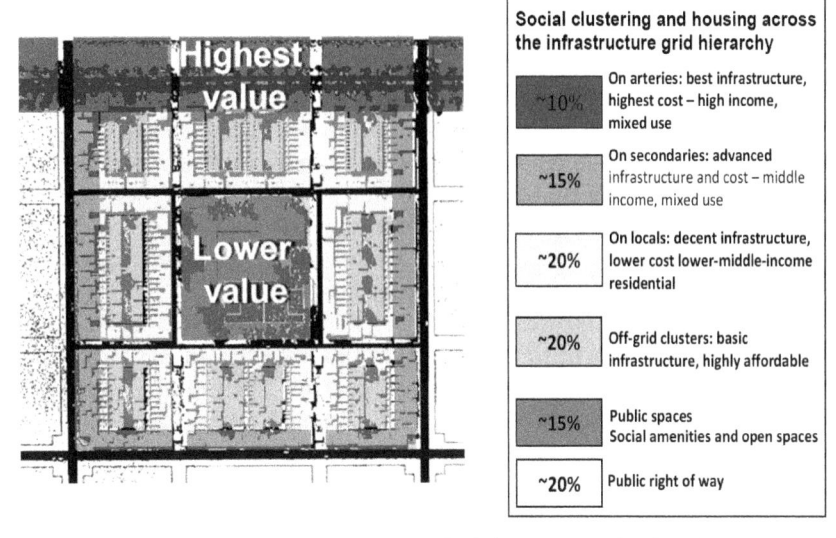

~10%	On arteries: best infrastructure, highest cost – high income, mixed use
~15%	On secondaries: advanced infrastructure and cost – middle income, mixed use
~20%	On locals: decent infrastructure, lower cost lower-middle-income residential
~20%	Off-grid clusters: basic infrastructure, highly affordable
~15%	Public spaces Social amenities and open spaces
~20%	Public right of way

Figure 16.1 Social clustering and housing across the infrastructure grid hierarchy
Credit: With thanks to Matthias Nohn for producing this diagram for this book showing social clustering and housing across the infrastructure grid hierarchy, based on Caminos and Goethert (1976)

opportunities to accommodate lower income households without the need for expensive lifts and costs can be reduced if the ground floor is allocated for commercial use. Where individual plots are feasible, the key consideration is plot size, though plot shape is also important. An obvious option for reducing plot costs is to reduce plot area to the minimum considered appropriate to meet social and cultural needs. In both cases, the key objective should be to minimize the proportion of land required for circulation and provide a mixture of housing types and land uses. However, in locations where significant densification is likely, minimal street widths can limit flexibility.

Attributing costs

Having identified project costs and levels of affordability, a second priority is to determine which costs should be attributable to the project. Consider the following situation in which an area of 100 hectares has been designated as part of an urban expansion proposal. The designated area is 2 kilometres from a major highway and land has to be acquired to provide an access road 20 metres wide. Should the cost of land needed for the 2 kilometre road be: 1) paid for out of city revenues, given that the additional housing will meet increased need and prevent price inflation; 2) paid for by the residents of the area to be developed who are the primary beneficiaries; 3) distributed between the city and the residents; or 4) some other arrangement?

In many cases, one of the first three options would be applied. However, a truly 'smart' urban authority would approach the owner or owners of the land required for the road and negotiate a solution that required that the land for the road be provided free of cost, together with an additional area adjacent to the road for the provision of public facilities such as schools and parks, in return for which the land owner/s would receive planning permission to develop the remaining land on each side of the road for urban uses, including housing and some commercial development. The key for success is to ensure that the costs, risks, and benefits from a development are allocated equitably and in a way that maximizes the public benefit.

Unlike settlement layouts and plot sizes, levels of services provision can vary enormously from initial to fully consolidated levels. In fact, progressive improvement is the norm in many urban areas. The objective should be to provide the minimum initial level to permit permanent occupation of individual plots. The provision of on-plot water will be a major cost threshold, since it will lead to increased consumption and therefore the need for improved disposal systems. Initial provision should be designed to facilitate subsequent upgrading, though apartments will require full initial provision.

The land, buildings, and services for public facilities and amenities, such as schools and health clinics, are normally provided and paid for by the agency concerned and should therefore be provided in accordance with local norms and excluded from the project budget. By adopting these approaches, the logic of the market can be applied in a way that maximizes public benefit.

Although the provision of public open space does not directly generate revenues, it can provide a strong indirect opportunity since many people will be willing to pay a premium for direct access. It is no coincidence that the highest residential values in New York are next to Central Park and in London are next to Hyde Park. The distribution of small landscaped open spaces can dramatically enhance an area if designed in a way that reflects cultural norms.

Even more important than its potential contribution to project finances, public open space provides a vital basis for public wellbeing. Suresh Gogte, a senior planner of Navi Mumbai, the new satellite city for Mumbai developed in the 1970s, once recalled how he would spend time sitting in a small local public space watching as people met and moved through. After a while, he noticed a pattern to the way the space was used. Early in the morning, maids would meet on their way to work and exchange complaints about the women they worked for. Mid-morning the upper-income women would meet and complain about their maids; lunchtime, office workers would meet to complain about their bosses; mid-afternoon, mothers would meet to complain about their teenage children and in the evening, the teenagers would meet to complain about their parents and plan their futures. What he realized was that the space served a vital function as a social safety valve, a far more important function than simply being attractive.

Once the market or opportunity costs of land have been added to the unit costs of infrastructure and construction, initial estimates can be made of the likely unit costs for housing provision. These costs can be further reduced by maximizing opportunities for incremental, resident-led house construction or the expansion of initial 'starter homes', an issue explored in more detail in Chapter 17. Where levels of affordability and attributed costs are in balance, a project can be considered viable. Where this is not the case, every effort should be made to further reduce costs or increase the internal cross-subsidy. This iterative process is the key to successful project planning at neighbourhood level. In making decisions, the key reference point should always be to compare proposed provision with existing forms of land and housing in areas where the target population live, since these will provide invaluable evidence of the key priorities in terms of land, levels of initial infrastructure, and housing that will be relevant in new developments. Since the poor are the experts in coping with poverty, professionals should be careful to learn from them.

The principle of incremental development has been applied in many countries, including sites and services as pioneered by the World Bank in Nairobi and other cities in the early 1970s and applied at scale in the Rohini project in New Delhi in the 1980s. The Rohini project provided housing and serviced plots for approximately a million people, including those on low incomes, for whom small plots were grouped around communal courtyards replicating the approach adopted in many informal settlements. It remains a valid option in countries at all levels of economic development

Designing the public realm

Producing cost-effective development is essential in providing affordable housing. However, it is not the only objective of good spatial planning. Creating developments in which people feel at home and which reflect their social and cultural values is the central role of good urban design and planning. As discussed in Chapter 2, place-making is a complex process and needs to reflect the priorities and lifestyles of the projected residents. In a pioneering urban design publication, Bentley et al. (1985) propose seven criteria for achieving responsive environments:

1. *Permeability*, relates to the number of alternative ways through an environment. A good layout is one with many options.
2. *Variety*, a range of land uses, such as a mix of housing, offices, shops, and workshops.
3. *Legibility*, or the ease by which people can find their way around an area.
4. *Robustness*, places that can be used for different purposes offer their users choice and are likely to be more resilient in responding to change.
5. *Visual appropriateness*, or the meanings and interpretations that people put on a place.

6. *Richness*, or the visual and non-visual elements that enrich the sense of a place.
7. *Personalization*, or the ability of people to put their own stamp on an area.

The ability to create developments that are affordable and reflect these diverse elements in a culturally sensitive manner is the basis of good new urban development and is integral to effective place-making.

Detailed project design

The regulatory framework of planning standards and regulations exerts a major impact on project costs, affordability, and therefore the ability of people to access formal housing. Before preparing projects seeking to meet the needs of the poor, an audit or review should therefore be undertaken of urban planning and building standards, regulations and administrative procedures (Payne and Majale, 2004). If this reveals that the minimum official residential plot size is significantly larger than is widely applicable in a city, households will be denied legal housing through no fault of their own. Imposing space standards based on aspirations, rather than realities, does untold harm to a city. Similarly, planning regulations that prevent home-based economic enterprises, constrain residents from being able to use their homes as a resource. To be effective and acceptable to the general public, it is essential that planning regulations are not unduly restrictive and are relevant to the local context.

Another regulatory constraint that has attracted criticism is that of Floor Area Ratio[5] (FAR). Some analysts (e.g. Bertaud and Brueckner, 2005; Bertaud et al., 2005; Brueckner, 2009) consider it impedes the efficient development of urban land compared to what would have been the case had market forces determined the density and height of urban development. Applying their analysis to the conventional monocentric urban model, they conclude that the restriction results in urban sprawl, increased housing prices, and commuting. Clearly, a very restrictive FAR can generate these outcomes. However, while a "common-sense FSI" as advocated by Bertaud and Buckley (2005) is advisable, a degree of restriction can help in guiding development to what may be considered more appropriate locations and helping to create a multi-nucleated urban spatial structure, rather than the conventional Central Business District (CBD) of a mono-centric spatial urban structure Bertaud and Brueckner applied.[6]

Moving and living better

Transport policy is a major driver of economic, social, and spatial development. By far the most ambitious example to date is the Chinese-funded Belt and Road Initiative that aims to link Beijing with cities across Asia via Moscow to Europe, promoting increased trade and investment at numerous points in between. China is also a global leader in transport oriented development (TOD), linking cities through the construction of new domestic airports and a historically unprecedented network of high-speed trains and highways. This leadership extends beyond the domestic infrastructure build out and as Yang (2018: 41) notes, 'The two recently-founded development banks – the Asian Infrastructure Investment Bank and the New Development Bank, were established under the leadership of China to address the increasing infrastructure needs in Asia'. This approach is promoting economic growth in many countries, though it appears that the economic impact in China is reducing as the housing and infrastructure systems begin to reach saturation level (Deng et al., 2013).

At city level, extending transportation routes can dramatically increase peri-urban land values and the potential for attracting inward investment and opportunities to capture a reasonable proportion of the increment in value for allocation in the public interest. When developing the new Indian city of Navi Mumbai in the 1970s, the state-owned City and Industrial Development Corporation pioneered a TOD approach that financed the main road and railway infrastructure from central Mumbai to the new city centre by selling land around the new terminal, including air rights over the new railway station.

Expanding road transport networks can, however, have negative impacts. As we saw in Chapter 3, air pollution from private vehicles has killed millions of urban residents globally. In many Asian cities, such as Phnom Penh, Ho Chi Minh City, and Jakarta, most journeys are by motorcycle and journeys to work frequently take more than two hours each way. Once in the city centre, motorcycles not only occupy all road space, but also park in large numbers along footpaths, forcing pedestrians to walk along the road, exposing them both to danger from collisions and air pollution. As economies grow, motorcycles are replaced by private cars that take up more space, causing so much congestion in Bangkok that the traffic police are even trained in midwifery.

The need to reduce the carbon footprint and improve access by all social groups to locations for work and social amenities within cities has promoted the growth of TOD approaches in many countries.[7] This includes the 15-minute city concept in which all essential amenities should be available within walking and cycling distance, reducing the need for private vehicles and the expensive land that they consume both in movement and when parked. In Los Angeles, roads and parking account for nearly 50 per cent of all urban land (Transport Geography, n.d.) and in London, 6.8 million parking spaces take up nearly 8,000 hectares of expensive land (Bates and Leibling, 2012), an area that could go a long way to providing affordable housing. Levels of car ownership in London decline as housing density increases, suggesting that the need for individual car ownership is less where local access to places of employment and entertainment is enhanced. Higher density levels also improve the financial viability of public transport such as rapid transit bus or train networks to facilities not locally available. In this way, TOD can enable land use planning to stimulate local economic activity, provide for a range of housing, reduce overall transport, reduce carbon emissions, and, most importantly, improve health and wellbeing.

Proposals in London, Paris, and Madrid to reduce air pollution include the introduction of car-free days and ultra low emission zones which will require the replacement of older, polluting cars. Advocates of the status quo in affluent urban areas with high levels of car ownership may claim that the rapid development of battery-powered cars undermines the need for change. However, this ignores the fact that the electricity powering such vehicles will put renewable power systems, such as solar and wind, under great pressure at a time when they have not been able to meet demand for more basic needs. Also, electric vehicles are not entirely emission-free. They require large quantities of rare-Earth metals, such as cobalt, which need extensive mining which in turn imposes heavy environmental costs, thereby simply passing the problem further down the line. Replacing all existing motor vehicles with electric vehicles is also likely to require far more rare-Earth materials than the planet can provide. The development of peer-to-peer transport systems, such as Uber, Ways, and Grab, provide a good opportunity to reduce the need for individual car ownership. While they are often accused of an exploitative form of operation which also minimizes tax obligations, better regulation through the conditions by which local authorities grant and withhold licences can help to reduce these concerns. This would complement efficient public transport and enable them to provide socially, economically, and environmentally sustainable ways of moving around and between cities. Electric scooters and e-bikes provide other options to improve connectivity. Other European cities, such as Ljubljana in Slovenia, winner of the European Green Capital 2016, pride themselves on being 'green' by promoting and supporting other means of transportation than private vehicles while autonomous bus and bike sharing is provided in Kaohsiung (Photo 16.8).

The city of Curitiba in Brazil has been a global leader in the integration of transport planning and social development in ways that also helped to reduce carbon emissions. The mayor, Jaime Lerner, committed to decongesting the city centre in favour of development along public transport corridors from the city centre towards the urban periphery. These express buses connect with 'feeder buses' at a series of interchanges that enable people to move between suburban neighbourhoods without having to go to the city centre. Over time, development concentrated along the main bus routes, providing a wide distribution of nodes providing economic opportunities and services to residential communities throughout the city.

One challenge faced in Curitiba and in all cities developing public TOD systems is the arrangements for inter-modal connectivity. In Curitiba, the separate routes were managed by separate bus companies, creating operational problems. This was solved in 1990 by integrating all travel modes under the

Photo 16.8 Public bike sharing system and autonomous bus in Kaohsiung
Source: Itzel Obregon

Urban Development Authority of Curitiba (n.d.). In Bangkok, Ho Chi Minh City, and other major conurbations with mixed-mode bus and train networks, ticketing between publicly and privately owned networks presents an ongoing management challenge. However, these challenges are minor compared with the benefits of promoting public transport. As the Colombian politician Gustavo Petro apparently once said, a developed country is not one where the poor have cars; it's where the rich use public transportation.

Putting it all together

The examples illustrated in this chapter demonstrate that while the financialization of land and housing has severely constrained opportunities for reducing inequality, spatial planning and land use management can significantly overcome this barrier and also address the climate crisis. Committed local leadership that promotes compact, polycentric urban forms, well served by public transport and adequate public open space, can create socially mixed communities that enable urban areas to meet the needs of all and respond to change.[8] Reducing entry costs to officially sanctioned development is a key factor in realizing this goal and requires that planning and building standards, together with efficient administrative procedures, are realistic and reflect local needs. All these objectives can be financed through the effective regulation of land and housing markets.

Notes

1. SDG 11.3.1 is defined as the ratio of land consumption rate to population growth rate. It measures how efficiently cities utilize land, which is measured as a ratio of the rate at which cities spatially consume land against the rate at which their populations grow. Empirical evidence has shown that cities that are compact use land more efficiently and are better placed to provide public goods and basic services at a lower cost. See: <https://trends.earth/docs/en/background/understanding_indicators11.html>.
2. The trailer for a video summarizing the achievements of community-led urban settlement planning in the El Ermitaño neighbourhood in Lima can be found at https://vimeo.com/user90803557. Contact Kathrin Golda-Pongratz at k.golda-pongratz@coac.net to see the full film.
3. Inadequate regulation of building materials and construction resulted in the deaths of 72 people when Grenfell Tower in central London caught fire in 2017.
4. Tables 30–32 can be used to assess the impact of inflation on total costs and provide ways of assessing project affordability.
5. Also known as the Floor Space Index, or FSI.
6. Such a creative use of FSI can be seen in the case of Mumbai in India, where it has been combined with Transfer Development Rights (see Chapter 14) to divert investment to proposed growth areas.
7. TOD Institute (no date) Transit Oriented Development Institute [website] <www.tod.org> [accessed 12 May 2021].
8. These recommendations are also included in an excellent report by the German Advisory Council on Global Change (2016): *Humanity on the Move: Unlocking the Transformative Power of Cities.*

CHAPTER 17
Homes not housing

An estate agent in London is recently said to have told a potential client, 'we had a house within your budget, but we sold it in 1979'. Since then, house prices have increased many times, and far faster than incomes. Coincidentally, 1979 was the year that my wife and I bought our first house, a four-bedroom terraced house in poor condition, but close to shops, parks, and transport facilities in west London. As an academic and a journalist, we had steady incomes and were just able to afford a mortgage at 3.5 times our combined annual income. One move and decades later, we have a larger house and garden, and count ourselves very fortunate. However, options to repeat this process have become far, far more difficult for the younger generation starting family life. Buying their own place is out of the question unless they are in very well paid jobs or are able to draw from the 'Bank of Mum and Dad', and even renting somewhere decent is extremely difficult. The massive increase in housing prices combined with wage stagnation has been a defining feature of the UK economy for the past two decades and UK homes now cost almost eight times average earnings (UK Department for Communities and Local Government, 2017). In 2015 alone, the average home in the south-east of England increased in value by £29,000, more than the average annual pay in the region of £24,542 (ibid.: 9). House prices in two London boroughs of Westminster and Kensington and Chelsea are now equivalent in value to all of the homes in Wales (Osborne, 2021).

The chapters in Part One analysed how the political and economic choices made by governments have led to this situation, not only in the UK, but globally. The housing sector is considered 'robust' if prices continue to rise and a cause of great concern if prices stabilize, let alone fall. Yet who benefits from increased prices, apart from landowners and developers able to manipulate the sector to generate vast profits, invariably with government support? Certainly not those trying to get a home of their own for the first time and not even for those wanting to move, since other prices will have also risen. Tenants have also found rents increasing as demand increases. The only residents who benefit are comfortable home-owners downsizing to smaller properties, probably on retirement, or using the value of their property for equity release. So why is the whole global housing sector organized for the benefit of this small group and not for the vast majority that simply wants somewhere decent to live? Part of the answer is clearly related to the promotion of housing as a financial asset, not as homes in which to enjoy life protected from the elements and with access to services, a source of livelihood, and social facilities.

Clearly, any political party proposing that house prices be reduced to levels applicable decades ago is unlikely to gain power as nobody struggling to pay a mortgage would vote for a government that intended to make their home worth less than they were paying for it. While a repeat of the 2008 economic crisis cannot be ruled out and could lead to a catastrophe for those with mortgages, other options need to be available to meet increasing needs without destabilizing the wider economy. Providing a wide range of tenure categories as discussed in Chapter 15 and applying innovative approaches to spatial planning and land management as discussed in Chapter 16 can both generate substantial resources for the provision of non-market, incremental, and participatory forms of housing development. These are not only better able to meet people's needs, but enable them to exert greater control over the key elements of housing – location, cost, design, and use – so that housing becomes a means of realizing wider developmental goals of personal fulfilment, greater economic equality, household and family stability, and general wellbeing.

Taking back control

A paper exploring these issues (Payne, 1979) posed the question: if the objective of social and economic development is to increase the choice and control that people have over important aspects of their lives, how does one explain that low-income groups in poor countries frequently have a wider choice of housing options and a greater degree of control over them than is available to many families in rich countries like Britain? The answer was that the demand for housing in urbanizing countries was so great that conventional methods of urban housing and planning had proved totally ineffective, forcing the authorities to adopt pragmatic responses to a range of resident-led initiatives and restricting themselves to providing what people could not provide for themselves. In countries as diverse as Peru and Turkey, local leaders assumed a position of considerable influence over local development and housing became a means of social and economic development, only to be undermined when governments, and later the markets, asserted themselves.

If the bottom rung of the housing ladder was just reachable for us in 1979, it is now way out of reach for most people in the UK and most other G20 countries, and even more for those in the Global South. Conventional approaches by the state and the market have not only failed to meet needs, but dramatically intensified the problems of providing adequate housing for the majority of people. The challenge is to promote local control over housing provision more widely in all countries. Instead of encouraging urbanizing countries to adopt measures applied in the Global North, the former provides valuable examples for application in the latter.

How can this be achieved in ways that also address inequality and the climate crisis? Clearly, groups benefiting from the status quo cannot be expected to welcome a challenge to their position, so sustained public pressure will be vital in generating the momentum for change. Now that a broad section of the urban population in cities at all levels of economic development are finding it difficult to afford somewhere decent to live, traction for systemic change can hopefully be mobilized more easily. Campaigns to provide adequate housing for all need to draw upon a wide range of innovative, cost-effective, socially responsive, and environmentally sustainable options to restore the housing sector to one that promotes development in the wider sense of improving choice and control over such an important aspect of life.

Fortunately, there is a wealth of positive examples on which to build. While the costs of services, finance, labour, and materials will be inelastic across sectors, the one element that is highly variable is that of land costs. If some of the policy options outlined in previous chapters are adopted, substantial revenues can be generated from various forms of land value capture, or sharing, that can be allocated to provide effective, people-friendly options. However, to broaden the scope of options, some need to be applicable in high value locations where the cost of land cannot be offset by non-market forms of tenure. In such cases, options will need to provide high density, mixed land use options in which the unit costs of individual units can be affordable. Following the principle of 'long life, loose fit, low energy', such developments should be adaptable to different needs and uses over time. This can easily be achieved with medium-rise developments of up to six floors, especially when one is at basement, or lower-ground floor level, so that lifts are not essential (see images in previous chapters). Low or medium rise developments also make it far easier to meet carbon emission targets than is possible in high-rise housing with its associated high embedded energy requirements. Replacing steel and cement with wood in urban construction can also reduce greenhouse gas emissions and turn buildings into a carbon sink, though upscaling would be dependent upon sustainable forest management and governance (Churkina et al., 2020). To make apartments even more affordable, and maximize options for resident participation, one option could be to leave internal details, such as the arrangement of non-loadbearing internal walls and finishes to be completed by residents according to their preferences and affordability as is common in China. In the UK, the Primary Supports Structure Housing Action Kits approach advocated by Hamdi and Wilkinson in 1971 was adopted by the then Greater London Council (GLC) (Jenkins et al., 2009). A similar approach to flexible internal planning was applied by the Dutch architect Gerrit Rietveld when designing the Schröder house in Utrecht in 1924. Another option for reducing initial costs and increasing resident control over apartment housing is to design structures that are suitable for future household-funded extensions, as exemplified by the examples in Bangladesh, Egypt, Ghana, and Zimbabwe (Tipple, 2000). The examples Tipple cites are unauthorized extensions of government-built apartment blocks, but the option is equally valid for developments held under condominium or communal forms of tenure. Designing apartments for such future extensions can provide a valuable contribution to meeting future needs.

Increasing the range of adequate, affordable, and attractive housing can best be achieved by reducing the stranglehold that private developers have in many countries over housing provision and the outsized influence of private banks in the mortgage finance sector and their associated influence on housing markets and government policy, both of which are relatively recent trends (Jordà et al., 2014b).[1] Land supply limitations can partly be addressed by requiring developers to develop sites for which they already have planning permission on the basis of 'use it or lose it' and applying a tax and other incentives reviewed in Chapter 14 to ensure that the additional units are put to good use. All such developments should be required to meet rigorous environmental standards, such as passive house construction norms,[2] since any increase in capital costs can be more than offset by reduced energy consumption over the building's lifetime, a factor that can be taken into account when calculating housing finance costs and therefore affordability through the application of green mortgages (International Finance Corporation (IFC), 2019, 2020). Promoting locally based builders familiar with local environmental conditions, social needs, and vernacular traditions, and making publicly owned land available to 'not for profit' organizations to provide housing would also help to ensure that developments promote social integration and diversity. These measures can help housing reduce inequality, enhance local place identity, and address the climate crisis.

In areas where land prices permit the provision of individual homes, numerous options deserve consideration to suit specific contexts, including the following.

Starter homes

These provide basic immediate accommodation and can take many forms from mobile homes, shipping containers, or small permanent structures that can be expanded horizontally and vertically. The Tiny Homes movement in the USA (Kaufmann, n.d.; Abraham, 2021) provides options that are energy efficient, very inexpensive, and suitable for young families.

Sites and services

Being able to control the design of their home is a dream few in the Global North can fulfil, though the approach has been widely applied in the Global South. By providing clusters of serviced plots, households can control the design and construction of their own home and expand or improve these as economic circumstances permit. However, this requires funding to be available separately for the land and the construction of a home. If plots are large enough, it could even be possible for several households to undertake joint development by providing two or more units on a single plot, thus saving on the costs of land and utility connections. Large projects provide the opportunity to include mixed income groups and land uses, creating neighbourhoods and employment opportunities as well as improving accessibility for lower income groups through the application of project-based cross-subsidies.

Participatory planning of housing

Grouping plots around a communal open space would enable households to control not just the design of their homes, but also the immediate environment, making housing a real contribution to personal and community development in its widest sense. If a development provides for clusters of 8–15 plots, experience shows that households can collaborate in the design of the communal spaces as well as the allocation and development of plots and design of houses to suit individual preferences and budgets. Developments planned by 10 or so households in one day, can generate far more imaginative and demand-based developments than even the most capable professional could design in 10 days. This approach offers great scope for community-based technical assistance, including design-based charrettes, that can help build communities.

Co-housing

This enables individual households to share some facilities, such as communal open space and indoor facilities for social interaction such as day nurseries, meeting rooms for elderly residents, and fitness groups. Homes may be individually owned, but maintenance of communal spaces is the responsibility of all residents. Sensitive design advice can ensure a balance of privacy and community that makes the most of site conditions. A leading advocate of co-housing, Vestbro (2010) provides a review of examples around the world, and the Marmalade Lane co-housing project in Cambridge, UK (see Photo 17.1), won the 2020 Royal Town Planning Institute Jubilee Design Award for planning excellence.

Intergenerational housing

In countries with increasing numbers of young or elderly households, providing the option for them to meet their housing needs in a complementary manner offers potential benefits to both. The option of providing houses in which three generations can coexist with separate spaces for young families and elderly relatives can provide vital social support for all, with the option of renting out rooms when the young move out or the elderly pass on. A more institutionalized version has been developed in the form of intergenerational care housing: the practice of bringing the young and elderly together by introducing nurseries into care homes. This is thought to have

Photo 17.1 Communal space and individual houses, Marmalade Lane co-housing project, Cambridge, UK
Credit: Geoffrey Payne

officially started in 1976, when Shimada Masaharu merged a nursery school and care home in Tokyo with great success. The idea has since spread to many countries (Age UK, 2018) and some offer facilities such as restaurants that are open to the local community, benefiting both them and the elderly residents, though designs need to provide options for segregation if needed. In another example, a nursing home in the Netherlands allows university students to live rent-free alongside the elderly residents, as part of a project aimed at warding off the negative effects of ageing. In exchange for small, rent-free apartments, the Humanitas retirement home in Deventer, Netherlands, requires students to spend at least 30 hours per month acting as 'good neighbours' to the elderly residents. The students are allowed to come and go as they please, as long as they follow one rule: Do not be a nuisance to the elderly. The home-owner joked that this is not difficult for the students, since most of the older residents are hard of hearing (Reed, 2015). A similar programme that began in Barcelona, Spain in the late 1990s has been replicated in more than 20 cities throughout the country.

Housing for refugees

In addition to the proposals for accommodating international migrants and refugees in abandoned towns and villages in Europe summarized in Chapter 13, Czischke and Huisman (2018) present an imaginative approach to providing housing for refugees that helps them assimilate to their new surroundings and build a new life in Amsterdam, Netherlands. They report on a pilot project housing 500 young adults, half local and the others refugees, in a collaborative, self-managed community. By sharing facilities and a communal open space, social bonds are encouraged, enabling housing to provide opportunities for assimilation and personal development.

Putting Housing First

The options listed above are all applicable in a wide range of contexts to help the poor and other vulnerable groups obtain a place they can call home. They put land to socially, environmentally, and economically efficient use and can be adapted to widely diverse contexts. Since the challenge is global, it is fitting to include the example of the Housing First organization established to meet the challenge of homelessness in the USA (Tsemberis, 2010). Recognizing that extremely vulnerable groups and individuals needed a secure place to live and rebuild their lives, the priority is to provide somewhere safe to live without prior conditions and as part of a community: the key difference between providing homes, not just housing. Many other organizations also support and promote innovative, practical approaches, of which Slum Dwellers International, Habitat for Humanity, Habitat International Coalition, Asian Coalition for Housing Rights, the Community Organizations Development Institute, and the Transition Towns movement (Hopkins, 2008) are outstanding examples.[3] Other local initiatives are recognized by the annual World Habitat Awards.[4]

Rebuilding after conflicts or disasters

Whether as a result of political conflict, economic inequality, or climate change, housing provides an ideal opportunity to help people literally rebuild their lives. As Davis and Alexander (2016) note, a multi-disciplinary approach is vital to ensure that gender aspects and the cultural needs of diverse groups are included as part of rebuilding communities. They stress that at the heart of all effective recovery operations lie the needs of survivors and that a good recovery policy helps to reactivate communities and empower people. Relocation is rarely effective and pre-disaster planning should be used wherever possible to prepare for disaster events, especially where risks can be predicted, such as annual cyclones or areas vulnerable to earthquakes. People-centred reconstruction is also central to the recommendations by Lyons et al. (2010) and needs to include all victims, irrespective of what rights they may or may not have had prior to a crisis, since tenants and those without tenure security are the most vulnerable at any time, especially after a disaster. Finally, the massive funding and humanitarian support that often follows a major disaster is often delivered on a short-term basis, and when the immediate crisis has been addressed, may be withdrawn before local institutional capability has been established. Lloyd-Jones (2006: 72) argues for more attention to be given to restoring and improving local capacity, particularly the professional capacity within local government. Furthermore,

> Microfinance, social funds, compensatory and cash transfer payments all have an important role to play in allowing greater choice and ensuring that financial inputs respond to real need. If properly managed, and alongside cash for work programmes, they can ensure the recovery effort does not have a negative impact on local markets and economic institutions but rather contributes to sustainable economic recovery, income generation and restoration of livelihoods.

The ever-increasing frequency and intensity of disasters resulting from political and natural causes exposes the most vulnerable groups to ever greater threats to their future. Putting their needs and potential contributions at the centre of reconstruction is therefore vital in making progress and the example of post-conflict reconstruction in Sri Lanka (Royo-Olid et al., 2018) illustrates how sustained support for local initiatives can make a substantial contribution through long-term support from the international community. The recovery from Covid-19 in cities around the world will provide a useful comparative case study on pandemic housing policy responses.

Setting standards

The regulatory framework of planning standards and regulations exerts a major impact on housing costs and therefore the ability of people to access formal housing. Before preparing projects seeking to meet the needs of the poor, an audit or review should therefore be undertaken of urban planning and building standards, regulations and administrative procedures (Payne and Majale, 2004). International experience demonstrates that there is no correlation between housing space standards and levels of economic development, so if a regulatory audit or review reveals that a significant proportion of the urban population are living in various types of unauthorized housing, it may well be because official standards are based upon official aspirations, not economic realities and need to be revised, or that administrative procedures are too complex and time-consuming.

In preparing proposals for new projects affordable to low-income groups, a key consideration would be to compare their current living conditions and undertake surveys to ascertain household priorities regarding floor area, building design and standard, and levels of services provision. Balancing initial provision of these components needs careful consideration. For example, where land prices make individual plots affordable, given a choice between larger plots or prebuilt construction, larger plots are preferable, since buildings can always be improved, or expanded, and full services connected later. However, cultural factors need to be taken into account in determining plot sizes, with smaller minimum plot sizes common in Asia (e.g. 25 m^2 in India) and larger ones in sub-Saharan Africa (e.g. 150 m^2 in Uganda). Wherever possible, building standards should encourage the application of traditional materials and built forms, or their adaptation, since these maximize user control and invariably require less energy-intensive forms of construction. Applying these in housing for high-income groups and a range of communal buildings, as in the 'A Roof, a Skill, a Market' approach in the Sahel (Thakara, 2013; World Habitat, 2016), can build confidence in the application of such adaptive approaches. Where land prices make individual plots unaffordable, efficient land use will need to include adequate provision for apartment residents to access public open space for their health and wellbeing.

Unlike settlement layouts and plot sizes, levels of services provision can vary enormously from initial to fully consolidated levels. In fact, progressive improvement is the norm in many urban areas. To maximize affordability, the objective should be to provide the minimum initial level required to permit permanent occupation of individual plots. The provision of on-plot water will be a major cost threshold since it will lead to increased consumption and therefore the need for improved disposal systems. Initial provision should be designed to facilitate subsequent upgrading, though apartments will require full initial provision.

Of all the project elements that concern project planners, housing construction need not be a major cause for concern, since most households are capable of organizing their own dwelling and improving it over time out of future incomes as shown in the example of Ismailia in Chapter 16 and countless other examples globally. Standards should be flexible and public intervention concentrated on providing technical assistance when requested. Such an incremental, resident-driven approach provides developments that may not appear as architecturally attractive as professionals would like, but are far more likely to meet people's needs and aspirations and enable housing to be a means of social and economic development, not a welfare burden.

Density and layouts in many existing inner-city settlements may make it impossible to apply standards applicable in new developments when upgrading. However, substantial improvements can be made simply by installing water, drainage, sewerage, and electricity connections along narrow paths and lanes as shown throughout the Global South and even in the original areas of major cities in the Global North, such as London.

Procedural issues

While rigorous building space and safety standards need to be formulated and enforced for all developer-built housing, standards should be flexible for individually developed dwellings and public intervention concentrated on advice and technical assistance, rather than conventional development control and the imposition of inappropriate standards, no matter how well intentioned. As John Turner (1972) and Bertha Turner (1988) advocate, housing should be conceived as a process more than just a product, or a verb, not a noun and the beneficiaries should be actively engaged. Thus, a minimum initial dwelling can be expanded, providing additional rooms to rent, increasing incomes to finance more rooms and floors, possibly with commercial uses on the ground floor after many years and making housing a means of social and economic development, as millions of people do throughout the world. Such an organic, incremental, people-driven process is also an effective way to build communities.

Administrative procedures relating to individual or small-scale housing developments need to facilitate such approaches to housing and be simple and transparent to manage. An early example of this user-friendly and cost-effective approach was the E-Seva programme developed in Hyderabad, India in the early 1990s. This provided 'one-stop-shops' scattered throughout the city and were particularly popular in low-income areas since residents were able to access any administrative service with the help of staff with internet connections. Applications for any form of official permission were processed in accordance with clear guidelines and any problems resolved by contacting the relevant official in the same way that is used in sending a package by courier. Similar approaches are now applicable throughout the world and are particularly important in areas where individual internet connections are lacking.

The lessons of experience have shown that attempts to enforce inappropriate or unaffordable planning and building norms on housing development result in an increase in unauthorized development. The only effective way to reduce the need for such developments is to ensure that the regulatory framework for community-led or individually developed housing reflects socially, economically, and culturally accepted norms. The merits of community-led and owner-built housing have been acknowledged for decades, yet the opportunities for applying them are under ever-increasing threat as a result of neoliberal economic policies that focus on providing housing and associated mortgage finance products (Badev et al., 2014), rather than on building homes and communities. The focus needs to be on developing secure, affordable, habitable, culturally appropriate homes within easy reach of economic opportunities and social amenities. Even more importantly, this needs to be undertaken in ways that put the potential residents in a position to determine the elements that best meet their needs in building communities in which they can thrive. A society that can achieve this in an environmentally sustainable manner for all can justifiably claim to be developed.

Notes

1. Before the middle of the 20th century, commercial banks in most advanced economies were restricted from entering real estate lending. In the first half of the century, real estate lending averaged under a third of all bank lending. Yet by 2007 the proportion was around two-thirds in countries such as the US and UK (see Jordà et al., 2014b).

HOMES NOT HOUSING **257**

2. Passivhaus Institut website <https://passivehouse.com>.
3. Slum Dwellers International (SDI) website <http://sdinet.org/>; Habitat for Humanity (HfH) website <https://www.habitat.org/>; Habitat International Coalition (HIC) website <https://www.hic-net.org/>; Asian Coalition for Housing Rights (ACHR) website <http://www.achr.net/>; Community Organizations Development Institute (CODI) in Thailand website <https://en.codi.or.th/>.
4. World Habitat Awards website <https://world-habitat.org/world-habitat-awards/>.

CHAPTER 18
Making it happen

The evidence clearly shows that the way a society values land and housing reflects a wider set of values. The manifest limitations of market and state-driven forms of land and housing management highlight the urgent need for a fundamental change in the way that we treat the planet and each other. In this respect, at least, the Covid-19 pandemic has provided a salutary reminder that a fundamental reset is needed to ensure that humanity can not only survive but flourish. This means redefining what we mean by development and the roles of the state and markets, both globally and locally. The pandemic has exposed the extent of inequality and the failure of neoliberal economics to meet the needs of all but a small elite. It has also demonstrated that concerted, global collaboration is essential, that governments are more powerful than is often assumed, and that market forces need to be managed more effectively to achieve social, environmental, and economic goals. At the same time, the climate crisis demonstrates that we have no time to lose to change the way towns and cities are managed as part of a reset to reduce overall consumption and carbon emissions.

A precondition for change is to accept that the present forms of growth and development cannot continue without causing an existential crisis for humanity. While powerful forces remain in denial, there are encouraging signs that grassroots pressure for change is increasing, especially from the younger generation. As Meadows (2004: 237) notes, this can have connotations of revolution and changing existing power structures. However, 'the same combination of people, organizations, and physical structures can behave completely differently if the system's actors can see a good reason for doing so, and if they have the freedom, perhaps even the incentive, to change ... Such a transformation need not be directed centrally; it can be unplanned, natural, evolutionary. Exciting, joyful'. Presenting the challenges as a positive opportunity, rather than a threat, may prove to be the best way to generate the changes needed.

Raworth's 'doughnut economy', as discussed with other ideas in Chapter 13, provides both a vision and a practical framework for achieving a sustainable future. Recognizing that growth in many parts of the world has exceeded sustainable levels, Raworth and others highlight the benefits of spending more time and energy on activities that add real value to life: creating, repairing, and sharing. She points out that a growth in creativity is needed if humanity is not just to survive but to thrive. The circular economy she advocates requires all sectors – public, private, and civil – to establish a clear purpose and principles for operating within sustainable limits and addressing the shortfall in provision of basic services suffered by so many globally.

The Covid-19 pandemic has also provided a timely reminder of what we all value most, and which groups of workers make the greatest contribution to society. Several cities have already adopted the doughnut or circular economy principles and the approach is gathering momentum. Of course, cities have been the centres of social change and progress throughout history so they present an ideal basis on which to transition towards a more sustainable future. The 2020 *World Cities Report* (UN-Habitat, 2020b: xviii–43)[1] prioritizes a broad definition of values that include 'the totality of the economic, social, environmental and intangible conditions (institutional, governance, political, cultural and civic perception), outcomes that have the potential to improve quality of life of residents in meaningful and tangible ways'. By putting economics within a broader set of policy considerations, the report provides a key basis for reconfiguring urban planning policy and practice for the 21st century. It notes that '71 million people will be pushed back into extreme poverty this year, the first rise in global poverty since 1998. Some 1.6 billion informal workers, half the global workforce, have seen their wages affected' (2020: xv). At the same time, 'about 2.9 billion people are living in cities where income inequalities are currently more pronounced than they were a generation ago' (2020: xvii). To address these issues, 'national governments must create an enabling environment for cities to thrive, and local authorities must seize the opportunities given to them to flourish and develop' (2020: v). Migrants should be seen as providing an opportunity to be harnessed, minimum wages and the formalization of informal employment, and even cash transfer programmes as proposed by Bregman (2017) (see Chapter 13), should be within the purview of national governments,[2] while local governments must work to provide sanitation infrastructure in order to mitigate the health risk. As the examples of Ankara, Karachi, and Medellin demonstrate (see Chapters 5, 15 and 16), community-led approaches to infrastructure provision can contribute to improved health at minimum cost, and enhance wellbeing.

Countries currently generating the highest level of emissions, such as Brazil, China, and India, clearly have a lot to do, though countries of the Global North bear the greater responsibility since they not only generated high levels of consumption and emissions for more than a century, but promoted and imposed the neoliberal economic model that has generated so much global inequality. Their current high levels of consumption of non-renewable resources, and the images of urban development and housing they promote, have set the precedents for elites in the Global South to further exacerbate the crisis. Furthermore, it is the countries of the Global North that have the financial, institutional, and technical resources to make the changes necessary, not those in the Global South held back by unsustainable approaches.

When the combined interests of the political, commercial, and administrative elite coalesce around a shared vision of how society should be structured, they will inevitably seek to promote forms of urban development which reflect that vision. The examples highlighted in Chapter 6 illustrate how many new developments reflect elitist perceptions of progress rather than those of the majority, and the more that power is concentrated in an elite, the greater its ability will be to inhibit change, or channel its power in directions that protect its interests. This is where we can learn from the methods employed by neoliberal theorists to advance their cause. As discussed in Chapter 4, they created think tanks to alter the intellectual climate and influence academics, journalists, and teachers in favour of their ideas. Encouragingly, Chile, where Friedmann was able to impose neoliberal economics in 1973, has recently elected a young president on a mandate to address inequality and he has appointed a senior academic as minister to address the climate crisis.

Fortunately, pressure for change from those suffering from neoliberal policies elsewhere is also increasing, and this book seeks to contribute to the wealth of evidence by demonstrating, not only the damage neoliberalism has done, but also the immense range of alternative policy options that are available to realize the benefits of both state regulation and market competition. This needs to be part of international agreements to ensure the equitable distribution of costs and benefits in managing urban areas and housing development. The Sustainable Development Goals and the Paris Agreement provide internationally agreed frameworks for monitoring conformity by national governments to forms of urban development, land management, and housing provision that can create genuinely sustainable towns and cities. It is vital that these agreements are independently monitored and legally enforced, and that governments are encouraged, supported, and, if necessary, forced to meet their obligations.

Pressure from civil society, the built-environment professions, and the general public will be vital in holding those in power to account and countering reactionary messages and falsehoods from those who refuse to accept the evidence. As noted in Chapter 14, the countries of sub-Saharan Africa are likely to have to accommodate an additional 790 million residents between 2020 and 2050. This equates to finding homes for more than 100,000 people every working day over three decades (Durand-Lasserve et al., 2018). Even allowing for possible errors in such projections, the scale is greater than anything faced so far, by countries that are under-resourced and where corruption in the land sector is widespread (Durand-Lasserve, 2019). The scale of demand in other countries may be less, but is also enormous and increasing.

Conventional approaches by either the public or formal private sectors cannot be expected to meet even a small proportion of this immense need, and the prospects for a massive increase in already extensive slum areas are difficult to contemplate. Fortunately, the poor have repeatedly demonstrated that they are able to contribute substantially to meeting their need for somewhere to live. This suggests that the best – and possibly only – viable approach is for governments to focus on providing what people cannot provide for themselves. This involves providing land with basic services and security and allowing people to organize their own housing and improve them in an incremental manner as their circumstances change. This book has sought to provide both the evidence to justify change and a range of practical examples that can help to achieve it.

Collaborate rather than compete

Rather than competing in a race to the bottom to attract inward investment as proposed by the competitive cities approach (World Bank, 2015a), cities can benefit from collaboration in addressing the climate crisis and managing urban land and housing markets in ways that reduce inequality. Acuto and Rayner (2016) estimate that 49 per cent of a sample of 170 networks are nationally based, though regional and international networks are on the rise. Of these, the International Council for Local Environmental Initiatives (ICLEI) addresses sustainability, the C40 City Leadership Group is making great efforts to promote both climate action plans and digital democracy, the World Health Organization (WHO) European Healthy Cities network promotes health and wellbeing, the Mayors for Peace initiative includes over 5,000 cities in 152 countries seeking reconciliation, and the Cities Alliance focuses on both development and capacity-building. The authors also report that 29 per cent of the networks surveyed are principally focused on the environment, though poverty, gender, and inequality are also prominent concerns, somewhat ahead of energy and peace-building. However, the private sector is also increasingly active in global networks, and while they caution that this trend should not be reduced to simplistic accounts of a totalizing neo-liberalization, it is difficult to see other than commercial motives for their activities.

City networks, therefore, provide an effective means of strengthening urban governance in regulating commercial interests to address the climate crisis and inequality. They are also addressing the challenge of supporting and assimilating large numbers of migrants and refugees through city-led initiatives such as the Mayors Migration Council, which seeks to enable cities to learn from each other, supporting them to become more influential at the global level (Rees, 2020). Land and housing are central to these objectives and require public agencies to understand how markets operate and what options apply to maximize their regulation in the public interest. More needs to be done to create fiscal and regulatory frameworks that enable the state to generate a proportional benefit from the uplift in land values resulting from state action. Given the high price of land in and around urban areas, this provides a unique opportunity to generate the revenues needed to meet the needs of vulnerable groups. Land and property taxes need to be progressive and based on market values, updated regularly, and designed to discourage speculation by taxing second homes and empty properties at a higher rate, irrespective of where such properties are registered. Cities Alliance has also made progress in promoting City Development Strategies to reduce poverty and give urban residents a voice in the development of the place where they live. Building synergies between these and other international development organizations, particularly the World Bank, regional development banks, and UN-Habitat, can also enhance progressive forms of urban development.

One way of achieving progress could be for ministers or mayors to identify the key constraints to reducing inequality or carbon emissions in their urban areas and invite officials to propose examples from international experience to address them. By repeatedly market-testing different options for improving access to land, finance, services, or materials, public sector agencies can become innovative and powerful forces for change, and effective in regulating land and housing sectors. Public support will be essential in achieving this so urban authorities need to be transparent and democratically accountable to the populations they serve. In cases where ancient feudal practices remain, entrenched elites have succeeded in creating sufficient support for the status quo, which may constrain major change unless the crisis becomes even more extreme. A more likely source of pressure for change in such cases could be from the younger generation who have been effectively excluded from the benefits showered on the older generation. Where the state continues to exert control over land and housing sectors, as in the cases reviewed in Chapter 10, the prospects for creating demand-based forms of urban management will depend upon the ability of the authorities to continue meeting public needs. Those that exert unchallenged power will have no excuses for failure.

While socialist countries have enhanced the social value of land, ingrained paternalism has impaired their ability to identify and respond to changing needs. However, if convinced of the benefits of change, they have the power to change from paternalism to engagement with diverse stakeholders. Countries that have transitioned from state managed to market-based forms of economic management, as reviewed in Chapter 11, exhibit remnants of state control, though they are making rapid progress and embracing change. For them, the next challenge will require the state to become more effective regulators of land and housing markets in the public interest.

Finally, countries transitioning from customary to market systems face a major dilemma since the ethos by which land has been valued for centuries has been fundamentally undermined, exposing vulnerable groups to widespread exploitation. Progress is likely to depend upon creating 'win-win' solutions involving the active participation of customary leaders to build confidence for further change. Part Three chapters highlight a range of options for building trust and confidence between customary and statutory systems, raising the prospect of innovative arrangements that combine the customary ethos of trusteeship within statutory tenure regimes.

Building capacity and support

The ability of many urban authorities to prepare and implement innovative spatial planning and housing policies and programmes has not been helped by the limited capacity of many urban administrative authorities and a tendency for many to be insensitive to the needs of the poor. Overcoming this will often require a change of mindset on the part of senior officials and policymakers, providing an important role for international development agencies and lending institutions such as the World Bank. It also means that all available resources need to be extremely efficiently deployed, institutional duplication and overlapping responsibilities avoided, and new ideas encouraged for enhancing investment and access to land and housing for all those in need. While policies may be established at national or state level, detailed programmes and projects need to be planned and implemented by adequately resourced local governments to ensure they reflect local needs and conditions. This in turn will require an adequately resourced cadre of staff well trained in managing land and housing markets. Local authorities that adopt socially responsive approaches are likely to attract talented young professionals who otherwise may prefer to work in the private sector. The policy instruments listed in Chapter 14 provide a range of options applicable to different situations.

The blunt reality is that any attempt to improve access to land by low-income groups needs to address the vested interests and institutional inertia which constrain innovation. This was noted in a literature review of access to land markets by Williams (2008: 14), who found that 'there seems to be resistance to change and innovation among technicians and administrators. This resistance is fuelled by government, ministry and state officials' perceptions that changes in the legislations and programs will have a negative impact on their roles, their power and their jobs'. However, resistance to change is perhaps understandable if middle-level officials fear that senior officials will take the credit for success or pass down responsibility for failure, or if supportive senior officials may soon be replaced. When combined with possible changes of government, such concerns can have a seriously debilitating impact on the delivery of *any* policy. In this respect, innovative approaches need to be encouraged as part of a learning-by-doing culture, identifying and testing some of the examples of progressive and practical policy instruments identified in previous chapters.

For all these reasons, creating a professional cadre that is well equipped to manage and regulate urban land and housing sectors is extremely challenging. Promoting experienced professionals with private sector experience to positions of authority in urban management deserves consideration, since the ability to maximize a surplus can then be applied to maximizing the public benefit from a private investment. A clear remit to this effect will be essential to avoid the risk of private interests penetrating the public sector and undermining the ethos of public service.

Given the important role in urban development and housing played by the World Bank and other international agencies, scope exists for creating a routine 'feedback loop' that enables short-term consultants to learn what happened to projects on which they have contributed their best efforts. Ignorance of outcomes inhibits the ability of consultants to learn from experience and may also inhibit the Bank from maximizing its potential as a knowledge bank if staff are moved regularly to different departments or regions.

Promoting the benefits of the circular economy, in terms of health and wellbeing, can become a powerful means of addressing the climate crisis. Mass movements, especially by young people, have the power to change policies, and while some campaigns intentionally cause economic disruption, they point out that this is nothing compared to what will happen unless we change the way we live and work. The scope for making improvements to the environmental performance of cities in reducing CO_2 emissions is generally greater in more affluent countries where levels of car ownership are far higher and urban densities are generally lower than in currently urbanizing countries, and one study found that the density of lower-income cities was more than double that of wealthier cities (109 versus 52 persons/ ha) (Kenworthy 2003: 24). Since more affluent cities are likely to be better resourced financially, institutionally, and technically, they have a greater opportunity and responsibility to make the necessary adjustments than cities in less affluent countries.

For those seeking to influence decision-makers in favour of progressive approaches, providing evidence, as presented in this book, will be essential, but insufficient. After all, many of the proposals listed in previous chapters are already in the public domain. Progress will depend largely on presenting proposals in ways that reflect the concerns of those in power, or forcing them to change their mindset by putting them in the position of people directly affected by existing and proposed approaches. Presentational skills will therefore represent a key attribute of all those campaigning for change, and needs to be a key element of all educational programmes for the built environment professions. It should be remembered that neoliberalism succeeded by capturing the political agenda through retailing information supporting its case. The same needs to be done to promote policies addressing the climate and inequality. Education is a key component of change and a lead has been given by New Zealand, which is providing education materials about the climate crisis written by leading science agencies to every school in the country, including tools for students to plan their own activism. Another country taking a lead is Italy which is making sustainability and the climate crisis compulsory subjects for school students, with materials integrated into subjects such as mathematics and geography. Children have even taken to successfully suing governments for breaching their human rights on climate issues.

Arguments to generate support for change need to be context sensitive. In countries with high levels of individual home ownership, policies need to reassure the majority that the financial value of their asset will not be adversely affected – progress may best be made by introducing, or expanding, non-market forms of land and housing provision. In countries transitioning from state to market systems, many of the elite from the old system remain in positions of influence and continue to use land and housing as a means of perpetuating their influence and interests. Encouraging them to see that adopting a pro-poor approach will help to reinforce their positions may prove to be the most effective way of encouraging change. A major challenge will continue to be in those countries where customary systems of managing land and housing have been operating for long periods. The notion of trusteeship is central to the ethos of customary practice and is largely antithetical to market-based policies. The need to evolve forms of land tenure and land management that enshrine the customary ethos into statutory forms of urban development will be a major challenge during coming decades. Social and environmental sustainability deserve at least equal consideration to economic factors when formulating policies on land and housing. If there is a simple principle for professionals to adopt in order to contribute most, it is to find out what people want and can do for themselves, and what they want but cannot do for themselves. All professionals, including aid providers, should focus their efforts on understanding the former and providing the latter.

Urban management is key to success. While many cities have embraced the 'smart city' concept, this needs to be assessed not so much in terms of the application of hi-tech management, but in the creative ways land and housing markets are regulated to meet the needs of the most vulnerable. Market liberalists have promoted the concept of regulations as antithetical to market efficiency. However, unrestrained market actors have been acting like teenagers seeking short-term benefits without consideration of the long- or even medium-term consequences. Efficient regulation is needed to assert a form of parental guidance that is also in the interests of market actors by reducing risks and volatility.

A massive and sustained transfer of wealth from the Global North to the Global South that enhances opportunities for people to live a decent life in their own countries is the only way constrain global migration. OECD countries also need to honour their commitments to 0.7 per cent of GDP for international aid. However, many people will want, or be forced, to move in order to pursue the possibility of a better future. Good urban management will therefore require accepting in-migrants and refugees and enabling them to assimilate into new locations. This will understandably create ambivalence or even opposition if seen as undermining local values. However, international experience shows that those moving to urban areas tend to be relatively young, and the most resilient and ambitious social group, making it easier for them to adapt to a new environment. They provide the resources on which societies build their futures, and generate added value that can be redistributed to deprived locations, such as isolated rural areas. The degree to which the newcomers are able to quickly establish themselves exerts a significant influence over the degree to which urbanization is a positive process of development, or a drain upon it.

Whatever the political system and form by which land and housing are valued, the key to progress is to recognize that where we live exerts a major influence over every aspect of life, including our future prospects and those of other species. By regulating land and housing markets to maximize public benefit, rather than private profit, urban management can provide a basis for more equitable forms of social and economic development. Those cities that have made the greatest progress are those in which strong local leadership has applied innovative, pragmatic approaches to the provision of urban land and housing. If applied within the principles of doughnut economics and the circular economy, this can create cities that are congenial, socially diverse, and adaptable. The policy instruments identified and reviewed in Part Three provide a foundation for such policies. The challenge is now to turn these policies into practice. There is no excuse for failure and no time to lose.

Notes

1. The report mentions the word 'value' no less than 851 times.
2. The decision by President Biden to provide cash transfers to all US citizens as part of Covid-19 support provides a powerful precedent.

References

AACPPO (2017) *Addis Ababa City Structure Plan 2017–2027* [online], pp. 1–10 <https://c40-production-images.s3.amazonaws.com/other_uploads/images/2036_Addis_Ababa_Structural_Plan_2017_to_2027.original.pdf?1544193458> [accessed 22 September 2021].

Aalbers, M.B. (2016) *The Financialization of Housing: A Political Economy Approach*, Routledge, London and New York.

Abagissa, J. (2019) 'Informal settlements in Addis Ababa: extent changes and measures taken', *Journal of Public Administration, Finance and Law* 15 [online] <http://www.jopafl.com/uploads/issue15/INFORMAL_SETTLEMENTS_IN_ADDIS_ABABA_EXTENT_CHALLENGES_AND_MEASURES_TAKEN.pdf> [accessed 22 September 2021].

Abdo, M. (2014) 'Legislative protection of property rights in Ethiopia: an overview', *Mizan Law Review* 7(2): 165–206 <https://doi.org/10.4314/mlr.v7i2.1>.

Abood, M. (2018) *Wall Street Landlords turn American Dream into a Nightmare*, Americans for Financial Reform (AFR) [online] <https://d3n8a8pro7vhmx.cloudfront.net/acceinstitute/pages/100/attachments/original/1516388955/WallstreetLandlordsFinalReport.pdf?1516388955> [accessed 22 September 2021].

Abraham, R. (2021) 'San Francisco upgrades tent village to tiny home community', *Next City*, 28 October <https://nextcity.org/urbanist-news/entry/san-francisco-upgrades-tent-village-to-tiny-home-community?utm_source=Next+City+Newsletter&utm_campaign=99e7da35e0-DailyNL_2021_10_28&utm_medium=email&utm_term=0_fcee5bf7a0-99e7da35e0-44072537> [accessed 2 November 2011].

Abrams, C. (1966) *Housing in the Modern World: Man's Struggle for Shelter in an Urbanizing World*, Faber and Faber, London.

Acioly, C. (2019) 'Affordable housing provision: challenges and experiences in a global context' [PDF] UN-Habitat <https://www.ahisummit.com/wp-content/uploads/2019/07/14.-The-challenges-Experiences-with-Affordable-Housing-Provision-in-a-Global-Context.pdf> [accessed 26 April 2021].

Acioly, C. (2000) 'Can urban management deliver the sustainable city? Guided densification in Brazil versus the informal compactness in Egypt', in M. Jenks and R. Burgess (eds), *Compact Cities: Sustainable Urban Forms for Developing Countries*, pp. 127–40, Spon, London.

Acuto, M. and Rayner, S. (2016) 'City networks: breaking gridlocks or forging (new) lock-ins?' *International Affairs* 92(5): 1147–66 <https://doi.org/10.1111/1468-2346.12700>.

Adusumilli, U. (1999) 'Partnership approaches in India', in G. Payne (ed.) *Making Common Ground: Public-Private Partnerships in Land for Housing*, pp. 17–45, Intermediate Technology Publications, London.

Aga Khan Development Network (no date) 'East Wahdat Upgrading Programme' <https://www.akdn.org/architecture/project/east-wahdat-upgrading-programme> [accessed 26 April 2021].

Age UK (2018) 'How care homes and nurseries are coming together for good' <https://www.ageukmobility.co.uk/mobility-news/article/intergenerational-care> [accessed 06 May 2021].

Airey, J. and Doughty, C. (2020) *Rethinking the Planning System for the 21st Century* [PDF], Policy Exchange <https://policyexchange.org.uk/wp-content/uploads/Rethinking-the-Planning-System-for-the-21st-Century.pdf> [accessed 27 April 2021].

Almukhtar, A. (2018) 'Defining and enhancing place-identity in historic cities: embracing heritage, conflict and globalization in Erbil, Iraq', PhD thesis, Oxford Brookes University.

Alvaredo, F., Chancel, L., Piketty, T., Saez, E. and Zucman, G. (2018) *World Inequality Report 2018* [online], WID, Belknap Press <https://www.hup.harvard.edu/catalog.php?isbn=9780674984554> [accessed 22 September 2021].

Amirtahmasebi, R., Orloff, M., Wahba, S. and Altman, A. (2016) *Regenerating Urban Land: A Practitioner's Guide to Leveraging Private Investment* [online], World Bank, Washington, DC <https://openknowledge.worldbank.org/handle/10986/24377> [accessed 22 September 2021].

Amnesty International (2008) *Rights Razed: Forced Evictions in Cambodia* [online] <http://www2.ohchr.org/english/bodies/cescr/docs/info-ngos/AI_Cambodia_41_5.pdf> [accessed 22 September 2021].

Anderson, I. (2009) 'Challenges for housing policy in Cuba: case studies from Havana', *Journal of Iberian and Latin American Research* 15(2): 5–23 <https://doi.org/10.1080/13260219.2009.11090847>.

Anderson, I. and Serpa, R. (2018) 'Cuba: private home ownership recognised for first time since the revolution', *The Conversation*, 1 August <https://theconversation.com/cuba-private-home-ownership-recognised-for-first-time-since-the-revolution-100204> [accessed 22 April 2021].

Angel, S., with Parent, J., Civco, D.L. and Blei, A.M. (2011) *Making Room for a Planet of Cities* [pdf], Lincoln Institute of Land Policy, Cambridge, MA <https://www.lincolninst.edu/sites/default/files/pubfiles/making-room-for-a-planet-of-cities-full_0.pdf> [accessed 22 September 2021].

Apap, J. (2019) 'The concept of "climate refugee": towards a possible definition', European Parliament Briefing, February [online] <https://www.europarl.europa.eu/RegData/etudes/BRIE/2018/621893/EPRS_BRI(2018)621893_EN.pdf> [accessed 22 September 2021].

Archer, D. (2012) 'Baan Mankong participatory slum upgrading in Bangkok, Thailand: community perceptions of outcomes and security of tenure', *Habitat International* 36(1): 178–184. <https://doi.org/10.1016/j.habitatint.2011.08.006>.

Archer, R. (1999) 'The potential of land pooling/readjustment to provide land for low-cost housing in developing countries', in G. Payne (ed.), *Making Common Ground: Public-Private Partnerships in Land for Housing*, pp. 113–33, Intermediate Technology Publications, London.

Asian Development Bank (ADB) (2013) *Asian Development Outlook 2013: Pakistan* [online], Asian Development Bank, Metro Manila <https://www.

adb.org/sites/default/files/publication/30205/ado2013-pakistan.pdf> [accessed 12 May 2021].

Atkinson, A. (2007) 'Regional Planning in Viet Nam' <http://dpu-associates.net/node/120> [accessed 22 April 2021].

Badev, A., Beck, T., Vado, L. and Walley, S. (2014) 'Housing finance across countries: new data and analysis' [online], World Bank <http://documents.worldbank.org/curated/en/697351468165251669/Housing-finance-across-countries-new-data-and-analysis> [accessed 22 September 2021].

Baljmaa, T. (2019) 'Mongolian land exchange system launches', *Montsame*, 6 August <https://www.montsame.mn/en/read/197095> [accessed 23 April 2021].

Bandelj, N. (2016) 'On post-socialist capitalism', *Theory and Society* 45(1): 89–106 <https://doi.org/10.1007/s11186-016-9265-z>.

Bank for International Settlements (2016) 'Highlights of global financial flows', *BIS Quarterly Review*, September [online] <https://www.bis.org/publ/qtrpdf/r_qt1609b.htm> [accessed 13 April 2021].

Barder, O. (2012) 'What is Development?', 16 August [blog], Centre for Global Development <https://www.cgdev.org/blog/what-development> [accessed 28 April 2021].

Bardhoshi, N. (2011) 'An ethnography of land market in Albania's post-socialist informal areas', *Urbanities* 1(1): 11–20 [online] <https://www.anthrojournal-urbanities.com/wp-content/uploads/2016/05/4-Bardhoshi.pdf> [accessed 22 September 2021].

Barne, D. and Wadhwa, D. (2018) 'Year in review: 2018 in 14 charts', *World Bank*, 21 December <https://www.worldbank.org/en/news/feature/2018/12/21/year-in-review-2018-in-14-charts> [accessed 10 May 2021].

Barnes, Y. (2018) '8 things to know about global real estate value', *Savills Impacts* <https://www.savills.com/impacts/market-trends/8-things-you-need-to-know-about-the-value-of-global-real-estate.html> [accessed 30 April 2021].

Bastin, J.F., Clark, E., Elliott, T., Hart, S., van den Hoogen, J., Hordijk I., Ma, H., Majumder, S., Manoli, G., Maschler, J., Mo, L., Routh, D., Yu, K., Zohner, C.M. and Crowther, T.W. (2019) 'Correction: understanding climate change from a global analysis of city analogues', *PLoS ONE* 14: 2–3 <https://doi.org/10.1371/journal.pone.0224120>.

Batbileg, C. (2007) 'Does land privatization support the development of land market?' *International Workshop: Land Policies, Land Registration and Economic Development: Experiences in Central Asian Countries, Tashkent, Uzbekistan, 31 October–3 November*.

Bateman, M. (2020) 'Land titling improves access to microcredit in Cambodia: be careful what you wish for', *SSRN Electronic Journal* 1–42 <https://doi.org/10.2139/ssrn.3557083>.

Bates, J. and Leibling, D. (2012) *Spaced Out: Perspectives on Parking Policy* [pdf], RAC Foundation, London <http://www.racfoundation.org/assets/rac_foundation/content/downloadables/spaced_out-bates_leibling-jul12.pdf> [accessed 22 September 2021].

Bates, R.E. (2010) *When Things Fell Apart: State Failure in Late-Century Africa*, Cambridge University Press, Cambridge, UK.

Batta, S. (2020) 'Gulf States force India and other South Asian states to repatriate impoverished migrant workers', International Committee of the

Fourth International (ICFI), 25 May [online] <https://www.wsws.org/en/articles/2020/05/25/gulf-m25.html> [accessed 13 October 2021].

BBC (2012) 'Chinese revolt leader becomes village chief of Wukan', [online] <https://www.bbc.co.uk/news/world-asia-china-16571568#:~:text=Chinese%20revolt%20leader%20becomes%20village%20chief%20of%20Wukan,Chinese%20village%20has%20been%20appointed%20its%20new%20chief> [accessed 13 October 2021].

Bejtja (Muca), S. and Bejtja, D. (2013) 'The framework for restitution/compensation process in Albania', *Academic Journal of Interdisciplinary Studies* 2(8): 291–7 <https://doi.org/10.5901/ajis.2013.v2n8p291>.

Benjamin, J. (2016) 'When a mafia expert tells us Britain is the most corrupt country in the world, it's time to start listening', *The Independent*, 1 June <https://www.independent.co.uk/voices/when-a-mafia-expert-tells-us-britain-is-the-most-corrupt-country-in-the-world-its-time-to-start-a7057686.html> [accessed 11 May 2021].

Bentley, I., Alcock, A., Murrain, P., McGlynn, S. and Smith, G. (1985) *Responsive Environments: A Manual for Designers*, Architectural Press, Elsevier, Oxford.

Berg, A.G. and Ostry, D. (2011) 'Warning! Inequality may be hazardous to your growth', 8 April [blog], IMF <https://blogs.imf.org/2011/04/08/inequality-and-growth/> [accessed 22 September 2021].

Berrisford, S., Cirolia, L.R. and Palmer, I. (2018) 'Land-based financing in sub-Saharan African countries', *Environment and Urbanization* 30(1): 35–52 <https://doi.org/10.1177/0956247817753525>.

Bertaud, A. and Brueckner, J.K. (2005) 'Analyzing building-height restrictions: predicted impacts and welfare costs', *Regional Science and Urban Economics* 35: 109–25 <https://doi.org/10.1016/j.regsciurbeco.2004.02.004>.

Bertaud, A., Buckley, R. and Phatak, V.K. (2005) 'Reforming Mumbai's real estate raj: a prelude to a business plan', unpublished report, World Bank, South Asia Region, Sustainable Development, Urban, Water & Sanitation, and Hazard Risk Management (SASDU), Washington, DC.

Bird, R. (2006) 'Taxing land and property in emerging economies: raising revenue… and more?' ITP Paper 065 [online], University of Toronto <https://www.researchgate.net/publication/24137671_Taxing_Land_and_Property_in_Emerging_Economies_Raising_Revenueand_More> [accessed 22 September 2021].

Bird, R.M. and Slack, E. (2004) *International Handbook of Land and Property Taxation* (March): 1–311 <https://doi.org/10.4337/9781845421434> [accessed 11 May 2021].

Birkmann, J. and Welle, T. (2016) 'The World Risk Index 2016: reveals the necessity for regional cooperation in vulnerability reduction', *Journal of Extreme Events* 03(01): 21 <https://doi.org/10.1142/s2345737616500056>.

Bloomberg News (2022) 'Xi Reshapes China Property Market Paving Way for State Dominance' 13 January. <https://finance.yahoo.com/news/xi-reshapes-china-property-market-210000896.html?fr=sycsrp_catchall&guccounter=1&guce_referrer=aHR0cHM6Ly9zZWFyY2gueWFob28uY29tLw&guce_referrer_sig=AQAAAFqX1FjFheGRBpDWGpUpzQ3FJa2NHy_qpm50UWSmeQbNpqLfqZ5QdR2-DstVw5rRkFiFAYtfNSNCF_b4OFTG9SL0FSYPQ_PoNtWP8IVscDHGplz1JzDkB4RxB9jnMmVEGnATrh-HwRgAFNkyJ0B4dko6mmA5P32IEdoGbaw9fyJd> [Accessed 14 January 2022].

Boonyabancha, S. (2005) 'How upgrading of Thailand's informal settlements is spear heading a community-driven, city-wide, integrated social development process' [online], Community Organizations Development Institute (CODI) <http://www.codi.or.th/downloads/english/Somsook5-23-06.pdf> [accessed 22 September 2021].

Booth, C. (1892–97) 'Inquiry into life and labour in London' <https://booth.lse.ac.uk/learn-more/download-maps> [accessed 20 April 2021].

Boudon, P. (1972) *Lived-in Architecture: Le Corbusier's Pessac Revisited*, Lund Humphries, London.

Bourke, L. (2021) 'Britain mulls Australia-style offshore processing, but sees few takers to host migrants', *Sydney Morning Herald*, 19 March [online] <https://www.smh.com.au/world/europe/britain-mulls-australian-style-offshore-processing-but-scant-takers-to-host-migrants-20210318-p57c40.html> [accessed 22 May 2021].

Branigan, T. (2012) 'Chinese villagers clash with police in land-grab protests', *The Guardian*, 3 April <https://www.theguardian.com/world/2012/apr/03/chinese-police-land-grab-protests> [accessed 22 April 2021].

Bregman, R. (2017) *Utopia for Realists And How We can Get There*, Bloomsbury, London.

Briggs, A. (1963, rev. 1968) *Victorian Cities*, Pelican Books, Harmondsworth.

Brolich, M. (2021) 'Speculation and vacancy tax confirmation', British Columbia <https://www2.gov.bc.ca/gov/content/taxes/speculation-vacancy-tax> [accessed 14 April 2021].

Brown de Colstoun, E.C., Huang, C., Wang, P., Tilton, J.C., Tan, B., Phillips, J., Niemczura, S., Ling, P.-Y. and Wolfe, R.E. (2017) 'Documentation for the Global Man-made Impervious Surface (GMIS) dataset from Landsat' [online], NASA Socioeconomic Data and Applications Center (SEDAC) <https://sedac.ciesin.columbia.edu/downloads/docs/ulandsat/ulandsat-gmis-v1-documentation.pdf> [accessed 22 September 2021].

Bruce, J. (2007) 'Drawing a line under the crisis: Reconciling returnee land access and security in post conflict Rwanda', Humanitarian Policy Group Working Paper, Overseas Development Institute, London.

Brueckner, J.K. (2009) 'Government land-use interventions: an economic analysis', in S.V. Lall, M. Freire, B. Yuen, R. Rajack, and J.J. Helluin (eds), *Urban Land Markets: Improving Land Management for Successful Urbanization*, Springer, Dordrecht, Heidelberg.

Burt, C. (2019) 'Nigeria to receive $433M from World Bank for biometric national ID registration' [online], Biometric Update, 5 September <https://www.biometricupdate.com/201909/nigeria-to-receive-433m-from-world-bank-for-biometric-national-id-registration> [accessed 28 April 2021].

Cadavid, P.R. (2011) 'The impacts of slum policies on households' welfare: the case of Medellin (Colombia) and Mumbai (India) [online], ParisTech <https://pastel.archives-ouvertes.fr/pastel-00711971/document> [accessed 22 September 2021].

Cahill, K. (2001) *Who Owns Britain*, Canongate Books, Edinburgh.

Cahill, K. (2006) *Who Owns the World: The Hidden Facts Behind Land Ownership*, Mainstream Publishing, London.

Cajaptay, S. and Yalkin, M. (2018) 'Syrian refugees in Turkey', Policy Analysis, Policy Watch 3007 [online], The Washington Institute for Near East Policy

<https://www.washingtoninstitute.org/policy-analysis/syrian-refugees-turkey> [accessed 13 October 2021].

Calavita, N. and Mallach, A. (eds) (2010) *Inclusionary Housing in International Perspective: Affordable Housing, Social Inclusion, and Land Value Recapture*, Lincoln Institute of Land Policy, Cambridge, MA.

Calderón-Garcidueñas, L., González-Macie, A., Mukherjee, P.S., Reynoso-Robles, R., Pérez-Guillé B., Gayosso-Chávez, C., Torres-Jardón, R., Cross, J.V., Imad, A.M., Karloukovski, V.V. and Maher, B.A. (2019) 'Combustion- and friction-derived magnetic air pollution nanoparticles in human hearts', *Environmental Research* 17, September.

Caldiera, T.P.R. (2000) *City of Walls: Crime, Segregation and Citizenship in São Paulo*, University of California Press, Berkeley, CA.

Callaway, P. (2009) *Making Life Rich Without Any Money: Stories of Finding Joy in What Really Matters*, Harvest House Publishers, Eugene, OR.

Cambodia Urban Forum (2019) 'Smart, Sustainable and Inclusive Urban Development' Ministry of Land Management, Urban Planning and Construction, 27 November, Phnom Penh.

Caminos, H. and Goethert, R. (1976) *The Urbanization Primer*, Massachusetts Institute of Technology, Boston, MA.

Campbell, D. (2006) 'Vanuatu tops wellbeing and environment index', *The Guardian*, 12 July <https://www.theguardian.com/world/2006/jul/12/healthandwellbeing.lifeandhealth> [accessed 28 April 2021].

Canary Wharf Group PLC (no date) 'Film + photography permits' <https://group.canarywharf.com/media/filming-photography-permits/> [accessed 17 October 2021].

Cao, A.J. and Keivani, R. (2013) 'The limits and potentials of the housing market enabling strategy: an evaluation of China's policies from 1998 to 2011', *Housing Studies* 29 (1): 44–68 <https://doi.org/10.1080/02673037.2013.818619>.

Capitalism Common Sense (2011) 'Ronald Reagan describes Milton Friedman', YouTube, 2 October [video] <https://www.youtube.com/watch?v=F7HtZtwyn_c> [accessed 24 April 2021].

Carson, R. (1962) *Silent Spring*, Houghton Mifflin, Boston, MA.

Carter, T. (2020) 'Wealth of Amazon CEO Jeff Bezos surpasses US$200 billion', *World Socialist*, 9 September <https://www.wsws.org/en/articles/2020/09/09/amaz-s09.html> [accessed 12 May 2021].

Cassella, C. (2018) 'While we were busy debating climate science, we lost more than half the Arctic's permanent ice', *Science Alert*, 16 October <https://www.sciencealert.com/arctic-sea-ice-lost-thinner-more-vulnerable> [accessed 22 September 2021].

Castells, M. (2010) *The Power of Identity*, 2nd edn, Wiley-Blackwell, Chichester.

Centre on Housing Rights and Evictions (2011) 'Living under threat but with nowhere to go: A survey on the impact of forced eviction on women in Phnom Penh', pp. i–viii, 1–33. <https://landportal.org/node/36226> [accessed 17 October 2021].

Chapman, W. (2019) 'Ashgabat, Turkmenistan, is the world's most expensive city for expats', *US News*, 18 June <https://www.usnews.com/news/cities/articles/2019-06-18/ashgabat-turkmenistan-is-the-worlds-most-expensive-city-for-expats> [accessed 10 August 2020].

Chia, J. (2021) 'Offshore processing statistics' [online], Refugee Council of Australia <https://www.refugeecouncil.org.au/operation-sovereign-borders-offshore-detention-statistics/2/> [accessed 22 May 2021].

Christian, W. and Salong, J. (2018) 'Housing and climate change resilience: Vanuatu', in A. Nelson and F. Schneider (eds), *Housing for Degrowth: Principles, Models, Challenges and Opportunities*, pp. 80–95, Taylor and Francis, London.

Christie, W. (2017) *Safeguarding Indigenous Architecture in Vanuatu* [online], Paris <https://unesdoc.unesco.org/ark:/48223/pf0000248144/PDF/248144eng.pdf.multi> [accessed 22 September 2021].

Christophers, B. (2018) *The New Enclosure: The Appropriation of Public Land in Neoliberal Britain*, Verso, London.

Churchill, W. (1909) 'The mother of all monopolies' <https://www.cooperative-individualism.org/churchill-winston_mother-of-all-monopolies-1909.htm> [accessed 20 April 2021].

Churkina, G., Organschi, A., Reyer, C.P.O., Ruff, A., Vinke, K., Liu, Zhu, Reck, B.K., Graedel, T.E. and Schellnhuber, H.J. (2020) 'Buildings as a global carbon sink', *Nature Sustainability* 3: 269–76 <https://doi.org/10.1038/s41893-019-0462-4>.

Cities Alliance (2021) City Development Strategies (CDS) <https://www.citiesalliance.org/city-development-strategies-cds> [accessed 26 April 2021].

City of Vancouver (2020) *Empty Homes Tax Annual Report* <https://vancouver.ca/files/cov/vancouver-2020-empty-homes-tax-annual-report.pdf> [accessed 22 September 2021].

Climate Central (2020) 'Top 10 warmest years on record', 15 January [online] <https://www.climatecentral.org/gallery/graphics/top-10-warmest-years-on-record> [accessed 13 May 2021].

Climate Central (2021) 'Coastal Risk Screening Tool'. <https://coastal.climatecentral.org/map/3/-0.1016/51.5289/?theme=sea_level_rise&map_type=year&basemap=roadmap&contiguous=true&elevation_model=best_available&forecast_year=2030&pathway=ssp3rcp70&percentile=p50&refresh=true&return_level=return_level_0&rl_model=gtsr&slr_model=ipcc_2021_med> [accessed 03 November 2021].

Cockburn, J.C. (2002) 'The mystery of credit', *Land Lines* 14(2).

Colagrossi, M. (2019) '10 reasons why Finland's education system is the best', *Big Think* <https://awaken.com/2019/06/10-reasons-why-finlands-education-system-is-the-best/> [accessed 08 May 2021].

Constable, S. (2019) 'Borrowing binge: world debt hits record of more than $250 trillion', Forbes, 14 November [online] <https://www.forbes.com/sites/simonconstable/2019/11/14/borrowing-binge-world-debt-hits-record-of-more-than-250-trillion/> [accessed 02 May 2021].

Cosman, J. and Quintero, L. (2019) 'Fewer players, fewer homes: concentration and the new dynamics of housing supply' [online], Carey Business School, Johns Hopkins University <https://www.housingonline.com/2019/10/30/fewer-players-fewer-homes-concentration-and-the-new-dynamics-of-housing-supply/> [accessed 13 April 2021].

Couldrey, M. and Peebles, J. (2020) 'Cities and towns', *Forced Migration Review* 63, February [online] <https://www.fmreview.org/sites/fmr/files/FMRdownloads/en/cities/cities.pdf> [accessed 22 September 2021].

Cousins, B., Cousins, T., Hornby, D., Kingwill, R., Royston, L. and Smit, W. (2005) 'Will formalising property rights reduce poverty in South Africa's "second economy"? Questioning the mythologies of Hernando de Soto', PLAAS Policy Brief No. 18, pp. 1–6 <https://www.academia.edu/1966235/Will_formalising_property_rights_reduce_poverty_in_South_Africas_second_economy> [accessed 18 October 2021].

Cresswell, T. (2014) *An Introduction to Place*, Wiley-Blackwell, Chichester.

Credit Suisse (2021) *Global Wealth Report 2021*, Credit Suisse, Zurich.

Crowfoot, Chief of the Blackfoot (c.1853) 'Native Americans describe traditional views of land ownership', *SHEC: Resources for Teachers* <https://herb.ashp.cuny.edu/items/show/1543> [accessed 5 May 2021].

Cunningham, E. and Zakaria, Z. (2018) 'Turkey, once a haven for Syrian refugees, grows weary of their presence', *The Washington Post*, 18 April <https://www.washingtonpost.com/world/turkey-to-syrian-refugees-you-dont-have-to-go-home-but-dont-stay-here/2018/04/04/d1b17d8c-222a-11e8-946c-9420060cb7bd_story.html?utm_term=.9aaf46909884> [accessed 15 April 2021].

Czischke, D. and Huisman, C.J. (2018) 'Integration through collaborative housing? Dutch starters and refugees forming self-managing communities in Amsterdam', *Urban Planning* 3(4): 156–65 <http://dx.doi.org/10.17645/up.v3i4.1727>.

Dasgupta, S. (2018) 'Risk of sea-level rise: high stakes for East Asia & Pacific region countries', 3 September [blog], World Bank <http://blogs.worldbank.org/eastasiapacific/risk-of-sea-level-rise-high-stakes-for-east-asia-pacific-region-countries> [accessed 08 May 2021].

Davidson, F. and Payne, G. (2000) *Urban Projects Manual*, Liverpool University Press, Liverpool.

Davis, I. and Alexander, D. (2016) *Recovery from Disaster*, Routledge, London.

De Cesare, C.M. (1999) 'Challenges to property tax administration in Porto Alegre, Brazil', *Land Lines* 11(5): 4–5 [online] <https://www.lincolninst.edu/sites/default/files/pubfiles/329_linc_landlines 8.99.pdf> [accessed 22 September 2021].

Del Carpio, X.V., Seker, S.D. and Yener, A.L. (2018) 'Integrating refugees into the Turkish labour market', *Forced Migration Review*, June [online] <https://www.fmreview.org/sites/fmr/files/FMRdownloads/en/delcarpio-seker-yener.pdf> [accessed 22 September 2021].

De Paulo, F. (2021) 'Horta gigante complementa refeições em favela do Rio durante pandemia', YouTube, 26 April [video] <https://www.youtube.com/watch?v=g_ujjyVz8no> [accessed 29 April 2021].

Deng, T., Shao, S., Yang, L. and Zhang, X. (2013) 'Has the transport-led economic growth effect reached a peak in China? A panel threshold regression approach', *Transportation* 41(3): 567–87 <https://doi.org/10.1007/s11116-013-9503-4>.

de Rivero, O. (2010) *The Myth of Development: Non-viable Economies and the Crisis of Civilization*, 2nd edn, Zed Books, London.

de Soto, H. (2000) *The Mystery of Capital: Why Capitalism Triumphs in the West and Fails Everywhere Else*, Basic Books, New York.

Deuskar, C. (2013) 'George Washington and land readjustment', Sustainable Cities, 31 July [blog], World Bank, Washington, DC <http://blogs.worldbank.

org/sustainablecities/george-washington-and-land-readjustment [accessed 10 May 2021].
Deuskar, C. (2015) 'Despite expectations, cities in East Asia are becoming denser', Sustainable Cities, 23 February [blog], World Bank <http://blogs.worldbank.org/sustainablecities/despite-expectations-cities-east-asia-are-becoming-denser> [accessed 13 April 2021].
Diallo, B. (2018) 'Ethiopia to build "True Wakanda", a $3 billion tech city, in partnership with Hub City Live', Africa Tech, 22 August <https://www.afrikatech.com/misc/ethiopia-to-build-true-wakanda-a-3-billion-tech-city-in-partnership-with-hub-city-live/> [accessed 8 May 2021].
Disney, R. and Luo, G. (2014) *The Right to Buy Public Housing in Britain: A Welfare Analysis*, Institute for Fiscal Studies <https://www.ifs.org.uk/uploads/publications/wps/WP201505.pdf> [accessed 26 April 2020].
Dorling, D. (2015) *Inequality and the 1%*, Verso, London, New York.
Dou, L. (2018) 'les 8 villes les plus futuristes d'Afrique', YouTube, 15 September [video] <https://www.youtube.com/watch?v=tmhWGALy-sI> [accessed 8 May 2021].
D'Souza, J.B. (1989) 'Will Bombay have a plan? Are planners and their plans relevant?' paper no 47 presented at an international workshop on *Planning and Management of Urban Development in the 1990s*, Birmingham University, September 1989.
Durand-Lasserve, A. (2006) 'Market-driven evictions and displacements: implications for the perpetuation of informal settlements in developing countries', in M. Huchzermeyer and A. Karam (eds), *Informal Settlements: A Perpetual Challenge?* pp. 207–27, University of Cape Town Press, Cape Town.
Durand-Lasserve, A. (2019) 'Addressing corruption in land administration: the experience of West African cities', *Conference on Land Policy in Africa: Winning the Fight against Corruption in the Land Sector*, UNECA – Land Policy Initiative, Abidjan, 4–8 November.
Durand-Lasserve, A. and Royston, L. (eds) (2002) *Holding Their Ground: Secure Land Tenure for the Urban Poor in Developing Countries*, Earthscan, London.
Durand-Lasserve, A., Selod, H. and Sylla, O. (2018) *Challenges and Risks of Accelerated Urban Expansion in Sub-Saharan Countries: A Policy and Research Discussion on Mobilizing Land for Urban Development*, The World Bank, Washington, DC.
Eastman, E. (2019) 'Saudi Arabia to unveil controversial utopian city Neom by 2025', Globetrender, 21 October <https://globetrender.com/2019/10/21/saudi-arabia-neom/October. https://globetrender.com/2019/10/21/saudi-arabia-neom/> [accessed 8 May 2021].
Economist (2017) 'Why 80% of Singaporeans live in government-built flats' *The Economist*, 8 July <https://www.economist.com/asia/2017/07/06/why-80-of-singaporeans-live-in-government-built-flats> [accessed 23 September 2021].
Economist (2018) 'China has built the world's largest water-diversion project', *The Economist*, London <https://www.economist.com/china/2018/04/05/china-has-built-the-worlds-largest-water-diversion-project> [accessed 12 May 2021].
Economist (2020) 'The horrible housing blunder: why the obsession with home ownership is so harmful', Special report, 16–24 January <https://www.economist.com/special-report/2020/01/16/housing-is-at-the-root-of-many-of-the-rich-worlds-problems> [accessed 16 April 2021].

Edkins, J. (2019) 'The Grenfell Tower fire', in *Change and the Politics of Certainty*, Manchester University Press <https://www.regulation.org.uk/specifics-grenfell_tower.html> [accessed 26 April 2021].

Edmond, C. (2020) 'China's air pollution has overshot pre-pandemic levels as life begins to return to normal', World Economic Forum, 20 July <https://www.weforum.org/agenda/2020/07/pollution-co2-economy-china/> [accessed 29 April 2021].

Egypt Real Estate Hub (2019) 'A closer look at Egypt's new capital city', Egypt Real Estate Hub, 28 March, London <https://www.egyptrealestatehub.co.uk/closer-look-egypt-new-capital-city?gclid=CjwKCAjwztL2BRATEiwAvnALcsayYIU6jf-jI7o8u2DWuY3uy7gMhA0_UxMVDz6eIZS3OzqqAtRJvxoCoy8QAvD_BwE> [accessed 16 April 2021].

Elliott, L. (2019) 'Billions of UK aid failing to reduce poverty, report finds', *The Guardian*, 4 February <https://www.theguardian.com/global-development/2019/feb/04/billions-of-uk-aid-failing-to-reduce-poverty-report-finds> [accessed 28 April 2021].

Ellmers, B. (2021) 'Broad consensus, paltry results: the UN Forum for Financing for Development 2021', Global Policy Forum, April <https://www.globalpolicy.org/sites/default/files/download/Briefing_0421_UN_Forum_Financing_for_Development.pdf> [accessed 23 September 2021].

Elmouelhi, H. (2019) 'New administrative capital in Cairo: power, urban development vs. social injustice – an Egyptian model of neoliberalism', in A. Al-Hamarneh, J. Margraff, and N. Scharfenort (eds), *Neoliberale Urbanisierung Stadtentwicklungsprozesse in der arabischen Welt*, pp. 215–254, Bielefeld Verlag.

Engels, F. (1975) *The Housing Question*, Progress Publishers, Moscow, p. 20 [original publication 1872–73].

Eshete, Z.S., Abebe, T.K. and Wolde, K. (2010) 'Performance, challenges, and prospects of real estate financing in Addis Ababa', *SSRN Electronic Journal* <https://doi.org/10.2139/ssrn.2335525>.

European Commission (2016) 'Migration and Home Affairs: Action plan on the integration and inclusion', European Commission <https://ec.europa.eu/home-affairs/what-we-do/policies/legal-migration/integration/action-plan-integration-third-country-nationals_en> [accessed 12 May 2021].

European Commission (2020) 'Circular economy action plan', European Commission <https://ec.europa.eu/environment/strategy/circular-economy-action-plan_en> [accessed 28 April 2021].

Fathy, H. (1973) *Architecture for the Poor: An Experiment in Rural Egypt*, University of Chicago Press, Chicago, IL.

Field, E. (2005) 'Property rights and investment in urban slums', *Journal of the European Economic Association* 3(2/3): 279–90.

Field, E. and Torrero, M. (2006) *Do Property Titles Increase Credit Access Among the Urban Poor? Evidence from a Nationwide Titling Program*, Harvard University, Boston, MA.

Fioramonti, L. (2013) *GDP Gross Domestic Problem: The Politics Behind the World's Most Powerful Number*, Zed Books, London.

Fishman, R. (1977) *Urban Utopias 20th Century*, Basic Books Inc., New York.

Food and Agriculture Organization (FAO) (2002) *Land Tenure and Rural Development* [online], FAO, Rome <https://doi.org/10.1080/03768358708439359>.

Friedman, M. (1962) *Capitalism and Freedom*, University of Chicago Press, Chicago.

Fukuyama, F. (1989) 'The end of history?' *The National Interest* 16: 3–18

Fukuyama, F. (1992) *The End of History and the Last Man*, The Free Press, New York.

Fullerton, K. (2013) 'Birth rates decrease as people rise out of poverty', Borgen Project, 30 May <https://borgenproject.org/birth-rates-decrease-as-people-rise-out-of-poverty/> [accessed 28 April 2021].

Fung, S. and McAuley, B. (2020) 'Cambodia's property tax reform: policy considerations toward sustained revenue mobilization', Governance Brief 38 <https://www.adb.org/sites/default/files/publication/561136/governance-brief-038-cambodia-property-tax-reform.pdf> [accessed 23 September 2021].

Gabbatt, A. (2019) '"Traitors to their class": meet the super-rich who want to be taxed more', *The Guardian*, 13 December <https://www.theguardian.com/us-news/2019/dec/13/patriotic-millionaires-super-rich-want-to-be-taxed-more> [accessed 28 April 2021].

Geddes, M. (ed.) (2021) La Feuille des Feuilles, quarterly bilingual newsletter of the Association Patrick Geddes France.

Geddes, P. (1915) *Cities in Evolution*, Williams & Norgate, London.

Geissdoerfer, M., Savaget, P., Bocken, N.M.P. and Hultink, E.J. (2017) 'The circular economy: a new sustainability paradigm?' *Journal of Cleaner Production* 143: 757–68 <http://dx.doi.org/10.1016/j.jclepro.2016.12.048>.

Gentleman, A. and Meikle, J. (2013) 'Grant Shapps accuses United Nations housing rapporteur of political bias', *The Guardian*, 11 September <https://www.theguardian.com/society/2013/sep/11/bedroom-tax-housing-benefit> [accessed 20 April 2021].

George, H. (1881) *Progress and Poverty: An Inquiry into the Cause of Industrial Depression and of Increase of Want with Increase of Wealth – The Remedy*, D. Appleton and Company, New York.

German Advisory Council on Global Change (WBGU) (2016) *Humanity on the Move: Unlocking the Transformative Power of Cities*, WBGU, Berlin.

Ghebreyesus, T.A. (2018) 'Air pollution is the new tobacco: time to tackle this epidemic', *The Guardian*, 27 October <https://www.theguardian.com/commentisfree/2018/oct/27/air-pollution-is-the-new-tobacco-time-to-tackle-this-epidemic> [accessed 03 August 2021].

Gilbert, A. (2002) 'On the mystery of capital and the myths of Hernando de Soto: what difference does legal title make?' *International Development Planning Review* 24(1): 1–19.

Gilbert, A. (2009) 'The rise (and fall?) of a state land bank', *Habitat International* 33(4): 425–35 <https://doi.org/10.1016/j.habitatint.2009.01.003>.

Gillespie, T. (2015) 'Accumulation by urban dispossession: struggles over urban space in Accra, Ghana', *Transactions of the Institute of British Geographers* 41(1): 66–77 <https://doi.org/10.1111/tran.12105>.

Girardet, H. (1990, 2019) 'The metabolism of cities', in D. Cadman and G. Payne (eds), *The Living City: Towards a Sustainable Future*, pp. 170–80, Routledge (first published 1990, reprinted 2019).

Giradet, H. (1996) *The Gaia Atlas of Cities: New Directions for Sustainable Urban Living*, Gaia Books Limited, London.

González-Couret, D. and Payne, G. (2020) 'Cuban experiences on urban sustainability and resilience', in C. Ween and C. Murray (eds), *Real State and Urban Development in Central America and the Caribbean*, Routledge, London.

Gore, A. (2006) *An Inconvenient Truth: The Planetary Emergency of Global Warming and What We Can Do About It*, Rodale, Emmaus, PA.

Gough, K.V. and Tran, H.A. (2009) 'Changing housing policy in Vietnam: emerging inequalities in a residential area of Hanoi', *Cities* 26: 175–86.

Government of China (2020) *Annual Monitoring and Investigation Report of Migrant Workers*, National Bureau of Statistics, Beijing <http://www.stats.gov.cn/tjsj/zxfb/202104/t20210430_1816933.html> [accessed 20 October 2021].

Government of the Republic of Vanuatu (2019) *National Land Subdivision Policy of the Republic of Vanuatu* <http://documents1.worldbank.org/curated/ru/833591561010682026/pdf/National-Land-Subdivision-Policy-of-the-Republic-of-Vanuatu.pdf> [accessed 23 September 2021].

Gov.UK (no date) 'Council tax: second homes and empty properties' <https://www.gov.uk/council-tax/second-homes-and-empty-properties> [accessed 19 April 2021].

Gov.UK (2014) 'Guidance: viability' <https://www.gov.uk/guidance/viability> [accessed 26 April 2021].

Green, R.K. and Wachter, S.M. (2005) 'The American mortgage in historical and international context', *Journal of Economic Perspectives* 19(4): 93–114 <https://doi.org/10.1257/089533005775196660>.

Greenwood, X. and Adams, R. (2018) 'Oxford and Cambridge university colleges own property worth £3.5bn', *The Guardian*, 29 May <https://www.theguardian.com/education/2018/may/29/oxford-and-cambridge-university-colleges-own-property-worth-35bn> [accessed 1 April 2021].

Grimsditch, M. and Schoenberger, L. (2015) *New Actions & Existing Policies: The Implementation and Impacts of Order 01* [online], The NGO Forum on Cambodia <https://www.researchgate.net/profile/Laura_Schoenberger/publication/278467781_New_Actions_and_Existing_Policies_The_Implementation_and_Impacts_of_Order_01/links/55812bc808aed40dd8cd400a/New-Actions-and-Existing-Policies-The-Implementation-and-Impacts-of-O> [accessed 23 September 2021].

Guppy, D. (2010) 'Divorce, a way round China's second-home restrictions', *China Daily*, Xinhua, 13 May, pp. 13–15 <https://www.chinadaily.com.cn/business/2010-05/13/content_9845715.htm> [accessed 23 September 2021].

Gurría, A. (2008) 'The global dodgers', *The Guardian*, 27 November <http://www.guardian.co.uk/commentisfree/2008/nov/27/comment-aid-development-tax-havens> [accessed 28 April 2021].

Gurría, A. (2016) 'The integration of migrants and refugees: challenges and opportunities', OECD, 7 October <http://www.oecd.org/migration/integration-of-migrants-and-refugees-challenges-and-opportunities.htm> [accessed 15 April 2021].

Hague, C. and Jenkins, P. (2005) *Place Identity, Participation and Planning*, Routledge, London.

Hajjar, B. (2020) 'The children's continent: keeping up with Africa's growth', in *World Economic Forum Annual Meeting, 21–24 January, Davos-Klosters, Switzerland* <https://www.weforum.org/agenda/2020/01/the-children-s-continent/> [accessed 13 May 2021].

Hall, D. (2004) 'Regulatory frameworks governing access to legal low-income housing in Maseru' in G. Payne and M. Majale (eds), *The Urban Housing Manual: Making Regulatory Framework Work for the Poor*, Earthscan, London.

Hall, D. (2020) 'Inside the UK ghost towns that time forgot – including Britain's Atlantis and whole towns that time forgot', *The Sun*, 1 September <https://www.thesun.co.uk/news/12513890/uk-ghost-towns-abandoned-villages-britains-atlantis/> [accessed 27 April 2021].

Hallmann, C. (2021) 'Vacant properties throughout Ireland: Learning from Denmark', Medium <https://medium.com/spaceengagers/vacant-properties-throughout-ireland-learning-from-denmark-f540bdaf3151> [accessed 15 April 2021].

Happy Planet Index (2021) Vanuatu – Happy Planet Index <happyplanetindex.org/countries/vanuatu/> [accessed 17 October 2021].

Haregewoin, Y.M. (2007) *Integrated Housing Development Programs for Urban Poverty Alleviation and Sustainable Urbanization (The Case of Addis Ababa)* [pdf], European Network on Housing Research <https://www.academia.edu/2154526/Integrated_housing_development_programs_for_urban_poverty_alleviation_and_sustainable_urbanization_the_case_of_Addis_Ababa> [accessed 18 October 2021].

Harpaz, B. (2015) 'AirBnB is booming in Cuba', *Business Insider*, 02 June [online] <https://www.businessinsider.com/airbnb-is-booming-in-cuba-2015-6?r=US&IR=T> [accessed 23 September 2021].

Harris, L. (2019) 'Entire abandoned Spanish villages being sold cheap to raise money', *The Vintage News*, 25 April <https://www.thevintagenews.com/2019/04/25/spanish-villages/> [accessed 27 April 2021].

Harris, N. (2014) *From Master Plans to City Development Strategies*, Development Planning Unit: Working Paper 162/60, London <https://www.ucl.ac.uk/bartlett/development/sites/bartlett/files/wp162.pdf> [accessed 23 September 2021].

Harvey, D. (1973) *Social Justice and the City*, Edward Arnold, London.

Harvey, D. (2008) 'The right to the city', *New Left Review* 53, September/October: 23–40 [online] <http://www.hlrn.org/img/documents/Harvey_right_to_the_city.pdf> [accessed 23 September 2021].

Hasan, A. (2020) 'What has emerged from 30 years of the Orangi Pilot Project', *Oxford Research Encyclopaedia of Global Public Health*, April [online] <https://doi.org/10.1093/acrefore/9780190632366.013.150>.

Hatton, T. and Williamson, J.G. (1992) *What Drove the Mass Migrations from Europe in the Late Nineteenth Century?* National Bureau of Economic Research Working Paper <https://www.nber.org/system/files/working_papers/h0043/h0043.pdf> [accessed 11 May].

Hausfather, Z. (2018) 'Factcheck: how global warming has increased US wildfires', Carbon Brief, 9 August <https://www.carbonbrief.org/factcheck-how-global-warming-has-increased-us-wildfires> [accessed 29 April 2021].

Hawksley, H. (2009) *Democracy Kills: What's so Good about Having the Vote?* Macmillan, New York.

Haworth, R. (2000) 'Patrick Geddes' concept of conservative surgery', *Architectural Heritage* 11: 37–42.

Hayek, F. (1944) *The Road to Serfdom*, Routledge Press, London.

Hayek, F. (1949) 'The intellectuals and socialism', *The University of Chicago Law Review*, Spring: 417–33.

He, C. and Yang, L. (2011) 'Urban development and climate change in China's Pearl River Delta', *Land Lines*, July, Lincoln Institute of Land Policy, Cambridge.

Healey, P. (2010) *Making Better Places: The Planning Project in the Twenty-First Century*, Red Globe Press, London.

Health Effects Institute (2019) *State of Global Air 2019: Special Report*, Health Effects Institute, Boston, MA.

Herz, G. (2021) 'Social housing is becoming a mainstream policy goal in the US', Jacobin <https://jacobinmag.com/2021/02/social-housing-public-affordable-california-maryland?fbclid=IwAR2bRAgJMk4Py k9Bhibay4ebLS-VferHCj8JXwfgkDpfSHSr-CiZ5j32VE4> [accessed 20 April 2021].

HM Land Registry (2021a) 'UK House Price Index' <https://landregistry.data.gov.uk/app/ukhpi/browse?from=1991-08-01&location=http%3A%2F%2Flandregistry.data.gov.uk%2Fid%2Fregion%2Funited-kingdom&to=2020-08-01&lang=en> [accessed 15 April 2021].

HM Land Registry (2021b) 'HM Land Registry: about us' <https://www.gov.uk/government/organisations/land-registry/about> [accessed 14 April 2021].

Ho, V. (2019) 'The Californians forced to live in cars and RVs', *The Guardian*, 5 August <https://www.theguardian.com/us-news/2019/aug/05/california-housing-homeless-rv-cars-bay-area> [accessed 29 April 2021].

Hodson, H.V. (1972) *The Diseconomics of Growth*, Pan, London.

Home, R. (2004) 'Outside de Soto's bell jar: colonial/postcolonial land law and the exclusion of the peri-urban poor', in R.K. Home and H. Lim (eds), *Demystifying the Mystery of Capital: Land Titling and Peri-Urban Development in Africa and the Caribbean*, pp. 11–30, Cavendish Publishing, London.

Hopkins, R. (2008) *The Transition Handbook: From Oil Dependency to Local Resilience*, Green Books, Totnes.

House of Commons (2016) 'Land Registry Privatisation', Library Briefing Paper [online] <https://commonslibrary.parliament.uk/research-briefings/cbp-7556/> [accessed 18 October 2021].

House of Commons (2016) *Proceeds of Crime: Fifth Report of Session 2016–17*, Home Affairs Committee [online] <https://publications.parliament.uk/pa/cm201617/cmselect/cmhaff/25/25.pdf?platform=hootsuite> [accessed 17 October 2021].

Howard, E. (1898) *To-Morrow: A Peaceful Path to Social Reform*, Swan Sonnenschein & Co. Ltd, London.

Howard, E. (1902) *Garden Cities of To-Morrow*, Swan Sonnenschein & Co., London.

Human Rights Watch (2019) 'Turkmenistan: events of 2018', Human Rights Watch <https://www.hrw.org/world-report/2019/country-chapters/Turkmenistan> [accessed 10 May 2021].

ICRC (2018) 'Sustained humanitarian action still needed in Myanmar and Bangladesh: ICRC President: Speech to UNGA High-Level Event'

<https://www.icrc.org/en/document/sustained-humanitarian-action-still-needed-myanmar-and-bangladesh> [accessed 15 April 2021].

Inman, P. (2013) 'Economics students aim to tear up free-market syllabus', The Guardian, 24 October <http://www.theguardian.com/business/2013/oct/24/students-post-crash-economics> [accessed 28 April 2021].

Innovations for Poverty Action (2015) 'Urban Property Rights Project Evaluation: Design Document', 22 June.

IPCC (2019) *Climate Change and Land: An IPCC Special Report on Climate Change, Desertification, Land Degradation, Sustainable Land Management, Food Security, and Greenhouse Gas Fluxes in Terrestrial Ecosystems*, P.R. Shukla, J. Skea, E. Calvo Buendia, V. Masson-Delmotte, H.-O. Pörtner, D.C. Roberts, P. Zhai, R. Slade, S. Connors, R. van Diemen, M. Ferrat, E. Haughey, S. Luz, S. Neogi, M. Pathak, J. Petzold, J. Portugal Pereira, P. Vyas, E. Huntley, K. Kissick, M. Belkacemi, and J. Malley (eds) [online] <https://www.ipcc.ch/srccl/> [accessed 13 April 2021].

IPCC (2021a) *Climate Change 2021: The Physical Science Basis*, <https://www.ipcc.ch/report/sixth-assessment-report-working-group-i/> [accessed 16 November 2011].

IPCC (2021b) 'Climate change widespread, rapid, and intensifying – IPCC', 9 August [press release] <https://www.ipcc.ch/site/assets/uploads/2021/08/IPCC_WGI-AR6-Press-Release_en.pdf> [accessed 24 September 2021].

International Finance Corporation (IFC) (no date) 'Access to essential financial services' <https://www.ifc.org/wps/wcm/connect/industry_ext_content/ifc_external_corporate_site/financial+institutions/priorities/access_essential+financial+services/access+to+essential+financial+services> [accessed 23 September 2021].

IFC (2005) *Developing a Housing Microfinance Product: The First Microfinance Bank' s Experience in Afghanistan* [online] <https://www.ifc.org/wps/wcm/connect/809de349-a8ee-4b5a-a45d-95b8b898542d/Housing+Microfinance+Afghanistan.pdf?MOD=AJPERES&CVID=l3dKwNt> [accessed 23 September 2021].

IFC (2019) *Green Buildings: A Finance and Policy Blueprint for Emerging Markets*, Washington, DC [online] <https://www.ifc.org/wps/wcm/connect/a6e06449-0819-4814-8e75-903d4f564731/59988-IFC-GreenBuildings-report_FINAL_1-30-20.pdf?MOD=AJPERES&CVID=m.TZbMU> [accessed 23 September 2021].

IFC (2020) *Green Buildings: Policy Pathways for Emerging Markets*, Washington, DC [online] <https://edgebuildings.com/wp-content/uploads/2020/06/IFCs-Green-Buildings-Policy-Pathways.pdf> [accessed 23 September 2021].

International Labour Organization (ILO) (2019) *Global Wage Report 2018/19: What Lies Behind Gender Pay Gaps*, International Labour Organization, Geneva, Switzerland <https://www.ilo.org/wcmsp5/groups/public/---dgreports/---dcomm/---publ/documents/publication/wcms_650553.pdf> [accessed 10 May 2021].

International Organization for Migration (IOM) (2020) *World Migration Report 2020*, International Organization for Migration, Geneva [online] <https://www.un.org/sites/un2.un.org/files/wmr_2020.pdf> [accessed 13 October 2021].

IQ*Air* (2020) 'World Air Quality report: Region & City PM2.5 Report', IQAir <https://www.iqair.com/world-most-polluted-cities> [accessed 13 May 2021].

Janda, M. (2019) 'China's empty homes may prove a bigger threat than Donald Trump's tariffs', ABC News, 14 May <https://www.abc.net.au/news/2019-05-14/china-vacant-property-empty-homes-donald-trump-tariffs/11082900> [accessed 22 April 2021].

Jenkins, O., Milner, J. and Sharpe, T. (2009) ' A brief historical review of community technical aid and community architecture', University of Salford, Manchester [online] <http://usir.salford.ac.uk/id/eprint/10468/1/Chapter2_Historical_pjlf_Feb2009%283%29pdf.pdf> [accessed 23 September 2021].

Jenkins, P., Smith, H. and Wang, Y.P. (2007) *Planning and Housing in the Rapidly Urbanising World*, Routledge, London.

Jenks, M. and Burgess, R. (eds) (2000) *Compact Cities: Sustainable Urban Forms for Developing Countries*, Taylor & Francis, Spon Press, New York.

Joint Center for Housing Studies (JCHS, Harvard University) (2011) *Rental Market Stresses: Impacts of the Great Recession on Affordability and Multifamily Lending*, President and Fellows of Harvard College, July [online] <https://www.urban.org/sites/default/files/publication/27011/1001550-Rental-Market-Stresses-Impacts-of-the-Great-Recession-on-Affordability-and-Multifamily-Lending.PDF> [accessed 23 September 2021].

Jones, S. (2019) '"Empty Spain": country grapples with towns fading from the map', *The Guardian*, 22 April <https://www.theguardian.com/world/2019/apr/22/empty-spain-government-urged-to-act-as-towns-fade-from-map> [accessed 27 April 2021].

Jordá, Ò., Schularick, M. and Taylor, A. (2014a) *The Great Mortgaging: Housing Finance, Crises, and Business Cycles*, Working Paper 2014-23, Federal Reserve Bank of San Francisco [online] <https://www.frbsf.org/economic-research/files/wp2014-23.pdf> [accessed 22 September 2021].

Jordà, Ò., Taylor, A. and Schularick, M. (2014b) 'The great mortgaging', *VoxEU CEPR*, 12 October [blog] <https://voxeu.org/article/great-mortgaging> [accessed 6 May 2021].

Kaganova, O. with Zenebe, S. (2014) *Land Management as a Factor of Urbanization*, Ethiopia Urbanization Review Background Paper, World Bank, Washington, DC.

Kagawa, A. and Turkstra, J. (2002) 'The process of urban land tenure formalisation in Peru', in G. Payne (ed.), *Land, Rights and Innovation: Improving Tenure Security for the Urban Poor*, ITDG Publications, London.

Kallis, G., Paulson, S., D'Alisa, G. and Demaria, F. (2020) *The Case for Degrowth*, Polity Press, London.

Kamata, T., Reichert, J., Tsevegmid, T., Kim, Y. and Sedgewick, B. (2010) *Managing Urban Expansion in Mongolia: Best Practices in Scenario-Based Urban Planning*, World Bank, Washington, DC [online] <https://openknowledge.worldbank.org/bitstream/handle/10986/2464/550280PUB0Urba100Box34943B01PUBLIC1.pdf?sequence=1> [accessed 23 September 2021].

Kaufmann, C. (no date) 'Tiny houses are becoming a big deal', AARP Livable Communities <https://www.aarp.org/livable-communities/housing/info-2015/tiny-houses-are-becoming-a-big-deal.html> [accessed 26 April 2021].

Keffa, S. (2014) *Integrated Housing Development Program as Instrument to Alleviate Urban Poverty: The Case of Addis Ababa*, June <http://www.fig.net/resources/proceedings/fig_proceedings/fig2014/papers/ts07k/TS07K_keffa_7359.pdf> [accessed 23 September 2021].

Kelm, K. (2009) 'Study on Security of Registered Titles in Albania', Land Administration and Management Project Component A: Security of Tenure and Registration of Immovable Property Rights, December.

Kenworthy, J.R. (2003) 'Transport energy use and greenhouse gases in urban passenger transport systems: a study of 84 global cities', *Third Conference of the Regional Government Network for Sustainable Development, Notre Dame University, Freemantle, Western Australia*.

Keynes, J.M. (1930) *Economic Possibilities for our Grandchildren*, Yale University Department of Economics <http://www.econ.yale.edu/smith/econ116a/keynes1.pdf> [accessed 6 May 2021].

Khemro, B.H.S. (2014) 'Housing Policy and Circular No. 3 on Squatter Settlement Resolution', *Rethinking Sustainable Cities* 16 (June): 1–60.

Khemro, B.H.S. and Payne, G. (2004) 'Improving tenure security for the urban poor in Phnom Penh, Cambodia: an analytical case study', *Habitat International* 28(2): 181–201 <https://doi.org/10.1016/S0197-3975(03)00067-5>.

King, A.D. (1976) *Colonial Urban Development: Culture, Social Power and Environment*, Routledge and Kegan Paul, London, Henley and Boston.

King, A.D. (1995) *The Bungalow: The Production of a Global Culture*, Oxford University Press, Oxford.

King, A.D. (2015) *Urbanism, Colonialism and the World Economy: Cultural and Spatial Foundations of the World Economic System*, Routledge Library Editions, London.

Kingdom of Lesotho (2004) *Lesotho Vision 2020* [online] <https://www.gov.ls/wp-content/uploads/2018/04/National_Vision_Document_Final.pdf> [accessed 23 September 2021].

Kingdom of Lesotho (2015) *Habitat III National Report 2015*, Ministry of Local Government and Chieftainship Affairs, May [online] <https://uploads.habitat3.org/hb3/Lesotho-Habitat-III-Report-08-June-2015.pdf> [accessed 23 September 2021].

Kingdom of Lesotho (2018) *National Housing Policy 2018*, Ministry of Local Government and Chieftainship [online] <https://riseint.org/ritc2018/wp-content/uploads/sites/4/2018/07/National-Housing-Policy-Lesotho-2018.pdf> [accessed 23 September 2021].

Kingston, K. (1996) *Creating Sacred Spaced with Feng Shui*, Piatkus Books, London.

Kingwill, R., Cousins, B., Cousins, T., Hornby, D., Royston, L. and Smit, W. (2006) *Mysteries and Myths: de Soto, Property and Poverty in South Africa* [online], IIED Gatekeeper Series No. 124 <https://www.researchgate.net/publication/45581476_Mysteries_and_Myths_De_Soto_Property_and_Poverty_in_South_Africa> [accessed 18 October 2021].

Klein, N. (2007) *The Shock Doctrine: The Rise of Disaster Capitalism*, Picador, New York.

Klein, N. (2019) *On Fire: The (Burning) Case for a Green New Deal*, Allen Lane, London.

Klopp, J. (2000) 'Pilfering the public: the problem of land grabbing in contemporary Kenya', *Africa Today* 47(1): 7–26.

Kolokotroni, M, Ren, X., Davies, M. and Mavrogianni, A. (2012) 'London's urban heat island: impact on current and future energy consumption in office buildings', *Energy and Buildings* 47: 302–11.

Krugman, P. (2009) *The Conscience of a Liberal: Reclaiming America from the Right*, Penguin Books, London.

Kumar, S. (2012) 'Membership in co-operative businesses reaches 1 billion', Worldwatch Institute <https://www.commondreams.org/newswire/2012/02/22/membership-co-operative-businesses-reaches-1-billion> [accessed 30 April 2021].

Kwok, R. (2018) 'Arctic sea ice thickness, volume, and multiyear ice coverage: losses and coupled variability (1958–2018)', *Environmental Research Letters* <https://iopscience.iop.org/article/10.1088/1748-9326/aae3ec/pdf> [accessed 09 May 2021].

Labbé, D. and Musil, C. (2014) 'Peri-urban land redevelopment in Vietnam', *Urban Studies* 51(6): 1146–61.

Lahoti, R. (2021) 'A method to measure perceived tenure security in low-income settlements in India', *International Journal for Urban Sustainable Development* 51(6) <https://doi.org/10.1080/19463138.2021.1964972>.

Lam, A. and Tsui, S. (1998) *Policies and Mechanisms on Land Value Capture: Taiwan Case Study*, Lincoln Institute of Land Policy Working Paper [online] <http://scholar.google.com/scholar?hl=en&btnG=Search&q=intitle:Policies+and+Mechanisms+on+Land+Value+Capture:+Taiwan+Case+Study#0> [accessed 23 September 2021].

Land Tenure Reform Association (1871) 'Report of the inaugural public meeting …': 9-10, in Avner Offer, *Prosperity and Politics, 1870-1914*, p. 183, Cambridge University Press, Cambridge.

Langston, C. (2014) 'Measuring good architecture: long life, loose fit, low energy', *European Journal of Sustainable Development* 3(4): 163–74 <https://doi.org/10.14207/ejsd.2014.v3n4p163>.

Lave, L. (1970) 'Congestion and urban location', Papers of the Regional Science Association 25: 133–52.

Layard, R. (2005) *Happiness: Lessons from a New Science*, Penguin, London.

Leduka, C. (2012) *Lesotho Urban Land Market Scoping Study* [online] <https://housingfinanceafrica.org/app/uploads/scoping_study_gov_ulm_lesotho.pdf> [accessed 23 September 2021].

Lee, A. (2018) 'EU Member States in race to the bottom to sell golden visas to the super-rich', Transparency.Org, 10 October <https://www.transparency.org/news/pressrelease/eu_member_states_in_race_to_the_bottom_to_sell_golden_visas_to_the_super_ri> [accessed 19 April 2021].

Lewis, A. and Abdellah, M. (2019) 'Egypt's new desert capital faces delays as it battles for funds', Emerging Markets, 13 May <https://www.reuters.com/article/us-egypt-new-capital/egypts-new-desert-capital-faces-delays-as-it-battles-for-funds-idUSKCN1SJ10I> [accessed 10 August 2020].

Leyawdeen, S. (2017) *Assessing the Impact of Customary Land Brokers (Agents) on Land Market Price in Northern Ghana: The Case in Yendi Municipality*, Institute of Housing Studies, Erasmus University, Rotterdam.

Li, L. (2014) 'Zhaijidi Gage Shidian Weipo Liuzhuan Jinqu, 7000 Wantao Xiaochuanquanfang Zhuangzheng Wuwang' (The experiment reform on rural residential plots does not touch the conversion, 70 million small property rights housing cannot be legalized) [online] <http://finance.sina.com.cn/china/20141025/000320636961.shtml> [accessed 20 October 2021].

Liang, Y. (2018) 'China makes steady progress in urbanization', XinhuaNet, 10 September <www.xinhuanet.com/english/2018-09/10/c_137458990.htm> [accessed 22 April 2021].

Liegey, V. and Nelson, A. (2020) *Exploring Degrowth: A Critical Guide*, Pluto Press, London.

Lindert, P.H. (1987) 'Who owned Victorian England? The debate over landed wealth and inequality', *Agricultural History* 61(4): 25–51.

Ling, P. (no date) 'Ghost Towns of America', Geotab <https://www.geotab.com/ghost-towns/> [accessed 27 April 2021].

Liu, Z., He, C., Zhou, Y. and Wu, J. (2014) 'How much of the world's land has been urbanized, really? A hierarchical framework for avoiding confusion', *Landscape Ecology* 29(5): 763–71 <https://doi.org/10.1007/s10980-014-0034-y>.

Lloyd-Jones, T. (2006) *Mind the Gap! Post-disaster Reconstruction and the Transition from Humanitarian Relief*, Max Lock Centre for the RICS, June [online] <https://www.preventionweb.net/files/9080_MindtheGapFullreport1.pdf> [accessed 23 September 2021].

Loh, J. and Wackernagel, M. (2004) 'Informe Planeta Vivo 2004', WWF <https://wwf.panda.org/wwf_news/?109443/Informe-Planeta-Vivo-2006> [accessed 22 April 2021].

Long, O. (2018) 'The EU-Turkey deal: explained', Choose Love, 5 April <https://helprefugees.org/news/eu-turkey-deal-explained/> [accessed 22 May 2021].

Ludewigs, T., Brondizi, E. and Hetrick, S. (2009) 'Agrarian structure and land-cover change along the lifespan of three colonization areas in the Brazilian Amazon', *World Development* 37: 1348–59.

Lynch, K. (1981) *Good City Form*, Massachusetts Institute of Technology Press, Cambridge.

Lynch, J., Brown, M. and Baker, L. (1998) 'Public-private partnerships in transitional land and housing markets: case studies from Bulgaria and Russia', in G. Payne (ed.), *Making Common Ground: Public-Private Partnerships in Land for Housing*, Intermediate Technology Publications, London.

Lyons, M., Schilderman, T. and Boano, C. (eds) (2010) *Building Back Better: Delivering People-Centered Reconstruction at Scale*, Practical Action Publishing, Rugby.

McAuslan, P. (1985) *Urban Land and Shelter for the Poor*, Earthscan, London.

McGinty, L. (2011) 'World population to hit milestone with birth of 7 billionth person', PBS NewsHour, 27 October <https://www.pbs.org/newshour/bb/world-july-dec11-population1_10-27/> [accessed 13 April 2021].

McGranahan, G. (1991) *Environmental Problems and the Urban Household in Third World Countries*, Stockholm Environment Institute, Stockholm.

McGranahan, G., Balk, D. and Anderson, B. (2007) 'The rising tide: assessing the risks of climate change and human settlements in low elevation coastal zones', *Environment and Urbanization* 19: 17–37 <https://doi.org/10.1177/0956247807076960>.

McIntyre, D.A. (2019) 'China has 65 million empty apartments', 24/7 Wall Street, 8 January <https://247wallst.com/economy/2019/01/08/china-has-65-million-empty-apartments/> [accessed 22 April 2021].

M.A.D. Urban (2014) 'Safeguarding Ulaanbaatar's urban heritage: understanding the critical importance of the historic centre in the social fabric of UB' October, Ulaanbaatar.

Mahadevia, D. (2010) 'Tenure security and urban social protection links: India', *IDS Bulletin* 41(4): 52–62 <https://doi.org/10.1111/j.1759-5436.2010.00152.x>

Malthus, T.R. (1798) *An Essay on the Principle of Population*, J. Johnson, London.

Mangin, W. (1967) 'Latin American squatter settlements: a problem and a solution', *Latin American Research Review* 2: 65–98.

Mangin, W. (ed.) (1970) *Peasants in Cities: Readings in the Anthropology of Urbanization*, Houghton Mifflin, Boston, MA.

Manthorpe, R. (2018) 'Airbnb is taking over London – and this data proves it', *Wired*, 2 February [online] <https://www.wired.co.uk/article/airbnb-growth-london-housing-data-insideairbnb> [accessed 2 May 2021].

Marx, C. and Rubin, M. (2008) *The Social and Economic Impact of Land Titling in Selected Settlements in Ekurhuleni Metropolitan Area* [online] <https://www.birmingham.ac.uk/Documents/college-social-sciences/government-society/idd/research/social-economic-impacts/south-africa-case-study-report.pdf> [accessed 23 September 2021].

Maslow, A.H. (1943) 'A Theory of Human Motivation', Brooklyn College [online] <https://eranda1998.wordpress.com/2018/06/29/a-theory-of-human-motivation-a-h-maslow-1943-2/> [accessed 23 September 2021].

Mathéy, K. (2021) 'Housing in Cuba' *Trialog* 115: 181–216.

Maya, W. (2019) 'Eko Atlantic City Nigeria is the Dubai of Africa?' YouTube, 6 June <https://youtu.be/SmLavWHjl10> [accessed 10 May 2021].

Mazzucato, M. (2013) *The Entrepreneurial State: Debunking Public vs Private Sector Myths*, Penguin Books, London.

Meadows, D.L. (2004) *The Limits to Growth: The 30-year Update*, Earthscan, London.

Meadows, D.H., Meadows, D.L, Randers, J. and Behrens, W., III (1972) *The Limits to Growth*, Universe Books, New York.

Meadows, D.H., Meadows, D.L. and Randers, J. (1992) *Beyond the Limits: Confronting Global Collapse and Envisioning a Sustainable Future*, Chelsea Green Publishing Company, London.

Mgbako, C., Gao, R.E., Joynes, E., Cave, A. and Mikhailevich, J. (2010) 'Forced eviction and resettlement in Cambodia: case studies from Phnom Penh', *Washington University Global Studies Law Review* 9(1): 39–76.

Minton, A. (2017) *Capital City: Who is London For?* Penguin Books, London.

Mintrom, M. (2019) 'Is New Zealand's Wellbeing Budget worth all the hype?' Centre for Public Impact (CPI), 6 June <https://www.centreforpublicimpact.org/insights/new-zealands-wellbeing-budget-worth-hype-contributor-michael-mintrom> [accessed 28 April 2021].

Mishan, E.J. (1967) *The Costs of Economic Growth*, Penguin, London.

Mitchell, T. (2007) 'The properties of markets', in D. MacKenzie, F. Muniesa, and L. Siu (eds), *Do Economists Make Markets? On the Performity of Economics*, pp. 244–75, Princeton University Press <https://doi.org/10.1515/9780691214665-011>.

Mitchell, T. (2009) 'How neoliberalism makes its world: the urban property rights project in Peru', in P. Mirowski and D. Plehwe (eds), *The Road from Mont Pèlerin: The Making of the Neoliberal Thought Collective*, pp. 386–416, Harvard University Press, Cambridge, MA.

Moore, A. (2021) 'Constitutional Crisis People's Budget 1909', Intriguing History <https://intriguing-history.com/constitutional-crisis-peoples-budget-1909/> [accessed 14 April 2021].

Mora, C., Dousset, B., Caldwell, I., Dousset, B., Caldwell, I.R., Powell, F.E., Geronimo, R.C., Bielecki, C.R., Counsell, C.W.W., Dietrich, B.S., Johnston, E.T., Louis, L.V., Lucas, M.P., McKenzie, M.M., Shea, A.G., Tseng, H., Giambelluca, T.W., Leon, L.R., Hawkins E. and Trauernicht, C. (2017) 'Global risk of deadly heat', *Nature Climate Change* 7: 501–6 <https://doi.org/10.1038/nclimate3322>.

More, T. (1516) *Utopia*.

Morris, A.E.J. (1972) *History of Urban Form: Before the Industrial Revolutions*, Longman, Harlow, UK (2nd edn, 1979, 3rd edn 1994).

Morris, W. (1890) *News from Nowhere* (published in serial form in *Commonweal*).

Muggah, R. (2018) 'Cities need to welcome – not resist – refugees', Bloomberg, 2 October <https://www.bloomberg.com/news/articles/2018-10-02/understanding-the-rise-of-urban-refugees> [accessed 15 April 2021].

Mukwaya, P.I., Pozhidaev, D., Tugume, D. and Kasaija, P. (2018) *Losing Ground? The Unprecedented Shrinking of Public Space and Land in Ugandan Municipalities* [online], UNCDF and Cities Alliance <https://www.citiesalliance.org/sites/default/files/2019-02/Losing%20Ground.pdf> [accessed 17 October 2021].

Muller, M. (2018) 'Lessons from Cape Town's drought', *Nature* 559, 6 July <https://media.nature.com/original/magazine-assets/d41586-018-05649-1/d41586-018-05649-1.pdf> [accessed 12 May 2021].

Municipal Dreams (2014) 'The Lillington Gardens Estate, Westminster: "civilizing, elegant and exciting"' <https://municipaldreams.wordpress.com/2014/07/01/the-lillington-gardens-estate-westminster-civilizing-elegant-and-exciting/> [accessed 26 April 2021].

Musahara, H. and Huggins, C. (2005) 'Land reform, land scarcity, and post-conflict reconstruction: a case study of Rwanda', in C. Huggins and J. Clover (eds), *From the Ground Up: Land Rights, Conflict and Peace in Sub-Saharan Africa* pp. 298–307, Institute of Security Studies, Pretoria and Cape Town.

Nadeu, S. (2016) '5 abandoned French towns where time stood still', Solo Sophie, 26 November [blog] <https://www.solosophie.com/abandoned-french-towns-villages-france/> [accessed 27 April 2021].

Napier, M. (2009) 'Making urban land markets work better in South African cities and towns: arguing the basis for access by the poor', in S.V. Lall, M. Freire, B. Yuen, R. Rajack, and J.J. Helluin (eds), *Urban Land Markets*, pp. 71–97, Springer, Dordrecht <https://doi.org/10.1007/978-1-4020-8862-9_4>.

NASA (2020) 'Arctic Sea Ice Minimum', Nasa Global Climate Change, Earth Science Communications Team at NASA's Jet Propulsion Laboratory <https://climate.nasa.gov/vital-signs/arctic-sea-ice/> [accessed 9 May 2021].

Navaratnarajah, R. (2017) 'S'pore property developers face a dilemma after rule changes', PropertyGuru, 03 April [online] <https://www.propertyguru.com.sg/property-management-news/2017/4/149857/spore-property-developers-face-a-dilemma-after-rule-changes> [accessed 1 May 2021].

Neate, R. (2020) 'Jeff Bezos, the world's richest man, added £10bn to his fortune in just one day', *The Guardian*, 21 July <https://www.theguardian.

com/technology/2020/jul/21/jeff-bezos-the-worlds-richest-man-added-10bn-to-his-fortune-in-just-one-day> [accessed 24 April 2021].

Needleman, D. (2017) 'Who will save these dying Italian towns?', *New York Times*, 7 September <https://www.nytimes.com/2017/09/07/t-magazine/abandoned-italian-towns.html> [accessed 30 April 2021].

Nelson, A. (2011) *Life Without Money: Building Fair and Sustainable Economies*, Pluto Press, London.

Nelson, A. and Edwards, F. (eds) (2020) *Food for Degrowth: Perspectives and Practices*, Routledge, London <https://doi.org/10.4324/9781003004820>.

Nelson, A. and Schneider, F. (eds) (2018) *Housing for Degrowth: Principles, Models, Challenges and Opportunities*, Routledge, London <https://doi.org/10.4324/9781315151205>.

Nenquino, N. (2020) 'This is my message to the western world – your civilisation is killing life on Earth', *The Guardian*, 12 October <https://amp.theguardian.com/commentisfree/2020/oct/12/western-worldyour-civilisation-killing-life-on-earth-indigenous-amazon-planet> [accessed 28 April 2021].

Netzer, D. (1998) 'Land value taxation: could it work today?' *Land Lines*, March: 1–3 <https://www.lincolninst.edu/sites/default/files/pubfiles/422_linc_landlines 3.98.pdf> [accessed 23 September 2021].

Nilsson, S. (1973) *The New capitals of India, Pakistan and Bangladesh*, Scandinavian Institute of Asian Studies Monograph Series, Copenhagen.

Nitschke, G. (1964) 'The Metabolists of Japan', *Architectural Design* 34: 509–524.

Nitschke, G. (1966) '"Ma" the Japanese sense of "place" in old and new architecture and planning', *Architectural Design*, March: 117.

Noonan, L., Tilford, C., Milne, R., Mount, I. and Wise, P. (2018) 'Who went to jail for their role in the financial crisis?' *Financial Times*, 20 September <https://ig.ft.com/jailed-bankers/> [accessed 16 April 2021].

Nooraddin, H. (1998) *'Al-fina'*, in-between spaces as an urban design concept: making public and private places along streets in Islamic cities of the Middle East', *Urban Design International* 3: 65–77 <https://doi.org/10.1057/udi.1998.8>.

Nyasulu, T.U. (2012) *Governance and Customary Land Tenure in Peri-Urban Kasoa in Ghana*, PhD dissertation, University of Köln <https://d-nb.info/1045345776/34>.

O'Connor, S. (2018) 'Millennials poorer than previous generations, data show', *Financial Times*, 23 February <https://www.ft.com/content/81343d9e-187b-11e8-9e9c-25c814761640> [accessed 20 April 2021].

Organisation for Economic Co-operation and Development (OECD) (2008) 'Proposal for a Forum for the Future Workshop on The Future of International Migration to OECD Countries', OECD <https://www.oecd.org/futures/41539904.pdf> [accessed 12 May 2021]

OECD (2017) *Resilience in a Time of High Debt: Pre-Release of the Special Chapter of the OECD Economic Outlook* [online] <https://www.oecd.org/economy/outlook/Resilience-in-a-time-of-high-debt-november-2017-OECD-economic-outlook-presentation.pdf> [accessed 17 October 2021].

OECD (2018) *Inequalities in Household Wealth across OECD Countries: Evidence from the OECD Wealth Distribution Database* [online] <http://www.

oecd.org/officialdocuments/publicdisplaydocumentpdf/?cote=SDD/DOC(2018)1&docLanguage=En> [accessed 23 September 2021].
Ohio State University (2018) 'Climate change leading to water shortage in Andes, Himalayas', *ScienceDaily* <https://www.sciencedaily.com/releases/2018/12/181217101759.htm> [accessed 9 May 2021].
Oliver, P. (1969) *Shelter and Society*, Barrie and Rockliff, The Cresset Press, London.
Oliver, P. (1971) *Shelter in Africa*, Barrie and Jenkins, London.
Oliver, P. (1987) *Dwellings: The House Across the World*, Phaidon, Oxford.
Oliver, P. (1997) *Encyclopaedia of Vernacular Architecture*, Cambridge University Press, Cambridge.
Orozco, M., Isaacs, L. and Dwyer, P. (2018) 'Remittances to Latin America and the Caribbean in 2017', presentation at The Dialogue, Leadership for the Americas, 25 January 2018 <https://www.thedialogue.org/events/remittances-to-latin-america-and-the-caribbean-in-2017/> [accessed 15 April 2021].
Osborne, H. (2021) 'British homes worth four times the economy at £9.2tn', *The Guardian*, 14 October [online] <https://www.theguardian.com/money/2021/oct/14/britains-homes-could-be-worth-92tn-on-open-market-report-shows> [accessed 14 October].
Oxfam (2014) *Working for the Few: Political Capture and Economic Inequality*, Report to the DAVOS World Economic Summit, 20 January [online] <https://www-cdn.oxfam.org/s3fs-public/file_attachments/bp-working-for-few-political-capture-economic-inequality-200114-en_3.pdf> [accessed 11 May 2021].
Oxfam (2019) *Public Good or Private Wealth?* Oxfam Briefing Paper, Oxfam Digital Repository, January <https://oxfamilibrary.openrepository.com/bitstream/handle/10546/620599/bp-public-good-or-private-wealth-210119-en.pdf> [accessed 17 October 2021].
Patowary, K. (2017) 'The model villages of Britain', Amusing Planet <https://www.amusingplanet.com/2017/07/the-model-villages-of-britain.html> [accessed 25 April 2021].
Paviour, B. (2016) 'World Bank will resume funding to Cambodia', *The Cambodia Daily*, 21 May <https://english.cambodiadaily.com/editors-choice/world-bank-will-resume-funding-to-cambodia-112866/> [accessed 16 April 2021].
Payne, G. (1977) *Urban Housing in the Third World*, Leonard Hill, London.
Payne, G. (1979) 'Housing: third world solutions to first world problems', *Built Environment* 5(2): 99–110.
Payne, G. (ed.) (1999) *Making Common Ground: Public-Private Partnerships in Land for Housing*, Intermediate Technology Publications, London.
Payne, G. (ed.) (2002) *Land Rights and Innovation: Improving Tenure Security for the Urban Poor*, ITDG Publishing, London.
Payne, G. (2006) 'A journey through space: cultural diversity in urban planning', in L. Asquith and M. Vellinga (eds), *Vernacular Architecture in the Twenty-First Century: Theory, Education and Practice*, pp. 155–76, Taylor and Francis, London.
Payne, G. (2007) 'Making it home – Mehmet Ali and the growth of Ankara', in A. Mengi (ed.), *Kent ve Politika Antik Kentten Dunya Kentine*, vol. 3, Imge Kitabevi Yayinlari, Ankara.

Payne, G. (2020) 'Options for intervention: increasing tenure security for community development and urban transformation', in P. Van den Broeck, A. Sadiq, I. Hiergens, H. Verschure, F. Moulaert, and M. Quintana (eds), *Communities, Land and Social Innovation: Land Taking and Land Making in an Urbanising World*, pp. 41–58, Edward Elgar, Cheltenham.

Payne, G. and Majale, M. (2004) *The Urban Housing Manual: Making Regulatory Framework Work for the Poor*, Earthscan, London.

Pegg, D., Bengtsson, H. and Watt. H. (2016) 'Revealed: the tycoons and world leaders who built secret UK property empires', *The Guardian*, 5 April <https://www.theguardian.com/news/2016/apr/05/panama-papers-world-leaders-tycoons-secret-property-empires> [accessed 11 May 2021].

Peppercorn, I.G. and Taffin, C. (2013) *Rental Housing: Lessons from International Experience and Policies for Emerging Markets*, World Bank [online] <https://openknowledge.worldbank.org/bitstream/handle/10986/13117/7618 20PUB0EPI00LIC00pubdate03010013.pdf?sequence=1&isAllowed=y> [accessed 2 May 2021].

Persaud, A.D. (2017) 'London: the money laundering capital of the world', *Prospect*, 27 April <https://www.prospectmagazine.co.uk/economics-and-finance/london-the-money-laundering-capital-of-the-world> [accessed 11 May 2021].

Petanaj, E.S. (2018) 'The registration of the ownership of the illegal objects in Albania', *Academicus-International Scientific Journal* MMXVIII(18): 83–99.

Phang, S. and Helble, M. (2016) *Housing Policies in Singapore*, ADBI Working Paper, No. 559, Asian Development Bank Institute (ADBI), Tokyo.

Phonphakdee, S., Visal, S. and Sauter, G. (2009) 'The urban poor development fund in Cambodia: supporting local and citywide development', *Environment and Urbanization* 21(2): 569–86 <https://doi.org/10.1177/0956247809339661>.

Plender, J. (2020) 'The seeds of the next debt crisis', *Financial Times*, 4 March [online] <https://www.ft.com/content/27cf0690-5c9d-11ea-b0ab-339c2307bcd4> [accessed 2 May 2021].

Plimmer, F. and McGill, G. (2003) *Land Value Taxation: Betterment Taxation in England and the Potential for Change* [online] <https://www.fig.net/resources/proceedings/fig_proceedings/fig_2003/TS_9/TS9_4_Plimmer_McGill.pdf> [accessed 23 September 2021]..

Plummer, J. (2012) *Diagnosing Corruption in Ethiopia: Perceptions, Realities, and the Way Forward for Key Sectors*, World Bank, Washington, DC [online] <https://elibrary.worldbank.org/doi/abs/10.1596/978-0-8213-9531-8> [accessed 23 September 2021].

Pobsuk, S. (2019) 'Alternative land management in Thailand: a study of the Southern Peasants' Federation of Thailand (SPFT)', Focus on the Global South, Chulalongkorn University, Bangkok [online] <https://focusweb.org/wp-content/uploads/2019/07/SPFT_CaseStudy_final-nl.pdf> [accessed 17 October 2021].

Pojani, D. (2010) 'Public transport and its privatization in East Europe: the case of Tirana, Albania', *European Transport - Trasporti Europei* 45: 64–82.

Pollard, A. (2018) 'Living behind the wheel: More Americans are sleeping in their cars than ever before. Should cities make space for them?' Metropolis, 20 August <https://slate.com/business/2018/08/vehicular-homelessness-is-on-the-rise-should-cities-help-people-sleep-in-their-cars.html> [accessed 16 April 2021].

Poore, J. and Nemecek, T. (2019) 'Reducing food's environmental impacts through producers and consumer', *Science* 360: 987–92 <https://doi.org/10.1126/science.aaq0216>.

Private Sector Competitiveness and Economic Diversification Project (PSCEDP) (no date) 'The plan to reshape Maseru' <https://www.psc.org.ls/updates/the-plan-to-reshape-maseru> [accessed 1 May 2021].

Pyla, P. (2009) 'The many lives of New Gourna: alternative histories of a model community and their current significance', *The Journal of Architecture* 14: 715–30 <https://doi.org/10.1080/13602360903357120>.

Quackenbush, C. (2019) '40 years after the fall of the Khmer Rouge, Cambodia still grapples with Pol Pot's brutal legacy', *TIME*, 1 January [online] <https://time.com/5486460/pol-pot-cambodia-1979/> [accessed 23 September 2021].

Rabé, P. (2009) 'From squatters to citizens? Slum dwellers, developers, land sharing and power in Phnom Penh, Cambodia, Doctoral dissertation, University of Southern California.

Rama, E. (2012) 'Take back your city with paint', TEDxThessaloniki, Greece [video] <https://www.ted.com/talks/edi_rama_take_back_your_city_with_paint?language=en> [accessed 23 April 2021].

Rapoport, A. (1969) *House Form and Culture*, Foundations of Cultural Geography Series, Prentice Hall, Englewood Cliffs, NJ.

Rapoport, A. (1980) 'Culture, site-layout and housing', *Architectural Association Quarterly*, 12.

Rapoport, A. (2002) 'On the size of cultural groups', *Open House International* 7: 7–11.

Raworth, K. (2017) *Doughnut Economics: Seven Ways to Think Like a 21st-Century Economist*, Penguin Random House, London.

Redwood, M. and Wakely, P. (2012) 'Land tenure and upgrading informal settlements in Colombo, Sri Lanka', *International Journal of Urban Sustainable Development* 4(2): 166–85 <https://doi.org/10.1080/19463138.2012.734826>.

Reed, C. (2015) 'Dutch nursing home offers rent-free housing to students', *PBS NewsHour*, 5 April <http://www.pbs.org/newshour/rundown/dutch-retirement-home-offers-rent-free-housing-students-one-condition/> [accessed 26 April 2021].

Rees, M. (2020) 'Foreword: Time for cities to take centre stage on forced migration', in M. Couldrey and J. Peebles (eds), *'Cities and Towns' Forced Migration Review* 63(February) <https://www.fmreview.org/sites/fmr/files/FMRdownloads/en/cities/cities.pdf>

Rees, W.E. (1992) 'Ecological footprints and appropriated carrying capacity: what urban economics leaves out', *Environment and Urbanization* 4: 121–30.

Rees, W. (1999) 'Achieving sustainability: reform or transformation?' in D. Satterthwaite (ed.), *Sustainable Cities*, pp. 22–52, Earthscan, London.

Regenvanu, R. (2008) 'Issues with land reform in Vanuatu', *Journal of South Pacific Law* 12(1): 63–7.

Relph, E. (1976) *Place and Placelessness*, Pion, London.

Reuters (2020) 'OECD's corporate tax reform proposal gaining broad support – Scholz', Reuters, 9 October <https://www.reuters.com/article/germany-taxation-oecd-int-idUSKBN26U1N3> [accessed 28 April 2021].

Ritchie, H. and Roser, M. (2017) 'Obesity', The Unseen Effects of NAFTA, 11 August <https://unseeneffectsofnafta.voices.wooster.edu/documents/document-4/> [accessed 12 May 2021].

RNZ (2017) 'Kiribati to start farming its land in Fiji', RNZ, 18 January <https://www.rnz.co.nz/international/pacific-news/322637/kiribati-to-start-farming-its-land-in-fiji> [accessed 29 April 2021].

Roberts, G.D. (2003) *Shantaram*, Scribe Publishers, Australia.

Roberts, P. (2019) 'Can a project change a city and a country?' Design Exchange, 12 August <https://www.demagazine.co.uk/2019/08/12/can-one-project-change-a-city-and-a-country/> [accessed 23 April 2021].

Roitman, S. and Phelps, N. (2011) 'Do gates negate the city? Gated communities' contribution to the urbanisation of suburbia in Pilar, Argentina', *Urban Studies* 48(16): 3487–509.

Roitman, S. and Recio, R.B. (2020) 'Understanding Indonesia's gated communities and their relationship with inequality', *Housing Studies* 35(5): 795–819 <http://dx.doi.org/10.1080/02673037.2019.1636002>.

Rolnik, R. (2013) *Report of the Special Rapporteur on Adequate Housing as a Component of the Right to an Adequate Standard of Living, and on the Right to Non-discrimination in this Context*, UN General Assembly, 30 December <https://digitallibrary.un.org/record/766905?ln=en> [accessed 23 September 2021].

Rolnik, R. (2019) 'Urban Warfare: Housing under the Empire of Finance' Verso, London.

Rosenzweig, C., Solecki, W., Hammer, S. and Mehotra, S. (2011) *Climate Change and Cities: First Assessment Report of the Urban Climate Change Research Network*, Cambridge University Press, New York.

Royo-Olid, J., Fennell, S. and Skinner, R. (eds) (2018) *Building, Owning and Belonging: From Assisting Owner-Driven Housing Reconstruction to Co-production in Sri Lanka, India and beyond*, UN-Habitat and European Union, Publications Office of the European Union, Luxembourg [online] <https://op.europa.eu/s/oMF3> [accessed 23 September 2021].

Royal Government of Cambodia (2010) *Circular 03 on Resolution of Temporary Settlements on State Land Illegally Occupied in the Capital, Municipal and Urban Areas*, 53(9): 1689–1699 [online] <http://countrysafeguardsystems.net/sites/default/files/KH Circular 3 Resolution Temporary Settlements on Land 2010.pdf> [accessed 23 September 2021].

Rudofsky, B. (1964) *Architecture Without Architects*, Doubleday, New York.

Rudofsky, B. (1977) *The Prodigious Builders*, Secker and Warburg, London.

Sala, I.M. (2018) 'Senegal is building a futuristic city to deal with its congestion problems', QuartzAfrica, 29 August <https://qz.com/africa/1352926/will-senegals-diamniadio-city-solve-dakars-problems/> [accessed 8 May 2021].

Salewski, C. and Johannes, E. (2018) 'Life is good. Life is golden', Organized Crime and Corruption Reporting Project, 5 March <https://www.occrp.org/en/goldforvisas/life-is-good-life-is-golden> [accessed 19 April 2021].

Samad, T., Lozano-Gracia, N. and Panman, A. (2012) *Colombia Urbanization Review*, World Bank, Washington, DC [online] <http://documents1.worldbank.org/curated/en/527041468025227166/pdf/724620PUB0Publ067926B09780821395226.pdf> [accessed 23 September 2021].

Sammon, B. (2019) *Financialisation and Rental Housing: A Case Study of the Boroughs of Barking & Dagenham and Newham in East London*, MSc thesis, Institute for Housing and Urban Development Studies [online] <https://thesis.eur.nl/pub/51904> [accessed 20 April 2021].

Sandel, M. (2012) *What Money Can't Buy: The Moral Limits of Markets*, Allen Lane, London.

Sandel, M. (2020) *The Tyranny of Merit: What's Become of the Common Good?* Penguin Random House, London.

Sanyal, B. and Deuskar, C. (2012) *Town Planning Schemes as a Hybrid Land Readjustment Process in Ahmedabad, India: A Better Way to Grow?* Lincoln Institute of Land Policy Studies, Cambridge, MA.

Savills World Research (2015) *World Residential Markets* [online] <https://pdf.euro.savills.co.uk/global-research/world-residential-markets-2015-2016.pdf> [accessed 23 September 2021].

Says, L. (2018) 'A fifth of China's homes are empty. That's 50 million apartments', Bloomberg News, 8 November <https://www.bloomberg.com/news/articles/2018-11-08/a-fifth-of-china-s-homes-are-empty-that-s-50-million-apartments> [accessed 22 April 2021].

Scanlon, K. and Whitehead, C. (2016) The profile of UK private landlords [online] <http://eprints.lse.ac.uk/id/eprint/87131> [accessed 17 October 2021].

Scanlon, K., Whitehead, C. and Blanc, F. (2017) *The Role of Overseas Investors in the London New-build Residential Market: Final Report for Homes for London*, LSE, May [online] <https://www.london.gov.uk/moderngovmb/documents/s58640/08b2b LSE Overseas Investment report.pdf> [accessed 23 September 2021].

Scheck, J., Jones, R. and Said, S. (2019) 'A prince's $500 billion desert dream: flying cars, robot dinosaurs and a giant artificial moon', *Wall Street Journal*, 25 July <https://www.wsj.com/articles/a-princes-500-billion-desert-dream-flying-cars-robot-dinosaurs-and-a-giant-artificial-moon-11564097568> [accessed 8 May 2021].

Schirber, M. (2015) 'Cities cover more of Earth than realized', LiveScience, 11 March [online] <https://www.livescience.com/6893-cities-cover-earth-realized.html> [accessed 13 April 2021].

Schneiderman, A.G. (2014) 'A.G. Schneiderman releases report documenting widespread illegality across Airbnb's NYC listings; site dominated by commercial users', Office of the Attorney General, New York State [press release] <https://ag.ny.gov/press-release/2014/ag-schneiderman-releases-report-documenting-widespread-illegality-across-airbnbs> [accessed 2 May 2021].

Schumacher, E.F. (1973) *Small is Beautiful: Economics as if People Mattered*, Blond and Briggs Ltd, London.

Schumpeter, J. (1942) *Capitalism, Socialism and Democracy*, 2nd edn, Impact Books, Floyd, VA.

Scott, J. (1998) *Seeing like a State: How Certain Schemes to Improve the Human Condition have Failed*, Yale University Press, New Haven, CT.

Scrieciu, S.Ş. and Stringer, L.C. (2008) 'The transformation of post-communist societies in central and eastern Europe and the former Soviet Union: an economic and ecological sustainability perspective', *European Environment* 18(3): 168–85 <https://doi.org/10.1002/eet.480>.

Scurrah, N. and Hirsch, P. (2015) 'The political economy of aid and governance in Cambodia', *Asian Journal of Political Science* 15(1): 68–96 <https://doi.org/10.1080/02185370701315624>.

Sen, A. (1999) *Development as Freedom*, 1st edn, Oxford University Press, New York.

Sen, A. (2009) *The Idea of Justice*, Allen Lane, London and Harvard University Press, Cambridge, MA.

Sendra, P. and Sennett, R. (2020) *Designing Disorder: Experiments and Disruptions in the City*, Verso, London and New York.

Seto, K.C., Fragkias, M., Güneralp, B. and Reilly, M.K. (2011) 'A meta-analysis of global urban land expansion', *PLOS One* 6(8): e23777 <https://doi.org/10.1371/journal.pone.0023777>.

Shah, A. (2014a) 'Foreign aid for development assistance', Global Issues, 28 September <https://www.globalissues.org/article/35/foreign-aid-development-assistance> [accessed 28 April 2021].

Shah, A. (2014b) 'Official global foreign aid shortfall: $5 trillion', Global Issues, 28 September <https://www.globalissues.org/article/593/official-global-foreign-aid-shortfall-5-trillion> [accessed 28 April 2021].

Shanghai Municipal Public Security Bureau (2020) 'Total households, population, density of registered population and life expectancy (1978–2019)' <http://tjj.sh.gov.cn/tjnj/nj20.htm?d1=2020tjnjen/E0201.htm> [accessed 22 April 2021].

Shaxson, N. (2019) 'Tackling tax havens', *Finance and Development* 56(3) [online], International Monetary Fund <https://www.imf.org/external/pubs/ft/fandd/2019/09/pdf/tackling-global-tax-havens-shaxon.pdf> [accessed 14 April 2021].

Shaxson N. (2020) 'How to make multinationals pay their share, and cut tax havens out of the picture', *The Guardian*, 27 January [online] <https://www.theguardian.com/commentisfree/2020/jan/27/multinationals-tax-havens-britain-us-corporate-giants> [accessed 11 May 2021].

Sheppard, S. and Udell, A. (2018) *Do Airbnb Properties Affect House Prices?* [online] <https://www.aeaweb.org/conference/2018/preliminary/paper/sna9Y7s3> [accessed 24 September 2021].

Shifter, M. and Huerta, M. (2020) 'El impacto del Coronavirus en Perú', The Dialogue: Leadership for the Americas, 22 May <https://www.thedialogue.org/analysis/el-impacto-del-coronavirus-en-peru/> [accessed 15 April 2021].

Shrubsole, G. (2019) *Who Owns England? How We Lost Our Green and Pleasant Land & How to Take It Back*, William Collins, London.

Sims, D. (2011) *Understanding Cairo: The Logic of a City out of Control*, The American University in Cairo Press, Cairo and New York.

Sims, D. (2014) *Egypt's Desert Dreams: Development or Disaster?* The American University in Cairo Press, Cairo.

Sims, D. (2015) 'David Sims – The Future of Egypt', Vimeo, 10 April.

Skidelsky, R. and Skidelsky, J. (2012) *How Much is Enough? The Love of Money and the Case for the Good Life*, Allen Lane Penguin Books, London.

Smith, A. (1776) *The Wealth of Nations*, William Strahan and Thomas Cadell, London.

Smolka, M. (2013) *Implementing Value Capture in Latin America: Policies and Tools for Urban Development*, Lincoln Institute of Land Policy, Cambridge, MA.

Soliman, A. (2021) *Urban Informality: Experiences and Urban Sustainability Transitions in Middle East Cities*. Cham, Switzerland: Springer Nature <https://doi.org/10.1007/978-3-030-68988-9>.

Sovani, N.V. (1964) 'The analysis of "over-urbanization"', *Economic Development and Cultural Change* 12(2): 113–22.

State Bank for Foreign Economic Affairs of Turkmenistan (2013) 'Ashgabat – in the Guinness Book of Records', *State Bank for Foreign Economic Affairs of Turkmenistan*, 25 May <https://www.tfeb.gov.tm/index.php/en/2013-09-20-04-46-12/35-2013-06-10-16-09-00> [accessed 10 August 2020].

Stefanova, M., Porter, R. and Nixon, R. (2012) *Towards More Equitable Land Governance in Vanuatu: Ensuring Fair Land Dealings for Customary Groups* [online], World Bank <https://documents1.worldbank.org/curated/en/600051468038724435/pdf/722760WP0P12370iscussion0Note0Final.pdf> [accessed 17 October 2021].

Stiglitz, J. (2003) *Globalization and its Discontents*, W. W. Norton and Company, New York.

Stiglitz, J. (2012) *The Price of Inequality*, Penguin books, London.

Sudworth, J. (2016) 'Counting the cost of China's left-behind children', *BBC News*, 12 April <https://www.bbc.com/news/world-asia-china-35994481> [accessed 15 April 2021].

Sun, G., Webster, C. and Chiarada, A. (2017) 'Ungating the city: a permeability perspective', *Urban Studies* 55(12): 1–17 <https://doi.org/10.1177%2F0042098017733943>.

Sun, L. (2015) 'Homing city migrants', *RICS Land Journal*, October/November: 16–17 [online] <https://search.proquest.com/openview/341d6923a1e9a262055713903a381a31/1?cbl=2028823&pq-origsite=gscholar> [accessed 24 September 2021].

Sun, L. and Ho, P. (2018) 'Formalizing informal homes, a bad idea: the credibility thesis applied to China's "extra-legal" housing', *Land Use Policy* 79: 891–901 <https://doi.org/10.1016/j.landusepol.2016.10.024>.

Sun, L. and Liu, Z. (2014), 'Examining the urban-rural linkages in China', *Regional Development Dialogue* 35: 197–213.

Sun, L. and Liu, Z. (2015) 'Illegal but rational: why small property rights housing is big in China', *Land Lines* [online], Lincoln Institute of Land Policy Studies, Cambridge, MA, pp. 805–36 <https://www.lincolninst.edu/publications/articles/illegal-rational> [accessed 24 September 2021].

Tacoli, C. (2017) 'Migration and inclusive urbanization', United Nations Expert Group Meeting on Sustainable Cities, Human Mobility and International Migration, 5 September, International Institute for Environment and Development, London <https://www.un.org/en/development/desa/population/events/pdf/expert/27/papers/V/paper-Tacoli-final.pdf> [accessed 12 May 2021].

Telgu360 (2016) 'Amaravati Master Plan revolves around Naidu's Vastu fascination', Telgu 360, 2 January <https://www.telugu360.com/amaravati-master-plan-revolves-around-naidus-vastu-fascination/> [accessed 26 April 2020].

Tellis, O. (2015) 'Thirty years after a landmark Supreme Court verdict, slum dwellers' rights are still ignored', Scroll, 21 December <https://scroll.in/article/776655/thirty-years-after-a-landmark-supreme-court-verdict-slum-dwellers-rights-are-still-ignored> [accessed 15 April 2021].

Textor, C. (2021) Urban and rural population of China from 2009 to 2019, Statista <https://www.statista.com/statistics/278566/urban-and-rural-population-of-china/> [accessed 22 April 2021].

Thakara, J. (2013) 'A roof, a skill, a market - BSHF', Building and Social Housing Foundation World Habitat Awards <https://designobserver.com/feature/a-roof-a-skill-a-market/37855> [accessed 26 April 2021].

Thatcher, M. (1989) 'Speech to United Nations General Assembly (Global Environment)', Margaret Thatcher Foundation <http://www.margaretthatcher.org/document/107817> [accessed 29 April 2021].

Thu, T.T. and Perera, R. (2011) 'Consequences of the two-price system for land in the land and housing market in Ho Chi Minh City, Vietnam', *Habitat International* 35(1): 30–39 <https://doi.org/10.1016/j.habitatint.2010.03.005>.

Thurlow, R. (2016) 'Chinese investment in Australian real estate doubles', *The Wall Street Journal*, 10 April <https://www.wsj.com/articles/chinese-investment-in-australian-real-estate-doubles-1460265591> [accessed 30 April 2021].

Tian, M. (2014) 'The role of land sales in local government financing in China', CKGSB Knowledge, 3 September <https://knowledge.ckgsb.edu.cn/2014/09/03/policy-and-law/the-role-of-land-sales-in-local-government-financing-in-china/> [accessed 22 April 2021].

Tipple, G. (2000) *Extending Themselves: User-initiated Transformations of Government-built Housing in Developing Countries*, Liverpool University Press, Liverpool.

Transparency International UK (2017) 'UK remains global money-laundering capital with more work to be done', Transparency International UK, 16 October <https://www.transparency.org.uk/uk-remains-global-money-laundering-capital-more-work-be-done> [accessed 11 May 2021].

Trivelli, P. (2010) *Urban Structure, Land Markets and Social Housing in Santiago, Chile* [online] <https://cafedelasciudades.com.ar/imagenes109/012411 Informe final_PTrivelli.pdf> [accessed 24 September 2021].

Trust for London (2020) *Pretty Vacant: The Negative Impact of Wealth Investment on Access to Housing in London. Policy Analysis and Recommendations* [PDF] <https://www.actiononemptyhomes.org/Handlers/Download.ashx?IDMF=24ace1b7-b428-4fee-8dcc-6a7638f32eaa> [accessed 28 April 2021].

Tsemberis, S. (2010) 'Housing first: The pathways model to end homelessness for people with mental health and substance use disorders' [online], Dartmouth Psychiatric Research Center (PRC) and Hazelden Publishing <https://endhomelessness.org/resource/housing-first/> [accessed 24 September 2021].

Turner, J.F.C. (1988) 'Introduction', in B. Turner (ed.), *Building Community: A Third World Casebook*, pp. 13–6, Habitat International Coalition Building Community Books, London.

Turner, J.F.C.T. (1967) 'Barriers and channels for housing development in modernizing countries', *Journal of American Institute of Planners* 33(3): 167–81 <https://doi.org/10.1080/01944366708977912>.

Turner, J.F.C.T. (1968) 'The squatter settlement: an architecture that works', *Architectural Design* [online] <http://www.communityplanning.net/JohnFCTurnerArchive/pdfs/ADAug1968SquatterSettlement.pdf> [accessed 24 September 2021].

Turner, J.F.C. (1972) 'Housing as a verb', in J.F.C. Turner and R. Fichter (eds), *Freedom to Build, Dweller Control of the Housing Process*, pp. 148–75, Collier Macmillan, New York.

Turner, J.F.C. (1976) *Housing By People: Towards Autonomy in Building Environments*, Marion Boyars, London.

Turner, J.F.C. (1990) 'Barriers, channels and community control', in G. Payne and D. Cadman (eds), *The Living City: Towards a Sustainable Future*, pp. 181–91, Routledge, London and New York (reissued 2019).

UK Department for Communities and Local Government (2017) *Fixing Our Broken Housing Market* [online] <https://assets.publishing.service.gov.uk/government/uploads/system/uploads/attachment_data/file/590464/Fixing_our_broken_housing_market_-_print_ready_version.pdf> [accessed 24 September 2021].

UK Department for Work and Pensions (2018) 'DWP benefits statistical summary: two thirds of DWP benefit claimants were of state pension age' [PDF] <https://assets.publishing.service.gov.uk/government/uploads/system/uploads/attachment_data/file/734667/dwp-quarterly-benefits-summary-august-2018.pdf> [accessed 28 April 2021].

UK Houses of Parliament Home Affairs Select Committee (2016) 'Report on the UK property market' <https://publications.parliament.uk/pa/cm201617/cmselect/cmhaff/25/2506.htm#_idTextAnchor036> [accessed 26 April 20].

UK Ministry of Housing, Communities and Local Government (MHCLG) (2018) 'Local authority housing statistics: year ending March 2018' [PDF], Ministry of Housing, Communities and Local Government, 24 January <https://assets.publishing.service.gov.uk/government/uploads/system/uploads/attachment_data/file/773079/Local_Authority_Housing_Statistics_England_year_ending_March_2018.pdf> [accessed 27 April 2021].

UK National Archives (2005) 'The struggle for democracy' <www.nationalarchives.gov.uk/pathways/citizenship/struggle_democracy/getting_vote.htm> [accessed 25 April 2021].

UK Office for National Statistics (ONS) (2019a) 'Milestones: journeying into adulthood', Office for National Statistics, 18 February <https://www.ons.gov.uk/peoplepopulationandcommunity/populationandmigration/populationestimates/articles/milestonesjourneyingintoadulthood/2019-02-18> [accessed 27 April 2021].

ONS (2019b) 'UK homelessness: 2005 to 2018', Office for National Statistics <https://www.ons.gov.uk/peoplepopulationandcommunity/housing/articles/ukhomelessness/2005to2018> [accessed 27 April 2021].

UN-Habitat (no date) 'Best Practices Database: Award Winners' <https://mirror.unhabitat.org/bp/bp.list.aspx> [accessed 11 May 2021].

UN-Habitat (2004) *Urban Land for All*, Nairobi <https://mirror.unhabitat.org/pmss/(X(1)S(lbuotjomuwmnodsprkmj1uyo))/getElectronicVersion.aspx?nr=1706&alt=1> [accessed 24 September 2021].

UN-Habitat (2008a) *Secure Land Rights for All*, UN-Habitat, Nairobi.

UN-Habitat (2008b) *The Role of Government in the Housing Market: The Experiences from Asia* [online], Nairobi <https://unhabitat.org/sites/default/files/download-manager-files/The%20Role%20of%20Government%20in%20the%20Housing%20Market%20%2C%20The%20Experiences%20from%20Asia.pdf> [accessed 24 September 2021].

UN-Habitat (2010) *Uganda Housing Profile*, UN-Habitat, Nairobi.
UN-Habitat (2014a) *Vietnam Housing Profile*, UN-Habitat, Nairobi.
UN-Habitat (2014b) *Urban Planning for City Leaders*, 2nd edition [online], Nairobi <https://www.local2030.org/library/67/Urban-Planning-for-City-Leaders.pdf>.
UN-Habitat (2015) *Lesotho Housing Profile*, UN-Habitat, Nairobi.
UN-Habitat (2016) *Framework for Evaluating Continuum of Land Rights Scenarios: Securing Land and Property Rights for All* [online], UN-Habitat, Nairobi <https://gltn.net/download/framework-for-evaluating-continuum-of-land-rights-scenarios/?wpdmdl=8110&ind=0> [accessed 24 September 2021].
UN-Habitat (2017) The State of Addis Ababa 2017 [online] <https://unhabitat.org/sites/default/files/download-manager-files/State of Addis Ababa 2017 Report-web.pdf> [accessed 24 September 2021].
UN-Habitat (2019) *The Global Housing Affordability Challenge: A More Comprehensive Understanding of the Housing Sector* [online] <https://unhabitat.org/sites/default/files/2020/06/urban_data_digest_the_global_housing_affordability_challenge.pdf> [accessed 24 September 2021].
UN-Habitat (2020a) *The New Urban Agenda*, UN-Habitat, Nairobi.
UN-Habitat (2020b) *World Cities Report 2020: The Value of Sustainable Urbanization* [online], UN-Habitat, Nairobi <https://unhabitat.org/sites/default/files/2020/10/wcr_2020_report.pdf> [accessed 15 October 2021].
UN-Habitat (2021) *The Role of Land in Achieving Adequate and Affordable Housing* [online], UN-Habitat, Nairobi <https://unhabitat.org/sites/default/files/2021/09/the_role_of_land_in_adequate_housing_final.pdf> [accessed 15 October 2021].
UNICEF (2017) 'Dividend or Disaster: UNICEF's new report into population growth in Africa', UNICEF, 26 October <https://www.unicef.org/media/media_101150.html> [accesses 12 May 2021].
United Nations (no date) 'International Day of Happiness: About' <https://www.dayofhappiness.net/about/> [accessed 8 May 2021].
United Nations (1948) 'Universal Declaration of Human Rights', United Nations <https://www.un.org/en/universal-declaration-human-rights/> [accessed 6 May 2021].
United Nations (1972) 'United Nations Conference on the Human Environment', *Europhysics News* 3: 6–7 <https://doi.org/10.1051/epn/19720307006>.
United Nations (1973) *Urban Land Policies and Land Control Measures, Volume 1. Africa; Volume 11. Asia and the Far East; Volume 111. Western Europe; Volume 1V. Latin America; Volume V. Middle East*, United Nations, New York.
United Nations (2015) Sustainable Development Goal 11: Sustainable Cities and Communities [online] <https://sdgs.un.org/goals> [accessed 14 October 2021].
United Nations (2016) 'New York Declaration for Refugees and Migrants', *International Journal of Refugee Law* 28: 704–32 <https://doi.org/10.1093/ijrl/eew057>.
United Nations (2017) *Report of the Special Rapporteur on Adequate Housing as a Component of the Right to an Adequate Standard of Living, and on the Right to Non-discrimination in this Context* [online] <https://digitallibrary.un.org/record/861179?ln=en#record-files-collapse-header> [accessed 24 September 2021].

United Nations (2018) *World Urbanization Prospects, Demographic Research* [online] <https://population.un.org/wup/Publications/Files/WUP2018-Report.pdf> [accessed 24 September 2021].

United Nations (2021) 'SDG indicators: metadata repository', United Nations Statistics Division <https://unstats.un.org/sdgs/metadata/?Text=&Goal=&Target=11.3> [accessed 26 April 2021].

United Nations Department of Economic and Social Affairs (UN DESA) (2018) '68% of the world population projected to live in urban areas by 2050, says UN', United Nations, 16 May, New York <https://www.un.org/development/desa/en/news/population/2018-revision-of-world-urbanization-prospects.html> [accessed 29 April 2021].

United Nations Development Programme (UNDP) (2011) *Human Development Report 2011: Sustainability and Equity – A Better Future for All*, UNDP, New York.

UNDP (2020) Vanuatu <http://hdr.undp.org/en/countries/profiles/VUT> [accessed 1 May 2021].

United Nations Environment Programme (UNEP) (2021) *Making Peace with Nature: A Scientific Blueprint to Tackle the Climate, Biodiversity and Pollution Emergencies* [online] <https://wedocs.unep.org/xmlui/bitstream/handle/20.500.11822/34948/MPN.pdf> [accessed 12 October 2021].

United Nations Framework Convention on Climate Change (UNFCCC) (2016) 'Nationally Determined Contributions (NDCs)', UNFCCC <https://unfccc.int/process-and-meetings/the-paris-agreement/nationally-determined-contributions-ndcs/nationally-determined-contributions-ndcs#eq-5> [accessed 28 April 2021].

UNFCCC (2020) 'Race to Zero Campaign', UNFCCC <https://unfccc.int/climate-action/race-to-zero-campaign#eq-6> [accessed 28 April 2021].

United Nations General Assembly (1994) *Programme of Action Adopted at the International Conference on Population and Development, Cairo, 5–13 September* [online] <https://www.unfpa.org/sites/default/files/pub-pdf/programme_of_action_Web%20ENGLISH.pdf> [accessed 16 October 2021].

United Nations General Assembly (2012) 'The right to adequate housing: note by the Secretary-General' [online] <https://www.ohchr.org/Documents/Issues/Housing/A-67-286.pdf> [accessed 24 September 2021].

United Nations General Assembly (2013) 'Happiness: towards a holistic approach to development – note by the Secretary-General', United Nations, 16 January [online] <https://unstats.un.org/unsd/broaderprogress/pdf/Happiness%20towards%20a%20holistic%20approach%20to%20development%20(A-67-697).pdf> [accessed 29 April 2021].

United Nations High Commissioner for Refugees (UNHCR) (2019) *Global Trends: Forced Displacement in 2018*, UNHCR Headquarters, Geneva <https://www.unhcr.org/5d08d7ee7.pdf> [accessed 12 May 2021]

UNHCR (2021) 'Refugee data finder' [online] <https://www.unhcr.org/refugee-statistics/> [accessed 13 October 2021].

United Nations Office for the Coordination of Humanitarian Affairs (UN OCHA) (2017) *Rohingya Refugee Crisis*, ReliefWeb <https://reliefweb.int/sites/reliefweb.int/files/resources/2017_HRP_Bangladesh_041017_2.pdf> [accessed 12 May 2021].

University of Maryland (2018) 'The Sahara Desert is expanding: new study finds that the world's largest desert grew by 10 percent since 1920, due in part to climate change', *ScienceDaily*, Rockville, MD <https://www.sciencedaily.com/releases/2018/03/180329141035.htm> [accessed 29 April 2021].

University of Toronto (2009) 'G20 Information Centre: G20 Leaders Statement: The Pittsburgh Summit', G20 Research Group, 29 November <www.g20.utoronto.ca/2009/2009communique0925.html> [accessed 29 April 2021].

Urban Development Authority of Curitiba (no date) 'Public transportation: evolution of the public transportation network' <https://curitibacity-planning.weebly.com/public-transportation.html> [accessed 26 April 2021].

Urban Institute (2017) 'Mapping America's Futures' <http://apps.urban.org/features/mapping-americas-futures/> [accessed 13 April 2021].

Urbaplan (2008) 'Urban Regulatory Plan Tirana: Draft Diagnostic report' Municipality of Tirana, July.

USAID (2018) 'Investor Survey on Land Rights 2018', Land Links <https://land-links.org/document/investor-survey-land-rights/> [accessed 19 April 2021].

Vanelli, F. (2019) 'Social effect of land titling: the link between private property and social cohesion in the case of Greater Tirana, Albania' [online], MSc Thesis, Institute of Housing and Urban Development Studies (IHS), Erasmus University, Rotterdam <https://thesis.eur.nl/pub/51907/-1-41527.pdf> [accessed 24 September 2021].

Vestbro, D.U. (ed.) (2010) *Living Together – Cohousing Ideas and Realities Around the World, Proceedings from the International Conference in Stockholm, 5–9 May* [online] <http://www.gbv.de/dms/ub-kiel/683490370.pdf> [accessed 24 September 2021].

Vietnam Investment Review (2016) 'Mekong Delta: Many industrial zones built, but others left idle', 18 August [online] <https://www.vir.com.vn/mekong-delta-many-industrial-zones-built-but-others-left-idle-44069.html> [accessed 2 May 2021].

Vivid Economics (2019) 'Lesotho Special Economic Zones: feasibility study', report prepared for the Lesotho Ministry of Trade and Industry, December.

Von Benda-Beckmann, F. (2003) 'Mysteries of capital or mystification of legal property?' *European Journal of Anthropology* 41: 187–91.

Von Mises, L. (1944) *Human Action: A Treatise on Economics*, Yale University Press, New Haven, CT.

Wainwright, O. (2020) 'Welcome to the yurt-opolis! How Mongolia is helping its nomads adapt to big city life', *The Guardian*, 17 May <https://www.theguardian.com/artanddesign/2020/may/17/yurt-opolis-mongolia-city-life-ulaanbaatar-community-hub> [accessed 23 April 2021].

Wallace-Wells, D. (2019) *The Uninhabitable Earth: A Story of the Future*, Penguin Random House, London.

Walters, L.C. (2016) 'Leveraging Land: Land-Based finance for Local Governments: A trainer's Guide' [online], UN-Habitat <https://www.researchgate.net/publication/311847011_Leveraging_Land_Land-based_finance_for_local_governments_-_Trainer%27s_Guide> [accessed 16 October 2021].

Walters, L.C. (2020) *Where to Start? A Guide to Land-based Finance in Local Governance* [online], UN-Habitat <https://www.fig.net/resources/publications/un/2020_GLTN-guide_land-based_finance.pdf> [accessed 2 May 2021].
Ward, B. (1976) *The Home of Man*, Penguin, London.
Ward, B. and Dubos, R. (1972) *Only One Earth: The Care and Maintenance of a Small Planet*, W. W. Norton, New York.
Ward, E. and Lyons, K. (2021) 'Who's buying Vanuatu's passports? Crypto moguls, wanted men and even a prime minister', *The Guardian*, 15 July [online] <https://www.theguardian.com/world/2021/jul/15/whos-buying-vanuatus-passports-crypto-moguls-wanted-men-and-even-a-prime-minister> [accessed 24 September 2021].
Wargent, M., Parker, G. and Street, E. (2020) 'Public-private entanglements: consultant use by local planning authorities in England' *European Planning Studies* 28(1): 192–210 <https://doi.org/10.1080/09654313.2019.1677565>.
Watson, G. (1988) 'Cities of light', *The Hudson Review* 40(4): 543–50 <https://doi.org/10.2307/3851121>.
Watson, V. (2013) 'African urban fantasies: dreams or nightmares?' *Environment and Urbanization* 26: 215–31 <https://doi.org/10.1177/0956247813513705>.
Watson, G. and Bentley, I. (2007) *Identity by Design*, Butterworth-Heinemann, London.
Wilkinson, R. (2020) 'How do we 'build back better' after coronavirus? Close the income gap', *The Guardian*, 26 August <https://www.theguardian.com/commentisfree/2020/aug/26/build-back-better-coronavirus-income-gap-pandemic> [accessed 28 April 2021].
Wilkinson, R. and Pickett, K. (2010) *The Spirit Level: Why Equality is Better for Everyone*, Penguin Books, London.
Wilkinson, R. and Pickett, K. (2018) *The Inner Level: How More Equal Societies Reduce Stress, Restore Sanity and Improve Everyone's Well-being*, Allen Lane-Penguin, London.
Wilkinson, R. and Pickett, K. (2020) 'Why coronavirus might just create a more equal society in Britain', *The Guardian*, 4 May <https://www.theguardian.com/commentisfree/2020/may/04/coronavirus-equal-society-britain-wellbeing-economic-growth> [accessed 28 April 2021].
Williams, S.M. (2008) *Improving Access to Urban Land Markets Though Less Conventional Land Policy Instruments: Literature Review*, World Bank, Washington, DC.
Williamson, J.G. (1988) 'Migration and urbanisation', in H. Chenery and T.N. Srinivasan (eds), *Handbook of Development Economics*, 1st edn, vol. 1, pp. 425–65, Elsevier, Amsterdam.
Wily, L.A. (2018) 'The Community Land Act in Kenya opportunities and challenges for communities', *Land* 7: 12 <https://doi.org/10.3390/land7010012>.
Wolf, M. (2020) 'The world economy is now collapsing: a microbe has overthrown our arrogance and sent global output into a tailspin', *Financial Times*, 14 April <https://www.ft.com/content/d5f05b5c-7db8-11ea-8fdb-7ec06edeef84> [accessed 24 April 2021].
World Bank (1993) *Housing: Enabling Markets to Work*, World Bank, Washington, DC.
World Bank (2011a) *Vietnam Urbanization Review* [online], World Bank, Washington, DC <https://openknowledge.worldbank.org/bitstream/handle/10986/282

6/669160ESW0P1130Review000Full0report.pdf?sequence=1&isAllowed=y> [accessed 24 September 2021].

World Bank (2011b) 'World Bank Board of Executive Directors considers Inspection Panel Report on Cambodia Land Management and Administration Project', 8 March <https://www.worldbank.org/en/news/press-release/2011/03/08/world-bank-board-executive-directors-considers-inspection-panel-report-cambodia-land-management-administration-project> [accessed 16 April 2021].

World Bank (2011c) *Recognizing and Reducing Corruption Risks in Land Management in Vietnam*, National Political Publishing House, Hanoi <https://documents1.worldbank.org/curated/en/918551468322441320/pdf/591690WP0Recog10BOX358274B01PUBLIC1.pdf> [accessed 16 October 2021].

World Bank (2013a) *Taking Stock: An Update on Vietnam's Recent Economic Developments*, World Bank, Washington, DC.

World Bank (2013b) *World Development Indicators 2013*, World Bank, Washington, DC.

World Bank (2013c) *China 2030: Building a Modern, Harmonious, and Creative Society, China 2030* [online], The World Bank Group, Washington, DC <https://doi.org/10.1596/9780821395455_overview> [accessed 24 September 2021].

World Bank (2014) *Promoting Affordable Housing in Changning District, Shanghai* [online], World Bank, Washington, DC <https://collaboration.worldbank.org/content/usergenerated/asi/cloud/attachments/sites/collaboration-for-development/en/groups/affordable-housing-ksb-c4d/documents/jcr:content/content/primary/blog/promoting_affordable-qlZv/Promoting%20Affordable%20Housing%20in%20Changning%20District,%20Shanghai.pdf> [accessed 24 September 2021].

World Bank (2015a) *Competitive Cities for Jobs and Growth: What, Who and How* [online], World Bank <http://documents1.worldbank.org/curated/en/902411467990995484/pdf/101546-REVISED-Competitive-Cities-for-Jobs-and-Growth.pdf> [accessed 24 September 2021].

World Bank (2015b) *Ethiopia Urbanization Review: Urban Institutions for a Middle-Income Ethiopia* [online], Washington, DC <https://openknowledge.worldbank.org/bitstream/handle/10986/22979/Ethiopia000Urb0ddle0income0Ethiopia.pdf?sequence=1&isAllowed=y> [accessed 24 September 2021].

World Bank (2015c) *India Land Governance Assessment: National Synthesis Report* [online], World Bank Group, Washington, DC <http://hdl.handle.net/10986/24420> [accessed 15 April 2021].

World Bank (2015d) 'Vietnam Affordable Housing: A Way Forward' Washington DC. <https://documents1.worldbank.org/curated/en/240541467995097856/pdf/100706-WP-P150619-PUBLIC-Box393231B-2015-10-16-05-45.pdfl> [accessed 16 October 2021].

World Bank (2015e) *Land Administration and Management in Ulaanbaatar, Mongolia*, World Bank, Washington, DC.

World Bank (2016) *Investing in Urban Resilience: Protecting and Promoting Development in a Changing World*, World Bank Elibrary, Washington, DC <https://elibrary.worldbank.org/doi/abs/10.1596/25219> [accessed 12 May 2021].

World Bank (2018a) 'Decline of global extreme poverty continues but has slowed', World Bank, 19 September [press release] <https://www.worldbank.org/en/news/press-release/2018/09/19/decline-of-global-extreme-poverty-continues-but-has-slowed-world-bank> [accessed 29 April 2021].

World Bank (2018b) *Poverty and Shared Prosperity 2018: Piecing Together the Poverty Puzzle* [online], World Bank Group, Washington, DC <https://openknowledge.worldbank.org/handle/10986/30418> [accessed 24 September 2021].

World Bank (2018c) *Vanuatu Climate Resilient Transport Project*, World Bank, Washington, DC <http://documents1.worldbank.org/curated/en/402161542854905069/pdf/Concept-Project-Information-Document-Integrated-Safeguards-Data-Sheet-Vanuatu-Climate-Resilient-Transport-Project-P167382.pdf> [accessed 12 May 2021].

World Bank (2019a) *Unlocking Ethiopia's Urban Land and Housing Markets: Synthesis Report* [online], October <https://doi.org/10.1596/32756>.

World Bank (2019b) *Cambodia Economic Update: Recent Economic Developments and Outlook* [online] <http://documents.worldbank.org/curated/en/707971575947227090/Cambodia-Economic-Update-Upgrading-Cambodia-in-Global-Value-Chains> [accessed 24 September 2021].

World Bank (2019c) 'Spatial development challenges of Pacific Island countries', presentation at Side Event 4 at the *Pacific Urban Forum, Suva, Fiji, July* [online] <http://devpolicy.org/2019-Pacific-Update/Day_1_Panel_2A_Chair_Robert_Utz.pdf> [accessed 24 September 2021].

World Bank (2019d) *Land and Poverty Conference 2019: Catalyzing Innovation*, World Bank <https://www.worldbank.org/en/events/2018/08/13/land-and-poverty-conference-2019-catalyzing-innovation> [accessed 16 April 2020].

World Bank (2019e) 'GNI per capita, Atlas method (current US$) - Low income, High income, Upper middle income, Lower middle income', World Bank <https://data.worldbank.org/indicator/NY.GNP.PCAP.CD?locations=XM-XD-XT-XN> [accessed 28 April 2021].

World Bank (2020) *Networked: Towards Urban Resilience and Economic Growth in Vietnam's Mekong Delta* [online], World Bank, Washington DC. <https://openknowledge.worldbank.org/bitstream/handle/10986/35241/Net-worked-Towards-Urban-Resilience-and-Economic-Growth-in-Vietnam-s-Mekong-Delta.pdf?sequence=1&isAllowed=y> [accessed 2 May 2021].

World Bank (2021) 'Water: overview', World Bank, Washington, DC <http://www.worldbank.org/en/topic/water/overview> [accessed 8 May 2021].

World Bank and Development Research Center of the State Council, The People's Republic of China (2014) *Urban China: Toward Efficient, Inclusive, and Sustainable Urbanization*, World Bank, Washington, DC <https://openknowledge.worldbank.org/handle/10986/18865> [accessed 24 September 2021].

World Commission on Environment and Development (WCED) (1987) *The Brundtland Report: Our Common Future*, Oxford University Press, Oxford and New York.

World Habitat (2015) 'Caño Martín Peña Community Land Trust' <https://world-habitat.org/world-habitat-awards/winners-and-finalists/cano-martin-pena-community-land-trust/#outline> [accessed 30 April 2021].

World Habitat (2016) 'A roof, a skill, a market', World Habitat, Coalville UK <https://world-habitat.org/world-habitat-awards/winners-and-finalists/a-roof-a-skill-a-market/#award-content> [accessed 15 April 2021].

World Habitat (2020) 'World Habitat Awards 2020 for innovative housing ideas and projects', World Habitat <https://opportunitydesk.org/2020/01/01/world-habitat-awards-2020/> [accessed 16 April 2020].

World Health Organization (WHO) (2018) Air Pollution and Child Health: Prescribing Clean Air [online] <https://apps.who.int/iris/bitstream/handle/10665/275545/WHO-CED-PHE-18.01-eng.pdf?sequence=2&isAllowed=y> [accessed 19 October 2021].

World Population Review (2021) 'Obesity rates by country' [online] <https://worldpopulationreview.com/country-rankings/obesity-rates-by-country> [accessed 24 June 2021].

Yahya, S. (2002) 'Community Land Trusts and other tenure innovations in Kenya', in G. Payne (ed.), *Land, Rights and Innovation: Improving Tenure Security for the Urban Poor*, pp. 233–63, Intermediate Technology Publishing, London.

Yang, W. (2021) 'A Tale of Two Cities' [online] <https://www.rtpi.org.uk/blog/2021/may/wei-yang-a-tale-of-two-cities/> [accessed 1 June 2021].

Yang Y. (2018) *Transport Infrastructure, City Productivity Growth and Sectoral Reallocation: Evidence from China*, IMF Working Paper [online] <https://doi.org/10.5089/9781484389584.001> [accessed 19 April 2021].

Yaro, J.A. (2009) 'Customary tenure systems under siege: contemporary access to land in Northern Ghana', *Geojournal* 75: 199–214.

Yin, P., Brauer, M., Cohen, A., Wang, H., Li, J., Burnett, R., Stanaway, J.D., Causey, K., Larson, S., Godwin, W., Frostad, J., Marks, A., Wang, L., Zhou, M. and Murray, C.J.L. (2020) 'The effect of air pollution on deaths, disease burden, and life expectancy across China and its provinces, 1990-2017: an analysis for the Global Burden of Disease Study 2017', *The Lancet*, 17 August <https://www.thelancet.com/action/showPdf?pii=S2542-5196%2820%2930161-3> [accessed 12 May 2021].

Young, M. (2019) '"Help to Buy" builder Persimmon Homes exposed as worst in UK after investigation', *Daily Mirror*, 14 July [online] <https://www.mirror.co.uk/news/business/help-buy-builder-persimmon-homes-18209854> [accessed 14 October 2021].

Zelleke, A. (2019) 'Fifty years later, reflecting on the defeat of Nixon's Family Assistance Plan', Basic Income Today: Universal Basic Income News Hub, 8 August <https://basicincometoday.com/fifty-years-later-reflecting-on-the-defeat-of-nixons-family-assistance-plan/> [accessed 28 April 2021].

Zetter, R. and Deikun, G. (2012) 'A new strategy for meeting humanitarian challenges in urban areas', *Forced Migration Review* 38: 48–50, Refugee Studies Centre, Oxford <www.fmreview.org/technology/48-50.pdf> [accessed 13 October 2021].

Zhu, M. (2014) 'Managing house price booms in emerging markets', [blog], IMFBlog, 10 December <https://blogs.imf.org/2014/12/10/managing-house-price-booms-in-emerging-markets/> [accessed 19 April 2021].

Zucman, G., Fagan, T.L. and Piketty, T. (2015) *The Hidden Wealth of Nations: The Scourge of Tax Havens*, University of Chicago Press, Chicago.

Index

Page numbers in *italics* refer to figures and photos, those in **bold** indicate boxes.

Aalbers, M.B. 108–9
access to urban land and housing 3–5
Accra *see* Ghana
Addis Ababa *see* Ethiopia
administrative procedures 255–6
affordable housing
  assessing 236–9
  EAH programme, China 114
  regulatory framework setting 254–5
  Vanuatu Enabling Affordable and Resilient Settlements (VEARS) 161
  see also social housing/public rental housing
Africa/sub-Saharan Africa
  communal ownership or lease 216
  expansion of Sahara 25–6
  informal management systems 202
  urban population growth 47, 190
  see also specific countries
Aga Khan Award/Development Network 226
agricultural land sales and compensation
  Albania 139, 140
  China 116
  Ethiopia 122–3, 124
air pollution 28–9, 243
  Mongolia 136
  reduction 243–4
  see also greenhouse gas/carbon emissions
Airbnb
  case study in adaptive regulation **93**
  Cuba 119
Albania 86, 206, 235
  state to market system 139–45, 150
Almukhtar, A. 13–14
ALUIZNI agency, Albania 141–2
Alvaredo, F. et al. 36
Amman, *see* Jordan
Ankara *see* Turkey
Anticretico tenure system, Bolivia 215
apartment blocks 249–50
  Albania 144
  Ankara, Turkey 227–8
  Ulaanbaatar Master Plan (2020), Mongolia 137–8
Archer, R. 219
Ardern, J. 175
Ashgabat, Turkmenistan 61–2
Asia
  urban population growth 47
  see also specific countries

Asian Development Bank 25, 135
Asian financial crisis (1997) 34
Attenborough, D. 31
authoritarian regimes *see* state land and housing management; state to market system

Bangladesh 29, 174, 249
  Rohingyas 44–5
Bastin, J.F. et al. 28
Bentley, I. et al. 241–2
Bhutan: Gross National Happiness Index 24, 175
Biden, J. 177, 185, 218
Bird, R.M. and Slack, E. 193
Bolivia: Anticretico tenure system 215
Boonyabancha, S. 219
Booth, C. 103
Botswana: certificates of rights 215
Brazil
  CEPAC bonds 197
  integrated transport planning and social development, Curitiba 244–5
  intermediate tenure options 213
Bregman, R. 176, 184, 185, 260
building capacity and support 263–7
Building Ownership Land Use Certificates (BOLUCs), Vietnam 126–7, 128, 130
'Buy to Let', UK 91, 108

Cahill, K. 99–100
California Model of development 174
Cambodia, 9, 47, 82, 86, 126, 150
  land management and administration project (LMAP) 77–8, 145–9
  state to market system 145–9, 150
Cambridge, UK
  co-housing, Marmalade Lane 217, 251, *252*
  and Oxford universities 100
capitalism
  property ownership as foundation of 73–4
  see also global move to market; neoliberalism; state to market system
carbon emissions *see* greenhouse gas/carbon emissions
certificates of comfort (COC), Trinidad and Tobago 213
certificates of rights, Botswana 215

change 256–61
  building capacity and support 263–7
  collaboration vs competition 262–3
Chennai, India 28
chiefs
  land allocation, Lesotho 151–2, 154, 155
  land values, Ghana 163
Chile and Philippines: housing subsides **91**
China, 11, 35, 47, 86, 136, 195, 243
  Bank of 12
  carbon emissions 178
  Daoyan 28
  feng shui, concept of 11–12, 13
  investment in Portugal 92
  land sales and leases 198
  rural-urban migration 43, 49
  segregated developments 39–40
  Shanghai 113, 114, *115*, 116, 230
  state land and housing management 113–17, 131
  tourism 15, *16*
  urban land expansion 187
Christophers, B. 96
Churchill, W. 102, 196
circular economy 29, 181, 259–60, 26–6
  see also 'doughnut economy'
citizenship
  and land rights for sale 91–2
  and residential leases, Vanuatu 159
City Development Strategy (CDS) 234–5
civil society organizations/NGOs 64, 163, 203
class and public communal spaces 19
climate change/crisis 3–4, 6, 98, 133
  as driver of migration 28–9, 48
  education 265
  growth and sustainability 177–9, 180–1
  Mongolia 133, 136, 137
'closed'/'restricted' vs 'open' housing supply system 190–2
co-housing 217, 251
Cockburn, J.C. 74–5
collaboration vs competition 262–3
Colombia 225
  intermediate tenure options 212
  upgrading existing urban area, Medellin 225
colonialism 4, 14, 19
  and decolonization 162–3
  land tenure and legal plurality 68
  Ottoman Land Act (1858) 18, 50
communal open space
  participatory planning 251
  see also public open space
communal ownership or lease 216, 218–19
  Thailand 214
community cohesion, Vanuatu 156–7
community land trusts (CLTs) 216
compact development 229–30
competition vs collaboration 262–3

conflict
  as driver of migration 27–8, 48
  rebuilding after 253–4
Constitutional protection of tenure 212
cooperative ownership 216–17
corporate tax/multinational corporations 38, 94, 177, 180, 185
costs
  assessing 237–9
  attributing 239–40
Cousins, B. et al. 81
Covid pandemic 3–4, 35, 38, 39, 50
  as catalyst for change 110–11, 188, 194, 254, 259, 260
  growth and sustainability 170, 173, 175–6, 177, 183
  climate crisis 178, 180–1
  impact of 224, 229
'creative disruption' 171–2
Cresswell, T. 13
Cuba 198
  Human Development Index (UNDP) 120, 175
  leases 198
  state land and housing management 117–21, 131
cultural context 9–11
  connecting space, culture, and identity 18–19
  impact of tourism, migration, and lifestyles 15–18
  imposed concepts and built forms 14
  learning from experts 20
  place and identity 13–14
  place and space 11–13
cultural diversity 224
custom-made approach 162–4
customary tenure and legal plurality 208
customary to market system
  Lesotho 151–6, 162–3
  Vanuatu 156–62, 163–4
cyclones, Vanuatu 156, 157, 160

Dar es Salaam (New Kigamboni City eco-city), Tanzania 58
Davidson, F. and Payne, G. 237
de Rivero, O. 173–4
de Soto, H. 73–4, 141, 142
de-growth 181–2
developers
  charges and impact fees 198
  China 116–17
  land hoarding/banking 96, 201
  and private banks 250
  requests for proposals (RFPs) 199–200
  transfer development rights (TDR) 200–1
  UK 108
development
  definitions of 170–1, 175, 183

measures of 21–2, 175
see also growth and sustainability
development rights, sale of 197
development-based instruments 197–201
disasters, rebuilding after 253–4
displacement/forced relocation 96
  Cambodia 78
  China 115
  Ghana 162–3
  see also agricultural land sales and compensation
diversity
  of building types and settlement forms 9–10
  and infrastructure grid hierarchy 238–9
  see also tenure security and diversity
documentation, tenure security through 212
'doughnut economy', concept of 181, *182*, 259–60
droughts 25
  flooding and 26, 27–8, 45, 46
Durand-Lasserve, A. 96, 155, 197, 261
Durand-Lasserve, A. and Royston, L. 67
Durand-Lasserve, A., Selod, H., Sylla, O. 47, 56, 190, 261

ecological footprint, minimizing 229–30
economic growth and management 3–4
  climate change 29–31
  see also growth and sustainability; inequality
Economic Land Concessions (ELCs), Cambodia 147
Economically Affordable Housing (EAH), China 114
The Economist 27, 85, 88,
Edkins, J. 235
Edmond, C. 29
education about climate crisis 265
Egypt 209,
  Hekr tenure 215
  informal development, Cairo 202
  Ismailia 230, *231–2*
  NAC 'smart' city 59–60
  New towns 233
  New Gourna project 55
  Real Estate Hub 59
  security through documentation 212
  tourism 15
elitist aspirations 56–64, 260–1
emergency housing 20
empty property 107, 195–6
Engels, F. 37, 95, 101, 103
environmental movements 178
environmental standards 250
equity sharing 217–18
Erbil, Iraq 13, 14, 19
Ethiopia 25,
  industrial zones 94

state land and housing management 121–5, 131
European Central Bank 193
European Commission 45, 178, 181
European Court of Human Rights 142
Evergrande, China 116–17
expansion, planning for 229–35
experts, learning from 20

Fathy, H. 55
fee-based instruments 197
feng shui, Chinese concept of 11–12, 13
Field, E. 75
  and Torrero, M. 75
financial crisis (2008) 75, 76–7, 85–6, 87, 89, 90, 98
  public sector cuts 193–4
financialization 88, 108–9, 188, 205
Fioramonti, L. 24, 36
flooding and droughts 26, 27–8, 45, 46
Floor Area Ratio (FAR) regulations 242
Food and Agriculture Organization 67
food and resource consumption 22–4
forced eviction *see* agricultural land sales and compensation; displacement/forced relocation
France 100, 125, 176
  Pessac project, near Bordeaux 55
Friedman, M. 33–4, 73, 75, 77
Fukuyama, F. 37, 73

garden cities movement 54, 104–5
'garden towns', UK 100
gated communities 39–40
  Phnom Penh, Cambodia 148
Geddes, P. 53–4, 104
gender
  public communal spaces 19
  Vanuatu 157–8
George, H. 53, 102, 196
ger/ger settlements, Mongolia *10*, *134*, 135, 136–7, 138–9
Germany
  concept of *gemütlich* 13
  German Advisory Council on Global Change 47, 246
  rental housing 92–3
Ghana 162–3
global cities 86–7
global move to market 85–6
  citizenship and land rights for sale 91–2
  competition for investment capital and distortion of public policy 93–4
  as foundation of capitalism 73–4
  impact on urban form 94–6
  political economy of land and housing 86–9
  promoting property ownership with subsidies 90–1
  rental housing 92–3

role of global capital in transforming land and housing markets 89–90
role of international development agencies 97
summary and next steps 97–8
Global North–Global South 4, 260
  cities and climate change 28, 29–30
  migration 51–2, 179–80
  property taxes 194
  resource consumption 174
  sites and services 250–1
  wealth transfer 266
Gogte, S. 19, 240
'golden' residency visas/passports 91–2, 159
Gonzalez-Couret, D. and Payne, G. 120
Gordon, A. 224
Gore, A. 21, 22
greenhouse gas/carbon emissions 26, 260
  China 178
  reduction 243–4, 249, 265
  see also air pollution
gross national income (GNI) 23–4, 184
gross national product (GDP) 23–4, 36
  and global debt 98
  and mortgage markets 89–90, 205
growth and sustainability 169–70
  alternative approaches 175–7
  and climate crisis 177–9, 180–1
  and international development assistance 184–5
  and migration 179–80
  needs and wants 170–5
  towards a new economic future 180–1
guided land development (GLD) 199
Guinness Trust, UK 103–4

Hanoi *see* Vietnam
happiness and wellbeing 170–1, 174–5
  de-growth and 181–2
Harris, N. 234–5
Harvey, D. 96
Hasan, A. 211
Havana, Cuba *118*, 119, 120
Hayek, F. 33, 34
Health Effects Institute 28
heat islands, cities as 26, 29
Ho, V. 10
  Sun, L. and Ho 49, 114, 116
Ho Chi Minh City (HCMC), Vietnam 126, 128
Home, R. 74
homes not housing 247–8
  procedural issues 255–6
  standards setting 254–5
  taking back control 248–54
house prices 247–8
  and income ratio 195, 236–7, 247
  UK 107, 108
housing, broad concept of 10
housing benefit, UK 95, 109
Housing First organizations 253
housing subsides *see* subsidies
Howard, E. 54, 104
Human Development Index (UNDP) 24,
  Cuba 120, 175
  Vanuatu 158
Human Rights Watch 62
hurricanes 26
hutongs: Chinese courtyard houses 15, *16*

identity
  connecting space, culture and 18–19
  place and 13–14
inclusionary zoning/mandatory allocations 199
income inequality 34–6, 173
incremental development 226, 241
incremental regularization 210–11
India 4–5, 39
  Chennai: public sewage system and flooding 28
  fee-based instrument 197
  informal land tenure and housing development 71–2, 88
  intermediate tenure 212, 220
  Land Acquisition Act (1894) 4
  land banking 110, 199, 201
  Lavasa 28
  Mumbai
    communal spaces 19
    perceived tenure security *71*
    public open space 240
    street dwellers 50, 72
    upgrading existing settlement 228–9
  New Delhi 14, 241
    Rouse Avenue 16–17, *18*
  new towns 39
  'over-urbanized' 17
  pattas and short-term leases 217
  public rental housing 89
  Town Planning Schemes 199
  unauthorized settlements and incremental regularization 210–11
  urban land demand 49
  urban poor 5
  vastu, concept of 13, 224
indirect interventions 209–12
Indonesia
  Jakarta 27, 49, 219, 226, 230
  Kampung Improvement Programme (KIP) 213–14, 226, *227*
Industrial Revolution, impact of 100–1
inequality
  and development 170–5
  elitist aspirations 62–4
  Global North–Global South migration 51–2, 179–80
  income 34–6
  internationally constrained supply 188
  living with 39–41
  new global financial architecture 37–8

INDEX 311

rise of the right 33–4
wealth and land 36–7
see also poverty; tax
informal land tenure/unauthorized
    settlements 68, 88, 136, 187, 189, 190,
    201–2, 210, 211, 230
  Albania 140–3
  Cambodia 145, 146, 148
  India 71–2, 88
  'twin-track' approach to land and housing
    189–90
  see also land titling programmes; tenure
    security and diversity
innovative formal options 216–19
Integrated Housing Development
    Programme (IHDP), Addis Ababa
    123–4, 125
intergenerational housing 251–2
Intergovernmental Panel on Climate
    Change (IPCC) 21, 22, 178–9, 189
intermediate tenure options 212–15
internal planning 249–50
international development assistance/
    donor agencies 97, 135–6, 146,
    184–5, 263–4, 266
International Finance Corporation (IFC)
    90, 250
International Monetary Fund (IMF) 34,
    35, 193
International Organization for Migration 43
investment
  Albania 143–4
  Cambodia 147, 148
  casino capitalism 170
  and distortion of public policy 93–4
  Lesotho 155–6
  Mongolia 149–50
  Portugal 91–2
  public and private 177
  see also under London
Iraq 13, 14, 19
Italy: Sutera 180

Jakarta, Indonesia 27, 49, 219, 226, 230
Japan
  Metabolists 12, 54, 202
  place-making (ma) and urban forms
    12–13
Jenkins,P. et al. 36
joint venture companies 203
Jordà, O. et al. 87
Jordan
  East Wahdat Palestinian settlement,
    Amman 226

Kallis, G. et al. 181–2
Kamata, T. et al. 134–5, 137
Kampung Improvement Programme (KIP),
    Indonesia 213–14, 226, 227
Kaohsiung, bike sharing 244, 245

Karachi, Pakistan 211, 260
Kenya
  community land trusts (CLTs) 216
  cooperative ownership 217
  occupancy certifications 215
  temporary occupation licences (TOLs) 212
Keynes, J.M. 171, 174
Khan, A.H. 211
Khemro, B.H.S. and Payne, G. 146, 148
Khmer Rouge regime, Cambodia 77, 126,
    145, 146, 149
Kigali, Rwanda 56–8
King, A.D. 18–19
Kingston, K. 12
Kingwill, R. et al. 74
Klein, N. 33, 77, 180

Lagarde, C. 193–4
Lagos, Nigeria 59
land auctions, Ethiopia 122
land banking: development-based
    instrument 201
land demand: rural-urban migration 49–50
land pooling/land readjustment (LP/LR):
    development-based instruments
    198–9
land sales and leases: development-based
    instrument 198
land tenure continuum and risk of eviction
    209–10
land tenure and property rights 67–8, 69
  analysis into action 75–7
  assessment 69–70
  evolving debate 72–5
  need for legitimacy 70–2
  see also land titling programmes; tenure
    security and diversity
Land Tenure Reform Association, Britain
    101–2
land titling programmes 205, 206
  Cambodia 77–8
  of informal/squatter settlements,
    consequences of 206
  Lesotho 153–4
  Peru 74–5, 82
  Rwanda (NLTRP) 78–80, 82
  South Africa 74, 80–2
  summary and next steps 82–3
land tribunals, Uganda 163
Land Use Rights Certificates (LURCs),
    Vietnam 126–7
land value, 68,117, 163, 192, 196–7, 216, 230
  Cambodia 146–7, 148
  cultural perceptions of 10–11
  increment tax 196
  Vanuatu 157, 158, 162
land value capture, 54, 192, 249
land value sharing 192
land value taxation, 102, 193
land and wealth inequality 36–7

landowners
  Albania 140, 141–3
  taxes 194–5
  transfer development rights (TDR) 200–1
Layard, R. 170
Le Corbusier 54–5
Lease Proclamation (2011), Ethiopia 122
Leduka, C. 152–4
legal plurality 68, 208
legality of tenure security 207–8
Leopold, A. 183
Lesotho, 37, 86,
  customary to market 151–6, 162, 163–4
  Form C 152, 215
Lima, Peru 230
Liu, Z.
  et al. 189
  Sun, L. and 35, 114
Lloyd Wright, F. 54–5
Lloyd-Jones, T. 254
local communities vs professionals, learning from 20
local scale, planning new development at 235–6
London 16, 29
  affordable housing developments 103–4, 105–6
  migration and assimilation 224
  private investment in property 86–7, 95
  money laundering 37, 38, 107, 159
  property prices 247
  rental housing 109
  transport 243–4
'long life, loose fit, low energy' principle 224, 249
Lutyens, E. 14

McAuslan, P. 73
Manchester: Industrial Revolution 100–1, 103
Manchester University: Post-Crash Economics Society 182
mandatory allocations/inclusionary zoning 199
market system
  change to 164–6, 263, 265–6
  see also customary to market system; global move to market; state land and housing management; state to market system
Maseru see Lesotho
master plans, limitations of 233–4
Mathéy, K. 119–120
Mazzucato, M. 177
Meadows, D.H. 21, 259
  et al. 21
measuring development 21–2, 175
meritocracy 172–3
Metabolists 12, 54, 64, 202
Mexico City: subsidence 27

Middle East
  concept of *al-fina'* 13
  gender 19
  Gulf States 50
  see also specific countries
migrant workers: Singapore and Dubai 62
migration 43, 50–2
  cities as magnets 46–8, 224
  contemporary drivers 43–6
  growth and sustainability 179–80
  official responses 48–50
  see also rural-urban migration
Mill, J.S. 101–2
Millennium Challenge Corporation (MCC)
  Lesotho 152–3, 154
  Property Rights project, Mongolia 135
mixed land use 135
money laundering 37, 38, 107, 159
Mongolia
  foreign investment 149–50
  state to market system 133–9
moral limits of markets 172–3
Morocco
  Ben Guerir 19
  Tangier 59
mortgages 75, 87, 217, 248, 250
  and GDP 89–90, 205
  informal land tenure and titling programmes 74–5
  'sub-prime' 76–7, 188
  tax relief 91, 106
multi-stakeholder partnerships 203
multinational corporations 38, 94, 177, 180
Mumbai see India
Myanmar: Naypyidaw 60–1

Native Americans 10–11
Naypyidaw, Myanmar 60–1
Needleman, D. 180
Nenquino, N. 183
neoliberalism 261
  and customary systems 165
  and elitist aspirations 63, 64
  and inequality 33, 34, 35, 37–8, 40
  land tenure and property rights 72–5, 76
Neom, Saudi Arabia 53, 58
Netherlands 252–3
New Delhi see India
New Towns Movement, Britain 105
New Urban Agenda (UN-Habitat) 4–5, 69–70, 203
New Zealand 175, 217, 265
NGOs/civil society organizations 64, 163, 203
Nicaragua 20
Nigeria: Eko Atlantic project, Lagos 59
Nilsson, S. 14
Nitschke, G. 12
non-market-based instruments for equitable land markets 201–2
Nyasulu, T.U. 163

OECD 51, 89–90, 180, 184, 266
  Common Reporting Standard (CRS) 193
Oliver, P. 18, 20
Oxfam 34–5, 41
Oxford and Cambridge universities, UK 100

Pakistan
  Orangi Pilot Project (OPP), Karachi 211
  Walled City of Lahore 17
Panama Papers 37, 159, 193
Paris Climate Agreement/COP26 4–5, 178–9
Parker Morris Committee: 'Design Bulletin 6 – Space in the Home' 105–6
participatory planning
  communal open space 251
  urban expansion 234–5
passive house construction 250
pattas and short-term leases, India 217
Payne, G. 17, 67, 69, 70, 74, 203, 207, 211, 248
  Davidson, F. and 237
  Gonzalez-Couret, D. and 120
  Khemro, B.H.S. and 146, 148
  and Majale, M. 242, 254
Peabody Trust, UK 103
Peru 18,
  Commission for the Formalisation of Informal Property (COFOPRI) 141
  land titling programme 74–5
  Lima 230
Philippines
  and Chile: housing subsides **91**
Phnom Penh, Cambodia 78, *145*, 146–9
place
  and identity 13–14
  and space 11–13
place-making 12–13, 241–2
planning for expansion 229–35
planning regulations 116, 242
political economy of land and housing 7, 86–9
population growth 22–4, 187
  cities 26–7, 47, 187
  food and resource consumption/GDP/GNI measures 22–4
  sub-Saharan Africa 261
Port Vila, Vanuatu 158–9, 160–1
Portugal: investment and residency visas, China 91–2
poverty
  extreme 35, 43–4, 169
  impacts of climate change 27, 29–31
  relative 98, 169
  rural and urban 17, 18
private developers *see* developers
private investment *see* investment
private rental housing 92–3, 107
  tourists **93**, 118–19

Private Sector Competitiveness and Economic Diversification Project (PSCEDP), Lesotho 155
private sector influence, UK 109–10
privatization of public space (POPS) 95–6, 110
professional expertise 220, 264
  vs local communities 20
project design, detailed 242
property developers *see* developers
property ownership
  as foundation of capitalism 73–4
  with subsidies 90–1
  see also investment; mortgages; UK as property owing democracy
property rights *see* land tenure and property rights; land titling programmes; tenure security and diversity
property taxes *see* tax
public land
  and private land: costs and allocating uses by category 237–8
  privatization, UK 96
  sales and leases 198
  see also state land and housing management; state to market system
public open space
  access 19
  Mumbai 19, 240
  privatization of 95–6, 110
  see also communal open space
public and private sector partnerships 192, 203
public and private space 17, *18*
Public Rental Housing (PRH), China 114

Rabé, P. 146
Rama, E. 144
Rapoport, A. 14, 18
Raworth, K. 181, 259–60
Reagan, R. 34, 73, 75, 76, 85
refugees 44–5, 48
  housing for 252–3
Regenvanu, R. 158
registration and free *khashaa* land plots, Mongolia 133, 134–5, 136–7
registration permit (*hukou*), China 113–14, 117
regularization, selecting settlements for 208
regulatory framework setting 254–5
Rehman, P. 211
rental housing *see* private rental housing; social housing/public rental housing
requests for proposals (RFPs) 199–200
residency visas/passports, 'golden' 91–2, 159
resistance to change 264
'Right to Buy', UK 106–7
right-wing politics, rise of 33–4
romance and idealism 53–4

Rudofsky, B. 11
rural-urban migration 47, 48–50
  Albania 139–40
  China 43, 49, 113–14, 117
  India 16–17
  Lesotho 151–2
  Mongolia 134–5
  Turkey 18, 50, *51*, 211
  Vanuatu 158
Russia: 118, 200
  and Commonwealth of Independent States 87
Rwanda 174,
  Kigali 56–8
  land titling programme (NLTRP) 78–80, 82

Sala, I.M. 58–9
Sandel, M. 40, 172–3
Saudi Arabia: Neom 58
Schumpeter, J. 171–2
Scurrah, N. and Hirsch, P. 147
sea level rises 24–6
second homes 107, 195–6
segregation 39–40, 94–6, 140
self-help construction
  Cuba 117–18, 119–20
  Turkey 50, *51*, 211
  Vietnam 130
self-planned and developed urban settlements 5
Sendra, P. and Sennet, R. 63, 202
Senegal 25, 58–9
Shanghai 113, 114, *115*, 116–7, 230
Shaxson, N. 193–4
'shock doctrine'/'shock therapy' 33–4, 142
Shrubsole, G. 108, 183
Silk Road 16
Sims, D. *64*, 202, 233
Singapore 62, 88–9,
site development briefs 200
sites and services: 241, Global North–Global South 250–1
Skidelsky, R. and Skidelsky, J. 171–2, 173
Slum Networking Programme (SNP), Ahmedabad, India 210–11
Small Property Rights (SPR) housing, China 113–14, 116
'smart' cities 28, 58, 59–60, 266
Smith, A. 33, 40
social clustering and housing across infrastructure grid hierarchy 238–9
social housing/public rental housing 88–9, 218
  UK 95, 105–7, 109
  see also affordable housing
Social Tenure Domain Model (STDM) 210, 215
South Africa: land titling programmes 74, 80–2
Soviet Union, collapse of 73, 87, 118, 134

space and place 11–13
spatial planning and land use for adequate housing 223–4, 245
  assessing affordability and costs 236–9
  attributing costs 239–40
  cultural diversity 224
  designing public realm 241–2
  detailed project design 242
  limitations of master plans 233–4
  new development at local scale 235–6
  planning for expansion 229–33
  strategic development plans and participatory planning approach to urban expansion 234–5
  transport oriented development (TOD) and wellbeing 242–5
  upgrading existing urban areas 224–9
standardized cities 63
standards setting 254–5
starter homes 250
state land and housing management
  China 113–17, 131
  common threads in case studies 130–1
  Cuba 117–21, 131
  Ethiopia 121–5, 131
  Vietnam 125–30, 131
state to market system 133
  Albania 139–45, 150
  Cambodia 145–9, 150
  Mongolia 133–9
  summary and implications 149–50
stewardship, concept of 183, 220
Stiglitz, J. 34, 40, 173, 176
strategic development plans 234–5
structural adjustment programmes 34
'sub-prime' mortgages 76–7, 188
subsidies 90–1, 108, 192, 205
Sun, L. 49, 116
  and Ho, P. 49, 114, 116
  and Liu, Z. 35, 114–115
Sustainable Development Goals (SDGs) 4–5, 90, 161, 181, 203, 229–30
Sutera, Italy 180

Tanzania: New Kigamboni City eco-city, Dar es Salaam 58
tax 192–7
  corporate/multinational corporations 38, 94, 177, 180
  inequalities 36–7, 38
  landholdings, Britain 100, 102
  per centage of GDP 194
  relief on mortgages 91, 106
  wealth 176, 177, 183
tax havens 36–7, 38, 193–4
  impact of closure 184
  Vanuatu 158–9
technology 54–6, 171–2
  public and private investments 177
temperature and sea level rises 24–6

temporary occupation rights/licences
  Cambodia 146, 148
  Kenya 212
tenure security and diversity 205–7
  five step approach towards enhancing 207–19
    1: assessing degrees of legality 207–8
    2: selecting settlements for regularization 208
    3: forms of indirect intervention 209–12
    4: intermediate tenure options 212–15
    5: innovative formal options 216–19
  summary and proposal 219–20
Thailand 77
  Baan Mankong programme 213, 226, 228
  Bang Kaen canal cooperative housing project 218–19
  communal land rental 214
  Communal Land Title regulation 216
Thatcher, M. 21, 34, 36, 73, 75, 85, 105–6
Thunberg, G. 31, 178
Tiny Homes Movement, USA 250
Tirana *see* Albania
tourism 15–16
  see also Airbnb
transfer development rights (TDR) 200–1
transport oriented development (TOD) 242–5
Trinidad and Tobago: certificates of comfort (COC) 213
trusteeship, concept of 165, 183, 220
Turkey 48,
  Ankara 18
  gecekondus: upgrading urban areas 226–8
  rural-urban migration and self-help/communal support 50, 51, 211
  Küraya post-earthquake emergency housing 20
  refugees 48
Turkmenistan: Ashgabat 61–2
Turner, J.F.C. 5, 18–19, 73, 192, 256
'twin-track' approach to land and housing 189–90

Uganda 44
  customary to market system 163
  Land Equity Movement of Uganda 163
  speculative land development 94
United Kingdom (UK) 4, 90, 247
  Archigram 12, 54, 64, 202
  'beds in sheds' 72, 108
  'Buy to Let' 91, 108
  cities as magnets 46
  co-housing, Marmalade Lane, Cambridge 217, 251, *252*
  council tax 91, 195
  Eden Project 54
  empty and second homes 107, 195–6
  equity sharing 217–18
  financial crisis (2008) 75, 76–7
  garden cities movement 54
  Greater London Council (GLC) 249
  international aid 184
    DFID and Rwanda (NLTRP) 78, 80
  land banking 201
  land registration (in notes) 204
  overcrowding and homelessness 85, 103–4
  privatization of public land or assets 88, 90, 95–6, 105–7, 110
  Unexplained Wealth Orders 38
  urban periphery/inner suburbs 95
  wealth tax 185
  wealth inequality and land 36–7
  see also London
UK as property-owning democracy
  historical perspective 99–103
  promoting social value of land 103–6
  reversal of progress 106–10
  structural change and policy options 110–11
Ulaanbaatar *see* Mongolia, state to market system
United Nations (UN)
  Cambodia 146
  climate crisis initiatives 21
  financialization 88
  Intergovernmental Panel on Climate Change (IPCC) 21, 22, 178–9
  land tenure and property rights 72
  migration issues specify refugees 44–5, 47, 48
  New York Declaration for Refugees and Migrants 45
  report on poverty in UK 109–10
  Universal Declaration of Human Rights 54
  urban population increase 26
  wellbeing and happiness 174–5
UN-Habitat
  2020 World Cities Report 260
  cooperative ownership 217
  Ethiopia 125
  housing affordability, definition of 107, 236–7
  land tax 196
  land tenure continuum and risk of eviction 209–10
  land tenure and property rights, definitions of 67–8
  'land-based finance' reports 97
  Lesotho 151–2, 155
  mixed land use 135
  New Urban Agenda 4–5, 69–70, 203
  Social Tenure Domain Model (STDM) 210, 215
  Uganda 163
  Vancouver Declaration on Human Settlements 72

Vietnam 126, 128, 130
zoning 234
unauthorized settlements *see* informal land tenure/unauthorized settlements; land titling programmes; tenure security and diversity
universal basic income 176–7, 185
upgrading [tautology] urban areas 224–9
Urban Design International 11
urban forms
  impact of global move to market 94–6
  Western and non-Western 11–13
urban influences and impacts 26–8
urban land expansion 187–8, 189
urban land markets and management 97, 187–92, 206, 212
  building bridges 203–4
  challenges and innovative approaches 187–92
  dealing with disorder 202
  development-based instruments 197–201
  fee-based instruments 197
  land value and uses/taxes 192–7
  non-market-based instruments for enhancing equitable land markets 201–2
Urban Poor Development Fund (UPDF), Cambodia 147
urbanization
  China 113
  Ethiopia 121
  Western and non-Western countries 165–6
  USA, 93, 125–6,
  California Model of development 174
  co-housing 217
  community land trusts (CLTs) 216
  embargo on Cuba 118, 120, 121
  equity sharing 217–18
  financial crisis (2008) 76–7
  Housing First 253
  Native Americans 10–11
  overcrowding and homelessness 85–6
  social rental housing 218
  Tiny Homes Movement 250
  and Vietnam 125–6
USAID *see* Millennium Challenge Corporation (MCC)
'utopian socialism' 53
utopian vs dystopian visions of urban development 53
  elitist aspirations 56–64, 260–1
  romance and idealism 53–4

technology, architecture and planning 54–6
Uzbekistan 15

Vanuatu 25,175
  customary to market system 156–62, 163–4
Vietnam 25, 164,
  Hanoi 126, 130
    Royal Vinh residential complex 56, 95
  Ho Chi Minh City (HCMC) 126, 128
  Investment Review 94
  Mekong Delta 93–4, 129
  state land and housing management 125–30, 131

Wallace-Wells, D. 22
Wargent, M. et al. 109
water shortages *see* droughts
wealth and land inequality 36–7
wealth taxes 176, 177, 185
Western and non-Western space/place concepts 11–13
Wilkinson, R. 173
  and Pickett, K. 39, 170–1, 173
Williams, S.M. 264
World Bank 25, 34, 35, 47, 94, 97
  Cambodia 77–8, 146–7, 148
  Competitive Cities report: private sector investment 94
  and Development Research Center report on urban China 116–7
  Ethiopia 123, 124, 125
  housing policy report (1993) 72–3
  incremental development 241
  land titling programmes 74, 77–8, 205
  Lesotho 155
  Mongolia 135, 136, 137
  rental markets 93
  role 264
  universal basic income 185
  upgraded Palestinian settlement, Jordan 226
  Vanuatu 160–1
  Vietnam 126, 128, 130
World Health Organization (WHO) 28–9, 262

younger generation 98, 110, 195, 205, 247, 259

Zambia 210
  occupancy licences 215
zoning 199
zoning plan: Port Vila, Vanuatu 160–1

Lightning Source UK Ltd.
Milton Keynes UK
UKHW022353100522
402781UK00007B/1428